D1170230

L. N. Cottingham 1787-1847
Architect of the Gothic Revival

FLORIDA STATE
UNIVERSITY LIBRARIES

MAY 1 0 2001

TALLAHASSEE, FLORIDA

Janet Myles

L. N. Cottingham 1787-1847
Architect of the Gothic Revival

Lund Humphries Publishers
London

NA
997
.C68
M95
1996

First published in 1996 by
Lund Humphries Publishers Ltd
Park House
1 Russell Gardens
London NW11 9NN

Copyright © 1996 Janet Myles

British Library Cataloguing in Publication Data
A catalogue record for this book is available from
the British Library

All rights reserved. No part of this publication may be
reproduced, stored in a retrieval system or transmitted in any
form or by any means, electrical or otherwise, without first
seeking the written permission of the copyright owners and
of the publishers.

ISBN 0 85331 678 3

Typeset in Monotype Ehrhardt
Designed by Alan Bartram
Made and printed in Great Britain
by BAS Printers, Over Wallop, Hampshire

An exhibition of Cottingham's work will take place
at the Ashmolean Museum, Oxford in 1998,
in which all the works discussed in this catalogue
will be displayed.

FRONTISPIECE
Details from *Working Drawings of Gothic Ornament*,
Plate XXVIII, 1823
Lithograph 24×17 in (61×43.25 cm)

3 1254 03526 4452

Contents

I dedicate this book to the memory of my parents,
Sandy and Jessica Laird.

Acknowledgements

There are many people to whom I owe thanks for their help during my work on L. N. Cottingham. Above all I would like to thank Mary Stewart, former Head of Art History at Leicester Polytechnic for her guidance and encouragement throughout my career. I also have to thank the following people for their generous help, for taking time to see me and to answer questions: the late Colonel Stanton of Snelston Hall who allowed me free access to the family archives, and his family for their continuing support; Lord Brougham and Vaux, Christopher Terry and Dawn Tyler of the Brougham Hall Trust; Dean John Crooks and Dean H. M. A. Cassidy of St Patrick's Cathedral, Armagh; Professor Campbell Laird and Dr Michael Lewis of the University of Pennsylvania; the Rt Hon The Earl of Harrington, Sir Brooke Boothby and Lt Col The Lord Wynford; Dr Clive Wainwright of the Victoria and Albert Museum; Professor Mark Girouard, Professor Howard Colvin, Professor J. Kerry Downes, and Anthony Smith, President of Magdalen College Oxford; Haward Birkin, Cynthia Brown and Olive Cook of Suffolk; the late Eric Hill of Boston; Joan Robertson of Victoria, Australia; Peter Walton and staff of the Bar Convent Museum, York; and John Myles who persuaded me to research Cottingham in the first place, for his help with the family research and his continuing support.

I would like to thank the many archivists, librarians and curators throughout the UK, Ireland, France, Germany and the USA who responded with interest and helped me in my research, naming in particular R. Gwynn Thomas of Suffolk R.O.; Andrew Saint of the survey of London; G. R. Beasley and Andrew Norris of the RIBA; Dr John Booker, archivist of Lloyd's Bank; C. J. Pickford of Bedford R.O.; Gillian Furlong of University College London; Sheila MacPherson of Cumbria R.O.; Maurice Dennett of Saddleworth Museum; James Sewell of the London R.O.; David Birks and Tony Rumsey of the NMRO; Joan Williams of Hereford Cathedral Library; Isobel Sinden of the V&A Picture Library; John Fisher of the Guildhall Library; Herbert Mitchell and Angela Giral of the Avery Architectural Library, New York; John Shaw Ridler of Essex R.O.; Frank Miles, archivist of King's College School; Mrs Parry Jones and Dr J. Cottis of Magdalen College Library; Timothy Wilson and Jon Whiteley of the Ashmolean Museum, Oxford; Margaret O'Sullivan of Derbyshire R.O.; and Roger Towe and Mary Weston of De Montfort University Library.

I owe thanks to many friends for their help and encouragement throughout, particularly Ian Spencer who also helped me with photography and computer technology, and W. E. Stober for his work in proof reading and editing the text.

I have to thank the team at Lund Humphries for their absolute professionalism and their guidance throughout the project, mentioning in particular John Taylor, Lucy Myers, Lara Speicher, John Gilbert and Alan Bartram. Finally, I thank my daughters and their families for their unfailing encouragement and for putting up with Cottingham and me for all these years.

I acknowledge with grateful thanks financial support for the book from The British Academy and the Research Committee of the School of Arts, De Montfort University, Leicester.

Introduction

L. N. Cottingham is the forgotten architect of the Gothic Revival in the nineteenth century. His work as an architect, antiquary, designer and restorer has been overlooked to a large extent in the twentieth-century accounts of architectural history. The obituary of Cottingham, 'this distinguished architect', in *The Art-Union* of 1847, gave a useful outline of his career, listing his appointment as Surveyor to the Cooks' Company from 1820, his major works of restoration to Rochester Cathedral in 1825 and Hereford Cathedral in 1841, mentioned his amazing Museum of Mediaeval Art, and noted his domestic architecture for such eminent patrons as Lord Brougham, the Lord Chancellor, Lord Dunraven, the Earl of Craven and others.[1] This eulogy established unequivocally the esteem in which Cottingham was held in his own day. Since then he has lapsed into obscurity, relegated to a role barely worthy of a footnote. The entries for Cottingham in the *Dictionary of National Biography* and Howard Colvin's *Biographical Dictionary of British Architects 1660-1840* added little to the *Art-Union* obituary. One reason for his neglect may be that to date no collection of personal or family papers and no archive material relating to the architectural practice that he ran with his son, Nockalls Johnson Cottingham, have yet come to light.

My attention was first drawn to Cottingham when I researched a family crest on a set of Gothic Revival hall chairs which appeared in a Derbyshire saleroom in 1984.[2] The crest belonged to John Harrison of Snelston Hall, a Gothic mansion built in Derbyshire in 1827 and since demolished. The architect was L. N. Cottingham. Judging by my first glimpse of the beautiful watercolour drawings and plans for Snelston Hall in the family possession it was plain that here was a designer of the highest quality whose work deserved to be investigated further. In fact, he became the subject of my doctoral research. My study of his known works and publications brought me into contact with a wide variety of sources scattered throughout England, Ireland and Wales and led to the discovery of unknown buildings, church restoration, interior designs, furniture, metalwork, letters, drawings, sketchbooks and watercolours. I sought material in private collections and the archives of patrons, friends, contemporary architects and antiquaries, in record offices, church archives, libraries, museums, local studies collections, the archives of societies and professional bodies to which he belonged – anywhere, in fact, that would provide the smallest clue or slightest shred of evidence. This book and the planned exhibition are thus the result of this long search for Cottingham.

I found little more than was already generally known in my research of Cottingham's family background. (The text of his obituary is to be found in the Biographical Appendix on p.167.) Cottingham was born on 24 October 1787 at Laxfield in Suffolk of a highly respected family; his father, John Cottingham, was a farmer and his mother, Mary Johnson, daughter of a surgeon. A family ancestor was master carpenter at York Minster until his death in 1457 and another was Abbot of St Mary's, York in 1483.[3] Cottingham may have been educated at Seckford Grammar School, Suffolk, where his cousins attended, and of his apprenticeship or professional training very little firm evidence has come to light.[4] In a letter Cottingham said that he had trained 'with a country architect and builder', and then continued his studies in London from 1810, 'in the various branches of the profession under different gentlemen most experienced in their respective departments of the art', but tantalisingly he gave no names.[5] He then started his own businesss as architect surveyor in 1814, living at 66 Great Queen Street, Lincoln's Inn Fields.[6] In 1828 he moved to 43 Waterloo Bridge Road, Lambeth, part of an extensive estate that he designed in 1825, where he housed his museum collection and lived until his death in October 1847.

It is fairly clear that Cottingham was in a comfortable financial position at the outset of his professional career. His accumulation over many years of a vast collection of mediaeval art seems likely to have been financed not merely from his professional income but also from private means: as we shall see later, he was to confess in middle age that he had 'expended his patrimony'. Cottingham married in 1822 Sophia Cotton (*d.*1871) by whom he had two sons, Nockalls Johnson and Edwin Cotton and a daughter Sophia. Cottingham's obituarist in *The Art-Union* referred to his 'amiable domestic habits'.

Cottingham, as an architect born in 1787, had trained in the classical tradition of the eighteenth century, and his early works reflect the prevailing neo-classicism and Greek Revival of the turn of the century, and also show elements of eighteenth-century Picturesque theory. Another influence, however, proved the strongest in his development. Among his friends, listed in his obituary, was John Carter, an antiquary and draughtsman to the Society of Antiquaries who wrote articles attacking the neglect, destruction and ignorant attempts at repairs of English mediaeval buildings and monuments. Carter imparted his ideas on preservation and his passion for the mediaeval to the young Cottingham, encouraging him in his archaeological studies of Westminster Hall and Henry VII's Chapel between 1818 and 1821. From this period on, Cottingham's interests and efforts were to be directed towards a serious and scholarly study of mediaeval art and architecture, as an aid to its preservation and as a source of inspiration for building anew. In a letter of 1832, Cottingham wrote:

From the earliest period of my practice, I have been ambitious of arriving at excellence in my profession. My leisure time and patrimony have consequently been expended in ardent research to qualify myself accordingly. I now have a studio and museum of models and practical designs which are considered to be unrivalled.[7]

This museum of mediaeval antiquities, the first major collection of its kind in England, amassed between 1814 and his death in 1847, reveals Cottingham as an extender of the term antiquities to cover works disdained by the cognoscenti of the eighteenth century. His publication of detailed studies of mediaeval architecture made plain his intention to preserve the reviled Gothic against the prevailing taste for classicism, and his structural analysis of Gothic, designed to educate and inform architects, made a contrast with such contemporary publications as A. C. Pugin's mediaeval studies which reflected the topographical work of the late eighteenth century. Cottingham's activities as an archaeologist, his passionate efforts as a preservationist to save threatened mediaeval structures through the publication of pamphlets, subscription and even the gratuitous donation of his services as architect, help to indicate his significance as an early appreciator and disciple of the art of the mediaeval period. He was one of the earliest promoters of the Gothic Revival, for he re-examined both the Romanesque and the Gothic styles and reintroduced them to the English repertoire at a crucial moment in stylistic development. His links with the mediaevalist architects in France and Germany demonstrate patterns of intellectual intercourse between England and the Continent which continued the close contacts shown in the eighteenth century, between such figures as Adam and Clérisseau, Chambers and LeRoy, and also provide evidence of how the taste of the nineteenth century developed in part out of that of the eighteenth century. Cottingham's work – his theory and practice of Revivalism, and the extending of antiquarianism and preservationism as an influence upon architectural practice – foreshadows that of A. W. N. Pugin and other mediaevalists of the later nineteenth century. These are aspects that serve to establish him as a figure of influence in the English architectural tradition.

In this study I have tried to include all areas of his known work: his antiquarian studies; his extensive church restoration practice viewed in the light of his own theories and compared with the work of his better known contemporaries; his domestic architecture and design from the Mediaeval Revival mansions to his estate village and country schools, which showed his adoption of the English mediaeval vernacular as a source of style, an important step predating the ideals of the Arts and Crafts architects of the later nineteenth century; and his competition entries, which give an insight into the complexities of the architectural context of the time, in terms of patronage and political influence, and reveal Cottingham's position in that context, notably his attitudes, integrity and strength of character. Throughout, I have drawn upon the extensive contemporary comment on his work in such journals as *The British Magazine*, *The Gentleman's Magazine*, the *Engineer, Architect and Surveyor*, *The Builder*, and the *Ecclesiologist*, which enables us to see Cottingham as his contemporaries saw him and to place him within the social and architectural context of his time in this country and abroad. Much of Cottingham's domestic work, his church interiors and design, have been swept away and his restoration work undone or overlaid by later 'improvers'; and in a working life of some thirty years, a great deal of it concerned with restoration work, his output, or rather all that has been discovered to date, appears small by comparison with his long-lived contemporaries such as Anthony Salvin or Edward Blore.

As much of Cottingham's work as possible is illustrated here and in the planned exhibition, based on material loaned from a variety of sources, and arranged thematically to embrace the range of his interests and activities. We learn most about Cottingham from his own writings, letters, publications and reports, which give an impression of the man himself – open, brave, generous, honest, gentlemanly, professionally meticulous and honourable – and of his passions, prejudices and attitudes to his work. The quality of his work, too, is evident in the visual material, the sketchbooks, watercolours, competition designs, plans and etchings, which together demonstrate his abilities as architect, designer, engineer, artist and antiquary. Above all, his writings and these materials serve to reinstate Cottingham as a figure of importance in the development of that overwhelming movement of the nineteenth century, the Gothic Revival.

I make no apology for the strength of my conviction in attempting to re-establish Cottingham as an architect of significance. He has been overlooked, misjudged and misrepresented for nearly 150 years. My aim in this book and in the planned exhibition is to offer the opportunity for a reassessment and reappraisal of his work and its quality. I believe the evidence for his reinstatement in the progress of nineteenth-century architectural history is clear from the work itself – work that is comprehensively described, analysed and assessed in this study for the first time since his death in 1847.

1   *The Art-Union*. Obituary of L. N. Cottingham, October 1847, p.377

2   Bury and Hilton, Auctioneers, Ashbourne, September 1984, *Catalogue of Sale*

3a Guildhall Library, Ref. MS F843, File 14, letter from LNC to the Fishmongers' Court, 15 Feb. 1832

3b Laxfield Parish Records, Suffolk R.O., FC80: John Cottingham and Elizabeth Johnson, married by licence, 16 Dec. 1782: Laxfield Parish Records, 27 Sept. 1804; Lease of land to John Cottingham, farmer, of Laxfield, Framlingham, Woodbridge. Little Glenham Records show Cottinghams engaged as farmers, builders, plumbers and teachers; and in 1844, *White's Suffolk Directory* records a John Cottingham who was relieving officer and Registrar at Hermitage Place, Framlingham. Other members of the Cottingham family, LNC's cousins, moved to Great Chesterford and farmed in Essex. A cousin of LNC's father, Joseph Orlibar Cottingham, of 9 St Peter's Hill, Humber, was a builder who undertook work for Cottingham in his capacity as Surveyor to the Cooks' Company. (See *Minutes Book*, Cooks' Company, 19 June 1829, MS31115)

3c Harvey, J., *English Mediaeval Architects*, 1954, p.74

4   Suffolk R.O., admissions to Seckford Grammar School, Crisp, F. A., 1900; LNC may have been tutored privately or attended Seckford School. The records of other Suffolk Schools have no entries for Cottingham in the late eighteenth century

5   *The Art-Union*. Research into Suffolk architects of the appropriate date has revealed no records of apprentices. Very few records remain of the architects and builders, and an examination of the archive material relating to country houses or public buildings of this time has disclosed nothing. Possible Suffolk architects who may have had Cottingham as a trainee are: Coleby Clarke of Woodbridge (Boyton Rectory, 1808); Robert Heffer (Wetherden Rectory, 1816); John Field who worked for the Bishop of Derry at Ickworth; Thomas Leverton (Culford, 1803); George Thompson (Castle House, Woodbridge, 1805); William Brown of Ipswich (Earl Stonham Rectory); Thomas Adler (Snettisham, 1808); Benjamin Catt (Helmingham Parsonage, 1812). [I am indebted to Birkin Haward of Ipswich (who later published a *Dictionary of Suffolk Architects*), for advice on possible lines of research, and to Cynthia Brown for her help and advice.]
See also letter from LNC to the Fishmongers' Court, 1832, Guildhall Library, Ref. 516/SAL(1)

6   Guildhall Library, Cooks' Company Minute Books, Ref. MS31114, 19 June 1829

7   ibid.

Part One

L. N. Cottingham: Life and Work

Chronology

For each year personal details, publications and the starting date of each project is given with the length of time of building.

1787
Born 24 October at Laxfield, Suffolk, 'of an ancient and highly respected family', to John Cottingham, farmer, and Mary Johnson, daughter of a surgeon. A family ancestor was Abbot of St Mary's, York in 1483 and another, William Cottingham, was master carpenter at York Minster until his death in 1457.

1797
Possibly educated at Seckford Grammar School, Suffolk where his cousins James and John attended.

1802
Began his studies with a 'country architect and builder'.

1810
Continued architectural studies in London in the various branches of the profession. No record of the architects to whom he was articled have yet come to light and Cottingham himself never named them.

1814
Set up his own business as architect and surveyor; address, 66 Great Queen Street, Lincoln's Inn Fields. Began his Museum of Mediaeval Art.

1820
Possibly travelled on the Continent. No documentary evidence has come to light but in his publication on *King Henry VII's Chapel* (1822) he referred to churches in France and Germany: he also had casts from European churches in his museum. Began an architectural survey of Westminster in preparation of publications.

1821
Entered competition for The Salters' Hall; no premium awarded.
Restored Snelston Parish Church in Derbyshire for his patron John Harrison.

1822
Married Sophia Cotton, second daughter of R. T. Cotton, architect of Finsbury, by whom he had two sons, Nockalls Johnson and Edwin Cotton, and a daughter Sophia.
Published *Plans etc of Westminster Hall*, London, 1822: Volume One, *Plans etc of King Henry VII's Chapel*. Advertised that he gave lessons in civil architecture. (See Preface, *Plans etc of King Henry VII's Chapel*.)
Appointed Surveyor to the Cooks' Company, a post he held until 1840. The records show that he undertook building works in the city and at Walthamstow throughout this period.
Commissioned by John Harrison to design a mansion: Snelston Hall and estate village.

1823
Published *Working Drawings of Gothic Ornament and a Design for a Gothic Mansion*, 1823; *The Ornamental Metal Worker's Director*, 1st Edition, 1823.

1824
Published *The Metal Worker's Director*, 2nd Edition.

1825
Book of watercolour drawings for Snelston Hall, *Cottages etc for the Domain and Estate etc at Snelston, Derbyshire*: unpublished.
Commissioned to build estate of houses, shops and a hotel in Waterloo Bridge Road for John Field: work continued until 1828. (Demolished 1951.)
Restoration of Rochester Cathedral, 1825-9, and further works at Rochester until 1840.

1826
Gothic designs, watercolour elevations and plans for Snelston Hall.
Exhibited at the Royal Academy, 'West Front of Rochester etc' (See *The Royal Academy of Arts: A Complete Dictionary of Contributors and their work from its foundation in 1769 to 1904*, compiled by A. Graves ; Vol.II, Carroll to Dyer, London, George Bell & Sons, 1905. All Cottingham's work is listed and that of the firm, LNC & Son, and that of N. J. Cottingham.)

1827
Snelston Hall: foundation stone laid 11 June 1827; work continued on the Hall, estate buildings and village, and furniture designs until 1842. (Snelston Hall demolished 1952.)
Exhibited at the RA: 'Snelston Hall, Derbyshire'.

1828
Moved to 43 Waterloo Bridge Road, part of John Field's estate designed by Cottingham in 1825. Museum of Mediaeval Art established at this address.
Exhibited at the RA: 'Entrance to Library, Rochester Cathedral'.

1829
Published *Plans etc of King Henry VII's Chapel*, Vol.II.
Won competition for the restoration of Magdalen College Chapel, Oxford; work continued from 1829 to 1835.
Exhibited at the RA: 'Entrance, Snelston Hall'; 'Interior, Magdalen College Chapel'.

1830
Brougham Hall for Henry Lord Brougham; extensions, interior design, church restoration: work continued until 1847. (Demolished 1935.)
Exhibited at the RA: 'Interior, Magdalen College Chapel'.

1831
Exhibited at the RA: 'Interior, Magdalen College Chapel'.

1832
Cottingham's son Nockalls Johnson attended King's College School. (He was taught drawing by John Sell Cotman; NJC won a prize for drawing in 1835.)
Published 'Reasons Against Pulling Down the Lady Chapel at St Saviour's, Southwark' with James Savage: published lithographs to aid restoration funds.
Crosby Hall restoration campaign.
Elected a Fellow of the Society of Antiquaries, 10 May.
Entered Fishmongers' Hall Competition; won 3rd premium.
Restored St Alban's Cathedral, 1832-3.
Designs for the restoration of St Saviour's, Southwark in conjunction with George Gwilt.
Exhibited at the RA: 'Part of Mr Cottingham's studio of English Antiquities'; 'New Hall, Fishmongers' Company'.

1833
Designs for alterations, extensions and interior designs for Coombe Abbey for the Earl of Craven (demolished).

Designs for cottages at Binley, Warwickshire, for the Earl of Craven. (Possibly executed.)

1834
Extensions and interior designs for Elvaston Castle, Derbyshire, for the Earl Harrington.
Restoration of Armagh Cathedral, 1834-42.
Exhibited at the RA: 'A Louis XIV drawing room at Coombe Abbey'; 'Entrance, Coombe Abbey' (two more drawings of Coombe Abbey).

1835
Interior designs at Matfen Hall, Northumberland, for Sir Edward Blackett, 1835-47.

1836
Entered the Houses of Parliament Competition.

1837
Exhibited at the RA: 'New Houses of Parliament'; 'Central Saloon, New Houses of Parliament'.

1838
Designed Gothic apartment as showrooms for Samuel Pratt & Sons, New Bond Street, London.
Exhibited at the RA: 'Monument in Armagh Cathedral to Colonel Kelly'.

1839
Restored Ashbourne Church, Derbyshire; designed monument to Lady Boothby (executed by Thomas Willement) in Ashbourne Church: 1839-46.
Designs for Eglinton Tournament.

1840
Designs for Adare Manor for Earl and Lady Dunraven.
Published *The Metal Worker's Director*, 3rd Edition.
Exhibited at the RA: 'A Village Church in Derbyshire'.

1841
Survey of Temple Church, London (published in *The Temple Church: an account of its Restoration and Repairs*, by William Burge, 1842). Discovered Norman wheel window and lead coffins of Knights Templar; communicated his findings in *Archaeologia*. Discovered mediaeval tiles in the Chapter House at Westminster. (See *Archaeologia*.)

Restoration of Hereford Cathedral, 1841-7 (completed by Nockalls Cottingham in 1849).
Restoration of Roos Church, Yorkshire, 1841-2; Great Chesterford Church, Essex.

1842
Elected hon. member of the Society for Promoting the Study of Gothic Architecture.
Restoration of the Norman Tower, Bury St Edmunds, 1842-9; St Mary's Church, Bury St Edmunds, 1842-6; Davington Church, Kent, 1842; Milton Bryan Church, 1842-4; and designs for bench ends for Temple Church, London.
Exhibited at the RA; 'The High Altar, St Alban's Abbey "After the second battle at St Alban's the Queen caused the King to knight his son before the High Altar etc."'; 'Choir of Hereford Cathedral'.

1843
Restoration and designs at St Mary's Church, Nottingham (work continued by Scott and Moffat).
Exhibited at the RA: 'Interior of Hereford Cathedral'.

1844
Built The Savings Bank and Bank Cottage, Crown Street, Bury St Edmunds, 1844-6.
Restoration of Louth Church, Lincolnshire; and Market Weston Church, Suffolk, restoration and all interior fittings.

1845
Built St Helen's Church, Thorney, Notts., 1845-9.
Restored Kilpeck Church, Herefordshire, 1845-8; Horringer Church, Suffolk.

1846
Restorations of St Mary's, Clifton, Notts.; Theberton Church, Suffolk; the Lady Chapel, Hereford Cathedral.
Built Tuddenham School, Suffolk; Great Chesterford School, Suffolk.
Extensions to Clifton Hall, Nottingham; extensions to the General Hospital, Bury St Edmunds, Suffolk (demolished).

1847
Died, 13 October, at home in Waterloo Bridge Road, of heart disease and dropsy.

Cottingham, despite ill health, worked until the week before his death when he attended a meeting at Hereford Cathedral on the progress of the restoration. He was survived by his widow Sophia who died in 1871. His will, witnessed by his son Edwin Cotton Cottingham, a medical practitioner, and his brother Lionel Cottingham, stipulated that his elder son, Nockalls Johnson Cottingham, should continue the business. This he did, completing such works as the restoration of the Lady Chapel at Hereford; the restorations of Barrow and Ledbury Churches; the Norman Tower at Bury St Edmunds; and the building of St Helen's, Thorney. Nockalls died in 1854 on his way to America, when the ship *Arctic* foundered off Cape Cod.

1

Gothic Revivalism, Antiquarian and Preservationist Pursuits

Development of Revivalism in England

Cottingham played a notable but, since his own time, largely unacknowledged part in the development of Gothic Revivalism through his publications of structural analysis of mediaeval buildings, and through his efforts as collector, preserver and Mediaeval Revivalist in the early nineteenth century. Yet if the influence and significance of his advanced ideas are to be fully assessed, his contribution should be viewed within the wider European context of Mediaeval Revivalism.

The background to the chronological development of the Gothic Revival, first written about by Eastlake in 1872 and Clarke in 1928, has been widely researched in the later twentieth century by Frankl, Germann, McAulay, Frew, Branner, Mowl, McCarthy, Cocke, Colvin, Crook and others.[1] The work of the eighteenth-century researchers such as Bentham and Essex, the analysis of Gothic found in the writings of French theorists such as de l'Orme, Perrault, Frézier, Lassus and Viollet-le-Duc, and the importance of Richard Gough's key contribution as President of the Society of Antiquaries, have been well documented. Gough first led the way when he committed the society to a leading role in publishing, initially plates and then the first volume of *Archaeologia* in 1770. He stressed the importance of accurate drawings to mediaevalist research and in the 1790s the number of publications of topographical works and volumes on monastic and cathedral antiquities increased significantly. John Carter, for example, a draughtsman and antiquary to the society, and friend and mentor to the young Cottingham, produced in 1795 his *Ancient Architecture of England*, the first history of mediaeval architecture ever published. He stated in the preface that his intention was 'to inform those embarked on insensitive and ignorant restorations of mediaeval buildings of the true character of mediaeval architecture'. Through Gough's influence and his campaign in the pages of *The Gentleman's Magazine*, a small preservationist group emerged intent on creating an interaction between mediaevalism and architectural practice.[2] This idea brought on a fierce debate in the society and growing criticism of James Wyatt's cathedral restorations developed. Gough had written to *The Gentleman's Magazine* from 1786 onwards to protest about the destruction of mediaeval remains and suggested that the society's activities should be widened to include protection and preservation of ancient monuments. It seemed illogical, he said, to 'study with interest' and yet allow 'without remorse to run to ruin'.[3] Frew has described this letter as the first coherent preservationist manifesto, for now the antiquary was perceived as a protector and not simply a researcher and a concern for the mediaeval had grown from a passive scholarly subject into an active force.[4]

Gough's ideas were taken up by younger members. The Reverend John Milner, a Roman Catholic priest, later to be Bishop of Wolverhampton, wrote a dissertation on the *Modern Style of Altering Ancient Cathedrals* in 1798, protesting at Wyatt's modes of restoration. John Carter, between 1798 and 1815, wrote some 380 articles published in *The Gentleman's Magazine* called 'In Pursuit of Architectural Innovation', in which he stressed the need to preserve mediaeval antiquities almost to the exclusion of other relics, and vehemently criticised Wyatt's work, such as the destruction at Lichfield of the altar screen and monuments, huge quantities of exterior and ornamental stonework at Hereford, and the demolition of the Hungerford and Beauchamp chantry chapels at Durham. These alterations were generally regarded as 'improvements' and Carter identified the difference between 'improvements' that usually involved some destruction of existing work and 'necessary repairs'. Improvements had a long tradition reaching back to the Middle Ages, and it was this tradition that formed the basis of the restorations of Inigo Jones, Wren and, later, Essex at Ely Cathedral, and even Wyatt's late eighteenth-century work on mediaeval fabric. Gough, Carter and Milner all criticised Wyatt on the grounds too of his ignorance of Gothic.[5] Milner described Wyatt's organ case and bishop's throne at Salisbury as 'an incorrect attempt at the florid Gothic whilst the style of the building itself is in plain Gothic two centuries earlier'. Gough wrote of 'many proofs of the grossest ignorance in almost every architect who has attempted to imitate, restore or repair the best specimens of Gothic architecture',[6] and Carter wrote that this 'want of true knowledge of our ancient Architecture ... shows professional ability at a stand or utterly worn out'.[7]

In this way preservationism transformed antiquarian opinion and guaranteed that Wyatt's activities, such as his restoration at Westminster of 1820, examined by the ever vigilant Carter, should be closely scrutinised.[8] It was also clear that a thorough knowledge and understanding of stylistic developments was essential for those undertaking works of restoration. The increased knowledge and research resulted in important publications. John Britton, a disciple of Carter's and a passionate preservationist, published fourteen volumes on the *Architectural Antiquities of Great Britain* from 1805 to 1810. A reviewer of the works in the *Quarterly Review* noted that a 'compact chronological view of the ancient styles of building in Britain has long been awaited and an enumeration of the criteria by which the different eras of our Gothic architecture might be accurately ascertained'.[9] Reverend Milner published in 1811 *A Treatise of Ecclesiastical Architecture of England during the Middle Ages* in which he 'mourned over the buried remnants of ancient art as

Fig.1 (see Cat.A1) *Westminster Hall*, Plate 1, 1822
Lithograph 34½×21 in (87.5×53.5 cm)

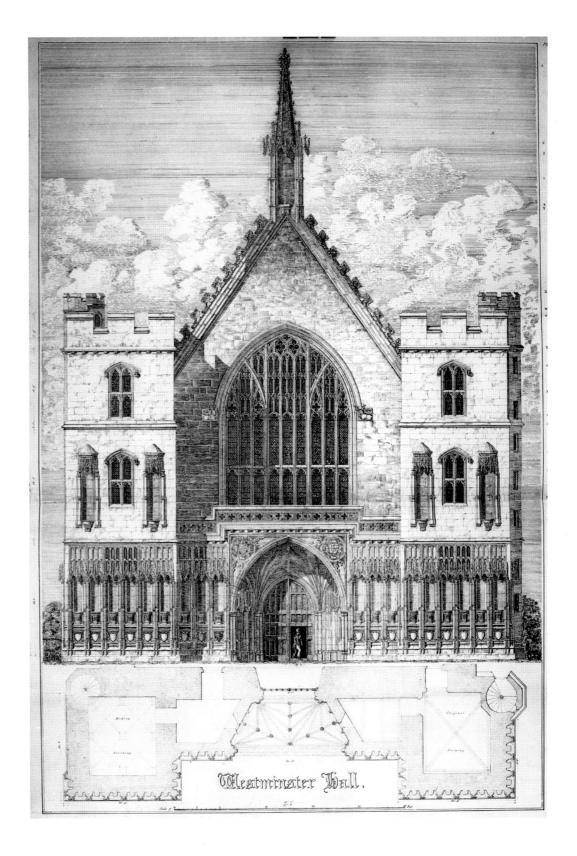

over the grave of a friend'.[10] An awareness of the structural properties of Gothic developed as opposed to the purely stylistic analysis used in the eighteenth century. Thomas Rickman's *Attempt to Discriminate the Styles of English Architecture* of 1817 was a culmination of the previous antiquarian research, and he produced the definitive chronological sequence and nomenclature of the various stages of development of Gothic. Other early innovators in structural analysis were T. Kerrich and G. Saunders who, in *Archaeologia* of 1811, gave an analysis of the construction of vaults in determining the Gothic style. However, it was L. N. Cottingham who, with his *Plans of Westminster Hall* of 1822 (Fig.1, Cat.A1) and *Plans, Elevations, Sections, Details, and Views of the Magnificent Chapel Of King Henry VII at Westminster Abbey Church, the History of its Foundation and an Authentic Account of its Restoration*, 1822 and 1829, produced the first works of major importance in the structural analysis of Gothic architecture – work intended to influence directly architectural practice in an archaeologically correct revival of the mediaeval style (Fig.2, Cat.A2). The volumes of A. C. Pugin and E. J. Willson, *Specimens of Gothic Architecture Selected from Various Edifices*, Vol.I of 1812 and Vol.II published in December 1822, although intended, as they said, 'to assist in perfecting the practical knowledge of Gothic architecture' and provide a chronological sketch of English architecture, were more in the tradition of the antiquarian studies of the earlier works of Britton and Carter and made no such forceful statements on Gothic related to architectural practice as Cottingham did in the Preface to his volume of *Henry VII's Chapel* (see Cats A1 and A2).

Many of Carter's fervently held beliefs are echoed in Cottingham's writing. Carter said of himself that he was 'an illustrator'; he did not have 'scientific knowledge', his 'technical knowledge of Gothic structure was limited' and he could not have attempted the systematic task of Henry VII's Chapel – it was too 'mighty' for him.[11] In these statements Carter was expressing recognition of the great importance of Cottingham's work, making plain the difference between the earlier appreciation of Gothic such as his own, and that contained in the studies of Cottingham – work of structural analysis that was to be continued in the writings of Robert Willis, Jacksonian Professor of Science at Cambridge, and an antiquary of note, and those of James Savage, Cottingham's friend and fellow preservationist, architect of St Luke's, Chelsea in 1821. Cottingham's importance in these developments was acknowledged in his own time. For example, in 1843, William Burge wrote in his account of the restoration of Temple Church that 'the lovers of Gothic architecture will acknowledge its obligation to Bentham, Carter, Rickman, Milner, Cottingham, Pugin and Savage',[12] and in a letter to John Glyde in 1852, an appreciation of Cottingham's influence was expressed by W. G. Colchester, an antiquary friend of his:

The published details of *Henry VII's Chapel* showed how laboriously he worked to make himself acquainted with the details of Gothic mouldings. At the present time owing to the works of Britton, Pugin, Le Kemp and others we possess accurate knowledge, but 50 years ago these details were unknown and Cottingham was one of the early workers. His *Henry VII's Chapel* was one of the first publications of details given to the public, before that all was chaos.[13]

Revivalism in Europe

It is significant that Cottingham's publications promoting an archaeologically correct Gothic Revival were widely consulted. Copies of his works were to be found in the libraries of major nineteenth-century architects or were accessible through the libraries of the Society of Antiquaries, the Oxford Society for Promoting the Study of Gothic Architecture after its founding in 1839, and the Magdalen College Library. Sir John Soane, who made a request for a copy of *Plans etc of Henry VII's Chapel*, Vol.I, in January 1822,[14] was working on the Law Courts at Westminster at the time and would have been interested in detailed drawings of the mediaeval buildings there. Sir Robert Smirke, who was to undertake a structural survey of Rochester Cathedral to confirm Cottingham's findings in 1825, and his brother Sydney, owned copies,[15] and a copy of *Henry VII's Chapel* was in the collection of Owen Jones, an influential contemporary design reformer.[16] Most significantly for coming events, A. C. Pugin owned copies of all Cottingham's publications, which were used not only in the education of his famous son A. W. N. Pugin (who in 1834 wrote in admiration of Cottingham's work) and of his other pupils Benjamin Ferrey, Thomas Walker, F. T. Dolman, and Talbot Bury, but also formed a strong link in the spreading of Gothic Revival influence to the Continent.[17]

Cottingham, in his Preface to *Plans etc of Henry VII's Chapel*, echoed Carter's sense of Romanticism in relation to Gothic architecture, urging the young architect to 'note down the impression made on his mind by their varied forms as a whole': in this way Cottingham was combining Romanticism with a rational concern for structure. Nikolaus Pevsner, in analysing 'Englishness and Frenchness' in the appreciation of Gothic, wrote that the French approach to Gothic is purely rational, and the English, by contrast, is emotional, and only in A. W. N. Pugin, being of French descent, are both tendencies to be found.[18] However, a careful consideration of these developments in Revivalism and preservationism in Europe shows that there were close links and mutual influences from the early nineteenth century onward and, in fact, Cottingham's structural approach to Gothic underlies many French ideas.

A Gothic Revival was slower to begin in France due to the upheavals caused by the French Revolution and fewer people were to recommend its adoption as a universal style, but by 1830 very strong influences flowed from England when the new conception of Gothic propounded by Cottingham was assimilated by émigrés. F. R. Chateaubriand was most important in this respect, his writing showing a fusion of supposed English Romanticism and French rationalism.[19] In his publication *Génie du Christianisme*, a key work in the development of Revivalism in France, he described the life-giving character of Gothic as opposed to classical, linking 'religion and the history of the motherland with such sweet memories'. He was acquainted with the theories of the origins of Gothic that had been debated fiercely in the pages of the *Quarterly Review*, for example in 1811 by Reverend Milner and Dr Whittington, and wrote of the Gothic churches evoking religious awe through the magnificent rationality of their structure, although he revealed no particular analytical appreciation of the formal properties of Gothic architecture. Like Chateaubriand, Count Montalembert spent part of his youth in England and maintained close connections with the Catholic Revival in England, with Ambrose Phillips, the

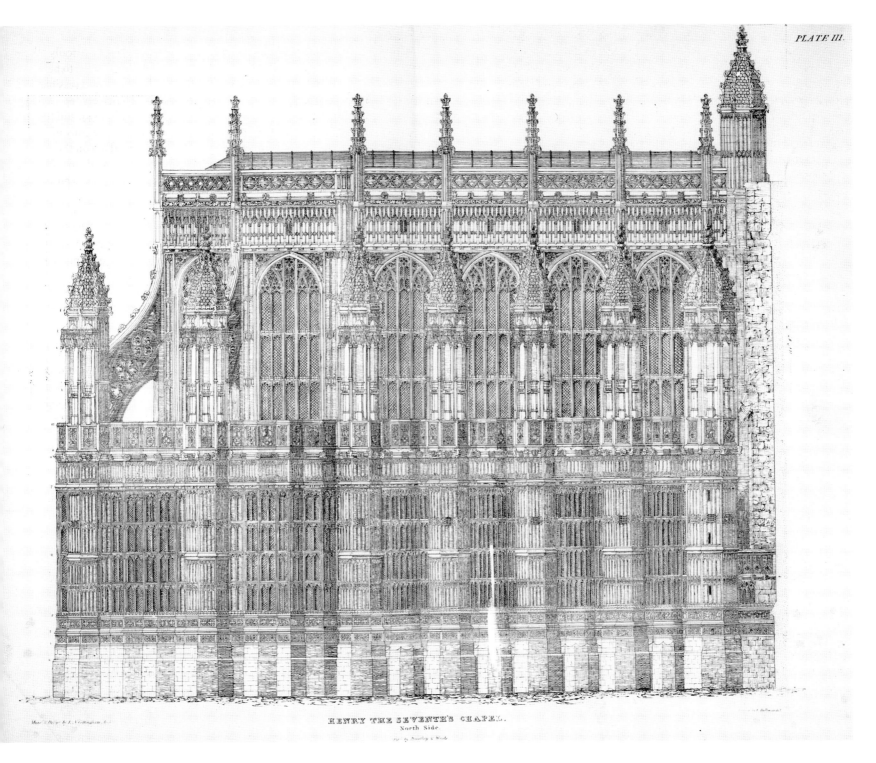

PLATE III.

HENRY THE SEVENTH'S CHAPEL.
North Side.

Fig.2 (see Cat.A2) *King Henry VII's Chapel*, Plate III, 1822
Lithograph 33× 23¾ in (84×60.5 cm)

Earl of Shrewsbury, both patrons of A. W. N. Pugin, and with Pugin himself, and he was a passionate preservationist and scholar of mediaeval art and architecture, writing in 1833 an article entitled 'Vandalism in France' in which he called for the preservation and imitation of mediaeval architectural monuments.[20] This article was written at a time when Cottingham's well-publicised efforts to save the Lady Chapel at St Saviour's and the fifteenth-century Crosby Hall were taking place, and his highly regarded and widely reported restorations of Rochester and Magdalen College Chapel were in progress. Montalembert formed links between the activities of antiquarian societies – such as the Society of Antiquaries and the Oxford Society for Promoting the Study of Gothic Architecture – and preservationists in England and France, and wrote about architectural developments occurring in England, spreading ideas that were subsequently influential in France when architects such as Viollet-le-Duc and Lassus became directly involved in Gothic Revival restoration and building. Montalembert was particularly interested in English Gothic Revival church architecture, writing in 1833: 'If these copies ... lack the vitality imparted by original inspiration, they nonetheless have the great merit of being completely in accord and harmonising with the ideas they represent.' He went on to note:

The Gothic reaction has now passed from religious architecture to secular architecture: wealthy estate owners are having castles built ... whilst private individuals, corporations, diocesan districts and committees are making enormous sacrifices in order to conserve in, or to restore to, their original condition any monuments that have survived from these periods.[21]

Other writers in France such as Alexandre de Laborde suggested the adoption of Gothic as a universal style.[22] Victor Hugo wrote of Notre Dame as a 'logical well-proportioned building', and expressed his aim to instil a sense of respect for the national mediaeval heritage. It is possible that Hugo was responding to Montalembert's 'Du Vandalisme' which took the form of a letter addressed to him.[23] Ludovic Vitet, another writer, associated Gothic with a sense of liberty and community, as Cottingham did in the Preface to his *Working Drawings of Gothic Ornament*. 'Gothic is bourgeois,' Vitet wrote, 'it is French, English, Teutonic.'[24] Chateaubriand and Montalembert both spoke in defence of Gothic in the first decades of the nineteenth century. Joined by preservationists such as Arcisse de Caumont, the Normandy antiquary, their main concern was with the conservation of mediaeval monuments rather than with the advocation of a Gothic Revival in new building.

In Germany, similar associationist and Romantic ideas about Gothic, strongly influenced by English theory, had developed in the eighteenth century – an aspect of the Gothic Revival described by Georg Germann. Christian Cay Laurenz Hirschfeld, a professor of philosophy and a landscape theorist, advocated the use of Gothic building as a means of heightening the atmosphere of Romantic landscapes, and Wilhelm Heinse, in his novel *Ardinghello* of 1787, wrote of the sublime feelings engendered by Gothic cathedrals, expressing the same emotion to be found in Carter's and Cottingham's impressions of Westminster. In Germany, Cologne Cathedral inspired Romantic ideas of the 'infinite nature of the universe', and Georg Forster, in 1790, wrote in

admiration of the 'splendid choir whose vault curves up towards Heaven', appreciating the sublime quality of the architecture as a work of art and regretting that 'such a magnificent building must remain unfinished'.[25] Goethe, in his work *Von deutscher Baukunst* of 1722, wrote of the impression made on him by Strasbourg Cathedral, seeing it as the epitome of German artistic genius, and stressing the national aspect of Gothic, a work 'stemming from the workings of a powerful, rugged German soul'.[26] The architect K. F. Schinkel, a close contemporary of Cottingham, was a fervent and notably early admirer of Gothic, making drawings of Italian mediaeval buildings in 1804 and in 1809 publishing a design for a Gothic church.

Nationalism in Germany, as in other countries, developed after the Napoleonic Wars and in 1814 Crown Prince Ludwig of Bavaria put forward the idea that the Germans should complete Cologne Cathedral as a monument to their liberation. The leading German architect and antiquary Sulpice Boisserée, another exact contemporary of Cottingham, and Ernst Zwirner were involved in the major work which led to communication and intellectual exchange and co-operation between architects and antiquaries in France and England, and between antiquarian societies such as the Oxford Society for Promoting the Study of Gothic Architecture.[27] Boisserée, who had begun drawings of Cologne in 1806, travelled in France in the 1820s, met other antiquaries, studied ancient mediaeval architecture, absorbed the developments stemming from England and produced a folio publication on Cologne Cathedral in 1823.[28] Acclaimed as one of the leading European antiquaries after the publication of *Domwerk*, Boisserée had restricted his archaeological studies to a single building, just as Cottingham had done in his *Plans etc of Henry VII's Chapel*, and his work formed the basis for the completion of Cologne Cathedral.

Although I have not yet found documentary evidence of Cottingham's travels in Europe, he wrote knowledgeably of Continental Gothic churches in his *Plans etc of Henry VII's Chapel*, and his Museum of Mediaeval Art housed items from Nuremburg, Cologne and Heidelberg. It is reasonable to assume that, as a leading mediaevalist architect of his day, he made journeys to the Continent for study, as did many of his contemporaries, and that he may have met Boisserée when he visited Cologne Cathedral. Boisserée, too, may have been familiar with Cottingham's work, for according to research undertaken by Michael Lewis, he appears to have been the principal conduit between English architects and Germany from the early 1820s to the 1840s. His diaries indicate that he was constantly visited by young English architects and consistently bought their books, promoting a scholarly interchange.[29]

In France particularly, notable similarities are to be found between local attitudes and the early Gothic Revival theory and practice of Cottingham and others, such as Willis and Savage, who showed none of the mediaevalising tendencies of the later Gothic Revival in England. Contrary to Pevsner's view of romantic and emotional English as opposed to structural and rational French, I find the English concern for structural analysis and use of materials close to that of the French, if not a direct influence upon it. Robert Willis, engineer and architectural historian, who confirmed Cottingham's assessment of structural damage at Hereford Cathedral in 1841, published works on Italian mediaeval architecture in 1835, and between 1842 and 1863 wrote articles explaining and illustrating the complexities of Gothic construction, particularly of vaults, as well as architectural histories of Hereford and other cathedrals. His article on vaults appeared in *Revue Générale de l'Architecture* in 1842 and Viollet-le-Duc in Vol.IV of his *Dictionnaire Raisonné* used sketches of vault surfaces reminiscent of Willis's drawings and made direct reference to Willis's article.

Reyner Banham has suggested that Viollet-le-Duc's rationalist approach to Gothic architecture was of English extraction from Willis, whereas we know now that it stemmed from the early work on structural analysis by Cottingham, and was only elaborated in France by Viollet-le-Duc.[30] I believe, however, that it is more likely a result of mutual influences: the traditional French rationalist view of architecture as expressed in the eighteenth century, for example, by Laugier in his *Essai Sur l'Architecture* of 1753: and the new conception of Gothic and an appreciation of its structural logic as the basis for a revival of architecture promoted in England in the early nineteenth century by Cottingham. Viollet-le-Duc and Willis both examined the construction of Gothic, but the former wrote of his search for universal principles in historic construction which might then be applied to current architectural design. He argued that Gothic elements such as rib vaults and flying buttresses were originally derived from structural engineering, and he proposed that modern architectural elements might be derived in the same way from the newly available materials of the age – theories very close to those expressed by Cottingham in his *Plans etc of Henry VII's Chapel* and his *Working Drawings of Gothic Ornaments*, and carried out in his practice.

Cottingham's friend James Savage, the architect of St Luke's Church, Chelsea, of 1821, with its stone-vaulted ceiling, was an architect engineer who also took up Cottingham's ideas of the importance of structural analysis of Gothic as the basis for a new style to suit modern requirements. In his *Observations of Style in Architecture* of 1836, he wrote:

The most splendid works of architecture, those which most affect and control the mind, have always been produced by men who were eminent for their full mastery of the principles of construction. This knowledge is absolutely essential to any design that should combine the most valuable of all qualities, originality and simplicity.[31]

In this publication he elaborated further ideas expressed by Cottingham in 1822 and 1829 on issues of copyism and fitness for purpose, ideas which are closely echoed in the writings of Lassus in France in the 1840s. Imitation of style, Savage wrote, was of value to pupils but 'a confession of incapacity in a professor'. The styles of the ancients grew out of a 'turn of thought' and arose from uniformity of purpose: 'We see the consequence of tamely copying and repeating forms, which copied, are destitute of that living principle which first prompted them.' The essential qualities, the 'harmony of the totality and the singleness of intention are thus lost'. Rules, Savage asserted, might act as guides, but the expression of the mind was the great essential. He went on to reiterate Cottingham's notion of fitness for purpose as the basic principle in building anew, addressing the 'young architect of the day', as Cottingham had done, and stressing that in Gothic 'every essential part is dictated by some

actual necessity'. Savage's writings also exerted influence through *Frazer's Magazine*, *The Quarterly Review* and *Blackwood's Edinburgh Magazine*, journals which conducted debates on 'imitation' and originality in design, and these notions of functionalism were taken up by A.W.N. Pugin in the powerful polemics of his *True Principles* of 1841.[32]

In France, Jean-Baptiste-Antoine Lassus, who collaborated with Viollet-le-Duc on the restoration of Notre Dame in 1842, wrote articles from 1845 for *Annales Archéologiques*, a journal edited by A. Didron and devoted largely to mediaeval archaeology.[33] Lassus expressed his views on Gothic in relation to architectural practice. He advocated a serious structural analysis of French national monuments, 'built for our needs and in our materials', for those qualities which are admirable in Gothic architecture stem, he said, from the technical perfection of the parts composing a unified whole, but unlike Viollet-le-Duc, who based his whole doctrine on the 'technical miracle' of Gothic, Lassus contended that the spirit and genius played an important part. Without it 'the architect would be nothing more than a machine for building'.[34]

On the subject of copyism, Lassus stated that it was ridiculous 'for our century with different needs and uses to take Gothic architecture as the model'. He despised 'pastiches of Gothic' and servile copying, but in building anew, architecture should take as its point of departure the finest period of France's national art. He wrote:

Build anew, but ask yourself how each question would have been treated in the 13th century. Search for, try to guess by analogy what form would have been employed ... if you have studied and understood the spirit of the art ... you benefit from the experience of the past, and as well, you will have responded to the needs of the present ... this will lead to a unity of style and a transformation of Gothic to a new expression of that art which is essentially national and of our time.

Lassus made quite different assertions in his theories of restoration, for he advocated a strictly archaeological approach, again coming very close to the English ideas of the early nineteenth century, and to those of Cottingham in particular. In this writing, Lassus expressed in remarkably similar language those same ideas and theories set out by Cottingham twenty-three years before and repeated by Savage and Pugin after him. In the use of materials, too, both Viollet-le-Duc and Lassus were close to Cottingham's practical approach of using techniques of engineering and new materials. Although the French attached great significance to masonry, they never made the mistake of regarding Gothic buildings solely as stone buildings. Restoration projects and archaeological studies had shown them the importance of iron cramps, which appear in mediaeval buildings. Cottingham used iron for structural restoration processes in many instances, and even in an inventive way, in the construction of the organ case at Magdalen College Chapel in 1829. Viollet-le-Duc wrote on the subject of iron in his *Dictionnaire Raisonné*, and earlier in the *Annales Archéologiques* Didron published a paper on 'chainage',[35] but, as Georg Germann points out, the Germans and Austrians were less enlightened on this subject for when Heinrich von Ferstel's Votivkirche in Vienna was completed in 1879 it was proudly pointed out that no iron cramps had been used in the construction.[36]

The growing appreciation of Gothic in England and on the Continent in the early nineteenth century, antiquarianism leading to Revivalism, attitudes to mediaeval Gothic both associationist and structural, the ideas of imitative architecture, the use of new materials, the relation of theory to practice: all this points to mutual influences and a scholarly interchange of ideas. But England was the leading force in the developments. Ruskin and Morris were later to change the emphasis of the Gothic Revival in England, but the ideas of A.W. N. Pugin, considered the most influential theorist of the nineteenth century, were firmly rooted in the early work of Gough, Carter, Britton and his father A.C. Pugin. A.W.N. Pugin's theories on the role of the architect and artist working in society to bring about change reflected the intellectual ideas of the age expressed in the early decades of the nineteenth century by such writers as John Stuart Mill, Thomas Carlyle, Robert Southey and Kenelm Digby, who in his *Broadstone of Honour* of 1822 recommended the mediaeval way of life. But Pugin's ideas of an archaeologically correct revival stemmed from the seminal work of Cottingham in structural analysis and through the example of his practice as antiquary, preserver, restorer and builder of the Gothic.

Cottingham's Antiquarian Activities

Mediaeval antiquarianism and a concern for national mediaeval antiquities – particularly the churches, domestic buildings and monuments that were being allowed to crumble to dust or were being demolished to make way for new bridges, banks and docks in the great expansion of commercial enterprises in the Regency period – led to works of restoration and campaigns to save threatened Gothic remains. Attempts were made to set up national societies for the conservation of antiquities in the early decades of the nineteenth century, but these were largely unsuccessful. Cottingham, from the time of his report (in *Plans etc of Henry VII's Chapel* of 1822) of Wyatt's archaeological restoration at Westminster, and increasingly from the beginning of his own works of restoration at Rochester in 1825, was an influential figure at the centre of these forces. The great triumph of the preservationist lobby in the early 1830s, the saving of the Gothic Lady Chapel of St Saviour's, Southwark, was largely due to his efforts and inspired further campaigns throughout the country.

In the early 1820s, when Cottingham was rising to fame, the pages of *The Gentleman's Magazine* gave evidence of the prevalent destruction of mediaeval buildings and also of the voices raised in protest. St Katherine's Church by the Tower, founded in 1148, which 'had survived the shocks of Reformation and the puritanical frenzy of the succeeding age', was demolished in 1825 to make way for the new St Katherine's Dock despite 'earnest appeals to Parliament' by the Society of Antiquaries.[37] E.I. Carlos wrote an emotional account of the last church service in *The Gentleman's Magazine*, adding 'your late ever to be lamented correspondent J. Carter is spared the pain of witnessing this destruction'.[38] Suggestions to remove the mediaeval church stone by stone to Regent's Park had been ignored, but during the demolition both Cottingham and A.C. Pugin rescued architectural features for their collections.[39] The destruction continued throughout the 1830s, *The Gentleman's Magazine* and the *Mirror* noting the destruction of St Bartholomew the Little, the monastic

buildings attached to St Saviour's that were removed for the London Bridge approaches, the threatened demolition of the French Protestant Church in Threadneedle Street, and the Church of St Benedict demolished 'on the slightest excuse' to make way for the Sun Fire Office, new banks and The Royal Exchange, creating 'a disgraceful precedent where ancient buildings fell prey to improvements'.[40] Even the monuments in Westminster Abbey were not safe from vandals. In 1825, a writer in *The Gentleman's Magazine* deplored the 'custom of playing football in the more curious parts of the Abbey which resulted in the mutilation of brasses and tombs'.[41]

In the face of such disregard for the mediaeval heritage, and the disinclination of the government to thwart powerful vested interest, any successful attempt to stay the demolition of a mediaeval building that stood in the path of 'progress' was a major triumph. The only one to be reported in the journals of the time was the campaign to save the Lady Chapel at St Saviour's, led by Cottingham and James Savage (see Cat.A6).

Following this campaign other preservation issues were raised. A.J. Kempe wrote in *The Gentleman's Magazine*: 'We have saved the little gem of the Lady Chapel, but what about the nave? St Alban's is rapidly sinking into ruins, the gates of York, a fine specimen of ancient military architecture, are about to be removed, Waltham Cross is tottering, and Crosby Hall threatened.'[42] Cottingham was called in to save St Alban's, and he also supported the campaign to save Crosby Hall, a rare remaining example of a mediaeval courtyard house at Bishopsgate, built in London in 1466 by Sir John Crosby, a rich merchant and alderman of the City of London. Richard, Duke of Gloucester, lived there in 1483 and Crosby Hall was famous for the allusion to it made in Shakespeare's *Richard III*, Act III, Scene 1:

Gloster: Shall we hear from you Catesby, ere we sleep?
Catesby: You shall my Lord.
Gloster: At Crosby Place, there you shall find us both.

By 1832, the Hall was falling to ruin and was degraded to commercial use as a packer's warehouse. The trading company, Holmes and Hall, had made many alterations, removing walls, staircases, much of the carved work and panelling, and even caused further destruction by inserting floors beneath the springing of the roofs. By the time the lease of the trading company had expired, Crosby Hall was considered too dilapidated to be capable of repair and its demolition to make way for new houses was proposed.[43] A Preservation Committee composed of antiquaries and architects, most of them members of the Society of Antiquaries, was set up to raise subscriptions to save the Hall.[44] An anonymous benefactor, 'a member of a neighbouring family', donated sufficient funds to secure the purchase: publications on its architecture and historical background were prepared, to which Cottingham subscribed, as a means of funding the restoration work. Edward Blore on this occasion 'gave his valuable services gratuitously', and in collaboration with the architect, John Davies, Crosby Hall was gradually restored over a period of ten years, finally to be reopened as a Literary Institute.

Cottingham's efforts as a preserver of threatened mediaeval buildings led to his election in 1832 as an honorary member of the Society of Antiquaries, and

Fig.3 (see Cat.A5) Bishop Sheppie's Tomb, Rochester, 1825
Lithograph $7\frac{1}{2} \times 11\frac{1}{2}$ in (19×24 cm)

Effigy of Bishop Sheppie, *c.*1825

later, of the Oxford Society for Promoting the Study of Gothic Architecture. These prestigious societies and their journals, which disseminated theories and knowledge throughout Europe, had a strong influence in the widespread development of preservationism and mediaeval antiquarianism with a resulting effect upon architectural practice. Cottingham's election to the Society of Antiquaries occurred immediately following the St Saviour's campaign and a week after a paper was read to the society by A. J. Kempe describing the sepulchral effigy of John de Sheppie, Bishop of Rochester in 1352, whose tomb had been discovered by Cottingham during his restoration works of 1825.[45] In addition to the illustration for Kempe's paper in *Archaeologia*, Cottingham published a series of prints illustrating his discovery of the tomb and the fragments that he salvaged (Fig.3, Cat.A5). Cottingham himself in 1841 contributed to *Archaeologia* the results of further antiquarian research into Westminster, in particular the findings made during an examination of the floor of the Chapter House.[46] As the acknowledged authority on Westminster through his publications of 1822 and 1829, Cottingham had been requested by the Societies of the Inner and Middle Temples to examine the whole fabric of the Temple Church and make a full report to them on its condition.[47] Owing to Sir Robert Smirke's illness in 1839, the responsibility for the church's restoration fell to James Savage, architect to the societies, and advice was sought from 'the most eminent architects in London': L. N. Cottingham, Edward Blore, William Etty and Thomas Willement.[48] The restoration was described in *The Gentleman's Magazine* as being 'carried out with true antiquarian feeling' and the committee of the two societies were 'exceedingly anxious that every part of their Church should be restored and adorned in the most correct manner'.[49] In order to have a precedent for floor design of the right period, Cottingham and Savage obtained permission from Sir Francis Palgrave to examine the floor of the Chapter House, Westminster, for specimens of painted tiles. The Chapter House – of circular or polygonal form, a characteristic English type found for example at Worcester, Salisbury, York and Southwell – was possibly completed by 1253, close in date to the construction of Temple Church. Cottingham's report in *Archaeologia* described their finds. On lifting a portion of the boarded floor, they uncovered the original pavement in a 'perfect state with scarcely a tile broken and the colour as brilliant as when it was first laid'.

The tiles, of sizes from 5¾in to 9½in square, had incised coloured figures, patterns consisting of geometrical forms divided by narrow borders; and both the tiles and borders were decorated with leopards, lions, flowers and foliage. These tiles were to be described later by Lethaby as 'the finest of their time now existing' and are similar to some found at the abbeys of Chertsey and Halesowen. Cottingham included traced and copied drawings with his report, and gave a description of the most interesting tiles, such as one representing St John the Evangelist dressed as a pilgrim requesting alms of Edward the Confessor. Cottingham concluded his detailed analysis thus: 'The other designs show great delicacy in the pattern and execution, and the whole floor, when open to view must have presented a gorgeous display of the exquisite taste of the Gothic architects of the Middle Ages.' Cottingham's report displays his scholarly knowledge of the historical background and art of the

thirteenth century, and also conveys his passion for the Gothic in his obvious excitement at making these discoveries of 'delicate, gorgeous, exquisite' specimens of mediaeval art.

The designs of Cottingham's tiles were published in J. G. Nichol's *Examples of Inlaid and Encaustic Tiles* of 1845, with due acknowledgement to Cottingham, for 'the kindness with which he furnished the very careful drawings'. Copies were made by Minton's and widely used. Evidence of this can be seen at Davington Priory, owned and restored by Thomas Willement in the 1840s, where the tiles below the fireplace in the entrance hall have designs from the Chapter House; in Cottingham's own works of restoration; and in his Church of St Helen at Thorney (1845), for example, where he used geometric two-colour encaustic tiles which he based on the Westminster designs.[50] Nichol's book of 1845 was listed in publications recommended by A. Didron in *Annales Archéologiques*, in 1846, extending the influence to Europe, and such designs as the fabled Cock and the Fox found resonance in Viollet-le-Duc's major work of rebuilding and decorating the interiors and exteriors of Pierrefonds in 1857 in the mediaeval manner.

During his examination of the Temple Church itself, Cottingham discovered ancient lead coffins containing the bodies of Knights Templar under the spot where the effigies of the knights were placed. He communicated this find in *Archaeologia*, describing the coffins as very corroded, some 6ft 8in long with ornament of embossed crosses and foliage in patterns 'resembling the ornaments of Norman architecture', which had been cast in the solid lead sheets, and dating the coffins to the early 13th century'.[51] Cottingham took casts of the ornament for his collection and lot 1240 in the *Catalogue of Sale* of his museum read: 'Seven casts of very beautiful foliated Early English ornament taken from the leaded coffins of the Knights Templar in the Temple Church'. Another very important find was Cottingham's discovery of a Norman circular window in the Temple Church above the western doorway. He wrote a long article describing the window for *The Gentleman's Magazine* in 1841, which announced: 'The following communication from a distinguished architect whose well-known experience in ecclesiastical architecture has occasioned his opinion and co-operation to be solicited on the repairs to Temple Church.'[52]

Cottingham had begun his examination in the circular part of Temple Church, 'that being the most ancient'. The window had been bricked up on the interior and the exterior in 1700, when, Cottingham surmised, 'the ordinary buildings which press like an unsightly incubus against the north side of this unique edifice were erected', and he described it as 'an Anglo-Norman wheel window' of Caen stone, composed of eight spokes like small Romanesque columns of 3-inch diameter with a groove for glass on each side of the columns. Cottingham's phrase 'Anglo-Norman' demonstrates his knowledge of the Romanesque styles, as derived from northern Europe and varied in the hands of English masons. The construction of the window, he said, was 'a masterpiece of masonry' and he went on to give a detailed analysis of its structural features. He took the opportunity to promote an archaeologically correct revival by stressing the necessity of studying and understanding the historical development and construction of the different periods of the Mediaeval:

I beg leave to impress upon architectural draughtsmen, particularly those concerned with Gothic works, the necessity of accurately ascertaining the modes of construction used by the ancient masons at different periods. It will stamp a value on their works and be a sure stepping-stone towards a correct revival of the Middle Ages.

Clearly in these remarks Cottingham was suggesting that all mediaeval art was as worthy of study as the art of any other period and that it should not simply be accepted or appreciated through antiquarian interest, but should be given full architectural status.

The report of Cottingham's examination of the Temple Church, which he undertook at the request of the Societies of the Inner and Middle Temples, is now missing from the archive, but in 1843 William Burge of the Inner Temple wrote an account of its restoration and repairs, in which he quoted extensively from Cottingham's long and detailed report.[53] Burge had asked Cottingham for observations on 'the peculiar style and character' of the Temple Church, explaining that 'the acknowledged taste and skill of that gentleman and his intimate acquaintance with the Norman and Early English styles, give them great value'. Cottingham wrote that the Temple Church is the building which at once decides the long disputed point about the origin of the pointed style of architecture, at least in this country, for the structure proves that the pointed style was not imported into England in a perfect state. The transition from round to pointed arch was by no means sudden, Cottingham continued, and in the round part of the church, 'we find the Architect endeavouring to obtain an altitude and lightness in the character of his building which compelled him to trespass on the solemn grandeur of the Norman style'. He concluded his analysis by remarking:

How rejoiced every lover of our ancient church architecture must be to see the plague-spot of Gothic architecture (whitewash) swept from its painted ceilings, the 'pew-lumber' from its floors, the monstrous Pagan altar-screen, the glaring monumental tablets from its walls and pillars, and the 'preposterous' organ case from closing up its centre arch. If one step further could be taken, by removing the houses which crowded against the Church's north western front, it would be 'a glorious triumph for Gothic architecture indeed'.

Here Cottingham was listing aspects of restoration procedures that he had begun in his own works of restoration of 1825, for example at Rochester Cathedral, where he discovered mediaeval frescoes, and at Hereford Cathedral, where he found late fourteenth-century frescoes, walled-up monuments, aumbries, a piscina and the doorway to the chapel of Bishop Audley. In his reporting of these finds he was able properly to interpret and date his antiquarian findings through structural analysis and his knowledge of the art and sculpture of the different periods of the Middle Ages.

In addition to his membership of the Society of Antiquaries, Cottingham was elected honorary member of the Oxford Society for Promoting the Study of Gothic Architecture at their meeting of 9 May 1842. He acknowledged receipt of the communication announcing his election 'for which distinguished favour I feel most highly gratified'.[54] The society had grown out of the Oxford University Genealogical and Heraldic Society of 1835-9, changing its title in 1840 as the Gothic Revival gained impetus. This society predated the influential Cambridge Camden Society, founded in 1839, which published the periodical, the *Ecclesiologist*, and which changed its name to the Ecclesiologists in 1841, and there is evidence of close links between the two societies. There were members common to both groups – men of major importance to the later Gothic revival in the nineteenth century, such as John Ruskin and John Henry Newman and architects such as Anthony Salvin. Salvin, as a member of the Ecclesiologists, restored the Round Church, Cambridge, in 1842, as a model of the society's principles of restoration in 1842. The *Ecclesiologist* regularly reviewed the activities of the Oxford Society, and when the latter published a book on the model restoration of the Abbey Church at Dorchester in 1845, a copy was dedicated to the Cambridge Camden Society. The Report of *Proceedings of the Oxford Society*'s meeting of 9 May 1842 noted 'the interest in all parts of the country in promoting the taste for a study of Gothic architecture', and went on to discuss the report by Dean Merewether on the proposed restoration of Hereford Cathedral by Cottingham. At the meeting of 1848 this restoration was described as 'perhaps the very greatest work of Church restoration which has been witnessed for many years'.

The first president of the Oxford Society for Promoting the Study of Gothic Architecture was Dr Martin Routh, from 1839-44. It was he who, as President of Magdalen, initiated a highly influential Gothic Revival restoration of Magdalen College Chapel at the early date of 1829, on the basis of an open competition won by Cottingham.[55] Cottingham's election as an honorary member of the society reflects the esteem in which he was held in antiquarian circles, and in 1843, among the fifteen other distinguished honorary members were Sir Henry Ellis, Edward Blore, R. C. Hussey, Sir F. Palgrave, A. Salvin, Dawson Turner, William Twopenny, Thomas Willement, B. Ferry and J. O. Halliwell. The society's library possessed copies of Cottingham's publications and lithographs like his 'View of the Abbey Gateway at Bury St Edmunds' of 1843.[56]

Antiquarian societies, with an increasing emphasis on mediaeval studies, proliferated in the provinces in the 1840s, as a direct result of the efforts of the Oxford Society for Promoting the Study of Gothic Architecture, and were composed usually of the local landed gentry, with squires and clergymen as president and vice presidents and the majority of members aristocrats, gentlemen and noted scholars and antiquaries. The Bristol Society for Promoting the Study of Gothic Architecture, for example, was inaugurated in 1841. The *Minutes of Proceedings* note that messages of good-will were read from the Oxford Society – and demonstrating the close connections – from the Cambridge Camden Society as well. At the third meeting, a paper by J. Markland was read, entitled 'Past and Present Sepulchral Memorials with some Suggestions on improving the condition of our Churches', which contained a favourable report of Cottingham's recent restoration (1839-41) of the thirteenth-century Ashbourne Church. Markland noted that parts of Ashbourne Church had 'been strangely cut away and defaced in order that monumental tablets might be more conveniently put against them', and he went on to say that under the direction of Mr Cottingham these tablets 'were judiciously removed to places more suited to their reception'. For example, 'One large monument of the age of James I, which interfered with a beautiful lancet window, has been placed against a blank wall and partly sunk into the ground without any portion of it being hidden. This may be successfully followed in other places.'[57]

Markland drew attention to the qualities of Cottingham's work, a sensitive concern for the original mediaeval fabric and its restoration, but at the same time a sympathetic and sensible treatment of later intrusions. Markland's publications on restoration and antiquarian topics were widely publicised in European journals such as the *Annales Archéologiques*, further disseminating Cottingham's ideas and procedures of work. Cottingham himself was involved in the activities of the provincial societies, in particular through their publications which were often produced as fund-raising ventures for proposed works of restoration. Among those known to us, he subscribed to C. R. Lewis's *Illustrations of Kilpeck Church, Herefordshire, with an Essay on Ecclesiastical design and a descriptive interpretation* (1842), a small Norman church of great significance which Cottingham was to restore in 1846, and to H. Davy's *Antiquities of Suffolk* of 1840.

Oxford in the 1840s was a lively centre for the promotion of mediaeval antiquarianism. J. H. Parker was an important figure in antiquarian society and publishing circles. He succeeded his uncle as a bookseller and publisher, was a writer of architectural works such as his *Glossary of Terms used in Grecian, Roman, Italian and Gothic Architecture* of 1836, and was also Secretary to the Oxford Society for Promoting the Study of Gothic Architecture. His premises were used for their meetings and he was involved in their publications. He also published the *Archaeological Journal* begun in 1844 by Albert Way for the British Archaeological Association, and his many letters to Way from the 1840s onward indicate the development and growth of interest in mediaeval antiquities from its beginning in the early decades of the nineteenth century and reveal, too, the extent of the contacts and exchange of wide co-operation and involvement.[58] Parker described his tour of Normandy in 1843, following the prescribed route for English travellers from Le Havre to Rouen, visiting Caudebec, Jumièges, Ivreuse and Caen, as well as remote villages like Noré near Bayeux 'where Rickman and Whewell were once arrested as suspicious characters'. In a letter of March 1844 to Way he noted that 'there is a want of a good shop in Paris for architectural and artistic works. I found it out when I published the *Memorials of Oxford* of which I sold hundreds in Germany and none at all in France'. In the same letter Parker gives a clear picture of the increasing passion for the Mediaeval: 'The interest taken by the public in Gothic Architecture seems to increase daily and to spread more and more widely in France and Germany as much nearly as in England, even the Americans are beginning to catch the infection.' Because of this he regretted the title 'Archaeological' for Way's *Journal*. The words 'Middle Ages' should appear, he said:

Architecture, sacred emblems, costumes, stained glass – these are the subjects of the day, Archaeological suggests everything, Greek, Roman, Norwegian, South American, everything that nobody cares about – *Middle Ages* – arts, architecture are the subject on which all the information is wanted – it ought to stare them in the face.

The *Minutes of Proceedings* of the Oxford Society and the extensive correspondence addressed to Parker as the secretary indicate its importance to preservationism and attitudes to restoration, for the society, in common with the *Ecclesiologist* and the Incorporated Church Building Society, were overwhelmed with requests for advice on works of restoration and of church building throughout the land and as far afield as India and Australia. G. R. Lewis wrote in a letter to Parker of October 1840: 'You and the Cambridge Camden Society will in the end be the means of bringing much lost information on ecclesiastical design to light and having religious architecture established again in the Christian land.'[59] And A. W. N. Pugin himself wrote in 1843: 'I look upon the Oxford Society as being the means under God of working a great reform in ecclesiastical architecture.'[60]

Pugin, from the time he visited Cottingham's restoration of Magdalen College Chapel, which he admired without reservation, had been involved with Oxford, building the gateway at Magdalen in 1844, and making designs for Balliol College, and clearly approving of the aims and ideas of the Oxford Society in its promotion of Gothic architecture.[61] An extensive correspondence was also maintained with the Oxford Society and German antiquaries, including long reports from Dr Scholz and Dr Cloeggerault in Bonn on the progress of the Cologne Cathedral restoration, and requests for the Oxford Society to form an association for raising subscriptions for that major work.[62]

Antiquarianism in the European Context

These influential societies, with their reports and journals, in which Cottingham's major role in the development of a Gothic Revival was fully appreciated and acknowledged, led to similar developments in Europe. Publications, important to continental concerns for the preservation of mediaeval architecture and the promotion of a Gothic Revival, were begun in France in 1844 with the *Annales Archéologiques*, edited by A. N. Didron, secretary to the Comité Historique des Arts et des Monuments; and in Germany, in 1843, the *Kölner Domblatt* was published by Auguste Reichensperger as a monthly magazine. The aims and influence of these journals were similar to that of the *Ecclesiologist* although the French and Germans during the 1840s did not attempt to influence church-building design, liturgical arrangements or restoration practice to the extent of the Ecclesiologists and in general were more concerned with antiquarian and preservationist studies.[63]

In the first volume of *Annales*, for instance, Didron wrote of the growing movement for the preservation of ancient monuments, their study and repair, and deplored the 'vandalism' of unworthy restorations. He gave notice of his intention to report on such restorations as Notre Dame, St Denis, St Vincent de Paul and Rheims; he included such topics as the Musée de l'Hôtel de Cluny, Christian iconography and a detailed and swingeing criticism of the restoration 'inflicted upon the Church of St Denis'. In the early 1840s, he showed the French leanings towards restrained restoration at this date – an influence stemming from England, and directly from Cottingham, the 'most eminent Church restorer of the day'. Didron, in his first volume, included a model and plans of a church of the thirteenth century to encourage a revival of this early Gothic style, a style Cottingham had suggested in *Plans etc of Henry VII's*

Chapel for its simplicity. He published archaeological news from provincial societies; a bibliography of all works and periodicals of interest to the mediaevalist which had been published in France, England, Germany, Italy and Spain, reviews of works by Pugin, de Lassaulx, Heideloff and de Roisin; and reports from Reichensperger from Bonn and Cologne and Goertner and Ziebland in Bavaria. Didron also announced excursions to Oxford where Cottingham's restoration of Magdalen College Chapel would be viewed; to Birmingham, Cologne and Munich, the visits to be guided by Pugin, Boisserée, de Lassaulx and others; and he included many articles and illustrations in the first volume by Geefs, Overbeck, Albert Way and Thomas Wright on antiquarian studies.[64]

The *Kölner Domblatt* published extensive articles on the restoration of Cologne, theories by Boisserée of its conception from an original design by Master Gerhard disproved by discoveries of its relationship to Amiens; and articles by Zwirner, the architect in charge of works, and by Lassaulx, described by Didron as the 'Pugin in Germany', who favoured an eclectic approach to the design of the cathedral, 'combining the good elements of all periods providing they are basically compatible'.[65] The *Kölner Domblatt* also considered all aspects of preservationist concerns and considered the suitability of Gothic as a Revival style, and in contrast to the French and English views expressed in the *Annales* and *Ecclesiologist*, advocated the Romanesque as a style to be used 'for its rich and dignified construction' – views promoted by Prisac and Heinrich Hübsch. Cottingham, in his *Plans etc of Henry VII's Chapel* of 1822, had suggested the thirteenth-century Gothic as suitable for revival, views strongly promoted by Didron and Lassus in *Annales*, again showing himself as a true mediaevalist, with none of the prejudice of the *Ecclesiologist* and Pugin for fourteenth-century Gothic. He chose Romanesque for his own church of St Helen's, Thorney, in 1845, an approach that places him very close to the European tradition.

Close contacts between Didron, Reichensperger and Beresford Hope of the Ecclesiologists were maintained through visits, exchanges of articles, reviews, reports of church building, antiquarian discoveries and theories. Didron and Reichensperger visited England in 1846 for the consecration of Pugin's St Giles Church at Cheadle. Didron wrote a full account in the *Annales* of his visit.[66] He spoke of the freedom of the English in comparison to the over-governed French, delighting in the discovery that in England 'l'art national, c'est l'art gothique'; the pointed style appeared in churches, colleges, schools, hospitals and stations of ancient and nineteenth-century date. He described his visits to the cathedrals of Canterbury, Rochester and Salisbury, escorted by M. H. Gérente, an antiquary and stained-glass designer friend of A. W. N. Pugin, and he gave an extensive descriptive and critical analysis of Pugin's St Giles. At Oxford he visited J. H. Parker who wrote to Albert Way that M. Didron 'was very friendly'. Parker gave him numbers of the *Archaeological Journal* and arranged for future issues to be sent regularly and then took him to view Oxford, including Cottingham's Magdalen College Chapel.[67] Reichensperger spent time in London with G. G. Scott, Barry and Didron, and travelled widely in England and Scotland. At Cambridge he met Robert Willis, and also visited Parker at Oxford, the latter writing to Way that he was 'very

much pleased with him ... he would be a valuable foreign correspondent ...' Reichensperger regarded England as 'the land of the Gothic Revival ... England is more Germanic than Germany ...' Reichensperger's impressions were published in the *Kölner Domblatt*, *Annales Archéologiques*, and the *Ecclesiologist*, and in 1847 Beresford Hope visited him in Cologne.[68]

This evidence of the extensive communications between the various antiquarian societies establishes firmly the pattern of intellectual intercourse and mutual influences between the Continent and England. Contributions from the Archaeological Association, the Society of Antiquaries, the Oxford Society, and articles from *Archaeologia* and the *Archaeological Journal* were frequently published in the European journals; and reports of new buildings, criticism of restoration, advances in knowledge and research on many mediaeval topics were widely disseminated. Such outside reviews and reports are to be found throughout the *Annales* and the *Kölner Domblatt*, articles often circulating between the two as well as appearing in the *Ecclesiologist*. Reports of the *Annales*, *Kölner Domblatt* and extensive reviews of foreign publications are also to be found in the pages of the English societies' journals such as the *Archaeological Journal*. Among regular contributors abroad were A. W. N. Pugin, Roach Smith, Stapleton, Albert Way, Thomas Willement, Henri Gérente, J. H. Parker, Thomas Wright and Longueville Jones. Both Didron and Reichensperger published reports on the Society of Arts, Society of British Architects, Society of Antiquaries of Newcastle and the Yorkshire Architectural Society. Didron considered the Oxford Architectural Society, as the Oxford Society for Promoting the Study of Gothic Architecture became known, in 1848, to be the most important and prestigious, 'for its rich collection of books, etchings and models, and not least the importance of its members, high Anglican clergy, dignitaries of the University, professors, and eminent architects and archaeologists'.[69]

Cottingham, as an honorary member, clearly took a key role as one of such 'eminent architects and archaeologists'. His books and etchings were in the society's libraries. His celebrated restoration of Magdalen College Chapel of 1830 was visited by all who went to Oxford. And his restoration of Hereford Cathedral was described at a society meeting as 'perhaps the very greatest work of church restoration which has been witnessed for many years'. The archives of these societies show the astonishing extent of the co-operation and friendship in the widespread promotion of a Gothic Revival or – as Didron described it when stressing the benefits of exchange of work, memoirs, monographs and research – 'le rapport archéologique'. Many of the foreign architects and antiquaries were members of the societies from as early as 1822 when Francis Douce, the distinguished antiquary friend of Cottingham's, proposed Auguste le Prevost of Rouen for honorary membership of the Society of Antiquaries, praising his 'consummate skill and achievement as an antiquary, and his well known kindness to many of our countrymen'.[70]

Cottingham, from the 1820s onward, was widely known and respected through his publications, his preservationist and antiquarian activities, his museum of antiquities, and his early works of restoration 'to restore the legitimate character of Gothic buildings', all of which exerted an influence upon the Gothic Revival at a most crucial time in its development. Even after his death his work continued to receive favourable reports, for example, in the *Archaeological Journal* which was widely circulated in Europe, and which carried reports of visits to his works of restoration such as the Norman Tower at Bury 'recently preserved from impending decay under the skilful directions of the late Mr Cottingham' and St Mary's Church, Bury, which 'was in a very insecure condition and was repaired with much care by Mr Cottingham ...'[71] Some of Cottingham's close friends, too, played a leading role, and, as a man of 'generous, benevolent disposition', he gave them the benefit of his advice and made his collection available to them for study. These friends included Henry Shaw, author of a volume on ancient furniture (1836) and a work on cast-iron designs (1834) similar to Cottingham's *Founder's Director* of 1823; Sir Samuel Meyrick, the owner of Goodrich Court, famed author and collector of armour;

Sir Walter Scott, a leading inspiration in the passion for the Mediaeval; and William Capon, antiquary and stage designer who in the 1820s made drawings of Westminster Palace. All of these men were friends both of Cottingham and of Francis Douce, and surviving letters from Cottingham, Willement, Capon, Shaw, Meyrick, Scott and others to Douce in the 1820s and 1830s give an illuminating insight into the passionate fervour and dedication with which these gifted men pursued the preservation and revival of the mediaeval ideal.[72] This correspondence provides clear evidence of Cottingham's importance in the context of this group of scholars and antiquaries and in the dissemination of his ideas through the societies and their scholarly exchange, transforming the work and theories of a small preservationist and revivalist group at the turn of the century into a tidal wave of Gothic Revivalism by the end of the 1840s.

1 See Bibliography

2 *The Gentleman's Magazine*, 1786, p.1048

3 ibid.

4 Frew, J., 'An Aspect of the Gothic Revival in England *c.*1770-1815. The Antiquarian Influence with reference to the career of James Wyatt', PhD Thesis, Oxford, 1976, p.55

5 Cocke, T., 'The Rediscovery of the Romanesque', *English Romanesque Art*, RA Exhibition Catalogue, 1984, p.361

6 *The Gentleman's Magazine*, 1789, pp.1194-5

7 ibid., 1807, pp.216, 428

8 Cottingham, L. N., *Plans etc of Henry VII's Chapel*, Preface

9 *Quarterly Review*, Vol.4, Aug.-Nov. 1810, p.474

10 ibid., Vol.6, Aug.-Dec. 1811, pp.62-4

11 Crook, J. M., 'John Carter', paper read at Strawberry Hill, conference on 'The Gothic Revival', 27 Feb. 1988

12 Burge, W., *An Account of Temple Church*, London, 1843, p.9

13 Letter to John Glyde, signed 'Colchester', letter dated 31 Aug. 1832, Ipswich R.O., Glyde Papers. Cottingham acknowledges his obligation to W. G. Colchester of Ipswich for the many architectural casts he made in Suffolk and Norfolk. (See Cottingham, L. N., *Working Drawings of Gothic Ornament*, 1821, p.2)

14 Letter from George Hawkins to John Soane, 19 Jan. 1822, Cupd 1, Div. 1, Sir John Soane's Museum

15 *Catalogue of Library of Sir R. Smirke*, MUS Bib. 1118579(7), *Catalogue of Library of Sir Sydney Smirke*, 2591 and 51, Bodleian Library, Oxford

16 RIBA Library: The copy of LNC's *Plans etc of Henry VII's Chapel*, is inscribed, 'From the collection of Owen Jones'

17 'Catalogue of Original Drawings, Books of Prints, extensive general and Architectural Library etc of the late A. Pugin Esq, 4th June 1833', *Sale Catalogue*. Messrs Wheatley, London. (Sir John Soane's Museum, SCXXXIII No.3, see Lots 375-8)

18 Pevsner, N., *Ruskin and Viollet-le-Duc: Englishness and Frenchness in the Appreciation of Gothic Architecture*, 1969, p.42

19 Chateaubriand, F. R, *Œuvres Complètes*, 11, Paris, 1861; Poirier, Alice, *Les Idées artistiques de Chateaubriand, Les Sources*, Paris, 1930, pp.317-19

20 Montalembert, C. F. R., *Œuvres*, VI, *Mélanges d'art et de Littérature*, 1861, pp.7-75

21 ibid., pp.9-11

22 Germann, G., *Gothic Revival in Europe and Britain: Sources, Influences and Ideas*, London, 1972

23 ibid., p.80

24 Hautecoeur, L., *L'Histoire de L'Architecture Classique*, VI, 1955, p.285. See also Germann op. cit., p.80

25 Germann, op. cit., pp.40-1

26 Robson-Scott, W.D., *The Literary Background of the Gothic Revival in Germany*, Oxford, 1965, p.76

27 Oxford Architectural and Historical Society (OAHS) Correspondence, Bodleian Library

28 Germann, op. cit., p.48, pp.92-3

29 Lewis, M., personal communication (1989), information on the Cologne circle of architects from his doctoral thesis, University of Pennsylvania

30 Banham, R., *Theory and Design in the First Machine Age*, 1967, p.14

31 Savage, J., *Observations on Style in Architecture etc*, London, 1836, p.7

32 Kindler, R. A., 'Periodical Criticism, 1815-40: originality in architecture', *Architectural History*, 17, 1974, pp.22-37

33 *Annales Archéologiques*, ed. Didron, Paris, 1845, pp.70-5

34 ibid., p.47

35 ibid., 1846, p.47

36 Germann, op. cit., p.141

37 *The Mirror*, 6 Aug. 1825, p.97; *The Gentleman's Magazine*, July-Dec. 1825, p.391, 6 Feb. 1826, pp.9, 105; Society of Antiquaries, *Minute Book*, 1825, Burlington House

38 *The Gentleman's Magazine*, 1825, p.391. E. I. Carlos suggested that the Chapter 'with the advice of an architect of taste' could remove the church, 'the whole of the columns, arches, and other architectural details, removed and reconstructed as some atonement'. He also criticised the plan for the new church in Regent's Park to replace it, 'a Gothic Church, an edifice rich in all that compo and deal can make it, run up in some corner, next to a tall house in a different but not less ludicrous style, possessing an appearance so unequivocal it may be mistaken for a lodge or a dog kennel'.

39 *Sale Catalogues*, LNC and A. C. Pugin

40 *The Gentleman's Magazine*, 1840, articles by E. I. Carlos, May 1840, February 1841, February 1835, October 1832 and June 1835; *Mirror*, 26 April 1828, p.274

41 ibid., July-Dec. 1825, p.623

42 ibid., 1832, p.303, letter of 25 March

43 Hammon, H. J., *Architectural Antiquities of Crosby Place*, London, 1834

44 *Athenaeum*, 1832, p.338, account of Crosby Hall meeting on 8 May. List of subscribers included W. Cotton, R. Wigram, E. Blore, Sir R. Inglis, F. Chantrey, J. Gage, A. Salvin, W. Tite, W. Twopenny, E. I. Carlos, W. Etty, A. J. Kempe, T. Rickman

45 Kempe, A. J., 'Description of the Sepulchral Effigy of John de Sheppie, discovered in Rochester Cathedral, 1825'. Paper read 3 May 1832, *Archaeologia*, Vol.XXV, pp.122-6

46 Cottingham, L. N., letter communicating the result of the Examination of the Chapter House Floor, Westminster 14 Jan. 1841, *Archaeologia*, Vol.XXIX, 1841, pp.390-1

47 Cottingham, L. N., letter dated 17 Dec., *The Gentleman's Magazine*, Jan. 1841, p.18

48 Burge, W., *The Temple Church. An account of its Restoration and Repairs*, London, 1843, p.15

49 *The Gentleman's Magazine*, 1841, p.18

50 Wainwright, C., 'Davington Priory', *Country Life*, 9 Dec. 1971, pp.1650-3 and 16 Dec. 1971, pp.1716-19

51 Cottingham, L. N., letter to Sir H. Ellis, 18 March 1841, *Archaeologia*, Vol.XXIX, p.399

52 *The Gentleman's Magazine*, 1841, p.18

53 Burge, op. cit., pp.11-16

54 Cottingham, L. N., letter, 15 May 1842, OAHS, Bodleian Library, 1538

55 Magdalen College Archive, MS 735

56 *Report of Proceedings*, Oxford Society for Promoting the Study of Gothic Architecture, 22 Feb. 1843. Present received; View of the Abbey Gateway at Bury by L. N. Cottingham, p.22

57 Markland, H., 'Remarks on the Sepulchral Memorials Past and Present, with some suggestions on improving the condition of our Churches', Oxford Society for Promoting the Study of Gothic Architecture, 1840

58 Parker, J. H., letters to Albert Way, 15 April 1843 to Dec. 1845, Society of Antiquaries Archive, OAHS, Cat. of Correspondence, 1835-1900, by R. E. Poole, depd 538

59 ibid. (Society of Antiquaries Archive), G. R. Lewis to J. H. Parker, 26 Oct. 1840

60 ibid. (Society of Antiquaries Archive), A. W. N. Pugin to J. H. Parker, 13 May 1843

61 Ferrey, B., *Recollections of Pugin*, London, 1861, Reprint with Introduction and Index by C. and J. Wainwright, 1978; Colvin, H., *Unbuilt Oxford*, London, 1983, pp.105-16

62 Society of Antiquaries Archive, March 1843, Cat. no.140-5

63 My study of the three journals up to 1850 substantiates this view. Germann analysed the journals from a Gothic Revival viewpoint and does not expand on restoration issues in any great detail

64 *Annales Archéologiques*, 1844, pp.89-90; pp.2-4; pp.170, 264 and 268

65 *Kölner Domblatt*, ed. A. Reichensperger, 1843

66 *Annales Archéologiques*, 1846, pp.258-94; Beresford Hope replied in *Annales*, 1847, pp.65-70, pp.244-6

67 Society of Antiquaries Archive, letter from J. H. Parker to A. Way. Parker wrote that Didron bought a complete set of journals for his brother and paid for them ('a marvel from a French bookseller'!). They viewed the Bodleian, Radcliffe, New College, Magdalen, Christ's Church, Martyr's Memorial, The Univ. Galleries, St John's, Worcester College etc. Hence, Didron repeatedly said 'he must come again and stay for a week'.

68 Pastor Ludwig, *Auguste Reichensperger (1808-95)*, Freiburg im Breisgau, 1899, Vol.I, p.207. Reichensperger visited Canterbury, Salisbury, Cambridge (where he met Willis), Ely, Peterborough, Lincoln, Hull, Beverley, Ripon, Durham, Berwick, Melrose, Edinburgh, Glasgow, Oxford, Birmingham, St Marie's, Oscott, Worcester, Portsmouth etc

69 *Annales Archéologiques*, 1847, p.246

70 Society of Antiquaries Archive, Francis Douce to the Secretary, 20 May 1822

71 *Archaeological Journal*, Vol.XI, 1805, pp.305-7, Vol.XI, p.397

72 *The Douce Mss*, Bodleian Library, Correspondence

2

The Museum of Mediaeval Art

'The Museum of Mediaeval Art Collected by the late L. N. Cottingham FSA. Sold by auction by Messrs Foster & Son, on the premises, 43 Waterloo Bridge Road on Monday 3rd November, 1851 and subsequent days.'

In order to extend his knowledge, Cottingham spent thirty-five years building up a library and a vast collection of original specimens, models, casts of monuments and architectural features, furniture, stained glass and decorative arts, which formed 'a complete practical illustration', a study collection of Greek and Roman antiquities, and above all, of English and continental architecture, both ecclesiastical and domestic, of the mediaeval period from the Romanesque onward. It is typical of Cottingham that he was anxious to share his knowledge and promote a study of the Mediaeval, not only through his publications but through his museum which he made openly available to all to view and study. As early as 1822, in his Preface to *Plans etc of Henry VII's Chapel*, he announced that 'Mr Cottingham gives lessons on civil architecture for which purpose he has made an extensive collection of models and casts from the best remains of Grecian and Gothic buildings.' By 1840 his collection, now housed in his own house in Waterloo Bridge Road, had grown enormously. The *Civil Engineer and Architect's Journal* described a visit by a 'numerous party to a conversazione' at Cottingham's museum:

We were certainly never so surprised on passing through numerous rooms to witness such an immense collection of specimens, about 31,000 we understand, of domestic and ecclesiastical architecture, painting, sculpture and furniture. Every architect, artist and lover of antiquity should not fail to visit this museum.[1]

Cottingham himself wrote that his collection, the outcome of vast outlay of labour and cost, and the expending of his 'time and patrimony', was considered unrivalled, and had been viewed by 'several noblemen of acknowledged taste and many distinguished literary characters as well as by numerous professional friends'.[2]

The collection was sold by his family on 3 November 1851, four years after his death. The date of sale places it in the same year as the Great Exhibition, which opened in April, a coincidence that serves to set Cottingham's contribution to the Gothic Revival in sharp relief: his collection, begun in the early decades of the nineteenth century, when admirers of Gothic were few in number, was sold and dispersed barely a few months after the opening of the Great Exhibition at which A.W. N. Pugin's Mediaeval Court presented an expression of the passion for the Mediaeval at its height of influence. A *Descriptive Memoir* of Cottingham's museum was published by Christie and Manson, prior to the sale,[3] and this, with the Preface in the *Catalogue of Sale* itself, written and compiled by the distinguished antiquary and writer friend of Cottingham, Henry Shaw, together provide a comprehensive view of the contents and arrangement of his collection of mediaeval antiquities.[4] (Fig.4)

As the catalogue makes abundantly clear, the vast majority of items in the museum were carefully moulded and cast in composition, the moulds being afterwards destroyed to render the copies unique. Numerous examples of architectural details were cast from the cathedrals of Winchester, Salisbury, Lincoln, Hereford, Wells, Peterborough, Rochester, Rouen, Westminster, St Alban's Abbey, Melrose Abbey, St Stephen's and Henry VII's Chapels, the Painted Chambers and Speaker's Lodgings at Westminster, and innumerable churches in England and on the Continent. Not only were duplicates cast but details of the finest monuments of the thirteenth, fourteenth and fifteenth centuries had been carefully modelled, the mutilations restored and many of them 'fully emblazoned in imitation of the ancient colouring'. The examples were chosen to illustrate and exemplify the progression of style and were then arranged in room settings of each period.

The specimens of Anglo-Norman and transition decoration were described by Shaw as 'judiciously chosen for practical purposes but are not as numerous as those from the enrichment of later and more refined styles'. Shaw wrote of the illustration of Early English:

The most elegant, the most gorgeously beautiful of the various gradations of pointed architecture are almost endless, and comprise nearly every conceivable variety of Capitals, Bosses, Finials, Corbels and other details calculated to assist the architect in composing new designs, or guide the workman in carrying them out with appropriate character and feeling.

Examples of the Decorated and Perpendicular styles were equally numerous, varied and useful, particularly in the specimens of groining and 'other complicated features peculiar to the richly elaborate architecture of the fourteenth and fifteenth centuries'. Elizabethan architecture was represented by many and original features in the shape of ceilings, chimney pieces and panelling, besides copies from 'choice examples in various celebrated buildings'. Domestic architecture was also largely illustrated by many examples in wood and stone including whole ceilings, panelled rooms, fireplaces and windows which had been rescued intact before the demolition and destruction of the buildings themselves – an indication of Cottingham's appreciation of their use for antiquarian study, and also of their value to posterity.

The museum consisted of a range of apartments, an Elizabethan parlour and

Fig.4 Crosby Hall ceiling, 1851
Woodcut $7\frac{1}{4} \times 9\frac{1}{2}$ in (18.5×24 cm)

anteroom, two large galleries connected by an intermediate room, a chapel with a series of vaulted chambers, two rooms devoted to monumental sculpture and a number of studios filled with objects of architectural detail of every description. The richly panelled ceiling of Elizabethan plaster work with its surrounding frieze in the 'Elizabethan Parlour' was the original one from the 'ancient Palace of Bishop Bonner in Lambeth, many years since destroyed'.[5] The Palace of Bishop Bonner, described in a *History of Fulham* by Thomas Faulkener in 1812 as a mansion of the time of Henry VII, was traditionally known in the neighbourhood as the residence of Bishop Bonner. The property became an inn called the Anchor about 1500; it was variously known in the mid eighteenth century as 'The White House' and 'The Barge House', and finally became the Golden Lion tavern in 1787. It was demolished in April 1836. The walls of the Elizabethan room in the museum were decorated with brackets supporting busts, cast from various monuments, of Queen Elizabeth, Mary Queen of Scots, Sir Walter Raleigh, William Camden with his *Britannia*, and Lady Elizabeth Fane, Frances, Duchess of Suffolk, and Sir Thomas Bromley, Lord Chancellor to Queen Elizabeth, all cast from their monuments in Westminster Abbey. The elaborately carved oak door of six panels with medallions containing busts and foliage was complete with its surrounding framework of richly carved pilasters, frieze and entablature and a shield of arms with the date 1652 carved on a panel. The carved oak panelling and bookcases were of the same date as the door. The chimney piece was of carved stone with pilasters, and the mullioned window, carved inside and out, was filled with stained glass depicting the white rose en soleil of the House of York, the fleur-de-lis of Henry VII and the pomegranate of Catherine of Aragon. Furniture included a side-table of rosewood and lignum vitae 'formerly in the celebrated Palace of Nonsuch', a carved and embroidered sofa, reputedly used by Queen Anne Boleyn when she was imprisoned in the Tower, an elaborately carved walnut cabinet of the seventeenth century, a carved giltwood chandelier from the Palace of Heidelberg, and on the mantelpiece two early Flemish carved oak groups of mounted figures in armour of the time of Henry VI, formerly in the Church of St Sebald in Nuremburg and bearing the name of the artist 'Hendric Roose'.[6]

The adjoining anteroom was also in Elizabethan style with oak panelling, plasterwork ceiling, richly carved Caen-stone fireplace, mullioned window, furnished with Elizabethan oak trestle tables, fine carved oak cabinet and William III high-backed chairs. The anteroom was also ornamented with full-size cast figures of St George in armour and Henry VI with sceptre and ball, a pair of female figures reclining on couches, a pair of full-length figures of composition in imitation of bronze of St John the Evangelist and St James of Compostella, numerous busts, shields of arms, a Flemish chandelier and a pair of enamelled fire-dogs, formerly belonging to Sir Thomas More. Other curious items were a bust of Shakespeare from the monument at Stratford – 'the original mould very carefully made under the late Mr Cottingham's immediate super-intendance, and this was the only cast taken from it' – and a canette of German stoneware dated 1604, found in Shakespeare's garden at Stratford in 1818.

The First Gallery, according to Shaw, had 'obtained quite the rich subdued tone of an apartment of the Middle Ages, and may be considered the beau ideal of an Architect's Studio'. The highly enriched panelled ceiling of carved oak, with its corbels, spandrils and painted and gilt pendants, was originally from the Council Chamber of Crosby Hall and was purchased by Cottingham at the sale of Charles Yarnold's museum in 1825. The three stone windows of the First Gallery, one over the staircase leading to the basement and one measuring 9ft by 6ft, were Early English with tracery panels and mullions resting on moulded corbels and had all been saved from 'the Chapel attached to the Alms Houses of Queen Katherine in the Tower when that charitable foundation was removed to the Regent's Park'.[7] The Collegiate Church of St Katherine by the Tower, founded in 1148, was situated on the east side of the Tower of London and was attached to the oldest ecclesiastical community existing in England. It was demolished in 1825 to make way for the new St Katherine's Docks, despite pleas that 'with the advice of an architect of taste the whole of the columns, arches and other architectural details might with care be removed and reconstructed in a new situation as some atonement'.[8] Clearly Cottingham was able to salvage five of the windows and other architectural fragments. A. C. Pugin, also a collector of mediaeval remains, had acquired portions of the destroyed church as well, for they appear in the sale of his collection in 1833.[9]

Other features of the First Gallery included a magnificent altar-screen of Flemish workmanship of the date 1490, richly painted and gilt, containing one hundred and thirty figures in high relief, with fleur-de-lis surmounting each compartment placed there by the command of the Duke of Orléans (Philippe Egalité) while the screen was in his possession; a stone fireplace, 8ft wide and 15ft high, constructed from parts of the original one from the Star Chamber at Westminster; a series of panelling modelled from Winchester Cathedral and eighty-five linenfold panels in carved oak from the ancient Palace of Layer Marney in Essex; and a series of eight carved stone panels from the cathedral at Rouen and two pairs of stone capitals c.1200 from the Church of St George de Bocherville near Rouen.

The walls were covered with a series of models of saints, bishops and prophets on brackets, modelled to the same scale 'from authorities in countless Cathedrals'.[10] Thirty-one of these models had been made by Cottingham for the altar-screen at Magdalen College Chapel which he began to restore in 1829; but the models 'were not employed in consequence of objection taken to their introduction by the College authorities'.[11] Cottingham's saints had been rejected by Dr Ellerton, the Senior Fellow, who, although not an Evangelical, was bitterly opposed to High Church principles, and Cottingham had to exchange his saints for a frieze of angels, the niches remaining empty until 1865.[12] Ranged around three sides of the First Gallery were cases containing a vast collection of works of mediaeval decorative arts in stone, wood and metal, 'all of them examples of the utmost utility as studies'. The gallery also contained a colossal oak bookcase, carved with linenfold panels of 24ft in length and two others of lesser size, sets of William III carved chairs, screens, an oak reading desk, and 'a richly carved chair, of the time of James I presented to the late Mr Cottingham by Sir Walter Scott, Bart'.[13] This gift reflected the value that Scott must have placed on his friendship with Cottingham. Clive Wainwright points out in The Antiquarian Interior that at Strawberry Hill and Abbotsford antiquities presented to their owners played an important part in the creation of the interiors of these houses. 'It is a tribute to both Walpole and Scott that their friends thought highly enough of their friendship to present antiquities to them.' Scott, too, presented a Scottish sword to Sir S. Meyrick and 'was thanked in the Catalogue of Meyrick's collection'.[14]

The next room formed a small anteroom connecting this gallery with the North Gallery and had a carved oak pendant ceiling of the time of Henry VII, two stone-mullioned windows of two and three lights complete with label heads and glazing from St Katherine's Church, and numerous models and casts such as the children of Edward III from his monument in Westminster Abbey and Prophets from the tomb of Henry VII. The North Gallery again had a fine mid fifteenth-century ceiling with bold moulded principals, spandrels and elaborate bosses at the intersections, stone-mullioned windows, walls lined with compartments from tombs, a very large model with a figure from one division of the screen leading to Edward the Confessor's Chapel, a triple canopy of

elaborate design showing canopied niches with figures of St Anne, the Virgin Mary, St James and other saints, many canopies, niches with cast figures of bishops, pinnacles, corbels, colossal heads, shields, Flemish carved lions on pedestals, and fourteenth-century wood carving and examples from subsellae. This suite of rooms was terminated by an elaborate model, full size and 'executed with the greatest care', of the doorway to the Chapter House at Rochester Cathedral with its enriched arch mouldings containing niches with figures of prophets, praying angels and a figure representing the ascent of the soul to paradise.[15]

The staircase to the basement was lined with carved panels, perforated tracery and carved stoppings for beams, and the staircase itself had balustrades with quatrefoil tracery and newels surmounted by lions holding shields. The first part of the basement was arranged as a chapel with an altar-screen 12ft 8in by 10ft high, with eleven niches filled with angels, a rich cornice of angels and pierced tracery, and a panelled altar 6ft long with buttresses, pinnacles and polychromed monograms. There was also a set of six rare thirteenth-century stall ends, the return standard ends and portions of the throne with boldly carved groups of figures. Shaw wrote that 'they are of foreign manufacture and afford the strongest evidence of being the production of the same Artist as the matchless stalls of the Church of St Gereon de Cologne'.[16]

Shaw described the walls, ceilings, side-vaulted chambers, recesses and passages around this chapel as being completely filled with every conceivable detail connected with mediaeval architecture, from the most delicate fan tracery of a groined canopy to colossal specimens, including facsimiles of nine tombs, life-size figures of St George and the Dragon, 11ft-high equestrian figures of Edmund Crouchback and Henry V, a model of an angel with wings outspread from the destroyed St Stephen's Chapel under an elaborate triple canopy, with figures in niches on either side; the model of a 12ft-high doorway and its stone work surround with triple attached shafts with moulded capitals, the whole composition crowned by a panelled and embattled parapet. In addition to these recesses and vaulted chambers there were seven rooms containing even larger models and including 'a vast quantity of exceedingly fine casts of the grandest remains of Greece and Rome procured at vast expense, many of them direct from abroad', together with a large collection of carvings in detached pieces in cabinets, chimney pieces, panelling, tracery, an oak ceiling from the former cloisters at Westminster and an open timber roof of the time of Edward III which 'would admirably suit the requirements of any gentleman desirous of obtaining a Baronial Hall roof for his mansion'. Cottingham had prepared diagrams and measurements of this open timber roof to enable its accurate reconstruction.[17] Listed separately in the catalogue were architectural models of buildings. These were Cottingham's models of the restoration of St Stephen's Chapel which he constructed during the preparation of his plans for the Houses of Parliament competition, models to scale of Canterbury Cathedral, St Alban's Abbey Church, the screen of York Minster, one-half of the nave of Armagh Cathedral, one side of King's College, Cambridge, the end of Westminster Hall in its original state and 'a very beautiful model, by Salter, of St Stephen's Chapel, Westminster, shown as it originally existed; prepared for his late Majesty William IV'.[18]

As Shaw wrote, 'Nothing but the long, minute and careful inspection of a connoisseur could enable one to form an idea of the extent of Cottingham's collection' but from an analysis of the 2205 lots listed in the catalogue we can gain some sense of his passion for the mediaeval, his efforts to promote a knowledge and understanding of the architecture of the Middle Ages, his desire to preserve examples for posterity, the sheer colossal work and cost involved in collecting, modelling, casting, painting and gilding and researching his examples, and the extent of the travels he undertook in pursuit of his consuming interest. Some 700 lots, mainly models and casts, were from named English sources, of which forty-six are identified, including all major cathedrals, churches and abbeys. The evidence shows that he made models from 300 examples of architectural features, tombs, carvings, corbels, pillars, groining, tracery and statues in Westminster Abbey alone, from the Chapter House, Henry VII's Chapel, Westminster Hall, St Stephen's Cloister, the Painted Star and Jerusalem Chambers.

Nor were his interests confined to ecclesiastical work alone. He showed an understanding, rare at this time, of the importance of ancient domestic precedent; his studies included details of architectural features from unnamed domestic sources, and from Leeds and Hever Castles in Kent, great manor houses at Cobham, Barsham in Norfolk, Franks in Kent, Snelston Hall and others in Derbyshire and Herefordshire, the residence of Cardinal Wolsey in Fleet Street, and the Old Golden Lion in Fulham. As a fervent preservationist he rescued fragments as well as whole ceilings, rooms, windows from a number of named sources of ecclesiastical and domestic buildings that were falling into ruin or were actually demolished, such as Crosby Hall, Layer Marney, St Katherine's Church, the Chapter House, Cloisters and St Stephen's Chapel at Westminster, destroyed churches in Kent, the church at Westley in Suffolk, old London Bridge, Snelston Manor House, and other items such as lot 532, a cast full-size, complete with tomb, recumbent effigy and elaborate wooden canopy, of the monument of Philippa, Duchess of York, who died in 1433, 'all of which has been destroyed'.

As another source of items for the museum, Cottingham bought at auction from sales of other collections, or made models of items belonging to other antiquaries. He owned two 'cases of ornament' from A. C. Pugin's collection which was sold in 1833; a fine Elizabethan wrought-iron lock and handle with iron escutcheons and two pieces of iron railing from the tomb of Henry V from the antiquary John Carter's collection, sold by Sotheby's in 1818; other mediaeval fragments from the collection of Mr Gayfere, the Abbey mason; Roman and Greek remains such as a cast of the Elgin horse's head, a head of the Niobe and a cast of the Venus de Medici from the collection of Colonel Samuel Hayward; and a statue of Venus and a figure of Cupid from Robert Adam's collection.[19] Listed under a collection of 'Casts of Old French and Louis Quatorze Examples' was a 'very beautiful original model of two reclining figures, with a lyre between them, from the collection of Mr Nash, architect to George IV'. Cottingham had also studied mediaeval arms and armour, for among the items were figures in 'suits of armour very carefully modelled from the originals in the collection of Sir S. R. Meyrick at Goodrich Court, Herefordshire'. Sir Samuel, well-known antiquary, writer and armour expert,

had reorganised Queen Elizabeth's Armoury in its new museum at the Tower in 1828. No doubt Cottingham also bought from the well-known antique dealers of the day such as Edward Hall, John Webb and Samuel Pratt, who was a close friend of his.[20] Other friends supplied him with antiquities, collecting for him on their travels. A. W. N. Pugin, for example, made a note in his diary for December 1840: 'Figures for Cottingham';[21] and in a letter to R. B. Phillips, Cottingham's son Nockalls wrote that he and his father thought Heckington Church so perfect that they had spent £100 having casts and drawings made.[22]

As indicated earlier, it would seem most likely from the evidence of a large range of items from continental sources that Cottingham travelled widely. Some of the Greek and Roman casts were described as 'procured at vast expense many of them direct from abroad', and the catalogue lists mediaeval architectural fragments and casts from Germany, St Sebald's Church at Nuremburg, St Gereon de Cologne and the Palace at Heidelberg, churches in Belgium at Malines, many from France, from the Church of St George de Bocherville and the cathedrals of Rouen and Chartres, as well as many items from unnamed sources, Flemish carvings, screens, and 'French work of 1600 and Louis XIV examples'. Cottingham, with his knowledge of the development of continental Gothic church architecture, which he displayed in his volumes of 1822, and his passion for the Romanesque, undoubtedly would have been among those architects who visited northern France for the purposes of study. Many of Cottingham's friends in the Society of Antiquaries and the Oxford Society for Promoting the Study of Gothic Architecture travelled abroad and of course A. C. Pugin and his son Augustus also enlarged their collections of antiquities by bringing them direct from France.[23]

Cottingham's collection of casts and models was appreciated in his own time, but it is possible, however, to see how easily and quickly a reputation can be brought into disrepute by ignorant and inaccurate reporting. William Holman Hunt, for instance, in his influential volumes *Pre-Raphaelitism and the Pre-Raphaelite Brotherhood*, described a visit to the museum in 1850; he spoke of Gothic treasures in various chambers of the house: 'a magnificent fourteenth century balustraded flight of steps with pillars and groined covering, canopied tombs, statues, family effigies and brasses, stained glass of the choicest rarity'. Hunt then concluded with the statement: 'ALL OF WHICH had been improved off the face of the sacred edifices which the firm Cottingham & Son had been called upon to restore ... in those days this form of iconoclasm was regarded as meritorious rather than otherwise'.[24] This quotation, described as 'unkind but accurate', was used as recently as 1980 in comments on Cottingham's work.[25] However, as the evidence makes clear, the vast majority of items were carefully moulded from the originals and cast in composition or rescued from threatened buildings, indicating, not vandalism as Hunt implied, but an understanding of their value to posterity, and an advanced appreciation of the mediaeval at an early date in the nineteenth century.

In the *Descriptive Memoir*, Shaw pointed out the 'practical utility of the valuable assemblage of works of art' and continued: 'To the professional Architect it must be acknowledged to be the most perfect reference for study and analysis of the principles of Ancient art ever formed in this or any other country, indeed quite unique.' He hoped that the entire collection would be purchased by some patron of the arts sufficiently wealthy and liberal to procure it for one of the societies 'established throughout the Kingdom for the study of Mediaeval Architecture', or that the government might form the nucleus of a national museum of English architectural antiquities, 'the want of which has so long been felt by all engaged in the pursuit of the Architectural and Industrial Arts'. *The Gentleman's Magazine* of 1850 commented on the excuse that there was a problem of space for such a collection, 'yet the Parisians find space for their mediaeval antiquities, at the Palais des Thermes and L'Hôtel de Cluny and L'Ecole des Beaux Arts; even a suburban locality would do, even the terminus of a railway station, or like the riding house at Brighton.'[26]

The government failed to respond. This idea was not new. In 1844 Cottingham's pupil, E. B. Lamb, wrote 'a spirited letter' to the Trustees of the British Museum calling for the inauguration of a separate gallery for British Antiquities and the classification of Gothic architecture. He wrote: 'I have an earnest desire that both the public and the architectural profession should become more familiar with and better able to appreciate the architecture and arts of the Middle Ages.'[27] The reply then was the same as their reply in 1850-1; 'The Trustees are not prepared to recommend the Government to provide in the Museum for any collection or remains of the Gothic architecture of Great Britain.'[28]

This attitude in 1851 brought a sharp response. Reports in *The Gentleman's Magazine* and *The Builder* expressed 'regret and apprehension' at the sale, with bitter remarks about the British Museum's lack of interest and their failure to buy it intact.[29] In his Preface to the Sale Catalogue, Shaw wrote of the value of the Schools of Design 'having done much to improve the character of numerous articles', but such a collection as Cottingham's could supply a means of educating employers and employed in the principles of composition and the character of materials. As the government had failed to see this opportunity, he hoped that some of the collection might be procured as an adjunct to the Schools of Design. Other efforts to save the collection were made, including a subscription instigated by G. G. Scott, supported by Alfred Waterhouse, Norman Shaw, J. Clarke, E. Seddon and others, but to no avail. The collection was dispersed and sold to a variety of collectors and private buyers, *The Builder* noting on 8 November: 'It is a matter of regret that the members of the architectural profession have not yet availed themselves so extensively as they ought to have done, nor have representatives of any of the Schools of Design been present hitherto.'

A portion of the collection, however, formed the basis of the Architectural Museum at Cannon Row, Westminster, set up in 1852, and other buyers included those who were starting their own collections such as 'Mr Purnell of Stanscombe Park'. Purnell, according to the report in *The Builder*, bought the facsimile of the tomb of William de Valence for 21 guineas, lot 1531, a mediaeval cabinet which was illustrated in the catalogue, and lot 373, a fine marble cinerary urn. Sadly, the interiors of Stanscombe Park were destroyed by fire and presumably these items were lost then. A Mr Lacy of 'the New York Museum now forming' bought the cast of Shakespeare's bust at Stratford, and lot 374, a marble African girl's head 'brought from Pompeii'.[30] Many architectural casts found their way to the Architectural Association's museum

in Tufton Street, for in 1916 they were gifted to the Sculpture Department at the Victoria and Albert Museum.[31] In store are to be seen casts of architectural details from Westminster, foliate capitals, vaulting bosses, a carved and pierced arch moulding, and eighteen casts of half-length figures of angels from the soffits of the windows in the north transept. These were sold in pairs in the sale and correspond to lots 734 to 745. One of the soffits showing an angel playing on a dulcimer with a plectrum was illustrated in the catalogue. The total realised from the twelve-day sale of 2205 lots was £2009 13s 6d.

Cottingham's museum represented a life's work, 'the expending of his patrimony and his leisure time to qualify for excellence in his profession'. To this end he travelled to study, to collect, and to save from destruction examples of mediaeval antiquities: to understand fully, through minute analysis, the art and sculpture, and the historical background to the entire mediaeval period in Europe. The grasp he thereby achieved of the structure and development of the different stages of Gothic was fundamental to the character and high quality of his Gothic Revivalism. He used his study and his collection as a source for his publications on Gothic architecture, *Westminster Hall*, *Henry VII's Chapel* and the *Working Drawings of Gothic Ornament*, and for his designs in cast iron to which he brought his knowledge of classical antiquities. His study and collection also informed his work as a church restorer attempting to achieve an archaeologically correct revival of Romanesque and the true Gothic. In addition, they inspired his Gothic Revival domestic architecture and design. He made his collection available to antiquaries, architects, literary figures and his students for study and example in his efforts to promote a Gothic Revival, a revival to be achieved not through simple copyism, but through an understanding of the structure of mediaeval buildings and of the spirit and intention of the mediaeval architects. The mediaeval examples would be transformed to new uses and a new age.

The significance of Cottingham's museum becomes clear when seen in a wider European context. It followed the Renaissance tradition of a house museum in which the collector's private residence served as the repository for the collection, and also shared with other early nineteenth-century collections the characteristics of the Greek Mouseion, the idea of a Temple of Arts, a combination that David Watkin has described 'as an age of transition from the private collection to the public museum'.[32] The first private collections were founded in the villas of the ancient Romans with magnificent collections of paintings, sculptures and relics of antiquity looted from the entire Mediterranean world. In the Renaissance the idea of collecting was revived and the term 'museum' emerged to describe the collections formed by princes and artists, signifying great wealth, prestige and learning. A concern with antiquity showed in the assembling of antique statues and fragments in villas and gardens and soon cabinets and galleries were designed to house collections.[33]

Rubens designed an antiquarium at his Antwerp town-house based on the Roman Pantheon to accommodate his antique sculptures and this tradition spread to England in the early seventeenth century when Rubens's patron, Thomas Howard, Earl of Arundel, first assembled a vast collection of antiquities.[34] Neo-Palladian sculpture galleries were designed for the great collections at Holkham Hall, Castle Howard and Newby Hall and remained an influential prototype well into the nineteenth century. The curiosity cabinet, or chamber, for the display of smaller objects with its connotations of connoisseurship and study, foreshadowing the character of Cottingham's museum, stemmed from the Renaissance quest for universal knowledge. There were many examples of such cabinets throughout Europe including the 'closet of rarities' of John Tradescant and his son in the early seventeenth century, which formed the basis of the Ashmolean Museum, England's first public and pedagogical museum. By the end of the eighteenth century the passion for collecting antiquities of Greece and Rome was at its height, and as well as the famous collections of such dilettanti as Charles Townley, William Fitzmaurice, Charles Lennox and Richard Payne-Knight, many other small, private cabinets were to be found in London. John Timbs in his *Curiosities of London* of 1828 listed such museums:

Mr Chaffers with 1000 specimens discovered in London excavations; Saull's Museum in Aldersgate Street, a private collection of antiquities, open to view on Thursdays: Mr P. Marryatt's large collection of ceramics; Lord Londesborough's selection of antiquities, shown at conversationes given in the London season; the private collections of Mr H. Magniac, Mr Octavius Morgan, Mr Slade's and Mr Bernal's – all available to view upon written request.

Cottingham, in his work for his patron John Harrison of Snelston Hall in 1827, was required to design a large display cabinet or sideboard to house Harrison's collection of treasures, items of classical antiquity, mediaeval artefacts and Renaissance metalwork, a type of commission many architects in the first half of the nineteenth century were called upon to undertake.

A well-known house museum that also aspired to the Temple of Art ideal was that of Thomas Hope in Duchess Street, London. Cottingham, in his pursuit of knowledge, would no doubt have visited Duchess Street: his links through patronage with the Hope family support this supposition. Hope believed that a study of ancient art would improve standards of design and propagate a modern style, and he made his collection of classical antiquities, amassed during his Grand Tour and through such purchases as Sir William Hamilton's second collection of vases, available for study. He devoted a storey of his residence to a museum, open from 1804, and arranged a sequence of model rooms filled with antique paintings and furniture, composed of a sculpture gallery, a picture gallery, vase room, lavarium, Flaxman's room, and Egyptian and Indian rooms.[35]

M. Passavant, a German visitor to England in 1836, described the impact of Hope's museum: 'Luxuriously adorned in the usual style at the beginning of the century, when taste for the antique, however imperfectly understood, prevailed.'[36] Thomas Hope was a confirmed classicist but his intention to educate and improve design through his collection and his publication *Household Furniture* of 1807, as well as the French parallel, the *Recueil de Décorations Intérieures* of 1801 and 1812 by Percier and Fontaine, perhaps influenced Cottingham, whose museum was also concerned with the history, instruction and creation of architecture.

Sir John Soane's private museum in Lincoln's Inn Fields was another house museum established in the first decade of the nineteenth century, a 'perfect neo-classical miscellany,' as Susan Feinberg in her analysis of the museum described it, a shrine to its creator. John Britton in 1827 wrote an account of Soane's museum appropriately entitled the *Union of Architecture, Sculpture and Painting*, and Soane, in his own description of the house and museum, did not provide a catalogue of the 3000 exhibits but a descriptive account of his collection within its designed setting, as Shaw was to do later in his *Descriptive Memoir* of Cottingham's museum, stressing not simply the value of the objects but the manner in which the rich variety of objects was combined. Soane's museum closely followed the sixteenth-century tradition of the cabinet with its vast array and clutter of artefacts, pictures close-set, casts, sculpture and relics arranged with no attempt at chronology. G. F. Waagen, the director of the Royal Gallery in Berlin, gave in 1838 a personal view of Soane's museum, describing it as

a pattern card of the most diverse styles of architecture. Sometimes happy, for the most part failures – the whole, notwithstanding a certain picturesque fantastic charm in consequence of this arbitrary mixture of heterogeneous objects, something of the unpleasant effect of a feverish dream. As a splendid example of English whimsicalness which can only be realised by the union of colossal English wealth and the English way of thinking.[37]

Waagen in this description highlights the very qualities of Soane's museum, a highly subjective, whimsical, picturesque, fantastic mixture, a clear contrast to Cottingham's archaeologically correct approach. Soane's museum included a 'monk's parlour' or mediaeval closet which housed a collection of plaster casts and fragments of Gothic architecture, finials, crockets and grotesques. Some of the architectural remains were acquired by Soane in the early 1820s during his heavily criticised demolition of the old House of Lords at Westminster; but again, Soane's intention was not to imitate Gothic structural elements nor provide a visual history of the mediaeval, but to create a picturesque mock-period room, or, as John Summerson has suggested, a satire on Gothic antiquarianism.[38] Soane, of course, had suffered the humiliation of having to replace his Palladian façade to the new Law Courts with a Gothic design in 1825, and he condemned the 'blind attachment to modern Gothic structures'. He was critical of the 'incongruities so frequent in modern Gothic Buildings' although he scorned imitations of Gothic, and in his lectures to students at the Royal Academy in 1812 he advised them 'to study that style with the most serious attention, not for its taste, but for the same effect in mass and detail'. Perhaps in this attitude to the Gothic Soane was echoing the approach of Laugier in France, who in his *Essai* of 1753 wrote in appreciation of the structural rationality of Gothic but condemned the Gothic taste in ornament. Soane, however, showed respect for serious archaeological study of the Gothic, for he requested a copy of Cottingham's *Plans etc of Henry VII's Chapel* for his own library.

Cottingham lived close by in Lincoln's Inn Fields and no doubt knew the museum and its monk's parlour well. Certainly Soane, as well as creating picturesque effects and glorifying the art of architecture, intended his collection to function as a classroom or a private architectural academy, and his first recorded purchase of architectural plaster casts dates from 1792.[39] Other collections of casts had been amassed by Robert Adam, Henry Holland, Charles Tatham, Samuel Hayward and others, and as we have seen, both Cottingham and Soane bought items from these collections during the early 1800s as they came up for auction. John Britton wrote of the advantages of casts over drawings for the student to learn the subtleties of proportion, mass, light and shade, and Cottingham, in 1822, when advertising that he gave lessons on civil architecture, noted 'his extensive collection of models and casts from the best remains of Grecian and Gothic buildings'.

Soane's museum was predominantly classical, differing completely in arrangement and content from Cottingham's museum of mediaeval antiquities, which was specifically intended to promote an authentic archaeologically correct Gothic Revival. Others such as A. C. Pugin collected mediaeval remains with examples from England and the Continent as a means of instructing his son and his other students; and William Bullock, a Liverpool goldsmith, took his collection of curios from his private house museum and exhibited them to the public in the Egyptian Hall in Piccadilly prior to their sale in 1819. In his Liverpool museum, he had arranged a room 'in the Gothic manner' with a figure in a suit of armour under a Gothic arch, lit by a stained-glass window 'to kindle respect for the memory of our forefathers', but apart from these efforts little serious attention was given to the collection of mediaeval antiquities.[40] Cottingham's museum, therefore, was the first major museum of national mediaeval antiquities in the country, significant not only for its content at a time (1822) when in general Gothic was despised, but also for its chronological arrangement in suites of rooms, forming, as Shaw said, 'a complete illustration to the study of English Architecture, Ecclesiastical and Domestic, from the Norman Invasion to the end of Queen Elizabeth's reign, the most perfect reference for study and analysis ever found in this or any other country'.

The concept of period rooms as a means of display is rooted in antiquity, for example at Hadrian's Villa, Tivoli, where the emperor returned with his collection and re-created the finest monuments that he had seen in his ten years of travel, reproducing the celebrated halls of Athens and Delphi and the Vale of Tempe in Thessaly. An example of a museum designed as a sequence of period rooms that predated and may have influenced Cottingham (for it was devoted to the Mediaeval) was to be found in France in the late eighteenth and early nineteenth century. Laugier was an early appreciator of aspects of Gothic, but the true precursor of the Gothic Revival in France was Alexandre Lenoir.[41] In Lenoir's volume *Musée Royale des Monuments Français* of 1815, it is related in the Preface that Lenoir, during the revolutions of 1790 'at the peril of his life', saved from destruction a major part of the royal monuments. From that time he continued to buy, and save from being vandalised, other mediaeval antiquities, opening a museum in the converted convent of Les Petits Augustins, which he administered under the surveillance of the Minister of the Interior. Lenoir, during the twenty-four years of the museum's life, restored, re-created from fragments and arranged his exhibits in chronological order, 'composing a history of the French monuments through the arts, costumes and uses of the people of antiquity'.[42]

He explained in his volume that through a visual journey from one century to another all the variations of architecture, the monuments, the needs of life

and domestic usage would be clearly set out from the thirteenth to the seventeenth century. The Salle d'Introduction contained a chronological display of examples from all the centuries, a visual 'list of contents', the rooms lit by stained-glass windows to 'create a Gothic atmosphere', and then proceeded through a sequence of correct historical suites composed of original and facsimile monuments, ornaments and decorative arts of each era, exactly as Cottingham was to do in his museum of mediaeval antiquities.

Lenoir's Musée won international fame and was visited by keen antiquaries on their travels in northern France. Not all of them, however, approved of Lenoir's approach to archaeology. Charles Stothard, the antiquary friend of Cottingham, noted in 1818 in a letter to the Reverend T. Kerrick that he found the Musée 'a terrible disappointment':

I found Carloman, Pepin, Clovis and a whole lot of others as twins, all manufactured about the time of St Louis. Besides these I counted 16 or 18 substitutes for those figures which had been mutilated or destroyed in the revolution, made of Plaster of Paris, and to save trouble, all out of 1 mould, the variations being marked by divers ornaments scratched on the belts and fleur-de-lys stuck on the shields ... I thought this unpardonable in such pretenders as the French, when I learnt that sufficient of the originals still existed entirely to contradict their representations.[43]

The *Annals of Fine Art* of 1818 made the point, though, that it was an 'historic illustration of the arts, to which we have nothing in this country to compare', and Lenoir's description and catalogue which listed 572 entries was widely distributed, Soane having four different editions in his library.[44]

Lenoir's Musée was the first museum devoted to mediaeval works of art, inspired by his passion to preserve and restore remaining examples of the national art and architecture and by his desire to educate and inform. Hope and Soane, with their predominantly classical collections and subjective approach, cannot be compared to Lenoir, but Cottingham, with his unique collection of English mediaeval antiquities, his chronological arrangement from the Norman to Elizabethan age, his passion to preserve from demolition remaining monuments, his plaster casts and painstakingly modelled and painted replicas, and his declared intention to promote a Gothic Revival, is Lenoir's exact counterpart in England, in spirit if not entirely in execution.[45]

Later collectors in France acknowledged their debt to Lenoir. One such was Alex du Sommerard whose Hôtel de Cluny, a mediaeval building in Paris, housed his collection of mediaeval and Renaissance objects from 1832. In the prospectus to his five volumes *Les Arts au Moyen Age* of 1838-46, Du Sommerard noted the contribution of Montfaucon to antiquarian studies but he continued, it was Lenoir's Musée, 'so well described, so picturesquely classified which focused attention on the importance of these antiquities', an achievement that was exactly mirrored by Cottingham and his museum.[46] The Cluny exists today, and its present guidebook describes how Du Sommerard's museum was the haunt of litterateurs, artists and patrons, and it became the acknowledged centre of the growing cult for the Middle Ages among Romantics.[47] Cottingham wrote in 1832 that his collection had been viewed by 'noblemen of acknowledged taste, distinguished literary characters and numerous professional friends'. Among his noble patrons was Lord Brougham, the Chancellor, for whom Cottingham built a mediaeval baronial hall, and he was friend and mediaeval advisor to Sir Walter Scott, perhaps one of the greater influences on the European Romantic movement through his novels of the Middle Ages. Francis Taylor, writing of Lenoir, said that his Musée, as the first museum of mediaeval art in France, 'was the catalyst of the Romantic movement and the herald of the Gothic Revival in France'. Perhaps if the strenuous efforts of Scott, Waterhouse, Shaw, Clarke, Christian and Seddon in 1851 had been successful in saving Cottingham's museum of mediaeval antiquities from dispersal and persuading the government to fund it as a national collection, Cottingham's contribution as the catalyst of the Romantic movement and herald of the Gothic Revival in England through the far-reaching influence of his mediaeval museum would have been acknowledged before now.

1 Editorial, *Civil Engineer and Architect's Journal*, July 1840, p.249

2 Cottingham, L. N., letter to Fishmongers' Court, 15 Feb. 1832, Guildhall Library, MS F843, File 14

3 *Descriptive Memoir*, 'Museum of Mediaeval Architecture and Sculpture founded by the late L. N. Cottingham, FSA', Christie & Manson, 1850

4 *Catalogue of Sale*, 'The Museum of Mediaeval Art collected by the late L. N. Cottingham FSA'. Sold by auction by Messrs Foster & Son, on the premises, 43 Waterloo Bridge Road on 3 Nov. 1851 and subsequent days

5 ibid., Lot 61

6 ibid., Lots 47, 48, 73, 74, 79

7 ibid., Lots 365-7

8 *The Gentleman's Magazine*, 1825, p.391

9 *Sale Catalogue*, A. C. Pugin, Messrs Wheatley etc, Lot 20

10 ibid., LNC, Lots 295, 309, 327, 290, 243

11 ibid., Lot 83. Quote from entry for Lots 83-124

12 Boase, T. S. R., 'An Oxford College and The Gothic Revival', *Journal of the Warburg Institute*, Vol.XVIII, p.171

13 *Sale Catalogue*, LNC, Lot 303

14 Wainwright, C., 'The Antiquarian Interior', PhD Thesis, University of London, 1987, p.54

15 *Sale Catalogue*, LNC, Lots 162-234

16 ibid., Lots 347-51; 352-60

17 *Descriptive Memoir*, op. cit.

18 *Sale Catalogue*, LNC, Lots 829, 1508-14. Stephen Salter of Hammersmith was a celebrated model maker of the day

19 *Sale Catalogue*, 'The Collection etc etc of the late Mr Robert Adam' on 20-21 May 1818, Christie & Manson

20 *Brougham Papers*, Letters, diaries etc. University College Library, London

21 Wedgwood, A., *Catalogue of Architectural Drawings in the Victoria & Albert Museum. A. W. N. Pugin and the Pugin Family*, London, 1985, p.49

22 Cottingham, N. J., Letter to R. B. Phillips, 19 Oct. 1849, Belmont Abbey Collection, National Gallery of Wales, Bundle No.29

23 Ferrey, B., *Recollections of A. W. N. Pugin*, London, E. Stanford, 1861, p.xxiii

24 Holman Hunt, W., *Pre-Raphaelitism and The Pre-Raphaelite Brotherhood*, London, 1905, Vol.I, p.179

25 Cole, D., *The Work of G. G. Scott*, London, 1980, p.50

26 *The Gentleman's Magazine*, 1850, p.629

27 *Civil Engineer and Architect's Journal*, letter from E. B. Lamb, August 1844

28 ibid., 18 Nov. 1844, letter from I. Forshall, Secretary to the Trustees of the British Museum

29 *Civil Engineer and Architect's Journal*, June 1850, p.629; *Builder*, 27 Sept. 1851, p.742

30 Handwritten notes on the *Sale Catalogue*, LNC, V&A Library

31 V&A Museum, Sculpture Dept Archive, File; Tufton Street Casts, A1916 to 3906. Given by the Architectural Association. See p.10, Westminster Abbey. See also V&A Minute Paper, 9.3.1916, refers to offer from Professor Lethaby of drawings from his office in the Royal College of Art (RCA) of St Stephen's Chapel, possibly by Cottingham as part of the model he was having made. (E616 617-1916 A58)

32 Watkin, D., *Thomas Hope 1769-1831 and the Neoclassical Ideal*, London, 1968

33 Taylor, F. H., *The Taste of Angels*, London, 1984, pp.20-1

34 Baudouin, F., *La Maison du Rubens*, Antwerp, 1977, pp.14-16

35 Law, H. W. and I., *The Book of The Beresford Hopes*, London, 1925, pp.17-20

36 Feinberg, S., 'Sir John Soane's Museum, An analysis', PhD Thesis, University of Michigan, 1979, p.231

37 Waagen, G. F., *Works of Art & Artists in London*, 3 Vols, 1838, Vol.II, p.181

38 Summerson, J. ed., *A New Description of Sir John Soane's Museum*, 7th revised edition, The Trustees of Sir John Soane's Museum, 1986

39 Feinberg, op. cit., p.231

40 Bullock, W. A., *Companion of The Liverpool Museum*, 17th edition, 1816

41 Bazin, G., *The Museum Age*, New York, 1967

42 Stothard, C. A., *Memoirs, Including letters etc of the late C. A. Stothard*, London,1823. March 1818, letter to the Reverend T. Kerrick, p.262

43 Lenoir, A., *Musée Royale des Monuments Français*, Paris, 1815, Preface

44 *Annals of Fine Art II*, 1818, p.124

45 Feinberg, op. cit., p.263. Feinberg gives a brief description of LNC's museum taken from Shaw's *Descriptive Memoir*, and she rightly suggests that LNC rather than Soane is the 'English Lenoir'.

46 du Sommerard, A., *Les Arts du Moyen Age, Prospectus. L'Hôtel de Cluny, issu de ses ruines et les objets d'art de la collection du Sommerard*, Paris 1838-46, Preface

47 Wainwright, C., 'The Romantic Interior in England', NACF Review, 1985, p.88

3

Church Restoration

Cottingham's Approach to Restoration

The major part of Cottingham's practice between 1820 and his death in 1847 was concerned with church restoration, and the rebuilding and refitting of church interiors. He worked at Rochester Cathedral, Magdalen College Chapel, St Alban's Abbey, Armagh Cathedral, St Mary's Church, Bury St Edmunds and Hereford Cathedral as well as at many small parish churches throughout England. As far as we know, he designed and built only one church, St Helen's, Thorney, in Nottinghamshire. He had an extensive business in the design of church furnishings and was one of the first architects to promote the design and the use of encaustic tiles in churches.

His structural analysis and study of mediaeval architecture enabled him to bring to his works of restoration a scholarly understanding of the historical evolution of structure and design, an appreciation of the art of all periods, and a preservationist fervour to save as many parts of an ancient building as possible without reworking or rebuilding. In his *Plans etc of Henry VII's Chapel* he urged the young architects 'who might be called upon to restore' Gothic fabric to learn the relationship of the parts to the whole, to study the 'mechanical construction' and to observe with what strict propriety the character of each class of the Mediaeval was maintained through its structure and ornament. He deplored the 'ignorance of modern improvers' and stressed the need for accuracy, 'a sure stepping stone towards a correct revival of the Middle Ages'. He was aware of the value of saving even the smallest fragments of the English mediaeval heritage, noting:

It is a most fortunate circumstance for the revival of our national architecture that a certain impress or stamp is given to the minutest fragment of a moulding or vestige of enrichment so as to mark the era of a building and enable the architect to restore or design with certainty and the antiquary and historian to record with truth.

At every opportunity Cottingham pleaded for the preservation of all mediaeval remains, in terms of history, of style and as monuments to the past:

How truly admirable and honourable it is then to preserve these time honoured remains from total destruction for when perishable manuscript is lost and all record gone, a single capital or base of a column, a small fragment of foliage ... may serve to fill up a hiatus on the page of history.[1]

At times, for example in his work at Rochester and Bury St Edmunds, Cottingham carefully sifted through the dust and debris of centuries to find fragments to guide him to correct restoration of mouldings, tracery, tombs or sculpture. Unlike some restorers of the nineteenth century – for example, G. G. Scott, who wrote and lectured on the need for restrained restoration but at

times undertook drastic rebuilding work to return the fabric to some imagined ideal – Cottingham, in his works of restoration, invariably followed his own rules for the sensitive handling of the original mediaeval building. It is difficult to talk of a development or growing maturity in his approach to restorations apart from the authority gained through greater experience of ecclesiastical architecture, for Cottingham's principles of restoration were fully fledged when he began his major work at Rochester in 1825 and those principles and working methods he retained with the highest integrity throughout his career. For example, at the Magdalen College Chapel restoration, instructions were repeated throughout the *Bill of Works* to restore by mending the decay rather than by total renewal and to use only the finest quality of materials and craftsmanship.[2] Whitewash was removed from marble pillars and carved wood, pavements lowered to their original positions revealing the bases of columns as at Rochester in 1825, and funerary monuments and tablets, such as those at Ashbourne Church which disfigured piers and traceried windows, were removed to a more suitable part of the church. Some of the churches that Cottingham was to restore, Armagh and Hereford Cathedrals, St Alban's Abbey and the parish churches of St Mary's Bury, Market Weston and Milton Bryan, were in imminent danger of collapse after centuries of neglect or ill-judged repairs, and to these Cottingham brought his skill as innovative engineer. At Armagh and Market Weston he restored the leaning walls of the nave and towers 'by an ingenious application of science' of his own invention without dismantling or removing a single stone, and at St Mary's Bury and St Alban's he encased decayed roof beams in cast-iron shoes to avoid removing and renewing the ancient carved timbers. These were new processes and were widely reported upon at the time. When new work was required, Cottingham went to great lengths to find a precedent for his designs as at St Mary's Bury where 'every part of the old was restored with a faithful adherence to the original design, and all that was new was done in the same spirit and made to harmonise with the old'.[3]

Cottingham's techniques are shown clearly in his restoration work, his sensitive, informed and careful approach, and his Gothic Revivalist disdain for the fittings of the classical period, which he described as 'pagan' and which had obscured and damaged the structure and ornament of the original Gothic building. Other vital aspects of restoration work in this period were the influence of the Oxford Movement's doctrinal reform of the Anglican Church, dating from Keble's Assize Sermon of 1833, and from 1839 onward, the efforts of the Cambridge Camden Society to repair the neglected fabric of churches and to restore correct liturgical arrangements. Cottingham, as early as 1829 at

Magdalen College Chapel, Oxford, undertook a full Mediaeval Revival interior, predating A.W.N. Pugin and the Ecclesiologists. At Armagh in 1834 and Hereford in 1841, he met with some opposition to his plans to reintroduce the full imagery and symbolism of the Gothic church in the form of statues in niches and the reintroduction of rood screens. It was a measure of his authority as a mediaeval expert and of the force of his determination to restore the Gothic church in every detail that he was sometimes able to overrule his patrons.

Most importantly, Cottingham expressed an advanced appreciation and understanding of all periods of the Mediaeval, particularly the despised Romanesque, which even in the later nineteenth century was considered 'rude, shabby, bald, and grotesque'.[4] He viewed all stages of the Gothic as architectural developments worthy of serious consideration and recognised the relation of part to part and of part to whole, an approach which he stressed in his advice to architects who might be called upon to restore mediaeval buildings. Cottingham brought this understanding to his architectural practice, leading him to treat with respect the parts of a building that were of different dates, regarding each as a valid development and as an important part of the whole design. In this respect Cottingham introduced a new approach to mediaeval architecture, in complete contrast, for example, to the eighteenth-century works of restoration of James Wyatt and to the theories of Laugier. His innovatory approach was a vital element in the change of attitude to the Mediaeval and it marked the difference between the eighteenth and the nineteenth centuries. Indeed, the superior quality of Cottingham's work stands in notable contrast to much contemporary English and French restoration work of the nineteenth century.

Attitudes to Restoration and Contemporary Practice

As early as 1798 the Reverend John Milner, in his *Dissertation of the Modern Style of Altering Ancient Cathedrals as exemplified in the Cathedral of Salisbury*, deplored the destruction by James Wyatt of fifteenth-century tombs, the destruction of the proportions and the relation of different parts of the cathedral. He criticised the removal of the reredos and levelling of the chancel to create the classical ideal of space, and 'the introduction of uniformity' into a mediaeval edifice at variance with 'the original architectural mode'. And he objected to the combining in the restoration of the 'Third Pointed Order and the First Pointed Order'. In this work Milner showed an advanced historical understanding and an unbiased attitude in his demand that surviving distinctive architectural features be retained and respected, irrespective of their date of origin. This conservative concept was to become influential again later in the nineteenth century. This was the concept upon which Cottingham based his architectural theory and practice. In the great ecclesiological revival of the early nineteenth century, leading to a vast increase in works of restoration to rescue the many dilapidated ecclesiastical buildings, not all restorers followed these principles. T.S. Madsen has noted that despite Milner's proposals for restrained restorations, much drastic reparation of churches, totally unconcerned with historical congruence, was carried out; later additions were removed to obtain a unity of style. Such reparations did not arouse much

comment apart from Cottingham's and Savage's pamphlet of 1832 which stated their reasons for opposing the destruction of the Lady Chapel at Southwark.[5] They followed Milner's theories in objecting to demolition of parts of a mediaeval building on the grounds of its dilapidated state and stressed the importance of the later parts of the building in relation to the whole.

Restoration in general in the 1820s and 1830s was a matter of carrying out urgent repairs and whenever possible undertaking a radical return to a definite style: an example is Thomas Harrison's refacing of the south end of the transept at Chester Cathedral with the addition of squat corner turrets in 1818.[6] In 1834 George Austin at Canterbury destroyed Lanfranc's Romanesque north-west tower and replaced it with a copy of the existing south-west tower to create symmetry.[7] At Norwich in 1830 Anthony Salvin refaced the south transept in Bath stone, replacing the original Perpendicular work with a new design in Norman style to correspond with the north transept.[8] Edward Blore, also involved in restoration in the early decades of the nineteenth century, in 1830 replaced at Westminster Abbey the fourteenth-century bays of the cloister and refaced the north front of the nave.[9] In none of his restorations did Cottingham carry out such drastic removal of mediaeval work undertaken to achieve a supposed state of perfection. At Rochester, in his renewal of the tower, he replaced the repairs of 1798 with a design based on the broken fragments of the earlier tower, and at Magdalen College Chapel, with the authority of a mediaeval expert, he removed Wyatt's plasterwork niches in his reinstatement of an archaeologically correct Mediaeval in keeping with the remaining Perpendicular Gothic. He certainly removed the faulty repairs of 'modern improvers', such as clumsy shoring built in 'brickbat and tile' to support tottering fabric as at Hereford and Bury. But in all his works he respected the examples of the architecture and sculpture of different periods from the early Romanesque to the late Perpendicular. Lethaby, writing in 1902, said that 'if instead of this energy in pulling down and setting up, there had been carried on a system of patching, staying and repairs, a sort of building dentistry, much might have been handed on for other ages'.[10] The careful 'staying and repairing' that Cottingham carried out at Rochester, St Alban's, Hereford, Ashbourne and Ledbury was later obliterated by the more drastic rebuilding of G.G. Scott in his efforts to achieve a unity of style.

The more drastic works of restoration in the early decades were commented on by those in tune with Cottingham's enlightened views, such as the writer in *The British Magazine* of 1832 who deprecated the 'current type of restoration' arguing that 'all that is necessary to be done is not to make the building new, but so to repair it that all which is *original* may be preserved as much as possible from future decay, the principle upon which every repair should be conducted'.[11] Cottingham and his friends deplored the 'merciless demolition' undertaken at the Palace of Westminster under the direction of Soane from 1814 to the early 1820s. This involved the removal of a conglomeration of legal and administrative buildings surrounding Westminster Hall and the destruction of most of the buildings to the north-east and west of the hall and the Exchequer buildings on the east side of the New Palace Yard.[12] William Capon, Cottingham's antiquary friend, had made drawings of the demolished streets and palace which, he complained in a letter to Francis Douce in 1827, were wholly or in part destroyed or concealed by erections the tall Butcher who looks with an evil eye upon the remains of ancient art now left us, mediates even more destruction of our beautiful remains ... The whole eastern end will either be destroyed or concealed by the new gingerbread work or pastrycook work substituted for architecture.[13]

Cottingham, too, mourned the loss of so much mediaeval work and described a 'perfect reconstruction of the ancient royal Palace at Westminster' by his friend Mr Lee who had spent twenty-five years fitting up three rooms of his house with drawings and perspective views: 'By means of glasses this stupendous work showing the Royal apartments are made to appear the size of the originals'.[14]

Cottingham's archaeologically correct Gothic Revival interior of 1829-35 at Magdalen College Chapel had a considerable impact and influence upon the progress of the movement, an impact that preceded the similar ecclesiastical revival work of the Oxford Movement, the Cambridge Camden Society and A. W. N. Pugin. Pugin admired it 'as one of the most beautiful specimens of modern design' and he was in frequent and continuous contact with his counterparts in France discussing modes of restoration and revival of the Gothic.[15] Parties of foreign visitors were conducted by Pugin and J. H. Parker during the 1840s to Magdalen College Chapel to see Cottingham's work. Moreover, it is clear from an examination of the proposed alterations or new chapel designs for other Oxford colleges that the Gothic interior of Magdalen was an influence upon English architects. For example, Blore's remodelled Chapel of St John's College of 1843 took the form of Cottingham's late fourteenth- to early fifteenth-century Gothic at Magdalen; and Pugin's design of 1843 for Balliol College Chapel is remarkably similar to Magdalen, though with a flowing traceried west window in place of the stone-carved reredos.[16]

It is clear that there was more communication and contact between Cottingham and Pugin than has hitherto been supposed. In his diaries, which provide sparse information on his work and friends, it is noticeable and perhaps significant that Pugin refers to Cottingham several times. Thus there is in 1842 a terse allusion to 'Figures for Cottingham', which could be interpreted as Cottingham's commissioning of Pugin to make casts for his collection; and Cottingham's name appeared in enigmatic notes accompanied by references to sums of money. Again, in complaining of Willement, whom he considered to be concerned only with money and not with quality, Pugin wrote: 'But Cottingham will make amends, and the glazing [at Alton Towers] will be done at half the cost.'[17] It appears, too, that Pugin and Cottingham undertook works of restoration in the same areas at the same time. For example, when Cottingham was restoring Roos Church in Yorkshire in 1842 Pugin was visiting the mediaeval churches in the area, including Patrington Church, in preparation for his works of restoration at St Mary's, Beverley in October of that year.[18] Cottingham had casts of Gothic features from Patrington and Beverley in his museum and it is more than likely that they collaborated.[19]

Pugin, in his works of restoration, also followed Cottingham's example at Magdalen in his insistence on the finest quality in the use of natural materials (wood, stone) and on the highest craftsmanship. For example, at Peper Harrow in 1844 he removed the Roman cement to reveal the old rubble walls, renewed

the sedilia and piscina, erected a chantry chapel, and replaced a flat plaster ceiling with a wagon-headed timber roof ribbed and panelled with quatrefoils; and the old Norman chancel arch, 'greatly mutilated', was removed and replaced with one of 'richer character with double shafts and carved capitals'.[20] While Pugin certainly followed certain aspects of Cottingham's restoration procedures, his replacement of 'the old Norman arch' with one of 'richer character' separates Pugin the Gothicist from Cottingham the Mediaevalist, for Cottingham loved the massive simplicity of the Romanesque and its inherent characteristics, so knowledgeably described in his analysis of the Norman Tower at Bury, for example, and would never have replaced a Norman arch for one of later date. Perhaps Pugin's replacement of the chancel arch in 1844 reflected the beginnings of a move away from the strict historicism that characterised Cottingham's restorations towards the more drastic type of repair encouraged by the principles of the Ecclesiologists during the 1840s. Cottingham, on the other hand, remained faithful to his restrained and sensitive modes of restoration, for example in his restoration of the Norman church of Kilpeck in 1846, a work which earned Pevsner's grudging praise of 'a disciplined restoration': it was in the reparation of 1896 that more drastic work removed the remains of the ancient frescoes. Salvin's restoration of very early structures is in marked contrast to Cottingham's conservative and skilful approach. For example, at the Saxon church of St Nicholas at Worth in 1870, Salvin, on finding the north-east corner of the nave to be leaning 10in out of alignment and the apse supported by shoring buttresses, took the building to its foundations and rebuilt it.[21] Cottingham brought leaning masonry to perpendicular without rebuilding and underpinned piers, enabling the removal of shoring. Pugin's work of restoration was even compared unfavourably to Cottingham's in his own time. The *Ecclesiologist* disparaged Pugin's method of supporting the tower of Jesus College Chapel and cited Cottingham's work at Hereford as an example of a preferable procedure.[22] Other friends of Cottingham such as Thomas Willement undertook restorations that followed his principles. At Davington Church in 1842, Willement cleaned the interior of whitewash, restored the roof, constructed a porch 'chiefly out of old carved materials' and restored the spire and upper part of the tower from careful drawings made prior to the work, possibly with Cottingham's help and advice.[23]

By 1843 the Ecclesiologists, whose first concern had been to repair the neglected fabric of churches and restore correct liturgical arrangements, had become alarmed at widespread destructive and over-zealous works of restoration: 'We are entering on an age of restoration ... how sad for the church if the current should take the wrong direction.' And again, they feared that 'the restoration of the 19th century may be classed with the sacrilege and indifference of the preceding and scarcely less dangerous to the consistency and original beauties of our ancient churches'.[24] However, the Ecclesiologists' own view that the most favourable procedure was to recover the original appearance of the church 'either from existing evidence or from supposition' in preference to retaining the additions and alterations of subsequent ages positively encouraged over-drastic methods of restoration.[25] E. A. Freeman, in his 'Principles of Church Restoration', described three theories of restoration: the Destructive, which advocated wholesale demolition to render a building in the favoured Middle Pointed style of Gothic: the Conservative, which called for repair of ancient work of whatever period: and the Eclectic, the theory most favoured by the Ecclesiologists, which allowed a combination of restoration and remodelling to the taste of the architect and his patron.[26] The Destructive, or rebuilding according to preference, and the Eclectic were the most widely practised. The Conservative approach found little favour with theorists, apart from the Reverend J. L. Petit, who in his *Remarks on Church Architecture* (1841) and *Remarks on Architectural Character* (1846) made a plea for universal restraint and sensitivity in restoration and condemned Scott's plans for St Mary's, Stafford as 'not conservative enough'.

The Ecclesiologists, with Salvin as the architect, undertook the repair of the Holy Sepulchre Church, Cambridge from 1841-4 as a model of their favoured mode of restoration; and the *Ecclesiologist* published many reports listing the full extent of its almost total rebuilding and remodelling in which the Norman structure was stripped of later additions, apart from the fourteenth-century chancel.[27] The Ecclesiologists exerted their influence through other bodies, such as the Incorporated Church Building Society, which administered the spending of £6 million pounds on church extension and building. The society, in 1842, consented to 'reconsider and alter' its 'Suggestions and Instructions' to comply with the Ecclesiologists' principles. The close links between the Ecclesiologists and the Oxford Society for Promoting the Study of Gothic Architecture led to further mutual influence.[28] The Ecclesiologists supported the Oxford Society's restoration project of the Abbey Church at Dorchester of 1845-6, and A. J. Beresford Hope, of the Ecclesiologists, at an Oxford Society meeting in 1846, read a paper on the 'Present State of Ecclesiological Art in England' and it was noted that 'the Committee must still point to Hereford Cathedral as an admirable example of the method in which such works should be conducted'. Cottingham's restoration of Hereford was again praised at a meeting of the Oxford Society in 1848 as 'the very greatest work of restoration seen in recent years'.[29]

Despite this, and despite the fact that his work was generally highly regarded in critical reviews by the *Ecclesiologist*, where he was described as 'the most eminent ecclesiological architect of the day', his name appeared on the *Ecclesiologist*'s list of 'Architects Condemned'. I believe this strange juxtaposition of praise and condemnation contributed to the decline of Cottingham's reputation which took place in the absence of any published examination of the reasons for it. He was criticised for his conservative mode of restoration which was not drastic enough to comply with the *Ecclesiologist*'s doctrines. For example, in his extensive restorations at St Mary's, Bury and at Ashbourne Church, Cottingham did not remove the seventeenth-century galleries. He was also considered by the *Ecclesiologist* to be more concerned with a restoration of the fabric of the church than with correct liturgical arrangements.[30] Of his work at Hereford we find the journal stating:

We have every reason to be satisfied with the advance of the restoration. It will be a great triumph to modern mechanical skill to supersede the unsightly masses of masonry ... while we admire the skill and boldness of Mr Cottingham in the mechanical branch of his art, we must confess to some suspicions as to the extent of his acquaintance with the theory and rules of internal arrangement as adapted to The Ritual.

The journal also noted, on learning that Cottingham was to restore Kilpeck Church, that 'several of our own members are among the Committee, though we are not sure that we agree that Mr Cottingham is the best architect who could have been chosen'.

The *Ecclesiologist* thus once again doubted whether he was concerned with altering the church in order fully to restore correct liturgical practice.[31] Cottingham was in fact well educated in liturgical and theological matters, and his son Nockalls had noted in a letter to William Brougham that Kilpeck Church was full of symbolic meaning, a subject of great importance to the Revivalists in England and France. Didron, for example, had sent his work on symbolism to J. H. Parker in Oxford for the *Archaeological Journal* and G. R. Lewis in his volume on Kilpeck Church, to which Cottingham subscribed, included a long translation from Durandus, the thirteenth-century ecclesiastic.[32]

It is possible that for these reasons Cottingham was on the 'Condemned List' because the *Ecclesiologist* recognised that he was not committed to undertaking drastic alterations in the service of restoring correct liturgical arrangements. The journal perhaps also suspected that Cottingham was not fully conversant with the religious significance and symbolism of the liturgy. Yet Cottingham was an Anglican, an educated man of catholic taste, and in no way bigoted or dogmatic.[33] He was a friend of the Roman Catholic Pugin, and in his church interiors he favoured a return to 'the beauty of Holiness' as promoted by the Oxford Movement and the Ecclesiologists. At Magdalen and Hereford he fell foul of the anti-High Anglican faction who were afraid of accusations of popery and he was obliged to modify his designs. Again, at Armagh, he had to insist on the removal of the organ from the nave crossing and restored the chancel screen in his revival of the true mediaeval Gothic church. Yet he had an equal respect, as a passionate admirer of mediaeval art and architecture, for the preservation of the original fabric wherever it was humanly possible.

Despite the equivocal attitude of the Ecclesiologists towards Cottingham, he was never the subject of fierce criticism directed by their journal against some of his contemporaries. Thus Blore is dismissed unequivocally: 'He is entirely unacquainted with the true spirit of Pointed architecture ... manifestly unfit for the charge of any works on Westminster Abbey ... his truly contemptible building, Christ Church, Hexton, to select one of this gentleman's architectural enormities.'[34] Even Salvin – despite being the architect chosen by Beresford Hope for the restoration of St Sepulchre, the Round Church! – did not escape harsh criticism: 'The church erected at Spitalgate, Grantham, is the worst class of modern design ... every single detail involves a solecism and the plan is as faulty as the design.'[35] Nor could the *Ecclesiologist* ever fault Cottingham's antiquarian knowledge of all periods of the Mediaeval, or the technical skill with which he avoided demolition and rebuilding as practised by Blore, Salvin and Scott, and even when criticising his choice of the Romanesque for his own church, the journal 'found more to admire than condemn'.[36]

George Gilbert Scott's restoration work also offers a contrast to Cottingham's principles in those churches and cathedrals such as Rochester, Hereford, St Alban's and Ashbourne where he continued repairs after Cottingham's death. Scott, who restored over 700 churches, wrote about the dangers of over-restoring, quoting Ruskin's maxim that it was better to take care of monuments than to restore them, and he tried constantly to improve standards of restoration. Yet he followed the 'Eclectic' system of restoring, a combination of restoring and remodelling to the taste of the architect and his patron. He also practised at times the drastic mode of 'unity of style', although he denied this.[37] At times he roundly condemned drastic restoration measures. For example, in correspondence with the Oxford Society, Scott criticised Barry's proposed works at St Stephen's Chapel and 'his reckless disregard for a valuable ancient monument', calling for pressure from the Ecclesiologists 'to have him relinquish the project'. Yet in 1877 it was in protest at Scott's proposed drastic restoration of Tewkesbury Abbey that William Morris gained the impetus to found the Society for the Protection of Ancient Buildings.[38]

Conservation in the European Context

A similar progression from careful restoring to drastic unity of style took place in France not long after the first efforts of the preservationists like Montalembert to save such remaining examples of art and architecture as the Church of St Denis and the cathedrals of Amiens and Bourges from dilapidation and the hands of inexpert restorers. Montalembert's 'On Vandalism in France' (1833) and his 'Account of the destructive and revived pagan principles of France' (1839), which Pugin included as Appendix III in the second edition (1841) of his *Contrasts*, warned of the dangers of over-restoring and promoted a conservative approach. Montalembert divided repair of buildings into two categories, 'destructive vandalism' and 'restorative vandalism', the latter being perpetrated by the clergy, the government, the municipal authorities and the private owners. Didron, too, favoured restraint and writing in the *Bulletin Archéologique* in 1839 as Secretary to the Comité Historique, he prescribed as follows: 'In works to ancient monuments, it is better to consolidate than repair, better to repair than restore, better to restore than remake, better to remake than embellish; in any case nothing should be added, above all, nothing taken away.' Didron added that this principle should be defended by the archaeologists. He used the words 'consolidation and reparation' in his report on the proposed restoration at Notre Dame and he further praised Montalembert's denunciation of 'wholesale restoration'. Montalembert had attacked the 'scandalous works done in the Church of S. Denis, in the Cathedral of Bourges, in the Cathedral of Amiens, in the Cathedral of Rheims, in all the churches of France by M. M. Debret, Pagot, Jullien, Godde, and Cheussey ... our most beautiful monuments have been the ones most ill-treated by architects'.[39]

S. Denis had suffered the worst type of restoration at the hands of M. Debret. In 1837, during a banquet at Versailles for the inauguration of the Musée Historique, Abbot Suger's spire of S. Denis was struck by lightning. Debret, who had begun work on the cathedral in 1830, announced that he would demolish and build the spire anew. The tower, enfeebled by Debret's inept restorations, was unable to sustain the weight of the new spire which had been built at vast expense in unsuitable material. Whilst Debret 'was busy with his creations, new windows, new wall paintings, tombs, royal statues, historic saints', cracks appeared running through the tower to the great portal 'and even

the unhappy Clovis, reduced to a caricature by Debret was also split by a fissure'.[40] Debret's work of 1837-40 provides a telling contrast to Cottingham's engineering skill as demonstrated in his restorations of the endangered towers of Rochester, Armagh and Hereford; of the Norman Tower, and of Louth, where, without building anew, he strengthened and repaired the spire which had been struck by lightning, leaving cracks 'as wide as a man's arm'.[41] Debret's efforts may be contrasted, too, with Cottingham's superior work at Rochester where he uncovered mediaeval frescoes, the 'whitewash painstakingly removed with a penknife'. A further comparison is suggested by Cottingham's treatment of the panelled roof of the crossing tower, of which an observer wrote:

The whole affords a specimen of Early English horizontal oaken roof, the bosses ... in strict accordance with those in various parts of the transept – a sure proof of real and pure taste, which, far from attempting to display any modern rivalry of the inimitable productions of the ancients, rather chooses to assist in handing on to posterity, the beautiful character of those models which they alone invented.[42]

Very different, this, from Debret 'busy with his new creations ... '

The *Ecclesiologist* took an increasing interest in French and German works of restoration, publishing extensive reports on the proposed restoration of Notre Dame by Viollet-le-Duc and Lassus and on the progress of Cologne Cathedral, offering criticism and advice. The journal praised Viollet-le-Duc's impassioned response to an official paper from the Institute of France expressing strong disapproval of the revival of Gothic. The *Ecclesiologist* published much of Viollet-le-Duc's argument, which strongly echoed Cottingham's plea in his Preface of 1822 for the study of Gothic 'as an inexhaustible source of instruction'. The journal congratulated Didron and Viollet-le-Duc 'on their exertions towards the revival and purification of mediaeval art'.[43] In 1839 the task of restoring the crumbling Romanesque Benedictine Abbey of Vézelay was entrusted to the twenty-five-year-old Viollet-le-Duc by Prosper Mérimée, the Inspector-General of Historical Monuments. Viollet-le-Duc and others such as de Caumont and le Prévost were admirers of the Norman. The increased study of this style led to an understanding of its forms and construction, and to an appreciation that Romanesque architecture was an end in itself and not simply a clumsy preliminary to the perfection of Gothic. In France, however, the favoured style for the Revival was the Gothic of the thirteenth century, a style eminently suitable for revival, as Cottingham said in his preface to *Henry VII's Chapel* in 1821.[44] The *Ecclesiologist* noted with relief: 'We must notice their gradual, but we trust final adoption of Middle Pointed which is the more remarkable as no longer back than the first number of Annales, a considerable penchant for Romanesque was exhibited.'

In Germany Prisac and Hübsch promoted Romanesque in favour of Gothic, and Semper, in arguing for his designs for S. Nicholas at Hamburg, presented a view of Romanesque as a preliminary stage in the emergence of Gothic. Schaase, too, wrote that the inclinations and sympathies of the Germans were aroused by Romanesque.[45] Cottingham, with respect to his restoration, showed no 'preference' for any particular styles, appreciating the intrinsic qualities and historical development of each, an advanced notion in the first part of the nineteenth century, and one that foreshadowed Ruskin and Morris.

Viollet-le-Duc had worked under Lassus at La Sainte Chapelle of St Louis, and in 1845 they were both commissioned, on the strength of their reputations as scholars of the art of the Middle Ages and their previous restorations to restore Notre Dame de Paris. Viollet-le-Duc defined his principles of restoration in these terms: 'To restore a building is to re-establish it to a completed state which may never have existed at any particular time, and in a style which is proper to it.' His was therefore almost the same approach as that of the Ecclesiologists, their concern in the restoration of a building being 'to return it to its original appearance on evidence or supposition'.[46]

Lassus also subscribed to unity of style but took a more strictly historicist approach than Viollet-le-Duc, who in many of his works interpreted 'not merely the words of the 13th century architecture, but the grammar also, and the spirit', a doctrine he applied to restoration.[47] In an article of 1845 in *Annales Archéologiques* Lassus proposed principles of restoration close to those of Cottingham. 'The architect in building anew,' Lassus wrote, 'must not copy servilely' but

when an architect is in charge of the restoration of a monument then it is a matter of science; the architect must be completely self-effacing, forgetting his tastes and preferences, his instincts; his aim is to conserve, consolidate, add as little as possible; with a religious respect he must study the form of the building, the materials, the means employed, for accuracy and historical truth are as important as the materials and the style. It is absolutely essential that the architect should leave no trace of his hand upon the monument. It should be seen quite simply as a uniquely archaeological science.[48]

English influence upon Lassus is visible not only in his absorption of the theories of Montalembert, but also in his own contacts and scholarly exchanges with English architects and antiquaries such as Robert Willis and J. H. Parker.[49] With his archaeological approach, Lassus despised the eclecticism advocated by the German art historian Schaase. Didron reinforced Lassus's view in his criticism of the eclecticism of Pugin's Cheadle.[50]

The report by Montalembert on the Notre Dame restoration was published in *Annales*, the *Kölner Domblatt* and the *Ecclesiologist*. The reparation was to be limited 'to only what was necessary'. This included cleaning away all whitewash and cement, replacing modern water spouts by gargoyles, the replacement of twenty-eight statues from the principal front destroyed in 1793, and of 'the bastard pointed Arch and deformed columns of Soufflot', and the reproduction of the mutilated portal and the central pier and tympanum after a faithful drawing, such as 'came forth from the thoughts of the architects of the 13th century'. Soufflot's unarchaeological efforts at Gothic were condemned and the work of Viollet-le-Duc and Lassus would be 'in the spirit of and in harmony with the originals', reminiscent of Cottingham's achievement in his new work at St Mary's, Bury. Finally, a new sacristy was to be built against the south side of the choir. Interior works were planned as funds were made available. Montalembert objected to the replacement of the statues, for as the *Ecclesiologist* noted, he was the head of an archaeological school 'which proclaims the inutility and impossibility of making again statues which no longer exist'.[51]

The *Ecclesiologist* raised other controversial matters which highlighted the restrained approach of Montalembert and Didron in comparison to that publication's own unity of style preference. The *Ecclesiologist* argued for the addition of the western towers 'which we know were once intended' to S. Ouen, in contrast to Didron's opposition to the proposal, and continued:

Why should not the spires, which, as it is a Middle Pointed Church, must have been intended for it, be upon the western towers at Rheims? ... It is no argument to assert as M. Montalembert does that Rheims Cathedral should not have spires given to it because it has done very well without them for six centuries.[52]

Didron was considered to be 'too much an antiquarian' in these arguments on restoration practice, a criticism that was levelled at Cottingham.

Montalembert and Didron demonstrated the careful and restrained early French restoration philosophy, which reflected the theories of the English writers such as Carter, Britton and Cottingham, and was exemplified in Cottingham's work. But French restoring moved away from these well-formulated theories, and unity of style came to dominate French thinking, with Viollet-le-Duc as the foremost exponent, imitated by less able followers. In Germany the efforts of architects were directed towards interpretations of Gothic Revival in their new buildings, the major restoration of Cologne being regarded as the apogee of German art and architecture. At Cologne the idea of the late Gothic Bauhütte was revived in order to encourage the re-creation of schools of craftsmen for the rebuilding of the cathedral, a mediaevalising attitude akin to Ruskin's and Morris's later efforts to revive the mediaeval guilds. The attachment to traditional techniques of the stonemason caused Reichensperger bitterly to oppose Zwirner's proposal to build an iron roof for Cologne Cathedral. Reichensperger's insistence on the use of mediaeval materials in preference to cast-iron characterised an approach which later in the century drew the German and English closer together. It was in marked contrast to Viollet-le-Duc's rational and unbiased approach to the use of iron which linked him to the early nineteenth-century functionalist theories of Rickman, Cottingham, Willis and Savage.[53]

In France the government's centralised system of controlling works of restoration to mediaeval monuments played a role in encouraging and supporting the easily applied unity of style. Once a decision was taken by the Committee of General Inspectors, it became difficult to obstruct or influence its implementation, whereas in England the flexibility and more haphazard nature of the system gave greater opportunity for criticism and objections from clergy, architects, antiquaries and subscribers to the restoration. Criticism of Viollet-le-Duc and the French mode of restoration grew in England. G. E. Street noted with relief in 1858:

Fortunate indeed is it for us in England that the state is not so careful for us as in France, for then we should see here, just as we do there, a people utterly careless of the noble buildings which surround them, in place of as here, a people whose care of their monuments is enhanced and in part created by the fact that they themselves are perpetually invited to help in their restoration and repair.[54]

Street inherited Cottingham's passion for the Mediaeval and its preservation whatever its condition or style. From the time he first expressed his firm belief in Gothic as worthy of serious study and of elevation to the same level as classical architecture, and his ideas of a Gothic Revival through sympathetic restoration and understanding of all stages of the Mediaeval, Cottingham exerted an influence through his theories, writings and the example of his major works of restoration, an influence that can be seen in Europe. His works of restoration, conservative, skilful, archaeologically correct, were so much in harmony with the spirit of the original that some of his interiors and extensions are today not known as nineteenth-century work. Yet Cottingham was a man of his time in his attitude to the work of the eighteenth century. He left seventeenth-century galleries in mediaeval churches, but the 'pew lumber', dismissed as 'monstrous pagan deformities' and whitewash, 'that plague spot of our Cathedrals', were systematically removed. The plasterwork trivialities of the eighteenth century were replaced through a true revival of the Mediaeval in the use of materials, craftmanship and construction, and in the spirit and intention of the Gothic builders. Cottingham appreciated the classical works of ancient Greece and Rome. But he saw the use of classical motifs and the panelling, plasterwork and monuments of the eighteenth century as intrusions which had obliterated or threatened the beauty and structure of the Mediaeval architecture, widely regarded at that time as debased and barbaric. From the retrospective standpoint of the late twentieth century, we may condemn Cottingham's removal of classical accretions as vandalism. Yet in our day, over one hundred years after the founding of the SPAB (Society for the Protection of Ancient Buildings), evidence abounds of no lesser and perhaps less excusable vandalism perpetrated in a twentieth-century spirit of reform which has already swept away much of the best nineteenth-century work, including Cottingham's.

The works of restoration which occupied so much of Cottingham's time, energy and study and to which he brought his passion for the Mediaeval, retain their validity, and compare favourably with those of his contemporaries in England and France. These achievements make him the true precursor of the movement generally acknowledged until now to stem solely from the enlightened efforts of Pugin, Ruskin and Morris.

King Henry VII's Chapel,
Plate IV, 1829
Lithograph 33×23¾ in
(84×60.5 cm)

1 Cottingham, L. N., *Report on the Norman Tower at Bury, and the Necessary Repairs Thereof*, London, Dec. 1842

2 *Bill of Works etc at Magdalen College Chapel*, 1830-3. Atkinson and Brown, Goswell St, London. Magdalen College Archives MS 735

3 *Bury and Norwich Post*, 4 Dec. 1844, 'Reopening of St Mary's Church, Bury St Edmunds'

4 *Ecclesiologist*, Vol.I, July 1845, pp.133-4

5 Madsen, T.S., *Restoration and Anti-Restoration. A Study in English Restoration Philosophy*, London, 1976, pp.34-6

6 ibid., p.34

7 ibid., p.35

8 Allibone, J., *Anthony Salvin; A pioneer of the Gothic Revival*, Cambridge, 1987, pp.112-13

9 Fawcett, J., ed., *The Future of the Past: Attitudes to Conservation 1174-1976*, London, 1976

10 *Society for the Protection of Ancient Buildings* (SPAB) *Annual Report*, 1902, p.72, 'Westminster Abbey and its Restoration'

11 *British Magazine*, Vol.II, 1832, pp.455-6

12 Crook, J.M., and Port, M.H., *The History of the King's Works*, Vol.VI, HMSO, London, 1973, pp.436-50

13 *Douce MSS.* Letter from Capon to Douce, 13 June 1827

14 ibid., letter from LNC to Douce, 3 June 1831. Adam Lee was a Labourer in Trust of the Board of Works at Westminster. (See Crook and Port, p.499.) Cottingham had been invited to take a party of antiquaries to see Lee's construction and was inviting Douce. He had already asked Mr Hawkins (later to be involved with the British Archaeological Association with J.H. Parker) and W. Twopenny. I have not come across any other reference to Lee's extraordinary work in any book relating to this period

15 Ferrey, B., *Recollections of A.W.N. Pugin*, London (1861); reprint, 1978, p.86

16 Colvin, H., *Unbuilt Oxford*, New Haven and London, 1983, pp.112-13

17 Wedgwood, A., *Catalogue of Architectural Drawings in the Victoria and Albert Museum. A.W.N. Pugin and the Pugin Family*, London, 1985. Diary for Oct. 1842, p.88

18 Merewether, J.A., *A Statement on the Condition and Circumstances of the Cathedral Church of Hereford in the Year 1841*, Hereford, 1841. Letter of recommendation re LNC's work at Roos, from Reverend Hotham, 1841

19 Humberside Record Office, Pugin's restoration of St Mary's, Beverley, 1842-50. Pei/729-728

20 *Ecclesiologist*, Vol.XXXIII, Aug. 1844, p.154

21 Allibone, op. cit., p.130

22 *Ecclesiologist*, Vol.XVI, Dec. 1848, p.147. See also Belcher, M., *A.W.N. Pugin; An Annotated Bibliography*, 1987, p.260. Pugin commented on this report, defending his work on grounds of cost

23 Willement, T., Historical Sketch of the Parish of Davington in the County of Kent, MSCCLXII, p.40. See also: Wainwright, C., 'Davington Priory', *Country Life*, 9 Dec. 1971, pp.1650-3

24 *Ecclesiologist*, Vol.VI, April 1843, p.33

25 ibid., Vol.VIII, Feb. 1842, p.65. Criticism of Scott and Moffat's restoration of St Mary's, Stafford. It is interesting to note that Scott wrote to the OAHS on 3 June 1842 saying, 'I am glad the general plan proposed meets the approval of the society.'

26 ibid., May 1847, Vol.LIX, pp.161-7

27 ibid., Nov. 1841, 1st Series, Vols I-III, pp.5, 29, No.VI, April 1843, p.111

28 ibid., 1842, No.III, Jan. 1847; Nov. 1842, p.70: pp.153-7: *Incorporated Church Building Society* (ICBS) *Records*

29 Oxford Architectural and Historical Society (OAHS), Report of Proceedings, Bodleian Library, 9 May 1842; 23 June 1846; June 1848

30 *Ecclesiologist*, Vol.XXIX, Feb. 1844, p.113

31 ibid., Vol.IV, April, 1847, p.156

32 *Society of Antiquaries Correspondence*, J.H. Parker to A. Way, 2 Dec. 1843, 'The volume of M. Didron will no doubt be very interesting – but it is a subject I hardly dare mention for fear of getting out of my depth and becoming as cracked as poor Mr George Lewis who always seems to me quite beside himself when he gets on this hobby of his.'

33 Baptised at Laxfield Parish Church, 1787, Laxfield Parish Records

34 *Ecclesiologist*, Vol. XIII, Sept. 1842, p.99

35 ibid., July 1845, p.186

36 ibid., Vol.NVI, 1849, p.203, Vol.I, 1845, p.169

37 Scott, G.G., *Personal and Professional Recollections*, London, 1879, p.99: Pevsner, N., *Some Architectural Writers of the Nineteenth Century*, Oxford, 1972, p.173

38 OAHS Correspondence, Bodleian Library, letter from G.G. Scott to Reverend J.R. Bloxham, 20 Feb. 1842

39 *Annales Archéologiques*, 1844, p.3, Montalembert on vandalism; p.230, restoration of S. Denis

40 ibid., Vol.VI, 1846, 'The spire of S. Denis', p.175

41 *Illustrated London News*, Jan.-June 1845, 'Louth Spire', pp.180-1: Lincolnshire R.O., St James' Parish, 9/2/8, Oct. 1844, 11 April 1844, 6/7/12

42 Spence, C., *A Walk Through Rochester Cathedral*, London, 1840, p.8

43 *Ecclesiologist*, 2nd Series, Vol.II, 1846, pp.35-7; July, pp.75-9, No.LI, Sept., pp.81-90

44 *Annales Archéologiques*, 1847, p.65; 1846, p.129

45 *Kölner Domblatt*, 2, 9, 16 Oct. 1842

46 *Annales Archéologiques*, 1846, pp.1-5; *Ecclesiologist*, Vol.II, 1846, pp.55-6

47 *Ecclesiologist*, Vol.XV, Sept. 1846, p.88

48 *Annales Archéologiques*, 1845, pp.554-5

49 Lassus published a facsimile of Vilars de Honecourt's sketchbook (c.13th-century architect) with comments and descriptions. Willis translated it into English and edited Lassus's edition and included letters from Lassus to J.H. Parker concerning square-ended chapels, and others to Willis, Schaase of Berlin, and Montalembert in 1859

50 *Annales Archéologiques*, 1847, p.65

51 ibid., Aug. 1845; *Ecclesiologist*, 2nd Series, Vol.II, 1846, pp.55-9

52 ibid., *Ecclesiologist*, p.64

53 *Kölner Domblatt*, Sept. 1853; *Ecclesiologist*, 2nd Series, Vol.III, 1846, pp.75-8

54 Street, G.E., *Architectural Notes in France*, 1858; see also Madsen, S.T., *Restoration and Anti-Restoration, A Study in English Restoration Philosophy*, Oslo, Universitetsforlaget, 1975, p.83

4

Domestic Architecture and Design

The Mediaeval Revival

The revival of interest in the architecture of the Middle Ages in the early decades of the nineteenth century, after a long period of neglect, led not only to the restoration and revival of ecclesiastical buildings but also to a passion for the antiquarian study, restoration, rebuilding and revival of the styles of mediaeval domestic architecture. Cottingham, in the Preface to his *Plans etc of Henry VII's Chapel* (1822), had suggested an archaeological study of Gothic structure as a basis for a revival in domestic building. His own domestic work exhibited his concerns to create buildings suited to their age and to the patron's requirements, while reflecting an inspiration drawn from mediaeval precedents. Important sources of information were his own study of the mediaeval domestic architecture of England, evident in his museum collection and in his surviving sketchbooks, and lessons learned from his involvement with preservation issues, such as Crosby Hall in the 1830s. By the 1840s the influence of the preservationist lobby was having an effect. A further impetus to a revival based on archaeological study came from publications of works on mediaeval domestic architecture such as A. C. Pugin's and E. J. Willson's *Specimens of Gothic Architecture Selected from Various Edifices* (1822), in which they gave advice on imitation of styles:

Let ancient mansions serve for the decoration of modern ones ... Castles can very rarely be copied with success ... the imitation of an abbey requires exceptional circumstances, the towered gatehouse, cloisters and refectory may serve for modern uses without losing their proper character and towers, stair turrets will give picturesque effect without appearing as forced conceits.

Cottingham, in his publications of 1822 and 1823, advised architects to study the best examples of the mediaeval, but not to neglect contemporary usage, 'for no houses of mediaeval date would be habitable in the present day without considerable alteration ... ' Pugin and Willson shared this view, suggesting that 'modification of precedents allowed for absolute fidelity will prove incompatible with modern convenience ... but let the architect compare his designs with ancient examples'.

These ideas later formed the basis of A. W. N. Pugin's influential writings on domestic architecture in his *Contrasts* of 1836 and *True Principles* of 1841. A. C. Pugin's later work, *Gothic Ornament Selected from various buildings in both England and France* (1831), continued this theme, giving examples of details from many Oxford colleges, from ancient domestic dwellings such as Bond's Hospital and Ford's Hospital in Coventry and from gables on houses in the High Street in Rochester. Cottingham's friend, William Twopenny, also

produced a volume on the domestic architecture of the Middle Ages in 1840, giving descriptions and plans of manor houses of the twelfth century such as that at Boothby Pagnell, the Crown Inn at Rochester, the Jew's House at Lincoln, the thirteenth-century Aydon Castle owned by Cottingham's patron, Sir Edward Blackett, the fourteenth-century Markenfield Hall, the Mote Ightham and Little Wenham in Suffolk.[1] Other works of the 1830s and 1840s providing evidence of increased interest in the subject included publications by Hunt, Richardson and Nash on Tudor and Elizabethan architecture. Later works such as Hudson Turner's *Some Account of Domestic Architecture in England; the Conquest to the end of the 13th Century* (1851), which included an account of Cottingham's Brougham Hall with illustrations by Twopenny, Blore and Nesbitt, and Dollman's *Examples of Domestic Architecture, illustrating Hospitals, Bede Houses, Schools and Almshouses of the Middle Ages* (1849), were valuable sources of information on surviving examples of mediaeval architecture and became part of a tradition that led the way to the influential studies of Street, Shaw, Nesfield and Burges later in the nineteenth century.

The concern for preserving ancient domestic architecture became a subject of interest on the Continent during the 1840s. Didron, in *Annales Archéologiques*, wrote regular reports of 'Acts of Vandalism', deploring the destruction of mediaeval buildings such as the Hôtel de la Trémonville and others in Paris despite the outcry of scholars and artists. He published reports by Victor Hugo of 'barbaric and senseless destruction' at Saintes, and printed accounts of vandalism reported by Roisin in Bonn, Reichensperger in Cologne and Goertner in Bavaria.[2] 'The archaeological rapport' also promoted the study of domestic architecture in France and England in the first decades of the nineteenth century. Many English architects and antiquaries travelled and studied in France and published their work: for example, Cotman, A. C. and A. W. N. Pugin, Dallaway, Whewell, and Cottingham's pupils Truefitt and Vaux. The Preface to Hudson Turner's *Some Account of Domestic Architecture* pointed out that drawings of the French remains had been prepared by H. M. Didron, Bouet, Viollet-le-Duc and du Caumont of Caen. English publications on English domestic architecture and design by Pugin, Butterfield, Parker, H. L. Jones and M. A. Nichols (which included Cottingham's tile designs) were listed in the *Annales*. Important French publications on mediaeval domestic design were influential in England. For example, N. X. Willemin's two volumes, *Monuments Français Inédits, pour servir à l'histoire des Arts depuis le VI siècle jusqu'au commencement du XVII siècle*, which included drawings of French and German domestic architecture, dress, furniture, sculpture, mosaics, monuments, costumes of cavaliers and tournament stands, were subscribed to by 'Willemen(t) à Londres, Stothard à Londres, Hope (banker à Londres) and Gally Knight and Britton'. These were all friends of Cottingham's and copies of the work were to be found in the library of the Society of Antiquaries. Du Sommerard's volumes of 1836-46, *Les Arts au Moyen Age*, and the publication of the building manuals of the thirteenth-century architect Wilars de Honecourt were also widely known in England, providing a source of study of mediaeval architecture and interior design.

In France, perhaps the most notable work of restoration and rebuilding of a mediaeval castle was Viollet-le-Duc's work at the ruined late fourteenth-century Pierrefonds from 1857, a project similar to Cottingham's extension and development of Brougham Hall from 1830-46.[3] Viollet-le-Duc's work – a mixture of careful reconstruction and restoration based on the existing structure and fragments of ornament, of anachronistic elements such as the detached defensive towers built at the perimeter walls, and of a free and imaginative interpretation of the Mediaeval in his interior designs – makes a contrast with the earlier, more archaeological approach of Cottingham at Brougham. There Cottingham used the Bayeux Tapestry as the appropriate decoration for a Norman Revival interior and insisted on a mediaeval precedent for every feature in the construction of a castle where he attempted to show a gradual development in the styles of the Mediaeval.

Revival Mansions

Antiquarian, preservationist and revivalist influences contributed to the passion for the Mediaeval which developed in the 1820s and 1830s, and resulted in the building of Gothic mansions and battlemented castles. Other factors, too, played a part. Thus the wars with France revived feelings of nationalism while the overthrow in France of the whole traditional structure of society through revolution engendered a fear of radical democracy and change. The coronation of George IV on 19 July 1821 provided an opportunity for a revival of feudal customs, dress and splendour at a magnificent banquet in the setting of Westminster Hall.[4] At that very time, Cottingham was preparing his structural analysis of Westminster Hall for his publication of 1822: the full mediaeval pageant played out in the fourteenth-century Great Hall must have had a powerful effect on his imagination. Three years later Wyatville undertook the remodelling of Windsor Castle with its state sequence of the grand staircase, the armoury and the Waterloo chamber: the whole a mediaeval transformation in keeping with the mood of the times.

In literature, Sir Walter Scott's *Waverley* novels, romantic tales of the chivalrous Middle Ages, fuelled the Mediaeval Revival. A keen antiquary and scholar, Scott brought his scenes to life through vivid descriptions of interiors, armour, the dress of the period and particularly castles with drawbridges, battlements and armour-filled great halls with open timber roofs and the high table on a dais. J. R. Planché, the heraldic expert, claimed that 'honour is due to Sir Walter Scott for having first attracted public attention to the advantages of study of such subjects'. He questioned the accuracy of his descriptions of the dress and armour of the Anglo-Norman period but concluded overall that 'those scenes laid in the 16th and 17th centuries are admirable for their truth and graphic delineation'.[5]

We know that Scott made a gift to Cottingham of a Charles II chair for his museum. It is not unreasonable to suppose that Scott had consulted Cottingham on antiquarian and architectural matters, possibly to obtain background information for the descriptions in his mediaeval novels, and/or for advice on the building and interior design of his house Abbotsford, extended between 1812 and 1832.

Abbotsford, the subject of a study by Clive Wainwright in *The Antiquarian Interior*, was created by Sir Walter Scott in collaboration with Edward Blore and William Atkinson and with advice from others including Cottingham, Meyrick, Bullock and Douce. Francis Douce, Cottingham's friend, in handwritten marginal notes in an unabridged copy of *Sir Tristram* given to him by Scott, set down his impressions of Abbotsford and of its rich assemblage of 'materials borrowed from other places' such as 'a gateway from Linlithgow, a roof from Roslin, a chimney piece from Melrose, a postern from the Heart of Midlothian'. Douce delineated the house thus: '150 feet long in front, a tall tower at each end unlike each other with high gables, fantastic water spouts, balconies, painted glass windows, and projecting gateway'. He described the hall or armoury with two lofty windows of heraldic stained glass and the 'chimney piece copied from the Abbey of Melrose', and the 'Dining Room low roofed with a bay window a facsimile from Melrose.'[6]

Another description of Abbotsford is to be found in the diary of George Shaw, the Manchester architect and antiquary, who noted that the passage or lobby had a groined roof in plaster supported on figures, 'the whole cast from one of the aisles of Melrose'; and he stated that 'the fanciful edifice over the road at the reservoir is composed principally of the doorway of the French Ambassador's house in the Canongate of Edinburgh pulled down some years ago'.[7]

Cottingham's museum was filled with architectural fragments rescued from demolished buildings. His collection included casts of features from Melrose Abbey, linking him closely with Abbotsford. It is possible that he supplied Scott with facsimiles or advised him on these and other aspects of the work at Abbotsford. Cottingham used fragments and casts from his own collection at Snelston in 1829 and advised his patrons William Brougham and Earl Dunraven at Adare on acquisitions for their antiquarian interiors. The habit of incorporating early fragments, carvings and furnishings in the re-creation of mediaeval interiors was widespread by the 1830s and 1840s. Christie's held a sale of carvings for this purpose in 1826 and Pugin, too, used early Flemish carvings in his interiors at Scarisbrick in 1835.[8] Mediaeval stained glass was also used, as at Toddington in Gloucestershire, the Gothic mansion designed by Hanbury Tracy, the future Lord Sudeley. There the twelve pointed windows of the west cloisters were glazed with 'richly stained glass which formerly adorned monasteries in Switzerland, Germany and Holland'.[9]

Some castles and mansions built in the early decades of the nineteenth century showed little attempt to imitate the planning, internal arrangement, or organic development of the mediaeval buildings. Instead, symmetrical castles in the tradition of Adam's Inveraray Castle or Wyatt's Royal Castle at Kew were constructed, an example being Robert Smirke's Lowther of 1810-11 for the Earl of Lonsdale, with soaring towers at the four corners, and superficial mediaeval ornament. George Shaw, writing in 1834, compared it unfavourably to Cottingham's nearby Brougham Hall which appeared to him to be 'the epitome of an old baronial mansion'. Lowther, in Shaw's judgement, 'like most Smirke erections is spoiled for want of space at the first entrance, and the staircase coming close to the doors'.[10]

Smirke's Eastnor of 1812, of complex but rigid symmetry, again exhibited massive corner towers with unarchaeological round arch windows without mouldings to the first-floor windows of Early English lancet design to provide Gothic decoration, and no attempt to suggest organic growth or authenticity. John Britton criticised Smirke's work in 1840 claiming that he 'had not been successful in imparting the true architectural character of either the castle or the monastery to his work'. Of Eastnor, he feared that 'many details belong rather to church than to castle and do not combine well in the mansion'.[11]

After Smirke's Eastnor of 1812, perhaps the most notable Mediaeval Revival mansion was Thomas Hopper's Penrhyn Castle in North Wales of 1827. Here there was some approach to verisimilitude, with a great Norman keep and the main blocks arranged round courtyards. Penrhyn's owner, Spencer Stanhope, in a letter to George Shaw, wrote of its failings: 'The decorations of the Norman style are not at all in harmony with the requirements of modern times ... the finest part of the building is the keep which is almost a direct copy of Rochester.'[12]

Revivalism in the hands of lesser architects led to inconvenience. Convenience was not ignored by Cottingham, Pugin and Willson in 1822. In 1828–31 Edward Blore built a mediaeval castle, Goodrich Court in the Wye Valley, for Sir Samuel Meyrick. Its massive round towers and crenellations owed much to the early sixteenth-century Thornbury which was also used as a model for Costessey by John Chessell Buckler of 1826.[13] Sir Samuel and Lady Meyrick both made favourable comments on their new castle to their friend Francis Douce when writing to invite him to stay 'even though the house was not as far on as hoped'. Planché also visited and the antiquary J. H. Markland, who wrote in praise of Cottingham's restoration methods, 'expressed high approbation of the place'. But Lady Meyrick, left to deal with the problems of a new castle while her husband travelled for three months with lady companions, complained: 'We are much plagued by smokey chimneys, we couldn't light fires when the walls were streaming with wet.'[14] An anonymous visitor to Goodrich, writing from 'King James I's Chamber', described its

stately assemblages of towers and battlements, the buildings surrounding two courts and the whole erection taken from twenty existing specimens of the architecture which prevailed from the reign of Edward I to the close of that of Edward III, forming a perfect beau-ideal of an ancient castle bristling with all the fortifications of the chivalric ages.

The writer described the heavy arched entrance, approached by a drawbridge over a wide moat and defended by a portcullis, 'characteristic of the pedantry of the times ...'[15] The date range of the sources used by Blore reflected his attempt to suggest, in this new building, its growth over many years as in mediaeval times. Anachronistic features of the kind introduced by Blore at Goodrich, such as a defensive drawbridge and portcullis, were never employed by Cottingham.

Another of Cottingham's contemporaries whose Mediaeval Revival domestic architecture was criticised and compared unfavourably to his own was Anthony Salvin. Cottingham worked at Brougham from 1830 and Salvin built a new mansion at nearby Greystoke for Henry Howard from 1837, incorporating parts of the fourteenth-century pele tower, work that was not noted for archaeological correctness. William Brougham wrote that 'the work done at Greystoke is by no means what it ought to be' and he said he would be grieved if Naworth Castle, another of the Howard family properties, 'were restored in no better taste'.[16] Naworth was partly destroyed by fire in 1844 and William Brougham, anxious to see its rebuilding carried out 'with true antiquarian feeling', immediately wrote to George Howard, the 7th Earl of Carlisle, to recommend Cottingham for the work: 'I should strongly advise you to take advice from Mr Cottingham whom I have found the safest and most cognisant in this description of work of any architect I know at present.' Brougham, as brother of the Lord Chancellor, spent a great deal of time in London and on the Continent. He was a keen antiquary and amateur architect, and therefore able to speak with some authority on the architects of the day. He continued in praise of Cottingham: 'He is far better than Pugin, who is of the florid Church style, and Barry, whose Houses of Parliament turn out like conservatories.'

This observation is indicative of Cottingham's status in his own time while also alive to the difference between Cottingham the Mediaevalist and Pugin the Gothicist. Brougham, knowing that Salvin was already employed by the Howards at Greystoke, expressed his opinion of Salvin as 'a most estimable and liberal man, but I do not think he is sufficiently acquainted with the early style of Architecture to do the work at Naworth as it ought to be done'.[17] Naworth was described by Sir Walter Scott as one of 'those extensive baronial seats which marked the splendour of our ancient nobles'.[18] Indeed, Naworth was the very embodiment of the castle the Broughams were hoping to achieve through Cottingham's expertise. Brougham insisted that only Cottingham could 'do justice to' the restoration of the mediaeval Naworth Castle. He even suggested that if Salvin had already started on the work, the 'plans ought to be laid before Mr Cottingham, but I fear the custom of the profession would not justify it ...' The Earl of Carlisle thanked Brougham for his advice but explained that 'they were already advanced with Salvin'. As the whole exterior outline and detail were preserved after the fire there was 'little scope for architectural discretion' and Salvin's work was largely on interior reconstruction.[19] Salvin made no attempt to re-create the panelled ceiling of the Great Hall painted with portraits of the Kings and Queens of England. Instead he erected an open timber roof.[20] His reconstruction of the Great Hall was criticised by J. H. Parker in his *Some Account of Domestic Architecture in England* (1851) for its lack of archaeological correctness. It was, he judged, 'now of disproportionate length and the partition between the dais and the solar has been removed so that the latter is now thrown into the hall, which not only makes it too long, but makes the bay window appear out of place'.[21] At Peckforton Castle, built in 1844 for John Tollemach, Salvin achieved a massive Mediaeval Revival castle of pedantic correctitude, described by G. G. Scott as a 'real and carefully constructed fortress impregnable under mediaeval conditions and against an army ... the very height of masquerading'.[22]

Cottingham's Brougham Hall, extensively visited by influential friends of Lord Brougham and admired by contemporaries, clearly inspired other patrons and architects. George Shaw, writing in 1847 after his account of Brougham Hall had been published in *The Gentleman's Magazine*, the *Edinburgh Review* and the *Manchester Guardian*, reported that he had received letters from 'Sir Samuel Meyrick, Mr Tollemach, Mr Albert Way and many others', expressing their interest in Brougham Hall. He continued: 'Mr Tollemach speaks of flying off at once to see it – perhaps with an eye to some ideas there to be gained in reference to the Cheshire Castle of Peckforton now in progress.'[23]

A.W. N. Pugin, in his domestic work at Scarisbrick Hall from 1837 and in his alterations to Alton Towers, produced designs that were close in spirit to Cottingham's late Gothic Snelston Hall of 1829. Pugin was attempting to create the picturesque quality of the Mediaeval which arose from necessity and not 'the forced conceits' of the Picturesque eclecticism. At Scarisbrick Pugin built a new wing and in the south front used bay windows and oriels, lofty towers and lanterns and richly decorated Gothic interiors. At Alton Towers in the late 1840s he built the dining hall with a great oriel window, completed the chapel wing with sixteenth-century lights and endowed the tall tower with four pinnacles, work that linked him closely to Cottingham at nearby Snelston and the development of the antiquarian interior.[24]

The Antiquarian Interior

The armour hall played an important part in creating the ancestral baronial house and there was a great interest in armour in early decades of the nineteenth century. Sir Samuel Meyrick, who published three folio volumes in 1824 on *Ancient Armour as it existed in Europe, but particularly in England from the Norman Conquest to the reign of Charles II*, had arranged the royal collection of armour at St George's Hall at Windsor. In 1826 he supervised the erection and arrangement of a new armour gallery at the Tower of London.[25] At Meyrick's own castle of Goodrich, Blore designed a 'hastiltude chamber' with a tableau of a tournament and a Great Armoury, 86ft long, filled with mounted or standing knights in armour. Cottingham was a visitor to Goodrich. Suits of armour in his museum were modelled from those in Meyrick's collection. Cottingham's armour hall at Brougham of the 1830s, Pugin's armour hall for Lord Shrewsbury at Alton and others were designed with the archaeologically correct arrangement of dais and screen passage and were filled with every kind of heraldic device, weaponry, shields of arms and suits of armour, much of which was obtained in Wardour Street and Bond Street in London from dealers such as George Bullock, Daniel Terry and Samuel Pratt.[26] To Terry in 1822, Sir Walter Scott admitted: 'I wish I could take a cruise with you through the brokers which would be the pleasantest affair.'[27]

Among the publications used for designs was Henry Shaw's *Specimens of Ancient Furniture* of 1836. His intention was 'to further extend historical correctness in art', and Sir Samuel Meyrick suggested in the Preface that 'a feeling has now arisen for the ancient decorative style ... for however beautiful and elegant the simplicity of Grecian forms these are not sufficient to produce that effect that should be given to the interior of an English residence'. Shaw's later book *Decorative Arts of the Middle Ages* (1851) and other works such as

Planché's *History of British Costume* (1834), A.W. N. Pugin's *Gothic Furniture* (1835) and Richard Bridgen's *Furniture and Candelabra* (1838) enabled architects and designers to achieve archaeologically correct designs. William Brougham asked many questions of Cottingham in pursuit of authenticity and engaged in lengthy correspondence with George Shaw in his efforts to confirm precedents for his interiors at Brougham.

Cottingham and his son Nockalls worked closely with the leading designers and suppliers of the day like Thomas Willement. The Cottinghams and Willement shared many friends in antiquarian circles such as Francis Douce. Nockalls, exhibiting his father's characteristic generosity of spirit, recommended Willement to his own patron William Brougham: 'Have you paid our friend Willement a visit? I think you will much like him and will find him a most enthusiastic admirer of ancient art'.[28]

Designers, architects and professional antiquaries provided a link between private patrons and the many antique dealers and cabinet makers. Samuel Pratt and his sons Edward and James who made furniture, metalwork and upholstery and also dealt in armour were key figures in the early part of the nineteenth century, supplying work to Cottingham's and Pugin's designs for church restoration and domestic commissions.[29]

As Pratt's business expanded to supply the increased demand for furnishing mediaeval armour halls, he opened a new showroom in Lower Grosvenor Street in April 1838. Cottingham designed 'a truly Gothic apartment' for Pratt, its central feature consisting of 'six grim figures in full armour, apparently in debate', seated at a table.[30] The opening of the showroom was described in *The Times* and Cottingham's Gothic designs were highly praised. *The Gentleman's Magazine* went so far as to call the exhibition 'one of the most brilliant and interesting ever seen in London'.[31] The showroom designed by Cottingham had a great impact as did Pratt's catalogues published with illustrations and descriptions of the pieces offered for sale: 'To gaze at the plumed casque of the Mailed Knight, equipped for the Tournament', he wrote in his first catalogue, 'and to grasp the ponderous mace, yet encrusted with the accumulated rust of centuries, cannot fail to inspire admiration for the chivalrous deeds of our ancestors.' Pratt informed the public, in a catalogue describing 670 items, that his aim 'was to help revive the splendour of our ancient Baronial Halls'.[32]

Pratt's expanded armour business and his new showroom ensured that when Lord Eglinton planned his famous tournament of 1839, Pratt was put in charge of all the arrangements; of the supply of the equipment, armour, pavilions, tents, shields, banners, lances, swords, outfits for squires and pages and mediaeval costumes for the ball; and of the stands and marquees for the tournament as well. It is possible that Cottingham designed the marquees, depicted by J. R. Nixon for Richardson's *The Eglinton Tournament* of 1843, and by J. Aikman in his *Account of Eglinton*: the main grandstand was in the form of a Gothic arched canopy with crocketed finials and marquees giving the impression of towers and castellation.[33] These designs are very similar to drawings in Vol.II of N. X. Willemin's publication on civil and military costumes in mediaeval times illustrating a tournament depicted in a manuscript of 1466. Unhappily, the tournament was ruined by torrential rain and became the subject of satires. But the influence of the Mediaeval Revival continued through the 1840s with the redecoration of houses in the mediaeval manner and a revival of work for the College of Arms.

It was indicative of this revival that Cottingham's patron Lord Brougham went to great lengths to establish a much disputed ancient lineage, reviving the baronetcy of Vaux to which he claimed entitlement, while another patron, John Harrison of Snelston Hall, after first using a coat-of-arms without authority, was granted arms in 1852.[34]

Lord Brougham and Harrison, and others such as Sir Edward Blackett, the Earl of Harrington and the Earl of Dunraven – all of whom were antiquaries and interested in the architecture of the Middle Ages – commissioned Cottingham as the leading mediaevalist architect to create for them revivals of the mediaeval ideal between 1822 and his death in 1847.

Cottingham brought to his domestic architecture and design the same qualities that are shown in his ecclesiastical work: a desire to interpret the spirit of the mediaeval builders, the highest quality of workmanship and materials and a consideration for 'real practical utility'. He despised 'modern architects who considered their pockets more than the credit of their work', and made 'slight sketches and let the work take its chance in the hands of the workmen'.[35] Work on many of his commissions involved the design of all interior fittings, floorings, wall papers, lighting and furniture, and his extant letters reflect his attention to detail and his integrity in dealing with his patrons.

Cottingham's work shows a development from classical to Gothic Revival, beginning with his London estate for John Field of 1824 and his first drawings for Snelston Hall, which, like his Salters' Hall and Fishmongers' Hall competition plans of 1821 and 1832, reflect the neo-classicism of the early decades of the nineteenth century. The development continued with his Gothic Revival Snelston Hall of 1827 and the estate village built from 1827 to 1846; the mediaevalising of Brougham Hall in Cumbria from 1830 to 1846; Gothic extensions to the great houses Matfen Hall in Northumberland, Coombe Abbey in Warwickshire and Elvaston Castle in Derbyshire between 1830 and 1847; and finally his Tudor Revival Savings Bank and bank house at Bury St Edmunds of 1846 and two Gothic Revival schools, hitherto unidentified, Tuddenham School in Suffolk, 1845-7, and Great Chesterford School, Essex, 1846-9 (see Cats E1-4).

Much of Cottingham's work has been destroyed. Snelston Hall was demolished in 1952. Little remains of Brougham Hall or Coombe Abbey, of his extensions to Clifton Hall, Nottingham, or of the General Hospital at Bury St Edmunds. But from a study of original written sources, surviving drawings and plans and contemporary descriptions and opinions, and from an examination of some of his extant buildings such as the two schools, the Savings Bank, and the Snelston estate village, it is possible to measure the quality and the character of his work.

1 Twopenny, W., *Some Observations on the Domestic Architecture of the Middle Ages*, 3rd edition of *The Glossary of Architecture*, 1840

2 *Annales Archéologiques*, June 1844, pp.51-5

3 *Architectural Design*, 'Viollet-le-Duc', Academy Editions, London, 1980, pp.64-71

4 Girouard, M., *The Return to Camelot. Chivalry and The English Gentleman*, 1981, p.23-6, 34

5 Planché, J.R., *The Recollections of J.R. Planché*, 2 Vols, 1872, Vol.I, p.224

6 *Douce Mss*, letter from Sir W. Scott, E264: notes in Douce's handwriting inside a copy of Sir Walter Scott's *Sir Tristram*. Sir Walter Scott's letter to Douce thanks him for his kindness during 'a short stay in London' and reveals that Douce 'liberally communicated' information on antiquarian matters which Scott acknowledged contributed to the interest of the work. *Sir Tristram* was 'one of 12 thrown off without a castration which I had adopted in the rest of the edition, against my own opinion, and in compliance with that of some respectable friends. For I can by no means think that the coarseness of an ancient romance is so dangerous to the public as the mongrel and inflammatory sentimentality of a modern novelist.'

7 Shaw, George, *Diaries*, 1832-5, Manchester City Library, 19 May 1832

8 Wainwright, C., 'The Antiquarian Interior in Britain, 1780-1885' PhD Thesis, University of London, 1986, p.104; Jervis, S., *High Victorian Design*, Woodbridge, 1983, pp.16-17

9 Britton, J., *Graphic Illustrations with a History and Descriptive Account of Toddington, Gloucs*, London, 1840

10 Shaw, op. cit., *Diaries*, 30 Sept. 1834

11 Britton, op. cit., 1840, p.15

12 Shaw, G., *Shaw Correspondence*, letter from Stanhope to Shaw, 10 Oct. 1863, Saddleworth Museum

13 Girouard, op. cit., p.52

14 *Douce Mss*. Letters from Sir S. Meyrick, 12 Aug. 1930; Lady Meyrick to Douce 31 Aug. 1831, 20 Sep. 1831; 3 Oct. 1831; 7 Nov. 1831; 31 Nov. 1831

15 Shaw, op. cit. (unsigned and undated letter)

16 Brougham, W., letter to the 7th Earl of Carlisle, 25 Nov. 1844, *Castle Howard Archive*, J19/1/38/37

17 ibid.

18 *Illustrated London News*, 1844, p.340

19 *Brougham Papers*, UCL, letter, Earl of Carlisle to W. Brougham, 29 Jan. 1845

20 *Castle Howard Archive*, op. cit., letter from Salvin to 7th Earl, 2 Aug. 1844, J19/1/38/50; 13 Aug. 1844, J19/1/3854; 27 July 1845, J19/1/48/76

21 Parker, J.H., *Some Account of Domestic Architecture in England*, 2 Vols, Oxford, J.H. and J. Parker 1851, p.211. Salvin did, however, make an attempt at archaeological correctness, writing that the stone masons 'must make the new windows an accurate copy of the old ones'. See *Castle Howard Archive*, letter 2 Aug. 1844

22 Scott, G.G., *Personal and Professional Recollections*, London, 1857 p.14; Allibone, J., *Anthony Salvin: Pioneer of Gothic Revival Architecture*, Cambridge, Lutterworth, 1988, p.98. Allibone suggests that Tollemache was indeed fortifying his house against the civil unrest of the day

23 *Brougham Papers*, letter from George Shaw to W. Brougham, 27 Oct. 1847

24 Wedgwood, A., *Catalogue of Architectural Drawings in the Victoria & Albert Museum. A.W.N. Pugin and the Pugin Family*, London, 1985, Diary 1835, 1837

25 Girouard, M., *The Return to Camelot*, London, New Haven, 1981, pp.52-3

26 *Brougham Papers*, W. Brougham diaries, 1835-40

27 Wainwright, PhD Thesis, op. cit., p.69

28 *Brougham Papers*, letter NJC to WB, 7 June 1845

29 ibid., WB's diary, 22 Nov. 1844, 'Pratt says he cannot take less than £150 for the altar having refused this from Pugin for Lord Shrewsbury'

30 *The Times*, 16 April 1838

31 *The Gentleman's Magazine*, Jan.-June 1838, p.532

32 Anderson, I., *The Knight and The Umbrella*, London 1936, p.131. The Fine Art Pamphlets described by Anderson and Girouard (op. cit., p.92) are now missing from the V&A and British Library. No other copies have yet come to light

33 Girouard, op. cit., p.92. Cottingham is suggested as the likely designer but little documentary evidence relating to Pratt's business remains, beyond the references found in the Brougham Papers

34 Information from Maxwell Craven, Derby Museum and Art Gallery; *College of Arms Archives*

35 *Brougham Papers*, letter LNC to WB, 7 Sept. 1844

5

Cottingham and Patronage

Cottingham played an important role in the promotion of a Gothic Revival through his reputation as an expert on the Mediaeval, his archaeological studies, and the influence of his restorations and his domestic architecture, a role highlighted if viewed in the context of patronage and the intricate patterns of influence in the early nineteenth century. A scrutiny of his patrons' social and political standing, of the complex reasons for their desire to restore, extend or build, and of the extent to which they relied on Cottingham as an arbiter of taste, reveals much about patronage and the development of taste in the early decades of the nineteenth century. Cottingham's relationships with his patrons, in which he appeared as an absolute authority, rather than as a servant or retainer in the manner of the eighteenth century, and as one whose integrity was beyond doubt, are indicative of his professional standing at a time when architects in general were viewed with distrust. Those relationships also serve to underline changing trends from the eighteenth to nineteenth centuries.

During the eighteenth century the Crown ceased to be the most important source of patronage for architects and artists. Patronage was sought instead from the leaders of the political parties and from the aristocracy. The architect William Kent and his patron Lord Burlington provide an example. This trend continued into the nineteenth century. Cottingham's patron Lord Brougham was a powerful Whig with radical tendencies and Robert Smirke relied almost entirely for patronage on Sir Robert Peel, the great Tory leader.[1] The eighteenth century saw a change, too, in the role of the architect. A distinction arose between the master builder who could erect a building from the merest sketch and the increasingly arrogant architect, who now viewed himself as an artist above 'the vulgar and mechanical contrivances' of building, concerned with designing and interpreting contemporary taste: a precarious foundation, as Barrington Kaye has pointed out, on which to build a profession.[2]

Training for architects in the eighteenth century was limited, being essentially restricted to instruction in drawing, to which might be added a period of apprenticeship under an eminent architect and a Grand Tour. But most practitioners went into architecture from the position of clerk of works, mason, carpenter or surveyor, or from painting and sculpture. This system continued until well into the nineteenth century, when professional associations of architects were formed – examples being the London Architectural Society of 1806, the Architect and Antiquaries Club of 1819 and the Architectural Society of 1831 – and attempts were made to introduce proper training for architects through the Royal Academy or through examinations set by the Institute of British Architects, a campaign most forcefully run by James Savage in 1845.[3] Cottingham himself, coming from a family of master builders, was

trained in the traditional way through a period of practical apprenticeship with 'a builder and architect': he then gained further experience under various architects before setting up in business on his own, continuing his studies through his own researches so as 'to attain excellence in his profession'.

During the eighteenth and early nineteenth centuries patrons could rely on pattern books and folios of designs and on highly skilled master craftsmen to construct the buildings. But the development of a serious Gothic Revival in the early decades of the nineteenth century hastened the separation of builder from architect. Builders now had to demand detailed, exact scale drawings and the architects had to supply them. Seen in this context, the vital importance of Cottingham's publications of 1822, the first working manuals of the Gothic style for architects, becomes more readily apparent. It is crucially necessary to appreciate that Cottingham combined the two vital attributes, scholarship and fashion, that led to the change in taste from the eighteenth to the nineteenth century. Cottingham was in demand by patrons who were anxious to be part of this new trend and who wanted an architecture based on a correct revival of the Gothic from an architect known for his scholarship and the accuracy of his drawings. That this was so emerges clearly from the surviving correspondence between Cottingham and his patrons and from the Bills of Works (the architect's detailed instructions to builders).

Few contemporary architects possessed Cottingham's professional quality and integrity and during the 1830s and 1840s the profession in general, characterised by malpractices, was held in very low esteem. An article in the *Architectural Magazine* of 1834 described

the disgraceful practice whereby an architect deceives his employer by making pretty and attractive drawings and reporting the expense at $\frac{1}{2}$ or $\frac{2}{3}$ of what it actually turns out to be ... and their custom of exacting from the builder a commission for all works done under their direction and if refused, informing the builder his services are no longer required.[4]

The temptation of architects to under-estimate costs to attract clients led to problems for the builders who for their livelihood depended on the architects' estimates. The builder, in order to check the architect's figures, would therefore employ a 'measurer', who often found it advantageous to add to the estimates to increase his own commission. This state of affairs explains many of the contemporary comments by patrons or committees who employed architects to restore or to build. Questions were raised about the accuracy of drawings by the architect, the honesty of his estimates, and his relationship with builders and other merchants. In many instances Cottingham was forced to defend his position. This he did in forthright and unequivocal terms, showing him to have been a man of high principles and strength of character, refusing to be overawed by the patron's high rank or social standing, confident in the knowledge of his work's integrity. In a letter answering complaints from a client regarding costs – a universal problem – Cottingham defended himself firmly to William Brougham:

I regret you should think the charge I have made more than adequate recompense for the amount of time and expense I have bestowed in making the designs as correct in point of style, character, and taste as possible. You must consider that it has not been for 'plain wall work' that I have made drawings and models – far from it – nearly all that I have done has required the knowledge of Gothic architecture which nothing but years of study and experience would enable an architect to produce.

Here Cottingham stressed the quality of his work which at Brougham Hall involved the incorporation of an archaeologically correct revival of the various periods of Gothic. He went on to point out the difference between himself, skilled in every aspect of building and designing, and some of his contemporaries:

I could have done as many modern architects would consider the filling of their pockets more than the credit of their work do, namely have made slight sketches and let the work take its chance in the hands of workmen thereby giving to everything done the evident date of AD1844. Such has never been my principle. I have never, by serving my own interests neglected that of my employer, by letting anything go from my hands which was not well considered in every particular.[5]

Local criticisms and accusations of 'extravagant misapplication of funds' were made during the progress of the works at Hereford. One of the patrons and committee members, R. Biddulph Phillips, refuted these allegations based on wrong information, with evidence from Cottingham's estimates and completely vindicated the committee, noting that 'they adopted the recommendations of the architect instead of exercising their own opinion'.[6]

At Armagh the mistrust of architects and of the architectural profession in general was very evident in the intolerable treatment of Cottingham by Archbishop Beresford's agents, in their unsuccessful attempts to find a single discrepancy in the estimates or accounts, and, again, in the stormy vestry meeting at St Mary's, Bury St Edmunds, when local tradespeople tried to cast doubt upon the honesty of Cottingham's assessment of the works required and queried his estimate of the costs involved and his supposed favouring of certain contractors. At St Mary's, Nottingham, Cottingham's prompt action saved the great fifteenth-century tower from collapse and he subsequently drew up plans for the complete restoration of the church.[7] Difficulties arose during Cottingham's survey of the fabric of the church resulting in his writing a stern letter to the committee telling them that they were clearly 'unacquainted with the manner in which the restoration of buildings of such importance as the church of St Mary's should be conducted' and he would correct their 'erroneous opinions'. Finally, tenders were requested and three were very close to Cottingham's estimate of £5000. But the committee chose to accept a fourth, of £2800, a decision that raised protests from Cottingham who believed the works could never be undertaken properly for that amount of money.[8] The

committee then dispensed with his services and appointed Scott and Moffat who proceeded to undertake the work to Cottingham's plans, using his meticulous drawings, for his survey could not be bettered.[9]

Cottingham, in all his dealings with his patrons, appeared in a position of authority, achieving a certain degree of independence that was not possible in the eighteenth century when disagreement between architect and patron on the matter of style and design seldom arose because of the universal acceptance of Palladian architecture, the widespread use of textbooks and the uncertain status of the architect himself. Cottingham, by contrast, was the acknowledged expert in the early decades of the nineteenth century and as the Gothic Revival gained momentum, his work was in demand by patrons interested in the Mediaeval. The intricate pattern of patronage ensured that Cottingham was neither dependent for work on competitions, which he found unsatisfactory, nor on the open market conditions of the metropolis.

It is often assumed that patronage altered radically in the nineteenth century with the nouveaux riches taking over from the aristocracy as patrons. In fact, Cottingham's patrons were still drawn from the aristocracy, the landed gentry, the professional classes, politically prominent statesmen (although his patrons were not confined to one party) and the Church, traditionally controlled largely by the aristocracy. An examination of Cottingham's patrons reveals a web of connections through family and social ties, or shared concerns, that gained him his commissions. Many of his patrons had similar interests, for example, as amateur architects in rebuilding or extending existing houses in mediaeval style to enhance their social status, or as aficionados of heraldry, armour and genealogy. Many travelled widely to study Gothic architecture, of which they left descriptions in their letters, private diaries and journals. Keen interest was shown, too, in preservation of the mediaeval heritage through subscriptions to scholarly works and to campaigns to protect such buildings as the Norman Tower, Crosby Hall and Sir Walter Scott's Abbotsford. Membership of antiquarian societies and the promotion of mediaeval archaeology were common to most of Cottingham's patrons, as was an interest in the preservation and restoration of ecclesiastical architecture through patronage.

The patron of Cottingham's major works of restoration at Armagh from 1834, Lord John Beresford, Archbishop of Armagh, had connections that were important in the development of Cottingham's career. The archbishop was the uncle of Alexander Beresford Hope, a leading member of the Ecclesiologists from 1839, and his reports of Cottingham's restoration methods at Armagh and his perception that Cottingham was the most eminent restorer of his time undoubtedly contributed to the later ecclesiological crusade and its emphasis on the restoration of mediaeval art and architecture.

A. J. Beresford Hope's mother, Louisa Hope, had, on the death of Thomas Hope, married her cousin William, Viscount Beresford in 1832. He was Tory MP for Waterford from 1811-14. Archbishop Beresford also involved himself in politics, promoting Beresford interests in Ireland. The Beresfords remained Tory despite their opposition to the Roman Catholic Emancipation Act of 1829 and arguments with the government over disposal of patronage in Derry.[10] Cottingham's connections with leading Tory politicians such as Sir Robert Inglis and also his friendship with Sir Walter Scott may have stemmed from the

Beresford Hope connection, for in Louisa's journal, the *Deepdene Album*, she named Inglis and Scott as regular visitors.[11]

Cottingham's other aristocratic patrons offer evidence of close connections, again suggesting possible reasons for his employment. James Walter Grimston, 1st Earl of Verulam, Viscount Grimston and Baron Verulam of Gorhambury, was Tory MP for St Albans in 1830 and 1831, and the patron of Cottingham's restoration work at St Alban's Abbey in 1832. Verulam's diaries of 1819 to 1843 reveal that he was a close friend of both Earl Craven, for whom Cottingham undertook works of extension at Coombe Abbey in 1834, and of Sir Henry Hotham, a relative of the Reverend Charles Hotham of Roos in Yorkshire, where Cottingham restored the parish church.[12] The Hothams were also connected with Theberton Hall and Church in Suffolk: the Honourable Frederica Doughty, patron of Cottingham's works of extension and restoration at Theberton in 1846, was the daughter of the Honourable and Reverend Frederick Hotham and the cousin of the Reverend Charles Hotham.[13] Verulam was a keen antiquary and his diaries indicate that he visited Goodrich Court, the home of Sir Samuel Meyrick, the well-known antiquary and friend of Cottingham.

Church restoration was extensively patronised by the aristocracy, particularly when younger sons were churchmen. In Cottingham's home county of Suffolk, the sons of the Earl of Bristol (and grandsons of the amateur architect the Bishop of Derry) were the patrons for many of Cottingham's restorations and collected subscription funds to pay for the costly works. For example, one of the earl's sons, the Reverend Arthur Hervey, was involved as patron of St Mary's, Bury, Market Weston Church, Horringer Church and the Norman Tower restorations. As a keen mediaevalist antiquary, he belonged to learned societies and would have known of Cottingham's fame from the time of his publications of 1822 onward. Lord Arthur was president of the Suffolk Institute of Archaeology and was also a member of the Archaeological Association of London. The association's publication, the *Archaeological Journal*, reported a visit by a numerous party to Bury St Edmunds in 1850: the visitors were welcomed by Lord Arthur and conducted to view Cottingham's 'skilful' work at the Norman Tower and St Mary's Church 'which was in a very insecure condition, and was repaired with much care by the late Mr Cottingham'.[14] The Hervey family connection also ensured work for Cottingham through Lord Arthur's brother, the Reverend Lord Charles Hervey, at Great Chesterford where Cottingham restored the parish church in 1841.[15] As was often the case, ecclesiastical patronage led to other work. Thus Cottingham gained commissions to build the Savings Bank at Bury, the school at Tuddenham, and the school at Great Chesterford: at Snelston Cottingham began work on the small parish church and then went on to build the great mansion and the estate village.

Many of Cottingham's patrons were keen mediaeval antiquaries and knew of his work through the preservation campaigns, membership of antiquarian societies and through his publications, museum and works of restoration. The Earl of Dunraven, for example, was a member of the Oxford Society for Promoting the Study of Gothic Architecture. R. B. Phillips, patron of the Hereford Cathedral restoration, was also a member of the Oxford Society and a Fellow of the Society of Antiquaries (FSA), a member of the Cambridge Archaeological Association, and a member of the Arundel Society, to which John Ruskin and Lord Brougham also belonged. Sir Edward Blackett of Matfen was a FSA, a member of the British Archaeological Association and friend of Sir Robert Inglis. All these discriminating antiquaries employed Cottingham, in William Brougham's words, as 'the most cognisant architect of his day'. Lord Brougham was an important patron of Cottingham, and his brother William, also an antiquary of note, relied totally on Cottingham's authority as a mediaeval expert for every detail of the work at Brougham. Sir Robert Inglis, patron of Cottingham's restoration at Milton Bryan church, was a prominent politician, a Liberal of the Conservative school of Sir Robert Peel and a major figure in antiquarian and preservationist issues. He was vice president of the Society of Antiquaries, Professor of Antiquities at the Royal Academy, vice president of the Historical Society of Science, and President of the Literary Club. Inglis was associated, too, with Peel's Commission for Improving the Metropolis, which sought 'to provide increased facilities for communication within it', and with the Metropolitan Churches Fund, which considered the need for church accommodation in urban areas; he was also a commissioner of the Incorporated Church Building Society. As a major figure at the centre of key architectural and antiquarian developments, including the Committee for the Houses of Parliament Competition, Inglis was well placed to assess the leading architects of the day. He chose Cottingham for the task of rebuilding the dilapidated parish church of Milton Bryan in 1841, for which he was the patron. Sir Robert was a man of wide interests and contacts and a friend of many of Cottingham's patrons, including Sir Walter Scott. Scott, a leading influence in the revival of mediaeval taste in the early decades of the nineteenth century, was an important figure in antiquarian circles, with numerous connections and sharing with Cottingham many friends such as Francis Douce, Edward Blore, Lord Beresford of Armagh, A. J. Beresford Hope, Lord Brougham and the Hothams. Relationships and connections of this kind reflected the spread of influence through layers of patronage.

Cottingham's patrons were drawn, too, from professional classes and the landed gentry, such as John Harrison of Snelston. Harrison was a barrister of the Inner Temple, a keen antiquary and collector of mediaeval artefacts and a colleague of Sir Edward Blackett of Matfen, who was also a member of the Inner Temple and member of the British Archaeological Association.[16] Cottingham, as architect to such influential patrons as these, was in a position to promote change, and his ideas, so crucial to the Gothic Revival, were disseminated through the network and conduits of patronage available to him from 1821 until his death in 1847.

1   Crook, J. M., 'Sir Robert Peel; Patron of the Arts', *History Today*, Jan. 1966, pp.3-11; and 'The Pre-Victorian Architect. Professionalism and Patronage', *Architectural History*, 12, 1969, pp.62-73

2   Kaye, Barrington, *The Development of the Architectural Profession in Britain*, London, 1960, p.44

3   Savage, H., *A Memoir of James Savage*, 1852, RIBA MS, SPII (IV)

4   *Architectural Magazine*, 'On the Present State of the Professions of Architect and Surveyor and of the Building Trade in England', 1834, I, p.15-16

5   *Brougham Papers*, letter LNC to WB, 7 Sept. 1844

6   *Hereford Times*, 20 Jan. 1849, letter from R. B. Phillips, 27 Jan. 1849

7   Cottingham, L. N., 'Report on The Tower of St Mary's Church, Nottingham', *Architect, Engineer and Surveyor*, 1843, pp.43-5

8   *Vestry Minute Book*, St Mary's Church; entries by W. Tomlin, Secretary to the Restoration Committee; letter from LNC, 18 Dec. 1844

9   *The Builder*, 1845, p.299; *The Gentleman's Magazine*, Jan.-June 1843

10 Law, H. W. and I., *The Book of the Beresford Hopes*, London, Heath Cranton, 1925, pp.90ff. Curl, J.S., *The Londonderry Plantation 1609-1914*, Chichester, 1988, p.51

11 ibid., p.51

12 Verulam, *Diaries*, 20 Vols, 1830-45, Herts R.O., D/EV F44-45; F56-57; F346; F390

13 *Hotham Papers*, Brynmor Jones Library, University of Hull; Doughty, H. M., *Chronicles of Theberton*, London, 1910, p.233

14 *Archaeological Journal*, Vol.XI, 1850, p.397

15 *ICBS*, No.2985

16 See Myles, J., 'L. N. Cottingham 1787-1847, architect, his place in the Gothic Revival', PhD Thesis, Leicester Polytechnic, 1989, Part II, Chapters 2-9

Working Drawings of Gothic Ornament, Plate XXVII, 1823
Lithograph 24×17 in (61×43.25 cm)

6

Twentieth-Century Views of Cottingham's Work

The evidence of Cottingham's fame in his own time noted throughout this survey of his work is irrefutable. Yet by the late nineteenth century he was under criticism. In the twentieth century an uncritical disregard of his status has until now persisted with no new questioning or analysis of the documentary evidence. He has consequently been relegated to the position of an obscure architect barely worthy of a mention in passing. With regard to restoration practice, Holman Hunt sowed the seeds of Cottingham's marginalisation with his inaccurate reporting of the 'iconoclastic' methods used to fill Cottingham's museum. Worse still, he continued, 'the restorer had doubtless replaced everything considered necessary in what was decided to be the most correct Early English style, and loss of historic interest was then in no way accounted of'.[1]

In this account Hunt implicitly linked Cottingham to the worst mode of restoration, 'unity of style', drastic, unsympathetic, destructive. As the nineteenth century progressed, the restorations inspired by the ecclesiological crusade were increasingly attacked. Holman Hunt, with William Morris, was a founder member of the SPAB. Yet its archive reveals no analysis or discussion of Cottingham's major restoration works. By 1900, Benham, writing of Rochester, could claim that 'Cottingham's work was highly esteemed in its day but is no longer', an attitude that has prevailed until the present day.[2] The entry for Cottingham in the *Dictionary of National Biography* is taken directly from the obituary in *The Art-Union* of 1847, with the added comment: 'His enthusiasm for the Gothic Revival frequently overcame his discretion in handling the buildings entrusted to his care.' Criticism of his work at Rochester, even called 'mischievous meddling'[3] and 'stylistic barbarism', was directed at the lack of a spire, his reconstruction of Bishop Sheppie's tomb, and his replacement of missing parts of sculpture in the chapter house doorway.[4] To make matters worse, Cottingham's work at Rochester has also been confused with that of the heavily criticised Vulliamy who continued restoration in 1845.[5]

In twentieth-century writings on Hereford Cathedral, unity of style restoration is implied in a characteristic description of Cottingham's removal of the masonry shoring to the crumbling piers as 'the demolishing of all Post-Norman additions', and the work is wrongly attributed to N. J. Cottingham who, it is alleged, 'rebuilt rather than restored and allowed his workmen to rework ancient sculptures'.[6] An apologist for G. G. Scott wrote that 'Scott may be blamed unwittingly for earlier and less scholarly work such as Cottingham at Hereford',[7] and the restoration of Hereford was further dismissed in general misunderstandings: 'The Dean and Chapter had previously consulted William Burges as to Cottingham's fitness for the job. It is a tragedy that he and not

Burges was employed.' The writer, unhelpfully to accurate history and Cottingham's reputation, confused the architect Burges (only sixteen years old at the time) and William Burge of the Societies of the Inner and Middle Temple who wrote a testimonial to Cottingham at the dean's request.[8]

Some twentieth-century historians have afforded a more favourable assessment of Cottingham's contribution to church restoration in the early nineteenth century. Pevsner allowed Cottingham credit for 'a very creditable stone screen at Magdalen'. John Summerson and Clive Wainwright described him as 'one of the first careful restorers'. And T. S. R. Boase, writing of Magdalen in 1955, identified Cottingham as one of the chief Gothic practitioners in the country, his work characterised by 'extreme thoroughness and a far more scholarly approach' than had been evident previously in the college's Gothic undertakings, setting new standards of archaeological taste.[9] However, in 1983, Howard Colvin, in *Unbuilt Oxford*, described Cottingham's Magdalen as 'conscientious correctitude unalleviated by the slightest flight of fancy' and went on to praise A. W. N. Pugin's work at Balliol as a 'combination of scholarship and fantasy'.[10] Yet James Ingram, in 1837, had noted of Magdalen that 'though there may be as usual something to condemn there is much more to admire, whatever opinion may be entertained of the designs and fancies of the architect'.[11]

Views of correctitude have no doubt changed over time. But it is necessary to recall that Cottingham, and Pugin, who was influenced by Cottingham's theory and practice in restoration work, both believed that personal preferences and flights of fancy should be effaced in order to carry out a correct restoration of the style of architecture involved. The idea of imitation and strict historicism had been advocated in the early years of the nineteenth century by Carter and others. At the same time, 'slavish copying' had been seen as a denial of creative genius. Pugin's criticism of Wyatt's work at Lichfield in terms worthy of Carter and his own works of restoration demonstrate that Pugin also believed in the effacement of individual expression in works of restoration. His designs for Balliol, to which Colvin referred, included the restoration of the old hall and library, a new chapel in the style of the fourteenth century, new kitchens and interior design work that allowed creative expression in an interpretation of the Gothic spirit.

As to Cottingham's domestic architecture and design, Simon Jervis, writing in 1984 of furniture design, suggested that whereas antiquarian knowledge led to a more archaeological approach to Gothic design, 'only A. W. Pugin moved beyond simple copyism to forms convincingly Gothic, not only in ornament but also in structure'. He continued: 'It is clear that Cottingham never made this creative leap.'[12] Yet Cottingham stressed, just as Pugin was to do later, the need for draughtsmen to 'accurately ascertain the modes of construction used by the ancient masons. It will stamp a value on their work, and be a sure stepping stone towards a correct revival of the art of the Middle Ages.'[13]

In a letter to William Brougham, Cottingham showed his understanding that Gothic was not merely a style of applied decoration to be copied accurately but was a matter of structure; a furniture design provided the occasion for the expression of this insight: 'I thought you would like the table ... but only where the taste of those who have the designs prepared for them is sufficiently imbued with Gothic to advise it in its simplest form can an architect dare to make things so true to old character.'[14] A similar concern for simple form was shown by Pugin when he wrote to his cabinet maker Crace in 1850: 'I am anxious about this plain furniture, to introduce a sensible style of furniture of good oak, constructively put together that will compete with the vile trash made and sold.'[15]

Among Cottingham's pupils were E. B. Lamb and Calvert Vaux. Accounts of their work provide a further source of confused criticism of Cottingham's work in relation to his influence upon his pupils. Vaux went to America after his training with Cottingham to become a partner of A. J. Downing and F. L. Olmstead and was joint designer of New York's Central Park and others throughout America. Henry Hope Reed described Vaux as a British-trained architect 'who had so great an influence in America', his work representing 'a significant turn in American architectural history': and his volume *Villas and Cottages* of 1857 'remained a basic document of nineteenth-century American architecture'.[16] Yet in writings on Vaux, Cottingham's influence is dismissed; though 'technically meticulous', he 'was not an architectural thinker of any magnitude'. In work on E. B. Lamb, inaccuracies are perpetuated to an even greater degree. Cottingham's restorations qualified him to receive Wyatt's title of 'destroyer' and 'the historical accuracy does not seem to be of paramount importance'. Whereas Lamb, the pupil, 'unlike Cottingham saw the need to suppress his own instincts when restoring ancient buildings'. Previous assessments are repeated verbatim: 'He demolished the original tower and spire at Rochester', and at Hereford 'substituted three broad lancets for the original Perpendicular window at the east end, rebuilt rather than restored'.[17]

However, in his more recent work on Lamb, E. N. Kaufman attributes Lamb's qualities as a sensitive restorer and a Gothic Revivalist of originality and independence of thought to the training he received from Cottingham. But Kaufman noted that Lamb had a strong respect for vernacular building techniques and styles using 'sharply articulated volumes, high roofs, freely disposed windows and boldly massed chimneys, in a refined and vernacular Tudor style derived from ancient domestic building'. Kaufman, in ignorance of the previously unknown fact that Cottingham's domestic architecture was based on the vernacular, suggested that this area of Lamb's work was derived from A. W. N. Pugin.[18] In fact, Lamb's ideas and his use of the vernacular as a source of style stemmed not simply from Pugin, as Kaufman suggests, but primarily from his master Cottingham. Once again, lack of knowledge of the full extent of Cottingham's work has resulted in an obscuring of his role in the development of nineteenth-century architectural theory and practice and in the misattribution of his ideas.

The disturbing degree of confusion which has appeared throughout twentieth-century assessments of Cottingham's work and the dearth of knowledgeable appraisal suggest some reasons for Cottingham's neglect. That much of Cottingham's work has been destroyed or has remained unknown and unacknowledged has not been conducive to its proper reassessment. Another reason may be an almost total lack of readily accessible documentation relating to his architectural business. There are no holdings of archive material in his name, no extant personal papers, letters, daybooks, or diaries remaining. It seems likely that when his son Nockalls emigrated to America in 1854 and was lost at sea in the wreck of the *Arctic*, the family business records were lost as well. Nockalls and Calvert Vaux served their apprenticeship with Cottingham at the same time and it is possible that Nockalls was on his way to work with Vaux in America when the tragedy occurred.[19] Cottingham's advanced ideas and theories and his contemporary influence as a major figure of the early nineteenth century have, for a variety of reasons, been overshadowed and virtually lost to view: even when remembered he is usually misunderstood through ignorance. He was not a self-publicist with the literary power of a Pugin, Ruskin or Morris. A major part of his work lay in important tasks of restoration, work which consumed his time and energies in a comparatively short working life and which has been the subject of conflicting views, inaccurate preconceptions and very little close analysis or appraisal.

1   Holman Hunt, W., *Pre-Raphaelitism and the Pre-Raphaelite Brotherhood*, 2 Vols, London, 1905, Vol.I, p.179

2   Benham, W., *Rochester Cathedral*, London, 1900, p.33

3   ibid., p.33

4   Fawcett, J., ed., *The Future of the Past: Attitudes to Conservation, 1171-1974*, London, 1976, p.79

5   *Annales Archéologiques*, 1846, p.284, 'Promenade en Angleterre'

6   Fawcett, op. cit., p.79

7   Cole, D., *The Work of G.G. Scott*, 1980, p.50

8   Fawcett, op. cit., pp.79, 91

9   Pevsner, N. and Sherwood, J., *Oxfordshire* 1974, p.151; Wainwright, C., 'Davington Priory', *Country Life*, 9 Dec. 1971; Summerson, J., *Victorian Architecture*, 1970, p.56; Boase, T.S.R., 'An Oxford College and the Gothic Revival', *Journal of the Warburg Institute*, Vol.XVIII, 1955, p.172

10 Colvin, H., *Unbuilt Oxford*, 1983, p.109

11 Ingram, J., *Memorials of Oxford*, 3 Vols, 1837, Vol.II, pp.22-3

12 Jervis, S., 'Snelston Hall', *Victoria & Albert Museum Album*, 1984

13 Cottingham, L.N., letter to the Editor, *The Gentleman's Magazine*, Jan.-June 1841, p.18

14 *Brougham Papers*, letter LNC to WB, 5 Aug. 1844

15 Wainwright, C., 'The Architect and the Decorative Arts – Architect Designers, Pugin-MacIntosh' *Exhibition Catalogue*, Fine Art Society, 1981, p.5

16 Vaux, Calvert, *Villas and Cottages*, New York, 1857. Reprint NY, 1968, Preface by Henry Hope Reed

17 Winduss, M.A., 'E.B. Lamb, 1805-1869', MA Thesis, Manchester University, 1978 (unpublished)

18 Kaufman, E.N., 'Life and Work of E.B. Lamb 1805-1869', PhD Thesis, Yale University, 1984

19 King's College School Archives. I am indebted to Frank Miles, the archivist, for information, 16 July 1987 and 8 Aug. 1987. Nockalls was at the school from 1832-5, and Edwin from 1834-7. Other pupils at the school in Cottingham's sons' time were the future architects George Devey, Calvert Vaux who trained in LNC's office, Jacob Wrey Mould, Henry Crisp, William Lightly, William Burges, Dante Rossetti, E.M. Barry, Henry Bayly and Frederick W. Cumberland (designer of Toronto University in 1859)

PLATE I

A wall monument to the Hon. Frederica
Doughty, 1845-6, designed by Cottingham
in the style of fifteenth-century Gothic.
This monument hangs at St Peter's,
Theberton, Suffolk
Cat.CII

PLATE 2
L. N. Cottingham's proposal for the west
end of Magdalen College Chapel, Oxford,
new organ case and screen, 1829
Watercolour 24×19 in (61×48 cm)
Cat.B9

PLATE 3 OPPOSITE
Photograph of the west end of Magdalen
College Chapel, Oxford, 1985, showing
Cottingham's stone chair case of 1829
Cat.B14

DESIGN·FOR·A·GOTHIC·ELEVATION·FOR·SNELSTON·HALL
THE·SEAT·OF·IOHN·HARRISON·ESQ.·DERBYSHIRE

PLATE 4
L. N. Cottingham
Gothic elevation for Snelston Hall,
Derbyshire, 1826
Watercolour $18\frac{3}{4} \times 27\frac{1}{2}$ in (47.5×70 cm)
Cat.E5

Entrance Front of Snelston Hall   The Seat of John Harrison Esq.

PLATE 5
L. N. Cottingham
Entrance front of Snelston Hall, 1827
Watercolour 19×27½ in (48.25×70 cm)
Cat.E10

PLATE 6
L. N. Cottingham
Gamekeeper's Cottage, 1825
Number five in a series of seventeen designs
by Cottingham for plain and ornamental
cottages, gamekeeper's and bailiff's houses,
gate lodges and other rural residences for
Snelston Hall
Watercolour $9\frac{1}{2} \times 13$ in (24×33 cm)
Cat.E25

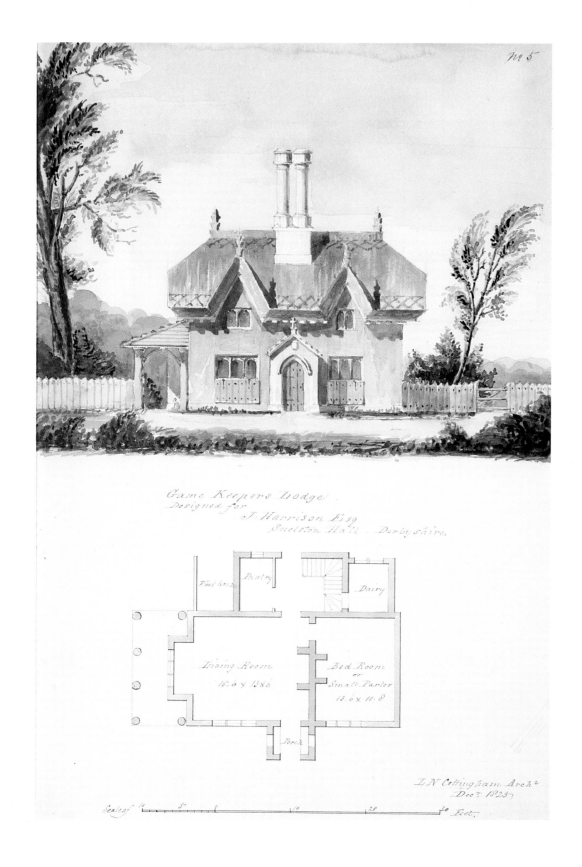

PLATE 7
L. N. Cottingham
View of the south front of Coombe Abbey, 1834
Pencil and watercolour 19¼×37 in (49×94 cm)
Cat.E38

PLATE 8
L. N. Cottingham
Design for a Louis XIV drawing room for
Coombe Abbey, 1834
Pencil and watercolour $19\frac{1}{4} \times 37$ in (49×94 cm)
Cat.E39

Conclusion

My intention in this book and the planned exhibition has been to bring to light the work of a neglected architect and to establish his contribution to the Gothic Revival while restoring to him the position he properly merits in architectural history. Most major figures of the nineteenth century – Pugin, Salvin and others – have been the subject of scholarly scrutiny, and their perceived influences and significance have now entered the accepted history of nineteenth-century architectural developments. Cottingham has remained a shadowy figure in the margins. Just as A. W. N. Pugin was rescued from obscurity in the 1960s by Phoebe Stanton, so, too, Cottingham deserves the posthumous award of his rightful place in the progression of events.

The attempt has been made in this book to cover the entire work of the man. Because Cottingham's work was largely unknown, it has been necessary to consider every aspect of his oeuvre in order to present an overall, if imperfect and incomplete, picture. Further discoveries may be made, and other works of restoration, missing watercolours and designs, extant buildings, or examples of furniture and interior design may come to light, enhancing our understanding of his theory and practice. In July 1992 a set of chairs appeared for sale in Christie's, their provenance being Brougham Hall; and in 1993 the two missing watercolours of Coombe Abbey which Cottingham exhibited at the Royal Academy in 1834 also came to light. Such examples are not unlikely to be replicated in the future.

An obvious pitfall in the endeavour to rehabilitate such a sadly neglected and maligned figure was a possible tendency to overrate his performance, over-estimate his influence or quality, or adjust the evidence to suit the hypothesis. The temptation was the greater since Cottingham emerges as a man of admirable personal qualities: passionate about the Gothic to the point of working without charge to preserve it, generous with his knowledge, never bigoted or narrow in his views, conscientious and utterly reliable, of unimpeachable integrity, possessed of a ready wit and a sense of humour and yet endowed with a strength of character and with authority in all his dealings with patrons. With this in mind, I have aimed at an impartial assessment on the basis of the work itself, drawing upon contemporary opinion and judgement, which I have sought to analyse and assess in the context of the time, and measuring Cottingham's achievement against the work of recognised figures such as Pugin, Barry, Salvin, Scott and others.

My study of Cottingham has also taken account of the broader context of European attitudes and developments. My argument is that the evidence fully justifies Cottingham's reinstatement as a leading figure of the Gothic Revival. He was one of the first analysts of Gothic directly to affect architectural practice by carrying forward the theories of Essex, Milner, Gough, Carter and Rickman, by going beyond the work of A. C. Pugin and Willson in his structural analysis of Gothic architecture, and by encouraging architects to move towards an archaeologically correct revival through restoration and building anew. As an historian of the whole mediaeval period, he appreciated every stage of its development without the prejudice that coloured the views of Gothicists such as Pugin and the Ecclesiologists. As early as 1822, he sought to establish the Mediaeval as architecture that conformed to certain definable structural and compositional developments, and as worthy of serious appraisal as the classical.

In his early work, Cottingham identified every major issue of the Gothic Revival in the nineteenth century: a revival through structural analysis; conservative restoration of the crumbling fabric of mediaeval architecture based on a sound historical knowledge; and the idea that the structural rules of Gothic might be applied without sterile copyism to a revival of domestic architecture based on a native tradition. His theories found faithful reflection in his practice as mediaeval archaeologist through his preservationist activities and his major works of restoration of all eras of the Mediaeval. These provided evidence of both his informed approach and his remarkable skills as a surveyor and engineer. His museum was the first major collection of mediaeval antiquities in England, comparable to that of Lenoir's Museé in France, identified as the main catalyst of the Romantic movement there. Cottingham's museum, though hitherto not unknown by historians of the period, can now be properly viewed as of similar importance in England. His vast collection was used as an informed historical account and illustration of the art and architecture of the Middle Ages at a time of general ignorance of that period. It provided a means of preserving examples that would otherwise have been lost in an age when the Gothic was reviled, and it was used as a source of study for students, architects, artists and such literary figures as Sir Walter Scott whose novels contributed to the growing passion for the Mediaeval.

Refocusing our perspective on the past, Cottingham comes into view as one of the leading mediaevalist architects of the first half of the nineteenth century, crucially influential in the Gothic Revival in a wide context. He was the key analyst of Gothic, its passionate promoter, preserver, collector, restorer and builder. He helped to reintroduce the Romanesque and Gothic to the English stylistic repertoire, leading the trend away from the classical dominance of the previous era. His importance in these developments was well recognised and widely acknowledged in his own time. Perhaps the most telling single evidence of this – though the evidence is cumulatively impressive – is the highly eulogistic judgement passed in 1834 by a young architect not then fully launched on his church-building career but now regarded as the most influential theorist and practitioner of the nineteenth-century Gothic Revival, A. W. N. Pugin. Pugin was much delighted by 'one of the most beautiful specimens of modern design that I have ever seen, and executed ... in the best manner'.

This study's raison d'être was to rescue, exhibit and illustrate the historical reality of Cottingham's achievements, status and influence: his exhumation from the vault of forgotten importance has been long overdue. The last word is left to Cottingham's obituarist in *The Art-Union* of October 1847 who wrote of this 'distinguished architect' and his significance, ending on a personal note:

His temper and feeling with regard to his profession might by the stranger be considered enthusiastic; but his heart and affections were equally ardent, and those who once knew him ever entertained the greatest esteem and friendship for his amiable domestic habits, and generous, benevolent disposition. Many who have enjoyed his friendship, and those who have received the advantage of his sound and able instruction, and since attained eminence in their profession, will feel this to be a just eulogy to the memory of so highly-gifted and true-hearted a man.

Part Two
Catalogue of Works

While the majority of the catalogue entries are illustrated here, there will be an opportunity to view them all in the exhibition on Cottingham to be held at the Ashmolean Museum, Oxford in 1998.

A Cottingham's Publications

A1 (Figs 1, 5 and 6)
L. N. Cottingham, *Plans of Westminster Hall*,
Rodwell and Martin, London, 1822
The British Architectural Library, RIBA, London

It was at Westminster that Cottingham developed his passion for the Mediaeval, studying, measuring, analysing the structure and making many models and casts of details from the timber-work of Westminster Hall. He filled his museum with tracery of windows, whole sections of vaulting from Henry VII's Chapel, minutiae of ironwork, mourning figures on the royal tombs in the Abbey, reproductions of whole monuments, tombs, statues, busts, and countless architectural and sculptural details. He was a close friend of Thomas Gayfere, the Abbey mason, and was on sufficiently close terms with the Reverend John Ireland, Dean of Westminster Abbey, for the latter to make him a 'Nomination', which resulted in a reduction in fees for Cottingham when he sent his sons Nockalls Johnson and Edwin Cotton to King's College School in 1832.[1] Another friend was antiquary William Capon, who made many drawings of the destroyed parts of Westminster and its surroundings. Cottingham was instrumental in selling these works to the Society of Antiquaries on behalf of Capon's widow, after Capon's death in 1827.[2] Cottingham's mentor John Carter, too, spent much of his time at Westminster before his death in 1817, ensuring that the restoration work under Wyatt, begun in 1793 and completed by 1822, was conducted in a properly sympathetic and sensitive manner and adhered strictly to the approved specifications. No doubt at the same time he encouraged Cottingham in his 'mighty task' of making measured drawings and undertaking structural analysis. The quality of this restoration, conservative and restrained by eighteenth-century standards, and those of Wyatt in particular, made an impression on Cottingham, for in his volume on Henry VII's Chapel he wrote a detailed account of the background and progress of the restoration, and the extent to which the work was archaeologically correct.

Cottingham's first publication, *Plans of Westminster Hall* (1822), consisted of four folio-sized plates, the first inscribed:

'This Print, representing a Geometrical Elevation of the Principal Entrance to Westminster Hall from actual admeasurements. Built in the 19th year of the reign of King Richard II 1397, And restored in the reign of his Most Gracious Majesty King George IV 1822' (Fig.1)

Plate II has detailed plans, sections and elevations showing roof timbers with full measurements of the scantling of the principal rafters, details of restoration work to be undertaken, drawings of the original Norman doors with restored mouldings, the 'Modern' door and steps leading to the House of Commons, the panelling in the doors taken from specimens in the hall, the mutilated niches restored, pinnacles above the niches 'too imperfect to be restored', and details of statues removed and placed in storage. Plate III is a transverse section through Westminster Hall looking north (Fig.5), and Plate IV shows elevations of one of the five-sided canopies in the Tower with detailed drawings of the cap and weathering to the buttresses, mullions and architraves of the north gable window, plans and elevations of the battlements, staircase, turret at the north end, the entrance doors, niches, and arms of Richard II in the spandrels of the large arch of the entrance door (Fig.6). There is no text to accompany these plates but in the Preface to his next volume of measured drawings, Cottingham clearly states his intention to bring, for the first time, structural as opposed to purely stylistic analysis into mediaevalist research in order to extend antiquarianism as a direct influence upon architectural practice.

A2 (Figs 2, 7, 8 and 9)
L. N. Cottingham, *Plans, Elevations, Sections, Details and Views of the Magnificent Chapel of King Henry VII at Westminster Abbey Church, the History of its Foundation and an authentic account of its Restoration*, Priestley and Weale, Volume I, 1822, Volume II, 1829
The British Architectural Library, RIBA, London

The first volume illustrates the exterior of the Chapel and the second, the structure and details of the interior. In the Preface to Volume I Cottingham explained that his aim was to present a work 'different from previous where embellishment, fine engraving and picturesque effect was of first importance', a work that was to be primarily 'really serviceable to the architect and practical builder'. At the outset he underlined the essential difference between his work of structural analysis and that of such writers as Roy, Hogg and Murphy who produced volumes of topographical views of mediaeval antiquities in the 1790s. He dedicated his volumes to

'the Young Architects of Great Britain for whose use and improvement the work is principally intended … I have endeavoured to present you with a set of accurate

working drawings of the exterior of this august pile, and of the interior, in which I shall endeavour to show you the principles on which it is constructed so as to render this, not only a work of real practical utility, but an epitome of the beauties of Gothic architecture.'

He continued: 'In speaking with admiration as I do of Gothic architecture, I am fully aware that I subject myself to the censure of some of my profession whose prejudice in favour of the Grecian style prevents them seeing merit in any other.'

This statement emphasises the fact that few architects at this date, apart from A. C. Pugin and James Savage, were prepared to consider Gothic architecture worthy of such serious consideration; Cottingham no doubt had in mind Greek Revivalists such as William Wilkins or Charles Barry. A. W. N. Pugin, in his publication *Contrasts* (1836), made this same point, naming the classicists Burton, Basevi, Wilkins and Inwood in comparison to mediaeval architects.[3] Making no apology for his decision to promote a revival of the Gothic, Cottingham went on to describe the chapel as 'allowedly one of the finest ecclesiastical structures of its age and size in the Kingdom'. He made reference to his own efforts and those of his friends at preservation: 'The desire evinced at present for the preservation of this species of building, and the probability that many of you may be engaged to repair or erect in the same style, must render the production on the subject calculated to promote and extend the enquiries of the young architect, of the greatest benefit.'

Perhaps he saw the costly restoration of Henry VII's Chapel funded from the national purse, and the £1 million voted by Parliament in the Church Building Act of 1818, as hopeful signs for the future; but here was Cottingham in 1822, pressing for a Gothic Revival in church building and restoration, pre-empting A. W. N. Pugin and the Ecclesiologists by some fifteen to twenty years. Cottingham went on to advise the young architects to consider the exterior of Henry VII's Chapel which was 'a perfect grammar of the architectural art', a grammar containing every rule necessary for 'the erection of a fabric of the same species'. To help them he had prepared a separate and detailed account accompanied by plates 'in which truth and accuracy should be studied rather than the fineness of the engraving'. The first volume contains forty-five plates of Imperial size, all drawn on a scale sufficiently large to 'exhibit the minutest decorations of the parts they relate to'.

Plate III of Volume I, for example, shows an elevation of the north side of King Henry VII's Chapel in a scale drawing of great detail and clarity (see Fig.2) and Plate XXV has details of Gothic ornament with oak leaves, a grotesque mask and winged angel (Fig.7).

Fig.5 (see Cat.A1) *Westminster Hall*, Plate III, 1822
Lithograph $34\frac{1}{2} \times 21$ in (87.5×53.5 cm)

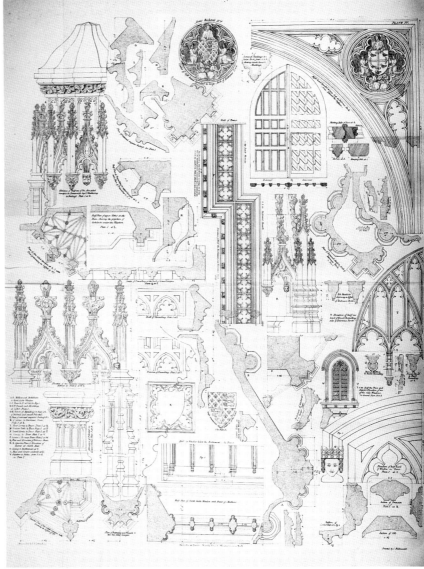

Fig.6 (see Cat.A1) *Westminster Hall*, Plate IV, 1822
Lithograph $34\frac{1}{2} \times 21$ in (87.5×53.5 cm)

Volume II, published in 1829, contains sixty-five plates devoted to the interior of the chapel, 'with all its multifarious decorations', showing geometrical diagrams and transverse and longitudinal sections for constructing the magnificent stone ceiling and different arches, and an elevation of the east end. The frontispiece is a perspective view of the interior of the chapel taken from the centre of the small eastern chapel at the end of the chancel looking west. Cottingham depicted Henry VII and his queen, Elizabeth, standing at the angles of their tomb in the royal costume of the period, and noted that the tomb itself 'presents a woful deviation from the architecture of the chapel and very poorly accords with the magnificent brass screen that surrounds it' (Fig.8). He was referring to Torrigiani's tomb of 1509, one of the first tombs in the Abbey to show the influence of the Renaissance; the new classical style contrasted 'wofully' with the mediaeval chapel and the screen of English Gothic designs by Thomas Ducheman.[4]

Plate IV illustrates a plan and elevation of the entrance gates inside the chapel, and Plate VIII a longitudinal section through the chapel showing the south side of the nave and entrance porch with part of the groining of Henry V's chantry (Fig.9). Three of the small chapels off the chancel are shown with niches and statues and the third with the screen work in front. These 110 plates, Cottingham noted, made an illustration 'more extensive, and its author thinks he may with truth aver, more complete than has ever yet been bestowed upon a single edifice in this or any other country'. Cottingham

Fig.7 (see Cat.A2) *King Henry VII's Chapel*, Plate XXV, 1822
Lithograph $33 \times 23\frac{3}{4}$ in (84×60.5 cm)

continued his Preface to Volume I with an account of the restoration of Henry VII's Chapel, instigated by a committee of eminent antiquaries, patrons and preservationists.

In Volume II Cottingham wrote a scholarly history of the development of Gothic architecture, based, as he said, on many years of studying 'the construction and gradual development of its character'. He wanted to point out to students of architecture that there are three distinct classes in which it ought to be studied,

'the confounding of which has brought so many of our modern imitators into contempt for it is just as barbarous to mix the first class of pointed architecture at the beginning of the 13th century with the 3rd class in the latter end of the 15th century as it was for architects of the 17th century to endeavour to unite the Roman and pointed arch in the same building'.

Cottingham described in detail the characteristics he had identified during his travels to study the ecclesiastical architecture of Europe; he particularly advocated the Early English style, 'simple in its conception, bold and solid in execution' as eminently suitable for 'churches and chapels on a modest scale'. He found it surprising that in a country abounding in specimens of this style 'scarcely

Fig.8 (see Cat.A2) *King Henry VII's Chapel*, Frontispiece, 1829
Lithograph $33 \times 23\frac{3}{4}$ in (84×60.5 cm)

70

Fig.9 (see Cat.A2) *King Henry VII's Chapel*, Plate VIII, 1829
Lithograph 33×23¾ in (84×60.5 cm)

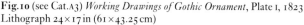

Fig. 10 (see Cat.A3) *Working Drawings of Gothic Ornament*, Plate I, 1823
Lithograph 24×17 in (61×43.25 cm)

Fig. 11 (see Cat.A3) *Working Drawings of Gothic Ornament*, Plate V, 1823
Lithograph 24×17 in (61×43.25 cm)

anything should have been done in restoration or imitation of it'. He continued his history with analysis of examples of the second class of style, dating from 1272 to 1377, and of the third class of Perpendicular Gothic, of 1377 to 1509; here he demonstrated his grasp of historical, structural and stylistic developments in the Mediaeval, and the extent of his knowledge of the mediaeval sites.

In these publications Cottingham's appreciation of all Gothic architecture through his work as a devoted antiquary is made clear: his understanding and study of its construction, and his strong promotion of a Gothic Revival through informed restoration of mediaeval buildings; and the taking of Gothic as a magnificent example and style for building anew. He continued his analysis in his publication of 1823 on Gothic ornament and also included designs for a Gothic mansion, bearing out his suggestion in the Preface to *Plans etc of Henry VII's Chapel* that a serious study of the principles of Gothic architecture could be 'applied to domestic architecture with the greatest advantage'. Once again the difference between Cottingham's archaeological study of the Mediaeval and all that had gone before is apparent.

A3 (Figs 10, 11 and 12)
L. N. Cottingham, *Working Drawings of Gothic Ornament, and Designs for a Gothic Mansion*, Priestley and Weale, London, 1823
The British Architectural Library, RIBA, London

Cottingham's volume of working drawings published in 1823 was enlarged and reissued in 1824, indicating that it was widely used as a handbook for many architects of the Gothic Revival. Cottingham paid tribute to his late friend Thomas Gayfere by using one of his working drawings of the chantry chapel of Edmund Audley at Salisbury Cathedral as the frontispiece to his volume. The drawing, with plans, sections and elevations, is of the west window of the elevation facing the chancel which is subdivided into an asymmetrical arrangement of a door and window, with tall narrow ogee-pointed crocketed niches, quatrefoil compartments, fruiting vine frieze above and cornice of cusped trefoils. Gayfere's elevation had been used in 1772 to form the façade of Horace Walpole's Chapel in the Woods at Strawberry Hill. Cottingham acknowledged the use of the drawing in his Preface, thanking Mr Gayfere, 'the present Abbey mason, for his liberality'.

Cottingham announced 'Working Drawings selected and composed from the best examples, consisting of capitals, bases, cornices, friezes, finials, pendants, crockets, corbels, spandrils, bosses, roses, battlements, doors, windows, various specimens of mouldings and a design for a Gothic Mansion'. He continued: 'Mr Cottingham, having been engaged several years in forming a collection of Gothic ornaments is desirous of offering a select portion of them to the public.'

The plates – with friezes of fruiting vines and cornices of cusped trefoils, brackets and pinnacles of Early English foliage, flowing tracery with a variety of ball-flower,

Tudor rose bosses, grotesque masks and elaborate mouldings of reverse ogee-form with intricately wrought foliage and angels' heads – show the very highest quality of draughtsmanship, fine examples of the new lithographic process (Figs. 10, 11). Forty plates show details drawn from Westminster Abbey, but Cottingham also included two more plates from Strawberry Hill, the cresting and frieze of fruiting vines and savage beasts from the Chapel in the Woods and the chimney piece in the north bedchamber which had been designed by Walpole and modelled on the tomb of Bishop Dudley of Durham at Westminster.[5] It is significant that Cottingham should have included Gayfere's drawings for Strawberry Hill for they forge a link with the eighteenth-century attempts at archaeologically correct Gothic and his own work. Walpole had seriously intended a faithful representation of the original in his Chapel in the Woods, and for that reason Cottingham included the designs in his book of Gothic Ornament. His plates were archaeologically correct working drawings clearly intended to educate and inform, and to be used by architects as a manual of Gothic design. Cottingham chose a 'select portion' of his collection as examples for architects to study, at the same time including in his volume an elevation and plan for a Gothic Mansion, a combination carrying the clear message that a Gothic Revival was not a matter of simple copyism (Fig. 12). A revival should stem from an archaeologically correct basis, but at the same time create an architecture that related to the needs of its own time,

ELEVATION OF THE PRINCIPAL FRONT.

Fig.12 (see Cat.A3) *Working Drawings of Gothic Ornament*, Plate XXXVI, 1823
Lithograph 24½ × 17 in (62.25 × 43.25 cm)

for as Cottingham stated in his Preface, no mediaeval house 'would be habitable for the nobleman of the present day'. In Gayfere's use of the mediaeval precedent accurately drawn from the original source but transposed to a new use, and in Cottingham's volumes of drawings promoting a Gothic Revival, we find the logical outcome of the efforts of such men as Carter and Britton to study the original mediaeval sources and transform the Gothic – 'the wild, false and fantastick' – for a new age, in the same way that Robert Adam used his study of the antique to re-create classicism in the eighteenth century.

In these first publications of 1822 and 1823, Cottingham is revealed as the first analyst of Gothic, and as a serious promoter of a Gothic Revival; a revival based on a combination of Romanticism, which expressed the beauty and spirit of Gothic as part of a national heritage that should be loved and preserved, and a sound archaeological knowledge and study of its development and construction, including an appreciation of all periods of Gothic. In later publications resulting from his antiquarian pursuits, Cottingham showed his understanding of the Romanesque, its history, development and construction, and chose the Romanesque style for the building of a new church in 1845. In 1822 he advised a study for those 'who may be called upon to restore or erect churches in the Gothic style' and suggested that the principles of Gothic architecture could be applied to domestic architecture without resort to a simple copying of its stylistic features.

Here is a statement of the utmost importance to the development of architecture in the nineteenth century. Cottingham suggested that there should be a break with the styles of the classical tradition, demonstrating a change in attitude towards the styles of the past with their incontrovertible rules, and one that looked forward to freedom from the trammels of style, whilst remaining firmly in the English mediaeval tradition. Cottingham, in a sense, was moving towards eclecticism in Gothic, and in so doing was foreshadowing the only uniting aspect of Victorian architecture. Equally, he was following the very English tradition of taking aspects of original sources, and using them to create an architecture for a new age. He was also expressing ideas that led to his examining the vernacular buildings of different regions such as Suffolk and Derbyshire, where he was to build houses that reflected mediaeval precedents. These ideas were taken up by A. W. N. Pugin, who wrote, 'It is not a style that we are trying to revive but a principle'; and by Butterfield, Webb, Morris and the later Arts and Crafts architects. Cottingham's writings at this date could be seen as the first manifesto of an archaeologically correct Gothic Revival, in which he set standards for restoration practice and for building anew that were to influence the course of nineteenth-century architectural theory and practice.

A4
L. N. Cottingham and J. Savage, *Reasons Against Pulling down the Lady Chapel at the East End of St Saviour's Church, usually denominated the Consistatorial Court*, Richard Taylor, Red Lion Court, 1832

In 1832, the introduction of a Bill into the House of Commons for the purpose of clearing the New Bridge approaches and the recommendations of the London Bridge Committee posed a serious threat to the Lady Chapel of St Saviour's, Southwark. The chapel, described by Cottingham as 'one of the most chaste and elegant specimens of thirteenth-century architecture', was part of St Saviour's, and was of major importance in the history of English mediaeval architecture. The choir and Lady Chapel were built by Peter de Rupibus, Bishop of Winchester, 1205-38; transepts and tower were altered in the fourteenth century, but the choir and Lady Chapel with their solid pillars, acute arches, lancet windows and simple groined roof were identified by Cottingham as unaltered buildings of the thirteenth century. The choir had been restored by George Gwilt in 1822-4, partly to Cottingham's designs, the choir vaults were remodelled using the old ribs strengthened with cast-iron trusses, and further repairs were undertaken to the choir in 1832. A report in *The Gentleman's Magazine* noted:

'The singular pinnacle at the north-east angle covering a staircase turret (which is now concealed by a casing of brick and crowned with a low tile roof) has been restored from a careful survey and measurement made by Mr Cottingham to whom indeed the credit of the restored design is justly due.'[6]

The nave of the church, however, was in a dilapidated state and narrowly escaped demolition in 1826. A letter in *The Gentleman's Magazine* from the Society of Antiquaries to the parochial authorities of St Saviour's regretted to learn that 'it was contemplated to demolish the nave of St Saviour's'. They praised Gwilt and Cottingham's restoration of the choir, continuing: 'We trust you will not harshly destroy the most important portion of this noble fabric which, if it can be preserved unmutilated and undefaced, will continue to be one of the most venerable and distinguished ornaments of the capital.'[7] The nave was not demolished at that time but in 1837 was still roofless, 'lying open to the Winds of Heaven, to sapping damp and frosts'.[8] By 1832 the Lady Chapel was under threat and the would-be destroyers wrote: 'There should be no national pride nonsense to deter them, the ratepayers should not be deluded by ancient fame or the magnificence of masonry, the removal would be a pecuniary advantage in making room for banking houses and commercial warehouses.'[9] Pleas were made to the vestry, passionate letters were printed in *The Gentleman's Magazine* in defence of mediaeval architecture and at a meeting on 28 January, Cottingham proposed a resolution seconded by James Savage to preserve from demolition and to restore the Lady Chapel. He refuted the claims of 'pecuniary advantages' through demolition by suggesting that if restored, the mediaeval church would enhance the neighbourhood by becoming an attraction to visitors, saying:

'St Saviour's is a splendid specimen of Gothic architecture and when restored will be a magnificent ornament to the southern approach to the new London Bridge and in conjunction with that object is well calculated to improve the neighbourhood and make the Borough the occasional resort of all persons of taste and curiosity and will consequently increase the trade and prosperity of the inhabitants.'[10]

This was a far-sighted comment, not only in recommending the preservation of mediaeval remains, but also the enhancement and prosperity of an area through its attraction as a resort. Cottingham went on to move that funds be raised for the restoration work, and the London Bridge Committee should be asked 'to allow more ample space for the view of the edifice by the public'.[11]

Cottingham and Savage then published a pamphlet at the request of 'some highly respectable gentlemen' entitled *Reasons Against Pulling down the Lady Chapel at the East End of St Saviour's Church, usually denominated 'the Consistatorial Court'*. They made their impassioned plea for its survival by listing seven reasons to support their case. They pointed out that it was one of the most important specimens of thirteenth-century architecture, it was a necessary appendage to the ancient collegiate church and could not be removed without destroying the architectural effect of the whole structure. They asserted that, far from being a later 'excrescence', it was in fact of the same date as the side aisles of the newly restored choir. A long and scholarly letter in *The Gentleman's Magazine* composed by Cottingham and Savage substantiated this view, and they gave a long and detailed explanation supported by their close analysis of the structure. They argued that if the chapel were removed a new design would be required for the parts then exposed 'to correspond with the able restoration already made of the choir ends above the roof of the Chapel, and for which new designs there is not nor can be any authority whatever'.

Despite the neglect of the building, in their opinion it was still stable and firm in all its bearings, its beautiful clustered pillars truly perpendicular, its pointed ribs not at all displaced from their centres, the walls and 'elegant windows' of the interior nearly perfect, while those of the exterior,

'although neglected have sufficient remains of their various parts to guide the architect to a perfect restoration of the whole, without the slightest innovation, a circumstance of the highest importance as it enables us to hand down to distant posterity, in all their original purity, these splendid works, illustrating the skill and imaginative genius of our forefathers, and which through neglect and want of taste, or more sordid motives, are daily suffered to crumble into dust'.

Here Cottingham and Savage were stressing the need for restoration work to be based upon and guided in every detail by the remains of the existing fabric, 'without the slightest innovation'. This was a plea for an archaeologically correct and conservative approach, one that Cottingham used in his own works of restoration. Further, and most importantly, Cottingham and Savage were treating the Gothic with the highest respect in using the arguments of the rationalists from Alberti and Brunellischi onward: in taking account of the relation of the part to part and part to whole, and of proportion, harmony and regularity, they were placing Gothic architecture on a par with others.

They concluded by condemning the 'unworthy motive in destroying the Chapel, for the building of houses would again encumber and obstruct the public view of this beautiful pile of building'. As the 'third Church of the Metropolis' it possessed sufficient merit to attract the attention of all foreigners of taste visiting the country, to whom 'it has ever been a subject of regret that our public buildings should, from an ill-judged parsimony, be exhibited to so little advantage'.

Their campaign was successful and public subscriptions were raised to fund the restoration. Cottingham himself produced a fine folio plate of the Lady Chapel which he published for the benefit of the restoration fund. This preservationist success helped to identify Cottingham as a leading authority on mediaeval architecture, a powerful advocate of its conservation. Through the reports of the work undertaken with Gwilt, in which cast-iron trusses were used to strengthen the original beams, it also established him as a pioneering restorer of technical skill who based his work on the archaeological study of the existing fabric.[12]

A5 (Figs 3, 13, 14 and 15)
L. N. Cottingham, *Some Account of an Ancient Tomb etc etc Discovered at Rochester Cathedral in 1825*, published by J. Taylor, 59 High Holborn, London, 1825
Illustrated by five plates by L. N. Cottingham
Kent Record Office

Cottingham's growing reputation as a leading mediaeval archaeologist, 'recommended to the Chapter as an Architect well skilled in Gothic Architecture' (Dean Robert Stevens's notebook, 1825) led to the commission he received to restore Rochester Cathedral. Cottingham carried out structural repairs to the ruinous building and also, in the course of the work, made important archaeological discoveries such as the thirteenth-century wall painting of the Wheel of Fortune (Fig.13).

The most important discovery at Rochester, however, on clearing away chalk and masonry from the blocked-up arches of the choir, was the tomb and effigy of Bishop Sheppie who was consecrated Bishop of Rochester in March 1352, appointed Chancellor of England in 1356 and died in 1360. An account of the discovery was written up in *Archaeologia* by A. J. Kempe (Vol.xxv, p.122), and Cottingham himself wrote an account of the discovery illustrated by his own engravings.

The frontispiece depicts the tomb surround as restored by Cottingham, using the fragments as a pattern; the first plate gives details of the effigy and fragments of the tomb, the figure of Moses, crocketed pinnacles and a frieze of rich scrolling and fruiting vines (Figs 14, 15). Cottingham dedicated this plate to his friend William Twopenny, barrister of the Inner Temple 'whose accurate sketches and observations on subjects of antiquity have afforded the Author much information'. The uncovering of the tomb aroused great interest and another etching depicts the handsome Mr Cottingham pointing out the beauties of the monument to the dean and worthies of Rochester while workmen carefully salvaged the shattered remains of the canopy from the surrounding

13

Fig.13 (see Cat.A5) Line drawing of thirteenth-century fresco at Rochester Cathedral, reproduced in *The Mirror*, 1825

Fig.14 (see Cat.A5) Fragments of the tomb of Bishop Sheppie, Rochester Cathedral, 1825
Engraving $7\frac{1}{2} \times 11$ in (19×24 cm)

debris. The caption and this image point to Cottingham's awareness of the significance of such a find and his excitement at the discovery: 'Representation of an ancient Tomb, with a magnificent Effigy and sundry rich sculptural remains of once splendid monument of John de Sheppie, Bishop of Rochester and Lord Treasurer of England. temp: Edward III. As discovered in Rochester Cathedral, January 15th, 1825' (see Fig.3).

Cottingham's concern for archaeological correctness in his works of restoration was fully developed in his work at Rochester, for now he used the fragments from the tomb as models for his reconstruction of Bishop Sheppie's canopy, and with the care of a committed antiquary he carefully preserved the original pieces in the crypt. The effigy itself was in a remarkable state of preservation. G.H. Palmer, in *Rochester, The Cathedral and See* (1897), wrote, 'Unfortunately Cottingham had it recoloured though the fact seems generally forgotten.' This was not the case. In fact, the dean wrote:

14

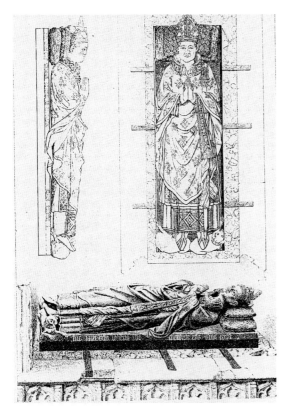

Fig.15 (see Cat.A5) Bishop Sheppie's tomb, Rochester Cathedral, 1825
Engraving $7\frac{1}{2} \times 11$ in (19×28cm)

'As the colouring of the Effigy (which was in most parts quite perfect, though at the most prominent parts entirely rubbed off by the rubble) was likely now it was exposed to the action of light and air, to fade and peel off, it was judged advisable by the Architect to prevent this if possible by means of a little varnish or by some process that might be recommended by a person well skilled in these matters.'[13]

Unfortunately, the dean continued, an artist was sent from London who either misunderstood or disobeyed orders and, in the absence of Cottingham and the dean, proceeded to recolour the effigy. Appalled at this, the dean sent for Cottingham who 'instantly came down and fortunately succeeded in almost entirely removing the mischief so that the colouring which was visible when the effigy was discovered appears to my eye nearly the same as it was before it was touched'.[14]

Far from recolouring the effigy in a vandalistic way, as Palmer suggested, Cottingham displayed a sensitive approach to the preservation of the mediaeval sculpture. This approach was in contrast to the work of previous decades when much art of the mediaeval period was obliterated by whitewash or destroyed in order to obtain a neo-classical uniformity, and was one that led to the revival of richly decorated interiors later in the century.

A6 (Figs 16, 17 and 18)
L. N. Cottingham, *The Ornamental Metal Worker's Director Containing a Series of Designs and Patterns of Ornamental Iron and Brass Work*, London 1823
Reissued in 1824 and 1840 under the title *The Smith and Founder's Director*
The British Architectural Library, RIBA, London

Cottingham, as a man of wide-ranging interests, concerned himself with many aspects of architecture and design, and in addition to his publications on Gothic architecture and ornament and antiquarian and preservationist issues, he published a volume of designs for cast-iron production in 1823.

In Europe iron casting as an industry was originally practised in the first half of the fifteenth century; accounts of foundry processes appeared in such works as *De Re Metallica* by Georgius Agricola of 1556, and in England it began at some time in the fifteenth century. By Henry VIII's reign the production of cast iron was fully understood and in 1532 London's Worshipful Company of Founders erected its first Hall.[15] Cottingham knew Penshurst Place in Kent, Haddon Hall and Compton Wynyates with their examples of sixteenth-century fireplaces with cast-iron firebacks and andirons, and in his museum he had examples of early cast metal such as iron locks, pieces of portcullis, sconces, escutcheons, cast-iron grates, iron casements, and even a fifteenth-century perforated door.

The use of ornamental cast ironwork in architecture dated from the early eighteenth century with such work as the railings of baluster form made to surround St Paul's Cathedral in 1710 by Richard Jones to Thomas Robinson's designs. Robinson had worked under Sir Christopher Wren and Jean Tijou, who had introduced the French mode of working iron in his publication of 1693, *A New Booke of Drawings*, and the French idea that ironwork could be used as a barrier but a transparent one.[16] The railings were cast in the Sussex Weald, an ancient ironmaking area before the Industrial Revolution, and the early designs for cast metal in general imitated the simple wrought-iron patterns. Other pattern books of the eighteenth century promoted the use of iron, such as the translation in 1723 of Sebastian Le Clerc's *A Treatise of Architecture with Remarks and Observations* in which he noted that 'balconies of iron will do much better than those of stone as being lighter and less subject to decay. If they be gilt they will be exceedingly magnificent and a proper ornament for a Palace.' This was a plea for the use of iron for practical reasons as a substitute material that could be disguised to give an impression of great richness. James Gibbs also used cast-iron railings for his church of St Martin's in the Fields, similar to the St Paul's railings, and gave designs in his 1728 *Book of Architecture*. Isaac Ware in his *A Complete Body of Architecture* (1756), a publication that Cottingham had in his library, made a promotional statement about cast iron:

'Cast iron is very serviceable to the builder and a vast expense is saved in many cases by using it. In rails and balustrades it makes a rich and massy appearance when it had cost very little and when wrought iron, much less substantial would cost a vast sum.'[17]

Now the implications of the economy of the casting process over hand-crafted wrought iron are stressed as well as the aesthetic qualities of its massive appearance for use as architectural ornament.

The use of iron became more widespread in the eighteenth century, encouraged by the London Building Act of 1774 which placed restrictions on wood ornament and, by the end of the century, cast iron had almost replaced wrought iron for architectural ornament such as the balconies that were a feature of the terrace houses of London. Robert and James Adam, in their *Works in Architecture* (1773 and 1779), gave examples of ironwork designs with classical ornament for balcony panels, railings, fanlights and lamp-holders incorporating urns, swags, round or oval paterae and an anthemion pattern.

The early nineteenth century brought a vast expansion in the use of cast iron, and there was a need for pattern books, a need that Cottingham saw as early as 1823 and fulfilled with his publication. Throughout the eighteenth and nineteenth centuries the London estates of such wealthy landowners as the Dukes of Bedford and Westminster were divided into streets and squares for building, and stucco became a fashionable surfacing material in the Regency period for entire public buildings such as Nash's terraces around Regent's Park and in the architecture of spa towns like Cheltenham and Brighton; the need for cheap ironwork for these vast new housing schemes promoted the production of cast ironwork. Repetitive architectural items of innumerable patterns could be produced at a fraction of the cost of wrought iron and answered the requirement of uniformity in the design of the terraces. The enormous increase in cast-iron production of architectural ornament and the demand for designs for the many interior and external fittings and furnishings led to Cottingham's publication of 1823, the first of its kind in England in the nineteenth century.

Cottingham's volume contained sixty plates, and a further twenty-two plates were added to the editions of 1824 and 1840. In the Preface to his 1823 volume,

Cottingham explained his purpose in producing this pattern book: 'The extensive application of metal in securing, decorating and furnishing every class of building, from the superb palace of the monarch to the social villa of the retired citizen, renders any apology for introducing a work of this description unnecessary.' He made it plain that he appreciated the uses of cast iron in the construction of buildings, for ornamental architectural purposes and for interior furnishings and fittings, applications to be employed in the widest possible range of buildings and for all classes of patron. He went on:

'The great improvement that has taken place in our Brass and Iron Foundries within these last twenty years has elevated this branch of English manufacture far above that of any country, and raised the articles which were formerly considered as merely gross and ponderous into the scale of ornamental embellishment in which utility and security are united with the lightness and elegance of classical designs.'

Iron foundries had developed in the eighteenth century under important ironmasters such as Abraham Darby who developed the iron industry in the Severn area and founded in 1708 the forerunner of the Coalbrookdale Company, which by the early nineteenth century was a very large and advanced foundry. Others like Isaac Wilkinson and the Walker brothers set up famous companies, and the Carron Works, begun in 1759 in Falkirk, Scotland, helped to build up the industry until its firm establishment in the nineteenth century with the growth of more companies such as the Phoenix Works in Sheffield. In mentioning the desirability of 'combining utility with the lightness and elegance of classical design', Cottingham was possibly referring to the fact that the Adam brothers were closely linked to the Carron Works, with John Adam as a partner in 1764; their contribution led to the production of high-quality design and delicacy and precision in manufacture. Also at the time of Cottingham's book in 1823, the classical style was universal. Designs for fittings and furnishings at this date would therefore show 'the elegance and lightness' of classical designs to be in keeping with the prevailing style, and Cottingham, as a man of his time, involved in every area of architectural development, set out to provide what was needed. His publication was intended, he said, to promote high-quality design, 'calculated to improve the taste of the Smiths and Ornamental Metalworkers' and to 'excite emulation in getting up their patterns'.

Cottingham wrote that he knew of patrons of discrimination and taste who sought high-quality design, and a 'correct' interpretation and usage of sources; he intended to help the tradesmen by providing means to achieve this end, for this was the only way to 'insure a

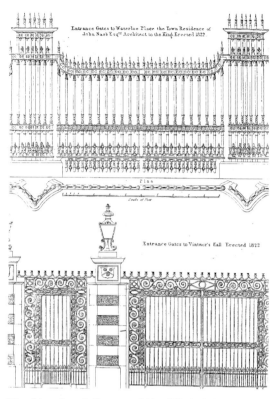

Fig.16 (see Cat.A6) *Ornamental Metal Worker's Director*, 1823
Lithograph 14×11 in (35.5×28 cm)

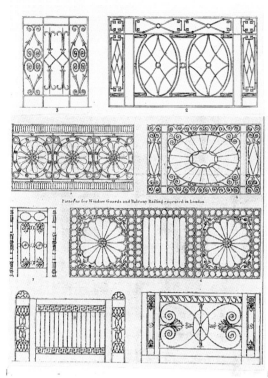

Fig.17 (see Cat.A6) *Ornamental Metal Worker's Director*, 1823
Lithograph 14×11 in (35.5×28 cm)

preference for British manufacture in every class, and prevent the inundation of foreign goods which have long obstructed the rising fame of our artists in the higher departments of their art'. He was no doubt referring to the supremacy of French design and industry at this date. Napoleon I had strongly promoted a revival of the decaying industries of France; and he instigated exhibitions of the finest products of French art manufacture, beginning in 1797 at St Cloud and continuing with the founding of a Temple of Industry and expositions in 1801, 1802 and 1806. After the revolutionary interlude, a major exposition was mounted in 1819 under Louis XVIII that lasted for thirty-five days and had 1700 exhibitors. Notably, too, in the early decades, French designers such as Jacob Desmalter were employed in the designing and furnishing of the interiors of Windsor Castle; they brought with them the influence of French classicism and the high standards of design and craftmanship promoted in France by Percier and Fontaine.[18] In his comments, Cottingham was reflecting the growing sense of nationalism in a desire to improve and promote British industry.

Many of the designs in the *Director* were taken from

the designs of the 'most eminent artists', and those by Cottingham himself were from accurate drawings and from casts in his possession. He used his museum collection as a source for his designs, looking at antiquity itself for inspiration, re-created for new needs. The 'eminent artists' were unnamed, but some of the designs were from named sources such as the entrance to 'Waterloo Place, the Town residence of John Nash Esq', erected in 1822, the entrance gates to the Vintner's Hall of 1822, and plans, elevations and details of Cumberland Gates, one of the entrances to Hyde Park (Fig.16). There were designs for 'Verandahs, Fences, Balcony, Area and Window Guards', those requirements determined by the prevailing form of building (Fig.17). Patterns for balustrades and newels for staircases and galleries were drawn, and fanlights, lamps and brackets for entrance doors. The nineteenth century had also brought an expansion of new uses for cast iron, and Cottingham included designs for lamp-posts for the newly developed coal gas and 'grand stands for gas lights', evidence that he was interested in all the technological developments. Heating systems were represented with designs for hot-air stoves for churches, chapels and public offices.

Fig.18 (see Cat.A6) *Ornamental Metal Worker's Director*, 1823
Lithograph 14×11 in (35.5×28 cm)

Cottingham, as an engineer architect, was to install entire heating systems in Magdalen College Chapel in 1830 and in Armagh Cathedral in 1834, and at Armagh would not entrust its insertion to the local 'Irish undertaker' but insisted on supervising every detail himself. 'Elegant stoves and fenders for drawing rooms', candelabra, candlesticks, chandeliers, vases and pedestals were drawn in profusion in meticulous detail. 'These designs,' Cottingham concluded, were to 'facilitate the operations of the professional artist and afford matter for the mechanic to study from, to whom it will be excellent practice to draw the smaller ornaments three or four times the size given in this work'.

Cottingham intended this publication (like his works on the Gothic, *Plans etc of Henry VII's Chapel* and the volume of *Gothic Ornament*) to be used as a means of improving design practice, to influence manufacture, and to educate and inform the artist and the 'mechanic'. He saw that through the advances in ferrous technology, the art of the carver of patterns and the craftsmanship of the technician, cast iron could be transformed by the founder's hands into complex patterns and forms creating architectural ornament of the highest quality and beauty, now widely available to all because of the economy of manufacture. The evidence of Cottingham's

influence through his *Smith and Founder's Director* is to be found throughout the world. Examples from his pattern book appear in Philadelphia and Boston in America; in Geelong, Cove West, Sydney and Tasmania in Australia; in Leningrad; and, of course, widely in towns throughout England and Ireland (Fig.18).[19]

Cottingham's concern in his *Smith and Founder's Director* was to elevate standards of design, encouraging taste to keep pace with an expanding industry, to suggest novel forms and designs for the new uses of iron in relation to technological developments, and through this to promote British manufacture in the face of competition from foreign goods. His designs were mostly classical, based on Greek, Roman and Etruscan precedents, and related to the prevailing style in architecture and design, showing influence from Europe and contemporary Regency England, although he also included some mediaeval designs for metalwork, stoves and altar fittings for Gothic churches. Among his sources for design he used the work of such designers as Robert Adam and John Nash and his own study collection: he may also have studied the publications of Thomas Hope and Percier and Fontaine, for there are similarities between the design motifs but not direct copies. *The Director* was largely concerned with ornamental architectural cast-iron work in response to the needs of the time. But Cottingham's training as an engineer, architect and surveyor and his understanding and familiarity with the properties of the metal led him to use it for structural purposes in his works of restoration.

Cottingham used cast iron in 1821 at Southwark Cathedral to reinforce the roof, renewing decayed beams by encasing the rotten ends in iron to avoid renewal of the ancient timbers; he invented a system of heating iron bars to bring leaning masonry back to upright, but he did not use cast iron as a substitute for the traditional building materials as Rickman did in his churches of the 1820s. In his church restoration work and building, he laid stress on the best quality of materials and craftsmanship, a characteristic of his work greatly admired by A. W. N. Pugin. Pugin was to take up the ideas of a Gothic Revival linked to nationalism, first propounded by Gough and Carter, and continued in the writings of Cottingham, but in his religious fervour and his passion for the Gothic above all else, he equated Gothic art and architecture with religion and morality. In his publications *Contrasts* (1836), *True Principles* (1841) and *An Apology for the Revival of Christian Architecture in England* (1843), he propounded his ideas of society, style and principles in architecture, of truthful materials undisguised in construction. 'Cast Iron', he said, 'is a deception, it is seldom or never left as iron.'[20] Pugin saw its value in the construction of new building types such

as railway sheds, but not in the revival of a Christian architecture. Cast iron could not be viewed as a mediaeval material; therefore its use was unjustifiable. Pugin may have accepted the fact that in mediaeval times iron cramps and tie bars, coated with lead, were used to bond pieces of stone, but he made no distinction between decorative and structural ironwork in architecture. Only carved wood or stone could convey the mass, the solidity and the sculptural and spiritual qualities created by the mediaeval craftsman. The slender proportions of cast-iron columns and Rickman's cast-iron work were viewed as thin, flat, unmeaning, repetitive imitations of the mediaeval materials; cast iron was also despised by the *Ecclesiologist* who closely paralleled Pugin's principles – influential views that led to bishops refusing to consecrate iron churches. The Ecclesiologists, however, allowed cast-iron, prefabricated churches to be sent to the colonies; practical necessity overcame their prejudice in the desire to promote church building, regardless of climatic considerations. John Ruskin, in his *Seven Lamps of Architecture* (1849), continued this disparagement of iron, arguing that only 'natural materials', stone, wood or clay, were permissible, and the moment 'iron in the least degree takes the place of stone or wood ... the building ceases to be true architecture'.[21]

The fact that iron was cast in a mould, could be quickly and economically made, enabling unlimited repetitive architectural components – the very features that prompted Rickman's and Cragg's use of it for church building in 1820 – was seen as a denial of the mediaeval qualities of joy in craftsmanship. Such joy would be stressed later by Ruskin and then by Morris, and underlay ideas basic to the emergence of the Arts and Crafts movement of the 1860s. Unlike wrought iron, which has to be hammered by hand – a process seen as craftsmanship – the casting technique of pouring molten metal into moulds is production and therefore a process of industry. Mechanical methods of production led, as Pugin said in 1841, 'to the present decay in taste', particularly in metalwork, and he castigated those 'inexhaustible mines of bad taste', Birmingham and Sheffield, the great industrial centres.[22]

These attitudes, stemming from Pugin, and culminating in great criticism, for example, of Paxton's iron and glass Crystal Palace of 1851, had little impact in France where the optimism and rationality of the eighteenth century regarding new materials and techniques continued into the nineteenth century; the architect Viollet-le-Duc, for instance, promoted an architecture that related to society, was secular, egalitarian, rationalist and progressive, and yet depended on a structural analysis of Gothic transformed through new techniques and materials.[23]

Cottingham's volume on cast ironwork was first published in 1823 before these English attitudes towards the use of iron developed. His intention was to make the best use of technological advances, an attitude inherited from eighteenth-century ideas of improvement through scientific discoveries and new industrial processes, and by this means to make a huge range of goods available to all, from the 'noble prince to the retired citizen'. Cottingham, in his approach to iron – a rational, practical approach close to that of the French – was not hidebound by the religious morality that developed in England with Pugin, Ruskin and others, and there is no evidence that his attitudes changed in later decades. Perhaps this approach indicated his independence of thought. Certainly Cottingham heralded the nineteenth-century concern to raise the standard of design and taste to match the manufacturing skills, in order to 'combine utility with elegance'. This was a concern of all design reformers from Pugin onwards, even though many shared moralistic ideas, including Cole, Redgrave, Owen Jones, Christopher Dresser and Ashbee and Lethaby later in the nineteenth century. Cottingham's ideas also foreshadowed the aims of a Select Committee of 1835 to enquire into the best means of extending 'a knowledge of the arts and principles of design among the manufacturing population of the country'.[24] His idea that British-manufactured goods should be improved through high quality of design, techniques and craftsmanship in order to prevent the 'inundation of desirable foreign goods' was also a notion well in advance of its time.

Cottingham's *Smith and Founder's Director* has been described by John Harris in his survey of English cast ironwork as the most comprehensive publication on ironwork that has appeared in England. It directly influenced the quality of ironwork in the first half of the nineteenth century, and it is noteworthy that this material came to be adopted universally.

B Church Restoration

Rochester Cathedral: Restoration from 1825

The Dean of Rochester, Canon Robert Stevens, wrote in his notebook in 1825 that it was agreed by the chapter at St Catherine's Audit that the interior of the choir of Rochester Cathedral should be restored and 'returned to its primitive state'. Cottingham, 'being recommended as an Architect well skilled in Gothic Architecture', was requested to make a report and estimate of costs. However, he found the state of the fabric of the Norman cathedral in such serious disrepair that it involved 'setting aside to a great extent of restoration in an ornamental sense'. The roof and supporting beams, oak roof plates of the choir and east transept, had dry rot and were in danger of collapse; part of the south wall between the main transept and the chapter was leaning out of perpendicular, with masses of birch shoring on the interior and exterior causing worse subsidence, and the central tower consisted largely of rubble and was incapable of supporting the spire which dated from 1790. Like many ecclesiastical buildings, Rochester had suffered from piecemeal repairs and 'the ignorance of modern improvers', and the *Chapter Acts Book* gives evidence of anxiety over the ruinous state of the building, the drastic repairs undertaken and the serious lack of funds. Robert Smirke, 'another architect of eminence', was called in as further justification for their proceedings, and in his survey of March 1825 he corroborated Cottingham's findings and endorsed his plans for restoring the crumbling fabric. Cottingham advised the replacment of brick repairs to the windows and restoration of the great west window, cornices, parapets, gutters and the external wall of St Edmund's Chapel, 'very carefully preserving all that remains of its original construction'.

He solved the problem of the south wall between the main transept and the chapter, which leaned 23 inches out of the perpendicular, by removing all the unsightly brick supports and building up the outer wall with a face of ashlar as an invisible buttress. This measure saved the demolition and rebuilding of the entire wall, and restored the leaning, ancient walls on the interior to their original condition (Fig.19). The decayed spire was taken down

and Cottingham began the repair of the tower. As Dean Stevens reported, 'the main timbers which perforated its walls were so entirely decayed that they would ere long have given way and if so, the Tower and Spire must have fallen down'. Cottingham renewed the belfry floors and began raising and encasing the tower. At this point the dean, due to 'apprehensions entertained by some that the Architect in raising the Tower was charging the piers with a weight they are unable to bear', decided to have the opinion of another architect. Jeffrey Wyattville was unable to attend and James Savage, 'who built the new Gothic Church at Chelsea', was sent for. Savage's long report was included in full in Dean Stevens's notebook and gave a detailed technical report on Cottingham's restoration of the tower. In his 'judicious repairs', Cottingham had removed the decayed beams of the belfry floor; iron-tied and strutted the walls of the tower 'in a very effectual manner'; lightened the weight over the centre of the arches by inserting a double window in the centre of each face of the tower; and removed the spire which, due to wind pressures, had 'shaken the masonry with the energy of great leverage'. The piers, Savage confirmed, were well able to support the proposed weight of the recased tower and pinnacles and he would not hesitate to 'raise the tower fifty feet higher on the same piers if required'. He endorsed Cottingham's work, praising the quality and thoroughness of the restoration without reservation.

Fig.19 (see Cat.B) Anon., South-East transept of Rochester Cathedral before restoration, 1825
Engraving, dimensions unknown

B1 (Fig.20)
L. N. Cottingham, 'West Front and Tower of Rochester Cathedral as it appeared previous to repairs in 1825'
Lithograph
National Monuments Record, © RCHME

B2 (Fig.21)
L. N. Cottingham, 'Restoration of the West Front of Rochester Cathedral with the ashlaring to the Tower when finished', 1825
Lithograph
National Monuments Record, © RCHME

During his structural repairs to the tower, Cottingham discovered, under the eighteenth-century recasing, fragments and rubble from the original tower of the Early English period. He used these as a basis for his design for rebuilding the tower above the belfry stage. He published a lithograph showing the rubble tower and spire of 1749, and his new tower, including drawings of the stone tracery and mouldings that he found, entitled 'Elevation of the Tower, as restored with sundry fragments found in the modern casing of the old one'. The style corresponded with the Early English date of the side aisles and transepts. Despite the expert knowledge of Cottingham and Savage, the dean was persuaded by local builders that the piers were being overloaded, and Cottingham was compelled to modify his designs, leaving the tower without a spire.

B3 (Fig.22)
L. N. Cottingham, 'Elevation of the Tower, as restored with sundry fragments found in the modern casing of the old one', 1825
Engraving $7\frac{1}{2} \times 11$ in (19×28 cm)
Published by J. Taylor, 59 High Holborn, London, 1825
Kent Record Office: DRC emf 135

This lithograph was part of the series published by Cottingham to illustrate his archaeological discoveries at Rochester, and shows the precedents that he used in his replacement tower designs. Cottingham carried out the main structural repairs within the year: he renewed the roof of the choir and transepts, the roofs of St Edmund's and St William's Chapels: repaired fractures in the north wall near the altar, the two west turrets and the crumbling parapets, 'laying new ones where there were none': renewed the great west window, 'which was reported in a very dangerous state and incapable of being repaired', and the battlements above it: and restored the great east window which was largely replaced 'with the exception of some parts of the tracery'. An engraving by John Coney of 1816 of the Norman west front before Cottingham's restoration shows the great Perpendicular Gothic window inserted in the twelfth-century façade. Although Cottingham had knowledge of Romanesque architecture

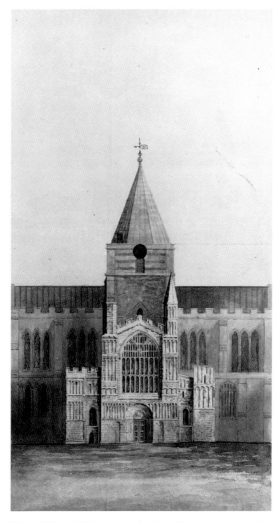

Fig.20 (Cat.B1) Rochester Cathedral before restoration, 1825
Lithograph, dimensions unknown

through his studies, he respected the work of later mediaeval periods, for here he retained the Perpendicular tracery in all its intricacy, merely repairing and renewing the crumbling stonework, and made no attempt to return the west front to its mid twelfth-century original state.

B4 (Fig.23)
Rochester Cathedral, west front, engraving by John Coney, 1816
Kent Record Office

B5 (Fig.24)
W.D., Rochester Cathedral, west front, 1826
Engraving $8\frac{1}{4} \times 11\frac{1}{4}$ in (21×28.5 cm)
Reproduced by permission of the Guildhall Museum, Rochester

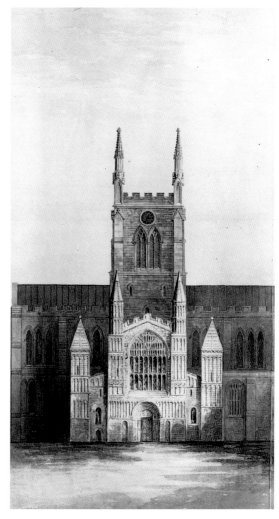

Fig.21 (Cat.B2) Proposed alterations to Rochester Cathedral, 1825
Lithograph, dimensions unknown

From the evidence of one of Cottingham's sketchbooks (1825) in the Avery Library, New York, showing Cottingham's studies for the restoration of the west window, a close analysis by Christopher Miele has demonstrated that Cottingham carefully numbered the stones of the spandrils dating from 1160, indicating his intention to put them back. The fact that he did not do so, Miele surmises, must have been because he realised that the pattern of the stones could not have been original, and the whole spandril area was a late Gothic pastiche. As a careful historicist, Cottingham preserved the stones in the crypt and returned the spandrils to a type appropriate to the date of the window.

In his repairs to the east end, Cottingham removed a large Corinthian altar-piece of Norwegian oak, and revealed the original composition of the east end of the choir, consisting of three Early English arched recesses and fifteenth-century windows that had been bricked up. Again he retained the windows and simply renewed the fourteenth-century tracery of the lower windows. In so respecting and repairing the alterations of later centuries, Cottingham's work was in direct contrast to G. G. Scott's restoration of Rochester in 1871. As J. G. Palmer wrote in 1897: 'Cottingham merely restored the ugly upper windows and left it for Sir G. G. Scott to erect in its stead the more appropriate tier of lancets ... '

Scott, in his report, deplored the state of the east end:

'The upper range of windows was taken out in the fifteenth century and a very uncouth window substituted, again renewed in our day ... I feel it ought to be restored to its original form ... I am inclined to think it should give way to the integrity of the Early English design. The stained glass which these windows contain could be fitted to some other windows.'

B6 (Fig.25)
East end of Rochester Cathedral, 1842
Engraving $6\frac{1}{4} \times 6\frac{1}{4}$ in (16×16 cm)
National Monuments Record, © RCHME

This interior view shows the east end after the unblocking and restoration of the windows discovered by Cottingham, and shows too Cottingham's carved oak pulpit, now situated in the nave, and the bishop's throne which was removed to St Alban's in 1877. The throne has since vanished. (See Catalogue C: Church Furnishings)

Cottingham worked throughout 1825 and 1826 on the restoration of the interior of the cathedral, as funds were raised. He removed a brick wall, characteristic of previous shoddy repairs, that had been built up to the ceiling over the doorway leading to St William's Chapel and which had obscured the range of arches; he reopened and partially restored the blocked-up windows to the left of the chapter room and the recesses to the right; and he reopened the arches of the crypt under the east window and two windows at the east end of the crypt for light and air, and had the build-up of earth dug away. A painting by Benjamin West, *The Angels Appearing to the Shepherd*, which partially obscured the altar-piece, was also removed and deposited 'pro tem in the Deanery as no determination is yet come to us as to what is to be done with it'. The dean added laconically: 'It is not an admired composition' – an interesting reflection of the changing taste from the eighteenth to nineteenth century.

At the same time, a heraldic shield of the king's arms over the west door which concealed the lower part of the west window and the upper part of the doorway arch was removed to the organ gallery. This was the beginning of Cottingham's practice of removing monuments which defaced or obscured the original mediaeval structure to a more suitable part of the church. He also took down a Grecian wooden cornice of the late eighteenth century that covered the mouldings of the wall over the side seats of the choir and the panelling below it to reveal a wall painting of 'a kind of Roman façade done in the time of Charles II'. *The Gentleman's Magazine* described the painting as consisting of 'birds and beasts, fleurs de lis, lilies, crescents, stars, foliage, fleury-crosses, and lacework borders arranged in the most beautiful order, and finely contrasted in the colours which consist of the brightest crimsons, purples, azures and greens'.[1] St John Hope, writing in 1900, stated that this discovery was obliterated by later restoration. In fact, despite Cottingham's obvious excitement at uncovering this 'display of architectural elegance', Dean Stevens would not tolerate it and wrote in his notebook: 'A most miserable and unsightly performance. This has been effaced'.[2] James Irvine, Clerk of Works to G. G. Scott, was later to comment on this aspect of working for cathedral authorities when he said:

Fig.22 (Cat.B3) The restored tower of Rochester, 1825
Engraving $7\frac{1}{2} \times 11$ in (19×28 cm)

Fig.23 (Cat.B4) John Coney, Rochester Cathedral, 1816
Engraving, dimensions unknown

Fig.24 (Cat.B5) W.D., Rochester Cathedral, 1826
Engraving $8\frac{1}{4} \times 11\frac{1}{4}$ in (21×28.5 cm)

Fig.25 (Cat.B6) East end of Rochester Cathedral, 1842
Engraving $6\frac{1}{4} \times 6\frac{1}{4}$ in (16×16 cm)

'They allowed excavation work to be done, but did not appreciate its significance and often ordered obliteration of painting and early work simply because they did not like them'.[3]

Further restoration work to the interior of Rochester involved the lowering of the altar and its pavement to its original position, uncovering the bases of the Purbeck marble pillars which Cottingham left in their unrestored condition: and the cleaning of whitewash from the Purbeck marble columns throughout the cathedral, revealing ornaments in the groups of vaulting shafts rising from finely carved brackets. The grouped corbels on the south side of the choir had been 'dreadfully mutilated' on the erection of a wooden episcopal throne, but were restored by Cottingham 'so completely as to defy the power of discriminating between the old work and that which has been renewed'.[4] Cottingham removed paint from the choir stalls, later to be discarded by G. G. Scott, and cleaned and restored the crypt, again revealing the bases of the original twelfth- and thirteenth-century columns. The chapter room doorway he found to be partially bricked up to allow a square-headed door to be inserted, 'a most barbarous arrangement', and he replaced it with a traceried oak door in keeping with the fourteenth-century surround. He restored the mutilated and headless figures in the niches of the archway, an aspect of his restoration at Rochester which has been criticised. Palmer wrote:

'Much fault has been found with him for turning the first, which is thought to have been a female figure, into a mitred Bishop holding a cross in his right hand, a model in his left to represent 'Church'. The blindfolded synagogue by her broken staff, tables of the Law reversed in her right hand typifies the overthrow of the Mosaic dispensation'.[5]

G. G. Scott later remodelled the figures when he restored the doorway, replacing 'the head of the bishop with a female head more suited to the body'. It is interesting to discover the lengths to which Cottingham went to research the origins of the mutilated figures and to find precedents for a restoration of the missing parts. William Twopenny had introduced Cottingham to the respected antiquary and Keeper of Manuscripts at the British Museum, Francis Douce, and Cottingham took sketches of the chapter house doorway to him together with 'two casts of the hands of the figure on the identity of which there is so much doubt'. Lengthy discussions and correspondence followed: only Cottingham's letters to Douce remain, leaving us to guess Douce's replies. Cottingham wrote to him in May 1826:

'I intend bringing with me a sketch for the restoration of the figures. The Dean is delighted beyond measure at the discovery you have made and begs to return you his best thanks for the trouble you have taken, but he agrees with me in regard to the male figure being a Bishop instead of a King and we hope to gain your sanction on this.'

Cottingham continued with his proposal:

'Our point is simply this, the female figure being symbolical of the obstinacy of the Jews at the coming of Christ, the male figure must be emblematical of his Church. I suppose the figure to be a Christian Bishop with a Church in one hand and a staff with the same ensigns as the York Bishop in the other. Would it not bear the following reading? As an emblem of Christianity the figure of a Bishop with a Church and pastoral staff surmounted by a cross under which Christ's banner of pure white linen is suspended in the other. The mitre you will observe in the York figure is inlaid with the bloody cross instead of the usual jewels. However, I will not attempt to stress my Hobby any further till I have the pleasure of seeing you for fear you should turn him into pasteboard'.

Douce had sent Cottingham a tracing from an old brass which had some bearing on the matter and clearly Douce agreed with Cottingham in favour of a bishop's head over that of a king. Cottingham wrote to him further:

'I think your judgement so correct when compared with Master Bradshaw's (a fellow antiquary and FSA) that I shall be able with the assistance of the Bishop to lay their Majesties' spirits should they attempt to rise up against

us ... to be serious, I have not yet been able to draw out the heads for your inspection.'[6]

At a later date, after Cottingham's restoration, other authorities argued that the figure of the Church should have been female, following the precedent of figures at Strasbourg and Amiens and not at York, as Cottingham and Douce had thought.[7] On the evidence of the continental precedents, Cottingham's reinstatement of the figures, clearly based, as we now know, on careful research and consultation, was branded as 'ignorant and uninformed'.[8]

Cottingham completed various works at Rochester over the next twenty years, including the substitution of a 'rich and elaborate' ceiling of the main crossing for his earlier plain one of 1825. Charles Spence, writing in 1840, described it as an 'elegant and appropriate' roof in keeping with the Early English clustered columns of the crossing.[9]

The expenditure up to the end of 1826 amounted to £9000, and the dean and chapter were so well pleased with their architect that in 1827 they awarded him an honorarium of £100 as a token of the ability and zeal he had shown in the much-praised restoration of their cathedral. Contemporary accounts of the work referred to the 'highly-talented architect of the Cathedral', noting the unusual quality of his restoration work, 'a more careful and attentive architect could not have been selected, as the result has amply proved in a more correct restoration of the architectural peculiarities of this very ancient Cathedral than is usually exhibited'.[10]

Cottingham's work at Rochester was overlaid by that of G. G. Scott in 1871-7, J. C. Pearson in 1888 and Hodgson Fowler in 1904. Cottingham's restoration of Rochester was a very early example of a restrained and sympathetic Gothic Revival restoration, one that, in contrast to others, showed an enlightened appreciation of all periods of the Mediaeval.

BIBLIOGRAPHY
Annales Archéologiques, 'Promenade en Angleterre', Vol.5, 1846, p.284
Chapter Acts Book Vol.2, pt.2: Kent R.O.
Cottingham, L. N., *Lithographs of Rochester Cathedral Restoration*, J. Taylor, 1825. Kent R.O. DRC emf 135
Cottingham, L. N., Letters to Francis Douce, Bodleian Library, *Douce Mss* D26
Fawcett, J., *The Future of the Past: Attitudes to Conservation, 1174-1974*, Thames and Hudson, 1976, p.103
The Gentleman's Magazine, January 1825
Hope, W. H. St John, *The Architectural History of St Andrew at Rochester*, 1900
Miele, C., Paper on Rochester read to the Society of Architectural Historians, Cincinnati, 1991
Palmer, G. H., *Rochester, the Cathedral and See*, 1897

Scott, G. G., *Report on Rochester Cathedral*, 20 April 1871, Kent R.O. DRC emf 65/4

Spence, C., *A Walk through Rochester Cathedral*, 1840

Stevens, R., *Repairs to Rochester Cathedral 1825-26*, 'Mr Cottingham, architect', Transcript of the notebook of Dean of Rochester, 1825. Kent R.O.

Magdalen College Chapel: Restoration 1829-33

In 1829 Cottingham was the successful candidate out of more than thirty competitors, including Anthony Salvin, for the restoration of Magdalen College Chapel, Oxford. He won the first premium of £105 and a young Oxford architect, 'Mr Plowman, junior', was awarded 25 guineas 'for a creditable design'. James Savage had been called in to advise on the designs and Edward Blore was consulted before the awards were made.[11] At Rochester Cottingham had shown his knowledge of the Romanesque and Early English architecture. Now at Magdalen he was to accomplish an archaeologically correct revival of fifteenth-century Gothic, reflecting the chapel's founding date of 1473.

The *Book of the Chapel*, which lists changes from the chapel's dedication on 2 October 1476 to the present day, described the classicising of the interior that had taken place from 1635 until James Wyatt's replacement of the open-framed timber roof with plaster rib vaulting in 1792. The chapel had suffered the vicissitudes of iconoclastic frenzy throughout the sixteenth and seventeenth centuries, and what was left untouched by these barbarous hands was dealt with by the hand of 'modern improvers'. In 1635 the floor of the choir had been laid with black-and-white marble; a new organ and screen with triangular pediments, a fanlight above the gateway and a great west window based on Michelangelo's *Last Judgement* were installed; the back row stalls with their lining and canopies alone remained. The remnants of the great Gothic reredos with its figures in niches, desecrated at the Reformation, were plastered over and covered by a huge Renaissance painting of the *Last Judgement* with wainscoting on the wall below, decorated with pilasters and swags.[12] As James Ingram, writing in 1837 in *Memorials of Oxford*, said

'A taste for foreign art was gradually introduced into England to the neglect and disparagement of our ancient architecture. Hence a large picture by Isaac Fuller (studied under Perrier in France) was thought a good expedient to cover the mutilated remains of the old tabernacle work.'[13]

B7 (Fig.26)

G. G. Cooper, interior of Magdalen College Chapel, the east end, 1811

Engraving 8¼×6¼ in (21×16 cm)

National Monuments Record, © RCHME

Reproduced by permission of the President and Fellows of Magdalen College Oxford

This view shows the classicising of the chapel before Cottingham's work. In 1740 the tapestry had been removed from the back of the altar and a Corinthian altar-screen was erected with elaborate reeded columns and decorated capitals, festooned with swags, cherubs and laurel wreaths; panelled stalls with classical entablatures and masks were also installed. James Wyatt, in 1790, inserted the plaster-vaulted ceiling to replace the decayed ancient timber roof and created niches with 'heavy obtruding canopies of plaster' in eighteenth-century 'Gothick' – work that drew the scorn of the Oxford antiquary John Buckler and his son John Chessel in their defence of mediaeval remains.[14] These alterations completed a transformation of the fifteenth-century chapel, creating an interior of the kind denounced as 'pagan' by Cottingham in his writings, and by A. W. N. Pugin in his *True Principles* (1841). The chapel underwent further repairs in 1794 and the many plans for

Fig.26 (Cat.B7) G.G. Cooper, East end of Magdalen College Chapel, 1811
Etching 8¼×6¼ in (21×16 cm)

its restoration were not carried out owing to lack of funds (Fig.27).

Dr Routh, the President of Magdalen and later the first President of the Society for Promoting the Study of Gothic Architecture, was clearly an early promoter of an archaeological Gothic Revival and had no doubt been influenced by the strenuous preservationist activities of John Buckler and his son. Buckler wrote that Dr Routh was a man 'of exalted talents, and refined taste whose knowledge of ecclesiastical architecture in particular is too profound to betray him into approbation of useless and expensive finery'.[15] Cottingham, too, found him sympathetic to the ideas of a Gothic Revival and presented him in 1830 with a copy of his *Plans etc of Henry VII's Chapel* for the college library, writing: 'should the few plain remarks I have made on the pointed style of architecture meet with your approbation I shall be highly gratified'.[16]

Later Cottingham involved the president in subscriptions to the restoration of the Lady Chapel at St Saviours's, Southwark and sent him a copy of his engraving 'A View of the Lady Chapel as Restored'.

B8 (Fig.28)

L. N. Cottingham, 'Proposal for the Restoration of Magdalen College Chapel: the east end', 1829

Watercolour 24×19 in (61×48 cm)

Magdalen College Archive

Photograph by Thomas, Oxford.

Reproduced by permission of the President and Fellows of Magdalen College Oxford

Cottingham's watercolour is so close to the built design that it is no doubt his finished proposal for the east end of the Gothic Revival interior. It shows his restoration of the reredos, stone-panelled walls, fifteenth-century carved pews, vaulted ceiling and, significantly, a floor laid with mediaeval armorial tiles to replace the black-and-white seventeenth-century marble flooring. At this early date of 1829 Gothic design encaustic floor tiles were not in production and were not available for such advanced restoration work as Cottingham's at Magdalen. After Cottingham's discovery of the mediaeval tiles in the Chapter House in Westminster in 1841, Minton and other firms such as Worcester began producing tiles based on mediaeval designs. The *Bill of Sundry Artificers' Works* drawn up by Atkinson and Browne of Goswell Street, London, the firm who worked for Cottingham at Rochester and who now carried out the Magdalen restoration to Cottingham's specifications, indicated the extent and the quality of the work. The instructions reflect Cottingham's concern to use only the finest seasoned oak, best Painswick and Portland stone, and to reuse and repair the old stone and timber wherever possible. The Bill of Works described how the floor of the choir was lowered to its original level, 'laying the Choir and High Altar with the ancient marble paving polished and laid in diamond form after the original manner providing and fixing solid marble steps of the same quality'.

The crumbling stonework of the altar-end, revealed after the removal of the Corinthian altar-piece and Fuller's *Last Judgement*, was restored where possible and replaced in Painswick stone, 'reinstating and firmly securing foundations, working mouldings, carving enrichments and fixing new altar-end in sound substantial manner'. Cottingham intended the triple row of niches which he based on the original fifteenth-century reredos to be filled with figures of saints. He had modelled these figures on 'the best authorities in countless Cathedrals', and Cottingham's reredos resembled the arrangement of niches at Henry VII's Chapel, of the same date as Magdalen, but the models remained in his museum due to Dr Ellerton's objections to High Church principles. The niches remained empty until 1865 when figures were supplied by Earp. A frieze of angels carrying heraldic shields was allowed, however, as was an Annunciation Visitation in the spandrels of the doorways in the eastern

end. A carved stone figure group in full relief, representing Christ meeting Mary Magdalen, 'executed in a most superior manner and under the immediate direction of Mr Chantrey', was placed above the reredos, and a 'splendid High Altar table' was supplied, carved to Cottingham's designs in a 'very select kind of Painswick stone and in the most superior stile of workmanship'. A lithograph by C.V. Richardson, made after completion of Cottingham's restoration, clearly shows the empty niches in the reredos, Chantrey's figure groups above the reredos, and the stone carved altar-table flanked by brass tripod candlesticks dating from 1858 (Figs 29, 30).

Cottingham removed Wyatt's cusped decoration from the vaulted ceiling, and his despised plaster canopies from the wall ribs and the stalls. Possibly the reinstatement of an open timber or stone-vaulted roof would have been too costly and Wyatt's ceiling was left. But Cottingham reworked the moulded ribs and corresponding bosses, lengthened timbers and rejoined the vaulting into the new masonry at the east end. For the carved oak choir stalls, Cottingham ordered 'the best Riga oak wainscot selected from a stock seasoned for four years', executed in a 'most superior stile of molded and enriched carved work'. Cottingham stated that they must

be executed 'from the originals', those remaining examples of mediaeval stalls spared in the reconstruction of 1635, with blind quatrefoil tracery and foliate carved finials; a clear example of his enlightened approach to restoration.

B9 (Fig.31; Colour Plate 2)
L. N. Cottingham, 'Magdalen College Chapel; proposal for west end, new organ case and screen', 1829
Watercolour 24×19 in (61×48 cm)
Magdalen College Archives
Photograph by Thomas, Oxford.
Reproduced by permission of the President and Fellows of Magdalen College Oxford

This watercolour is unsigned but may be attributed to Cottingham for it closely resembles the style of the signed watercolour of the east end, and it is close to the designs as built. The oak wall panelling behind the stalls, and the carved stone panelling of the chancel are ornamented with ogee-pointed blind tracery enriched with crocketed multicentred trefoils, designs of the late fifteenth century and similar to the work of Henry VII's Chapel. The doorways of the chancel have pointed arches

Fig.27 (see Cat.B7) Ackermann, Magdalen College Chapel, 1814
Print, dimensions unknown

Fig.28 (Cat.B8) 'Proposal for the Restoration of Magdalen College Chapel: the east end', 1829
Watercolour 24×19 in (61×48 cm)

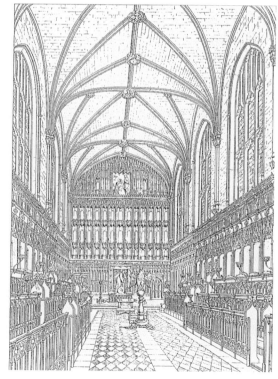

Fig.29 (see Cat.B8) C.V. Richardson, East end of Magdalen College Chapel, *c.*1850
Lithograph, dimensions unknown

under square moulds, the spandrels richly carved with foliage and tracery. The fan-vaulted canopies of the prebendary stalls rise in a wealth of intricate carving to tall crocketed pinnacles, and the stalls have blind traceried panels and finely carved *poupée* head finials in a variety of designs, with foliage, faces and winged figures. The finely carved doorways and stalls, the brass light fittings and the organ screen all show work of the highest quality and finest craftsmanship. Cottingham's concern for quality of materials was expressed in a letter to Dr Routh: 'I am happy to acquaint you that my researches for materials to refit your Chapel have been crowned with success.'[17] And in the estimates for costs of the furnishings, the contractor J. H. Browne, wrote:

'The new oak stalls and wainscotting to your Chapel with solid fixed seats molded in front to the patterns of the old seats with additional thicknesses to the tracery mouldings, ornaments, and panelling as described by Mr Cottingham will be at least £900 after deducting £150 included in the contract for repairing the old work.'[18]

Again, Cottingham was careful to reuse and repair, taking the originals as a model and allowing no skimping of materials.

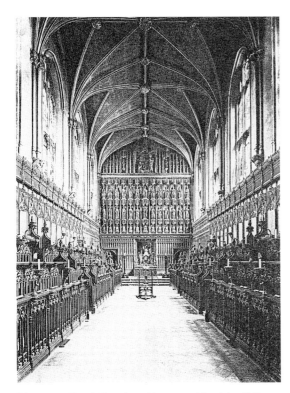

Fig.30 (see Cat.B8) Reredos with statues, Magdalen College Chapel, *c.*1865

Fig.31 (Cat.B9) 'Magdalen College Chapel; proposal for west end etc', 1829
Watercolour 24 × 19 in (61 × 48 cm)

B10 (Fig.32)
Magdalen College Chapel, carved stone screen by
Cottingham viewed from the Antechapel
Photograph by Thomas, Oxford
Reproduced by permission of the President and Fellows
of Magdalen College Oxford

Cottingham inserted a new carved organ screen and
entrance from the antechapel, using 'select Painswick
stone' with stairs leading to the organ loft in Portland
stone. In the screen he introduced a string course of
grotesque winged figures playing on musical instruments
modelled on fifteenth-century figures from the nave of
Worcester Cathedral, the whole finely carved with blind
quatrefoil tracery, crocketed ogee arches, relief-carved
ball-flower ornament and an intricately pierced cusped
frieze. The organ was an intrusion in mediaeval churches
that had known plainsong, and in many of his works of
restoration, for example at Armagh Cathedral in 1834,
Cottingham tried to resite the organ in a position where it
would detract as little as possible from the beauty of the
mediaeval architecture. At Magdalen, Cottingham's
solution for the organ, the incorporation of the chair
organ case into the new stonework, is still admired by
experts today, and has been described as a unique
example of a stone Rückpositiv, a remarkable piece of
engineering with cast-iron bracing, all cantilevered from a
cast-iron beam.[19] Cottingham's abilities as a structural
engineer and his knowledge of materials, in this instance
cast iron, enabled him to achieve a unity of design with
the organ case as an integral part of the stone screen. The
treatment of the great case was left to the organ builder,
for a college order of 1832 directed that 'Mr Blyth's
proposed alterations in the exterior Organ pipes be
adopted'. By 1834 the Swarbrick organ was enclosed in
Cottingham's finely carved intricate tabernacle work
stone chair case and a rearranged great case by Blyth.

In the antechapel Cottingham continued the careful
work, giving instructions throughout to retain as much of
the original woodwork as possible. The original oak stalls
with misericord were restored, 'cutting out all defective
plain and carved works, neatly reinstating the same with
new Riga wainscot'. The floor was lowered to its original
level and relaid with large slabs of Portland paving stones
inset with cast-iron gratings which were part of the new
heating system. The provision of suitable ironwork for
church heating systems and the heating arrangements
themselves were concerns that Cottingham had
addressed in his *Smith and Founder's Director* (1823). At
Magdalen he removed the heating stove that Buckler had
designed, and a new stone fireproof boiler house was
constructed at the south-west angle of the chapel with a
fireproof roof and a new door 'of ancient pattern'.
Cottingham had a concern for 'utility and convenience',

Fig.32 (Cat.B10) Stone screen designed by Cottingham,
Magdalen College Chapel, 1829

but at the same time utility could be made to harmonise with ancient precedent.

The ceiling cornices of the antechapel were removed, all crumbling plasterwork of the ceiling and walls renewed and the cornices and mouldings replaced. The decayed stonework of all windows and door surrounds was restored throughout the chapel and antechapel, and slender stone columns with enriched bases, capitals and corbel heads were reinstated between the windows of the choir. The doors, including the grand entrance and side doors, were cleaned of paint and varnish; rotten timbers were cut away and replaced to the original design; and all dilapidated stonework and timber of the small chantry chapel were also restored, 'making use of the old materials where possible'.

B11 (Fig.33)
L. N. Cottingham (?), 'Proposal for the tomb of Richard Patten', c.1829
Line and watercolour 64×46 in (162×115 cm)
Magdalen College Archive: B14/3.
Reproduced by permission of the President and Fellows of Magdalen College Oxford

A new recess was designed in the antechapel to receive the tomb of Richard Patten, father of the founder, on its return from Wainfleet in Lincolnshire, but this was eventually placed in the small chantry to the north of the sanctuary. A watercolour in the Old Library at Magdalen College, attributable to Cottingham, shows an alternative design for this niche set in the south wall by the altar, the tomb ornamented in the manner of Perpendicular Gothic with depressed arch opening, carved spandrels and cinquefoil-headed ogee arches in the blind tracery; it is

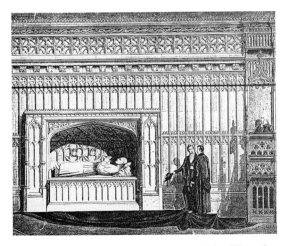

Fig.33 (Cat.B11) 'Proposal for the tomb of Richard Patten', c.1829
Line and watercolour 64×46 in (162×115 cm)

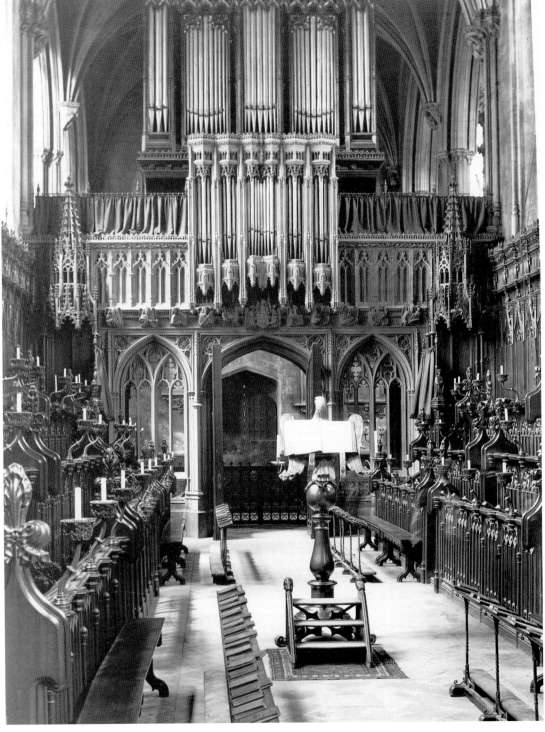

Fig.34 (Cat.B12) Magdalen College Chapel, Cottingham's stone screen and carved stone organ case, before the alterations of 1980

set against a wall identical to Cottingham's traceried panelling of the choir. Two figures in academic dress survey the tomb while a cleric looks on from the elaborately carved choir stalls.

B12 (Fig.34)

Magdalen College Chapel, photograph of the west end showing Cottingham's stone screen and carved stone organ case and the 1855 organ, before the alterations of 1980
Photograph by Thomas, Oxford
Reproduced by permission of the President and Fellows of Magdalen College Oxford

The Bill of Works noted the fixing of the candelabra in the choir, gilt-bronze fittings attached to the choir stalls, of single branching stems with quatrefoil decoration and cusped ornament to the rims of the cups: this photograph shows them in place before their removal in later alterations.

The Chapel Account Book lists a payment to 'Mr Pratt' in 1833 when the furnishings of the chapel were being completed. The reference is probably to Samuel Pratt of Lower Grosvenor Street. Pratt was a well-known antiquarian dealer, cabinet-maker and upholsterer who made furniture and fittings, both ecclesiastical and domestic, to Cottingham's designs over a number of years. A.W.N. Pugin, in following Cottingham in his demand for the highest quality work, also used Pratt and other top craftsmen to execute his designs.

B13 (Fig.35)

Gilt bronze candelabra from Magdalen College Chapel, designed by L.N. Cottingham 1829; possibly made by Samuel Pratt of Lower Grosvenor Street, London
V&A Museum
(See also Jervis, S., 'Furniture Designs for Snelston Hall', V&A Album, 1984.) Gilt-bronze candlesticks impressed Summers, listed as coppersmith and brazier at Herbert's Place, Waterloo Road, in 1835. Jervis also notes the similarity to candlesticks illustrated in L.N. Cottingham's *Sale Catalogue* and listed as 'fine branches of brass with pickets, time of Henry V'.

B14 (Fig.36; Colour Plate 3)

Magdalen College Chapel, view of the west end showing Cottingham's stone chair case of 1829 and Julian Bicknell's carved wood case of 1985
Magdalen College Archive
Photograph by Thomas, Oxford
Reproduced by permission of the President and Fellows of Magdalen College Oxford

The interior of Magdalen Chapel has changed little since Cottingham's restoration. The light fittings were replaced

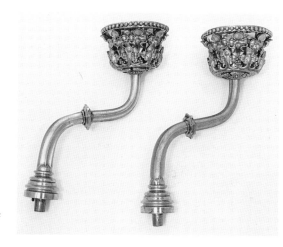

Fig.35 (Cat.B13) Gilt bronze candelabra, Magdalen College Chapel, 1829

Fig.36 (Cat.B14) West end of Magdalen College Chapel, 1985

with simple metal rods and plain glass light-holders. In 1855 a new organ by Gray and Davidson was installed with a case by J.C. Buckler which included 'the old work as far as practicable'. The installation of the organ proved a difficult task, for a bill itemises 'a second choir organ to suit the stone screen, as altered with new movements'; further modifications followed in 1866 and 1877-8. Gray

and Davidson's organ was recast in 1936, restored again in 1964, and finally removed in September 1985 to St Edmund's School, Oxford. All that remained was Cottingham's stone chair case. A new organ, built by Mander with a wooden case, designed by architect Julian Bicknell, to be in harmony with Cottingham's Gothic work, was installed in 1986.

Cottingham's work at Magdalen was greatly admired. James Ingram wrote in 1837 that 'though there may be as usual something to condemn there is much more apparently to admire, and whatever opinion may be entertained to the designs and fancies of the architect, it must be gratifying to behold, in aggregate, such accuracy and beauty of execution'.[20] It is hard to imagine what Ingram meant by 'fancies' but the accuracy reflected Cottingham's intention to bring a new standard of archaeological taste and knowledge to works of restoration. The detail and 'beauty of execution' shown at Magdalen is an embodiment of his *Working Drawings for Gothic Ornament* and a realisation of his instructions to architects in his *Plans etc of Henry VII's Chapel*, to study closely mediaeval precedents. Cottingham's surviving sketchbooks demonstrate his painstaking study of other mediaeval buildings in Oxford in preparation for his work at Magdalen, with architectural details drawn from St John's, Merton, University, Trinity, Magdalen and other colleges. Cottingham's work at Magdalen showed, too, a sensitive handling of the original fabric of the chapel, the use of good materials and a desire to restore by mending the decayed parts rather than by total renewal wherever possible, an instruction repeated throughout the *Bill of Works*. J.M. Crook has described the restoration of the Temple Church in 1840 – the removal of 'odious Wrenean overlayings of entablatures and fluted urns' – as an early landmark in the Gothic Revival, but Cottingham's complete transformation at Magdalen predates that work by eleven years. Clearly, too, his work predates the Ecclesiologists' principles and those of Pugin in his *True Principles* by some ten years. It is significant that Pugin was moved, in a letter of 1834 describing visits to Hereford and Lichfield Cathedrals where 'the villain Wyatt' had been at work, to invoke the language of praise when he came to write of Cottingham's work at Magdalen: 'At Oxford I was much delighted with the restoration of Magdalen College Chapel by Mr Cottingham which I can only say is one of the most beautiful specimens of modern design that I have ever seen and executed both in wood and stone in the best manner.'[21]

BIBLIOGRAPHY
Bill of Sundry and Artificers' Works etc., 1830, 31, 32, 33, agreeable to the Plans and Specs furnished by Mr Cottingham and Under his direction, Atkinson and Browne, Goswell St, London. Magdalen College Archives MS 735

Bloxham, Rev. J.R., *The Archaeological Changes at Magdalen College*, Magdalen College Archive, MS 732

Buckler, J.G., *Observations on the Original Architecture of St Mary Magdalen College*, (pub. anon.) 1823

Colvin, H., *Unbuilt Oxford*, 1983

Cottingham, L.N., *Letters to Dr Routh*, Magdalen College Archive; *Letters to Fishmongers' Court*, 1832; Guildhall Library

Cottingham, L.N., *Five Notebooks of Drawings, 1828-34*, Avery Library, Columbia, Ref AA2620C82

Crook, J.M., 'Restoration of Temple Church', *Architectural History*, Vol.VII, 1964

Ferrey, B., *Recollections of A.W.N. Pugin*, 1861

Harper, J., 'The Organ of Magdalen College, Oxford', *The Musical Times*, May 1986, pp.293-6

Ingram, J., *Memorials of Oxford*, 3 vols 1837

Magdalen College Archive, *New Building Account Book*, 1829, CP2, 152; *The Book of the Chapel*, MS 824

Myles, J., 'L.N. Cottingham at Magdalen', *Magdalen College Record*, 1991

St Alban's Abbey: Restoration 1832-3

Cottingham's reputation was further enhanced by his repairs to St Alban's Abbey Church, which attracted praise not only on account of his scholarly and able work but also of his integrity in completing the work at a cost of £5700, one-third of the original estimate. Cottingham appears as a man of unimpeachable honesty in all matters of finance, of estimating costs and keeping of accounts, who always gave of his best efforts in his aim of restoring the Mediaeval even to the extent of working without payment to achieve this end. *The Gentleman's Magazine* reported the dilapidated state of the Abbey and described how, on 3 February 1832, 'a large portion of the wall of the upper battlement on the south west side fell on the roof below with such weight that it drove in the leads and timber and everything in its way, into the south aisle of the building'.[22] The writer called for active exertions to create a fund for its repair before 'this matchless monument, admirable for the sublimity of its design would be numbered in the ruins daily crumbling to dust'. J.C. Buckler illustrated this event in a watercolour drawing entitled 'South Aisle of the Nave of St Alban's Abbey as it appeared in June 1832', a melancholy picture which underlined St Alban's long history of increasing dilapidation through lack of funds and general neglect and was also a reminder of the Abbey's long and eventful history (Fig.37; Courtesy Hertfordshire Record Office).

The Abbey had grown from a shrine on the site of St Alban's Martyrdom outside the Roman city of Verulanium and reflected every development of architectural style from the great Norman crossing and

Fig.37 J.C. Buckler, 'South Aisle of the Nave of St Alban's Abbey etc', 1832
Line and wash $9\frac{1}{2} \times 7\frac{1}{4}$ in (24×18.5 cm)

transept of Abbot Paul de Caen, begun in 1077, to the Early English nave of Abbot John of Cella, the Decorated work of the fourteenth century, and Perpendicular additions by Abbot John of Wheathamstead in the fifteenth century. Cottingham described St Alban's as 'the very Alphabet and Grammar of English Architecture, containing the grammar of an art which the genius of a Jones, a Wren, and a Kent failed to imitate, but whose praises a Chaucer, a Shakespeare, a Milton and a Scott delighted to sing'.[23] Here Cottingham was alluding to the fact that previous architects had no concern for the Mediaeval; even such great ones as Jones, Wren and Kent had failed to understand the qualities of Gothic architecture. Cottingham here echoed Horace Walpole who, while alluding to the 'unrestrained licentiousness of that which is called Gothic', and criticised the Gothic of Jones, Wren and Kent, could then ask: 'Is an art despicable in which a great master cannot shine?' Walpole seemed not to be inclined to dismiss Gothic out of hand. Cottingham, however, went further in saying that by contrast the poets and writers had appreciated the Mediaeval; perhaps he saw himself

doing for the Mediaeval in architecture what the poets had done for it in literature.

By 1720 the building was in a serious state of disrepair and money was collected to restore the ceilings; a legacy was used to repair the nave and block up the west end of the aisles with brick walls. Between 1721 and 1724, when Nicholas Hawksmoor was called in to advise, several thousand pounds were spent and in an engraving of the Abbey to raise subscriptions, Hawksmoor wrote: 'Support this Venerable pile from being Martyred by ye Neglect of a slothfull generation', a sentiment echoed two hundred years later by Cottingham in his engraving to raise funds.[24] Very little was spent after 1724. As an early eighteenth-century historian of Herefordshire remarked: 'This noble Fabric, hath, since it became a Parish Church, wanted its Abbot's Zeale and Purse too for repairs.' Lewis Wyatt was called in to survey the Abbey in 1818 and again in 1827 and found the fabric in such a ruinous state that his estimate for repairs and 'improvements' amounted to an impossible £30,000.[25] Nothing was done and it comes to us as no surprise that the nave roof finally collapsed in 1832.

Cottingham, 'the able and learned restorer of Rochester Cathedral and St Magdalen's Chapel Oxford', was immediately summoned to make a report.[26] Previous reports of 1818, 1827 and the opinions of an unnamed architect in 1832 had advised the total removal of the nave transepts and roofs of the side aisles, removal of the spire, total renewing of fifty-one windows, taking down and rebuilding the clerestory and other such drastic measures.[27] At a public meeting it was stated that this restoration could not be carried out for less than £15,000. *The British Magazine* commented on this in an article on 'Repairing and Restoring our ancient Buildings':

'An appeal was made to the public upon the report of a gentleman utterly unknown to them as having any knowledge of the ancient Architecture of this country ... a wiser course is to resort to the advice of three or four of those architects who are known to the world as having made ancient buildings their study.'[28]

The report and estimate of £15,000 were unacceptable and Cottingham was then called in to make a survey. G.G. Scott, in his *Personal and Professional Recollections*, wrote that the nave roof had been declared unsafe and would have met with a similar fate as the nave of St Saviour's Southwark, 'but another architect, Mr Cottingham, let us give him all praise for the act, offered to guarantee the safety of the roof and to give his services gratuitously to save it, which he effected by inserting cast-iron shoes to the decayed beam-ends'.[29] The writer in *The British Magazine*, however, disapproved of the committee accepting Cottingham's offer:

'It is for the mean consideration of saving their own pockets that these noblemen and gentlemen have condescended to accept Mr Cottingham's time and services, which by doing so they are putting themselves under an obligation to him, by taking from him, for their own benefit, so much of the means by which he supports himself and his family'.

Nevertheless, Cottingham reported that after a minute survey he found that the foundation walls and main arches were in a substantial enough state to last for centuries, with only trifling repair; but the roofs of the north and south transepts and the east end of the nave were insecure, the ends of many main timbers were rotten, and the great window of the south transept and several minor windows were in a ruinous state. He advocated the removal of the spire – the sixteenth-century 'Hertfordshire spike' – in order to relieve weight and wind pressure on the Norman crossing tower. Cottingham's friends John Gage and William Twopenny from the Society of Antiquaries had also visited the Abbey and examined the extent of the damage, corroborating Cottingham's findings.[30]

Cottingham's estimate for the work was £5700, of which £2000 had been subscribed, leaving £3700 to be collected. Cottingham prepared an engraving for subscribers to the appeal, dedicated to the Earl of Verulam, the Viscount Grimston.

B15 (Fig. 38)
L. N. Cottingham, proposed alterations to St Alban's Abbey, 1832
Engraving 14×24 in (35.5×61 cm)
Courtesy Hertfordshire Record Office D/EX50021

The print shows, in Cottingham's words, 'the lantern of the Great Norman Tower, now restored, the Choir of Edward III and the magnificent Altar screen of Henry VII, Wheathamsteads' Monument, and the splendid entrance of the Cloisters'.

Cottingham restored with archaeological accuracy the Romanesque tower, the fourteenth-century choir and the fifteenth-century altar-screen which was close in style to his newly restored reredos at Magdalen and at Southwark. He went on: 'The figures introduced are in the costume of the fifteenth century and may be supposed to represent one of the Royal Visits soon after the completion of the Altar.' He felt that his print gave but a faint idea of 'the rich and boundless variety in every gradation of style which composes this truly magnificent structure'. But he trusted that enough was shown to excite the feelings of all admirers of ancient architecture to contribute 'their mites towards its preservation'. He added that he had found no cause to suppose that the estimate would be exceeded, 'in which opinion we have

Fig. 38 (Cat.B15) Proposed alterations to St Alban's Abbey, 1832
Engraving 14×24 in (35.5×61 cm)

39

Fig.39 (see Cat.B15) West front of St Alban's Abbey, 1877

Fig.40 (see Cat.B15) West front of St Alban's Abbey after restoration, 1877

40

the concurring testimony of Mr Savage, an Architect also eminently conversant in the construction of Gothic buildings'.

Cottingham carried out his structural repairs as specified, beginning with the collapsed roof. He then turned his attention to the nave where his ingenious method of using cast-iron shoes to replace the decayed beam-ends saved a total removal and renewal of the roof. The large window of the south transept – blown in during the great storm of 1703 and replaced with wooden frames – and John of Wheathampstead's badly decayed west window of 1401 were also repaired. The progress of the work was again reported in *The British Magazine*:

'It may be stated as an interesting fact that Mr Cottingham in making repairs to the nave, opened twenty windows in that part of the building which had been rudely closed with common brickwork, probably since the days of Cromwell ... The flood of light thrown into the Church by this restoration has an effect indescribably beautiful'.[31]

Cottingham's concern was not simply to repair the structure through his engineering abilities and knowledge of Gothic construction, but to undo the bad restoration work of previous times and restore the beauty and effect of the original architecture.

The financial constraints allowed only the most crucial repairs, for although Cottingham unblocked twenty windows, early photographs taken before the restoration of 1870 showed the east and north-east windows of the Lady Chapel 'slated up whilst used as a grammar school', and the south-east aisle of Saint's Chapel bricked-up with an iron grating looking into the chapel.[32]

41

Fig.41 J. C. Buckler, North-West view of St Alban's Abbey, 1832
Line and wash $9\frac{1}{2} \times 8$ in (24 × 20.5 cm)

A comparison of St Alban's as Cottingham left it and its appearance after the restoration of G. G. Scott and Edmund Beckett, later Lord Grimthorpe, clearly demonstrates Cottingham's restrained approach (Figs.39, 40). The anonymous writer in *The British Magazine* who questioned the committee's choice of architect anticipated Ruskin and Morris when he wrote: 'No greater disaster can happen to an ancient building than that those who have its custody should, if they have ample funds, let loose a spirit of repair and restoration upon it.' The writer was fearful lest the dean and chapter should 'cause such a visitation of restoration to be inflicted upon it that it would stand transformed as a complete specimen of nineteenth century work'.[33]

At St Alban's, G. G. Scott was in charge of works from 1856 to 1877. The restoration began with necessary repairs to save the tower, reface the Lady Chapel and renew clerestory windows. But by 1876 the west front – with Abbot John's fine window repaired by Cottingham, its flat battlemented roofs, buttresses, and groined entrance porch, so sensitively drawn by J. C. Buckler in 1832 – was being dismantled (Fig.41).

Lord Grimthorpe, wealthy patron and amateur architect, continued the restoration after Scott's death, and his 'ample funds', amounting to nearly a quarter of a million pounds, ensured that St Alban's still stands today. But he left it utterly transformed by the depredations of unenlightened nineteenth-century restoration.

BIBLIOGRAPHY

The British Magazine, Vol.2 1932
Cottingham, L. N., *Preservation of St Alban's Abbey Church*, leaflet and print, Hertford R.O., D/228224
The Gentleman's Magazine, 1832, Report of 21 May, Society of Antiquaries
Perkins, T., *St Alban's Cathedral and See*, London, 1903
Pevsner, N., and Metcalf, P., *The Cathedrals of England; Southern England*, 1985
RCHM, *A Guide to St Alban's Cathedral*
St Alban's Abbey Archive, Hertford R.O., D/288; D/EX 50021; Collection of Photographs etc D/EX 50021; Reports by G.G. Scott etc
Walpole, H., *Anecdotes of the Arts in England*, 1762 and 1826, Vol.1

St Patrick's Cathedral, Armagh: Restoration 1834-41

Armagh Cathedral had suffered a tempestuous history from the time St Patrick established a church and school in 445 upon the hilltop called Ard-Macha. It was repeatedly sacked, burnt, pillaged, left roofless to ruin, and repeatedly rebuilt only to be destroyed again by war or 'the fire of God'. In 1261 it was in such a ruinous state that Archbishop O'Scannail rebuilt it completely. By 1268 he had added aisles, transepts, choir and crypt in a severe Early English lancet style similar to Kilkenny and Limerick Cathedrals. The shell of the present church dates from this time. Repairs were made in 1365 when the nave and aisles were rebuilt by Archbishop Sweetman, and following fires of 1405 and 1428 Archbishop Swayne undertook a complete restoration. In 1561 the cathedral was turned into a fortress by Lord Deputy Sussex in his wars against the O'Neills, protected by a stone wall 13ft high surmounted by looped battlements. But it was sacked by Shane O'Neill in 1566. It was restored again in 1631 by Archbishop Hampton, only to be burned by Sir Phelim O'Neill in 1642. Archbishop Bramhall began a restoration which was completed by his successor, Archbishop Margetson, in 1663. Margetson covered the nave with a high roof, enclosing the clerestory, and raised the steeple, adding battlements and a spire. Further extensive restoration work was carried out from 1765 by Archbishop Robinson, who employed architects Thomas Cooley and Francis Johnston to complete the tower and spire.[34] In 1802 Archbishop Stuart erected a gallery for choristers, slated the Chapter House and placed an altar at the west end of the nave, and in 1834 Archbishop Lord John George Beresford, Primate of All Ireland, began a complete restoration of the crumbling fabric, employing 'the most eminent ecclesiological architect of the day who had carried out the costly restoration of Magdalen Chapel', as Cottingham was described by the *Ecclesiologist*.[35] A picture of Cottingham's restoration at Armagh emerges from contemporary reporting in the *Ecclesiologist* and other journals, from his remaining thirty-four drawings, from his letters and those of Dean Jackson of Armagh and Lord Beresford himself, and from a report of a survey undertaken in 1886 by the architects R. H. Carpenter and B. Ingelow.

A major fund-raising initiative to restore the cathedral had begun in 1830. Archbishop Beresford contributed £8000 at the outset but by April 1834, Dean Jackson was writing about 'the instability of the tower' and hoping 'that the sum we may rely on will at any rate complete the choir – I should reluctantly abandon the most approved design of restoration'.[36] As the work progressed, with Cottingham making further estimates for major works such as the reroofing of the nave and restoration of the crumbling tower, more money was needed. By April 1836, £11,434 had been expended and £3500 more was required for 'stone carvers' wages in London'. Between 1837 and 1841 a further £8000 was raised, and by 1842 the total amount contributed to the restoration by Lord Beresford personally was £24,000, with a total overall cost in excess of £40,000.

Cottingham's archaeological survey of the cathedral showed the development of the building from the 1100s, identified the ruins of the old parish church and the site of the round tower destroyed in 1121, and listed his own discoveries such as the lancets in the transepts that had been hidden in earlier works. Carpenter and Ingelow wrote in 1886:

'By the inspection of the very valuable drawings made by Mr Cottingham, not only for the proposed works but also some of the plans of the church as he found it in 1834, one is clearly able to identify the several periods at which alterations were carried out from the 13th century to present time.'[37]

Cottingham's drawings showed that the walls were very dilapidated and bulging outward, requiring semi-circular arches on the south side as supports. The south arcade wall was 21 inches and the north arcade 7 inches out of perpendicular so that the roofs had to be fitted to the walls. The tower, too, was in need of major repair. Archbishop Robinson had decided in 1782 to build a tower of 100ft, like that of Magdalen College Oxford, but when it reached 60ft the tower piers showed signs of giving. The arches were reinforced and additional buttresses built, and the work would have gone on, 'but for the fears of some old ladies, out of respect for whom the Primate pulled down the whole tower'. Francis Johnston, in 1786, erected a copy of the original tower, introducing two windows instead of one in each face, and crowning it with a low spire.

Archaeological discoveries at Armagh

Cottingham made significant archaeological discoveries during his restoration work. *The Gentleman's Magazine* reported that he had discovered beneath the present edifice 'the original cryptic structure of the ancient cathedral'.[38] The crypt, restored by Cottingham and given a new door at the east end is 60ft by 24ft and supported by ten massive octagonal columns, which Cottingham attributed to Archbishop Robinson's restoration of 1765. The crypt was used in 1834 for burying remains disturbed during the works of rebuilding and 'specimens of art' – the scattered remains of monuments destroyed at earlier times – were deposited there for preservation. In 1888 these lay 'covered in dust'. A hundred years later, the remains of carved stone angels playing musical instruments, and pieces of foliated capitals, still lie covered in dust, but now the remnants of Cottingham's carved oak stalls are added to the relics. Cottingham also discovered a stone sculpture in a cavity near the foot of the choir rafters. According to E. Rogers in his *Memoir of Armagh Cathedral* (1888), the sculpture, attributed to the seventh century, depicted Saint Peter with his crozier in a compartment surmounted by shamrocks and Saint Peter with the keys in another surmounted by cocks. *The Gentleman's Magazine* of 1834 referred to a large slab of marble on which were engraved the effigies of Saint Peter and Saint Patrick, 'a very early work of art'. The archaeologists T. G. F. Paterson and O. Davies, writing in the *Ulster Journal of Archaeology* in 1940, suggested that two busts now in Belfast Museum might be the figures of Saints Peter and Patrick, but 'the fate of these statues is unknown'.

Remains of 'the ancient screen where the high altar stood', parts of 'highly ornamented windows' which Cottingham used as a model, shafts and octagonal columns, and fragments of heraldic shields were discovered in making the excavations to secure the foundations of the cathedral. There is no direct attribution in the *Sale Catalogue* of Cottingham's museum of the remains of the font, reputedly kept by him, nor of figures of Saint Peter and Saint Patrick. But listed as lots 190 and 214 were 'two busts of male figures' and 'a winged monkey playing a musical instrument from the choir screen at Armagh', while lot 216 described 'two Norman and one Early English stone capitals from Armagh Cathedral'. Many fragments, statues, capitals and other pieces of ancient stone have appeared in gardens throughout Armagh, suggesting that they were carried away at various times during the cathedral's many restorations or stages of extreme dilapidation. This was a widespread activity. Paterson and Davies suggested that Cottingham, presumably as one of the 'nineteenth-century vandals', succeeded in 'scattering much of the older work'. But Cottingham took pains to preserve examples of mediaeval work, or to reuse the old remains wherever possible. For example, in a letter to Archbishop Beresford, Dean Jackson wrote:

'A door case for the north transept has been also put together out of the mass of stonework lying in the north transept. The putting up of this Cottingham says will cost nothing but a few days labour ... He proposed to insert it without leave unless I positively forbade it. I did forbid it on the feeling, however, that as it lies there prepared we have no alternative but to make use of it.'[39]

Armagh Cathedral: Structural restoration

The first major task was the tower, in danger of collapse, with the walls above the pillars leaning 2ft out of perpendicular, and Cottingham brought his skills as an innovative engineer to this problem. The *Architectural Magazine* described how the vast superstructure, weighing 4000 tons, was supported during the relaying of the foundations of the piers without a single stone being removed from the upper part of the immense tower 'by means of some very ingenious mechanism invented by

Mr Cottingham'.[40] The model of the contrivance was apparently to be seen in the office of the Clerk of Works, Mr Smith. Great interest was aroused at Cottingham's 'bold mechanical skill' and reports of his 'singular operations' in shoring up the tower and straightening the nave walls were published in several journals with promises of 'figures of the modes of proceeding'. Carpenter and Ingelow wrote in 1886: 'It is to be wished that we could have the lost drawings and model of his clever shoring, showing the means by which he took out and rebuilt the piers and arches under it'.[41] The piers and restored tower were solidly built, and Cottingham reduced the weight upon them by removing the spire which was not replaced although drawings were made for its reinstatement. He did not alter the Early English design of the tower, retaining two windows of two lights in each face and a battlemented parapet, though he made alternative designs which were not used.

B16 (Fig.42)
L. N. Cottingham, west elevation of Armagh: proposal for tower with upper stage, 1834
Line drawing $15\frac{1}{2} \times 17\frac{1}{2}$ in (39×44 cm)
Armagh Cathedral Library
Courtesy the Dean and Chapter of St Patrick's Cathedral, Armagh

This drawing shows Cottingham's alternative design for the tower, with an upper stage, battlements and pinnacles, evidently inspired by St Mary's, Southwark. The reviewer in the *Ecclesiologist* noted that Cottingham's instructions to make the restoration archaeologically correct were most precise, but continued: 'It is a subject of great regret and criticism that Cottingham did not preserve the west doorway with its richly moulded and cusped arch, canopied niches on either side and pinnacles which filled the space up to the lancet windows.'[42]

Cottingham's first set of designs, described by Carpenter as 'conservative', showed precisely his intention to preserve such features as the west doorway and the original buttresses. This vindicating evidence supports the description of Cottingham as antiquary and preservationist. Carpenter, who had the benefit of studying all Cottingham's original one hundred drawings and plans, wrote: 'Indeed there are two designs of his which show the retention and restoration of this doorway and its side niches, but he was overruled for the present doorway and plain ashlar stonework took the place of the old rich work.' Cottingham had hoped to retain other features of the earlier fabric but again was overruled: 'For some such reason also the fine and bold buttresses at the west end were removed in order to make way for the present buttressed pinnacles though Cottingham retained them in his first design' (Fig.43). However, the aisle

buttresses, gables and finials were all modelled to the ancient designs, and again, in the chancel, with its fourteenth-century window openings, Cottingham adopted this period, 'designing admirable windows and buttresses in this style, following fine ancient precedents in his details'.

In the transepts Cottingham respected the evidence of different periods. He retained the two Early English lancets in the west and east sides of the north transept discovered on the removal of plaster, and the single broader lancet in the east side of the south transept. The end windows were of Decorated Gothic of three lights, with the mullions of the south window intersecting. The roofs of the nave, transepts and aisles were all restored, described in Carpenter's report of 1886 as 'the strong and efficient system of Cottingham's with triangular bracing by iron bars one and a half inches square, bolted to each other to butt ends of the tie beams'.

Cottingham continued the structural repairs by pulling the arcade walls upright without resorting to rebuilding by means of the contraction of iron bars, bolted and heated in successive operations, a technique he used later at Market Weston and the Norman Tower of Bury St Edmunds in Suffolk. The small, deeply recessed clerestory had been bricked up: Cottingham renewed the pointed two light windows with flowing tracery.

B17
L. N. Cottingham, drawing for the north transept with details of buttresses and pinnacles based on the remains of the existing ones, *c*.1839
$10\frac{1}{2} \times 18\frac{1}{4}$ in (27×46 cm)
Armagh Cathedral Library

B18 (Fig.44)
L. N. Cottingham, proposal for aisle windows, east end of Armagh Cathedral, 1834
Line drawing $10\frac{1}{2} \times 18\frac{1}{4}$ in (27×46 cm)
Inscribed no.4
Armagh Cathedral Library

The aisle windows, whose fifteenth-century tracery had been removed in 1765, were being renewed to a design by Cottingham when he discovered fragments of the windows broken up and buried. The new windows were abandoned. He redesigned them following the pattern of the original windows. Cottingham's drawing of the east end shows his intention to retain the fourteenth-century window opening.[43]

When Cottingham examined the pillars of the arches between the south aisles and the nave, he noticed corbels with 'different emblematic figures in stone'. The pillars were leaning out of perpendicular and 'underneath the clumsy covering ignorantly adopted to give them

Fig.42 (Cat.B16) West elevation of Armagh Cathedral, 1834
Line drawing $15\frac{1}{2} \times 17\frac{1}{2}$ in (39×44 cm)

Fig.43 (see B16) Details of west end of Armagh Cathedral, 1834
Line drawing $15\frac{1}{2} \times 17\frac{1}{2}$ in (39.5×44.5 cm)

support', he discovered clustered columns which he used as a model in his renewed columns and preserved two of the originals which supported the arches at the west entrance.

Armagh Cathedral: Interior restoration and furnishings

B19 (Fig.45)

L. N. Cottingham, 'View of the proposed restoration of the interior of the choir of Armagh Cathedral', published by Hulmandel, 1834

Etching $14\frac{1}{2} \times 23\frac{1}{2}$ in (37×59.75 cm)
Armagh Cathedral Library
Courtesy the Dean and Chapter of St Patrick's Cathedral, Armagh

Cottingham dedicated his view of the interior of the cathedral 'now in progress of restoration' to its patron, The Most Reverend John George, Lord Archbishop of Armagh, Primate of All Ireland and Metropolitan. The etching shows Cottingham's ideal of a restored interior including the carved pews, stone-panelled walls and carved stone screen, restored cluster columns, embossed

crossing ceiling and renewed flowing tracery, all of which were carried out to his designs by 1841.

Two designs were prepared for the choir, one for lengthening it by 30 ft. Cottingham made a model of the cathedral restored 'according to the present plan accompanied with a shifting piece to show the effect of the proposed addition'. Financial constraints prevailed and the east wall was rebuilt following the old design in line with the parish church. However, one of the five bays of the nave was used to lengthen the ritual choir, separated from the nave by Cottingham's finely carved stone screen.

Fig.44 (see Cat.B18) Proposal for east end of Armagh
Cathedral, 1834
Line drawing $10\frac{1}{2} \times 18\frac{1}{4}$ in (27×46cm)

Fig.45 (Cat.B19) 'View of the proposed restoration of the
interior of the choir of Armagh Cathedral', 1834
Etching $14\frac{1}{2} \times 23\frac{1}{2}$ in (37×59.75cm)

B20 (Fig.46)
L. N. Cottingham, 'A perspective view of the nave of
Armagh Cathedral (looking west) showing the Proposed
new Screens for enclosing Two Arches of the Nave', also
'A Design for a Coved Ceiling and new Western
Window', 1836
Line drawing $20\frac{1}{2} \times 28\frac{1}{4}$ in (52×71.5cm)
Inscribed no.3
Armagh Cathedral Library
Courtesy the Dean and Chapter of St Patrick's
Cathedral, Armagh

B21
L. N. Cottingham, 'Plan, Elevation and Details of the
Entrance Doors to the Screen', 1834
Line drawing $13\frac{1}{2} \times 18\frac{3}{4}$ in (34×47.5cm)
Armagh Cathedral Library

These drawings show Cottingham's designs of simple
trefoil tracery with a traceried door within a cusped arch
for the screen enclosing the west doorway. The stone
chancel screen was more elaborate with deeply panelled
canopied niches, coats of arms of the contributors in the
spandrels of the doors, and a frieze of fruiting vines
surmounted by a pierced cusped cornice.

B22 (Fig.47)
Photograph of Cottingham's chancel screen, now
removed to the side chapel, reredos and altar,
Armagh Cathedral c.1834-41
Photographs by Campbell Photography, Armagh
Courtesy the Dean and Chapter of St Patrick's
Cathedral, Armagh

The altar is richly panelled, buttressed and emblazoned
with the monogram. Behind it there is a reredos of
elaborate canopied niches, and above, a band of blind
quatrefoils and a frieze of joyful angels similar to those
on Cottingham's reredos at Magdalen.

B23

L. N. Cottingham, 'Second Design for the Throne', 1836
Line drawing $13\frac{1}{2} \times 18\frac{3}{4}$ in (34×47.5 cm)
Armagh Cathedral Library

Cottingham made three designs for the carved oak
bishop's throne. Existing drawings show details of the
spandrels and arch mouldings at the back of the throne,
an elevation of the second design illustrated here, plans
of the canopy, details of mouldings, elevations and plans
of the throne steps and ceiling.

B24

L. N. Cottingham, 'Armorial bearings on Panel at back of
throne' (half the full size), Armagh Cathedral, 1837?
Line drawing $20 \times 27\frac{3}{4}$ in (51×70.5 cm)
Armagh Cathedral Library

Two of the drawings inscribed 'Armorial Bearings' depict
the arms of Archbishop Beresford. The shield is held by
four winged angels with crowns and flowing locks. The
angels, well-rounded and of sweet expression, present a
most un-Gothic appearance and are unmistakably a
product of the nineteenth century. The throne depicted
in Cottingham's lithograph has a canopy with cinquefoil
pointed sides and elaborate crocketed finials. But the
throne actually made relates closely to the second design,
which has a square canopy pierced with trefoils and a
cusped and crocketed cornice. The pulpit was of carved
stone of polygonal form with blind tracery and a canopy,
the throne and pulpit facing each other against the north-
east and south-east angles of the crossing.

Fig.47 (Cat.B22) Cottingham's carved chancel screen,
Armagh Cathedral, c.1834-41

Fig.46 (Cat.B20) 'A perspective view of the nave of Armagh
Cathedral etc', 1836
Line drawing $20\frac{1}{2} \times 28\frac{1}{4}$ in (52×71.5 cm)

B25 (Fig.48)
Photograph of the choir of Armagh (looking west) previous to the removal of the screen in 1888
Armagh Cathedral Library, 798. W. L.
Courtesy the Dean and Chapter of St Patrick's Cathedral, Armagh

A photograph of the choir looking west, taken before alterations of 1888, shows Cottingham's interior intact with the screen, pulpit, throne and his carved oak stalls with pierced quatrefoils and foliate carved finials. Cottingham wrote in 1835 that he was engaged in making a complete model of the fittings of the choir and needed to know the exact number of stalls required and the Latin inscription to be put on the back panel of each. Other decorations, shown clearly in Cottingham's print and the photograph of 1888, were carved stone angels at the angles of the crossing, bearing shields. Cottingham wrote in November 1834: 'Having completed the eight angel corbels and shields for the great aisle of the Tower I am now having armorial bearings painted and gilded on the same.' He proposed the arms of the City of Armagh, those of the Dean and the Lord Primate, and those of leading subscribers and local nobility: Lord Caledon, Lord Charlemond and Sir Thomas Molineux. The font, standing 'properly in the most western bay to the south and side under the arch', according to the *Ecclesiologist*, was modelled on the remains of an octagonal fourteenth-century font discovered in 1805 in the grave of a Mr Lee at the north-west corner of the west entrance. E. Rogers, writing in 1888, noted that it was previously supposed to be part of a sepulchral pillar 'but Mr Cottingham, with that knowledge of ecclesiastical archaeology which he was well known to possess at one glance knew the object for what it was intended, sent it to London and from it designed the present baptismal font. The original stone was retained in Mr Cottingham's Museum'.[44] Other fragments of the font are preserved in Armagh Museum.

Relations with the cathedral authorities during the progress of the restoration of Armagh

In any undertaking of such magnitude as the restoration of Armagh, difficulties between the patrons, the architect, the dean and the church authorities were not unlikely to arise. The correspondence between Cottingham, Dean Jackson, Archbishop Beresford and his two agents Mr Paton and Mr Jones, give ample evidence of disputes over finance, the rendering of accounts before further expenditure, and matters of aesthetic, liturgical and historical precedents. On certain areas of the work, such as the glazing of the windows, interior fittings, the siting and rebuilding of the organ, Cottingham stood resolutely firm. He absolutely insisted

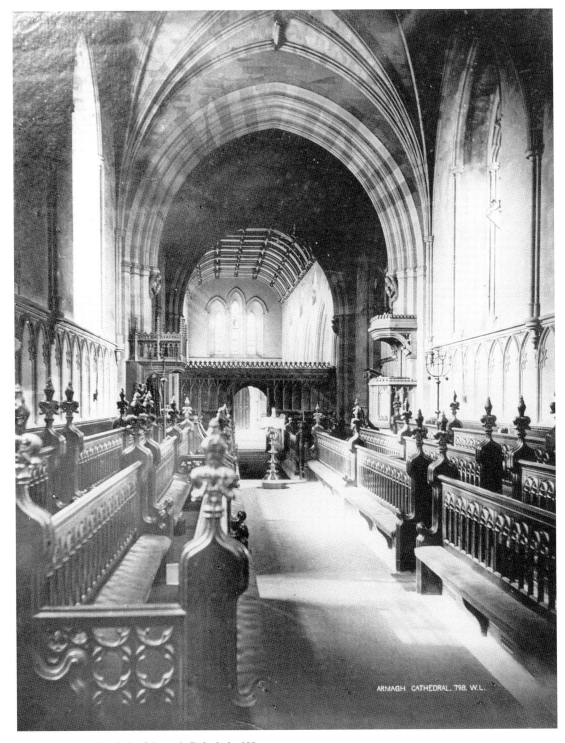

ARMAGH CATHEDRAL. 798. W.L.

Fig.48 (Cat.b25) The choir of Armagh Cathedral, 1888

97

on the integrity of his original designs, the materials used, the quality of construction and the value of his judgement as knowledgeable antiquary over other considerations. Most of the problems arose over money, lack of payments to Cottingham, and attempts to cut corners and compromise the quality of the restoration. The dean was in the difficult position of explaining expenditure to the archbishop who complained from a distance, while trying to raise money from subscribers in arrears, and allowing small payments to Cottingham at infrequent intervals. Cottingham's accounting was minutely examined. Archbishop Beresford's agents were despatched to Armagh with instructions to investigate the expenditure on labour and materials supplied for any signs of fraud, unnecessary expenditure and even embezzlement. Paton could find no irregularities whatsoever: 'Checked Mr Cottingham's vouchers – I find them all regular and correct, quantities and prices of all stone and other materials ... we can trust to Mr Cottingham's character for the correctness in all aspects.'[45]

Other disputes arose over economy measures through substitution of inferior materials. One aspect of the restoration of Armagh which has attracted criticism was Cottingham's apparent and most uncharacteristic use of plaster instead of stone in the columns of the north transept, the choir windows and the string course of the transepts. An explanation emerges from the correspondence. Dean Jackson wrote to the archbishop in June 1837 suggesting 'plaster instead of stone for economy' and proposing a simple label round the arches of the windows 'at not great expense', and a similar one for the lancet windows of the west entrance. The following April, Charles McGibbon, the contractor, deducted £90 from his estimate for 'finishing the north transept windows in the same manner as the choir in plaster instead of stone'. In June Cottingham wrote 'an angry letter to Mr Paton finding fault with Potts's execution of his part of the work as reported to him'. The dean, relating the contents of Cottingham's letter to the lord primate, continued:

'He is jealous of interference with what he considers his provinces as the architect – particularly in the unauthorised substitution of the plaster pillars in the windows for solid stone as in his specification. The man is evidently out of humour at the work not being conducted on the old plan.'[46]

The question of heating the cathedral was dealt with firmly by Cottingham. The dean wrote that 'in the construction of the boiler and position of the pipes Cottingham assures us there is more nicety required than we apprehend' and added dryly: 'His distrust of Irish undertakers is perhaps not unfounded.'

In the matter of the organ, its situation, and the organ case and screen, Cottingham was again adamant. He insisted that the organ should be removed from the south transept as it was 12ft in depth and there was no room for it near the new stone screen without producing 'a cumbrous deformity'. The dean agreed with the decision, assuring the archbishop: 'Your Grace will not regret the absence of the organ from the screen. You will agree on seeing the effect. The interior would have been entirely spoiled as to the view from the western entrance.'[47] Messrs Walkers of London were to supply the new organ donated by the archbishop. Walker made a design for the organ case as an alternative to Cottingham's design. Paton wrote that the case by Walker was to cost £150, 'but of which Mr Cottingham disapproves, and the other by himself which would cost £200. The latter is certainly very superior in appearance to Walker's.'[48]

Cottingham in fact 'urged strongly the impolicy of using Painted Woodwork and composition in the organ case', especially as the difference in expense between Walker's in deal and his own in oak would not exceed £50. He continued: 'The composition ornaments would be shaken and eventually destroyed by the powerful action of the instrument and the painting would require continual renewal.'[49] The two sets of drawings had been sent to the archbishop and Cottingham's plans were forwarded to Walker to work from without reference to Cottingham who had not finished the final measurements. He asked for their return, noting with some asperity: 'Until the candour and confidence which are necessary in works of this magnitude be restored nothing but mistakes and misunderstandings will occur.'[50]

The restoration was completed with the installation of the oak pews and choir stalls to Cottingham's designs, gas light fittings by Skidmore. Cast-iron gates and railings replaced the dilapidated perimeter walls. There are no remaining designs by Cottingham for the gates and railings but an existing account shows that they were made in 1840 by Thomas Edington and Son at the Phoenix Iron Works in Glasgow. The railings, of simple square section form with restrained crockets and Gothic finials, are supported by a low stone wall with repeating projections and cast-iron struts, a subtle reference to a Gothic flying buttress. Despite the difficulties that arose over costs, Cottingham's restoration of Armagh Cathedral was highly praised, particularly by the *Ecclesiologist*, not noted for approbation of any but their most favoured architects.

Archbishop Lord Beresford, the Lord Primate, whose effigy now lies under the third bay of the nave in the cathedral, was greatly pleased with the final results. His complaints during progress of the work were naturally those of a benefactor who had given £8000 and then found he had to give £16,000 more. A testimony to

Cottingham's work at Armagh is to be found in a letter from the archbishop to Dean Merewether of Hereford Cathedral; the dean was enquiring into Cottingham's fitness to undertake the restoration of Hereford:

'I do hereby certify that I employed L. N. Cottingham to restore the Cathedral of Armagh which had been dilapidated by time and violence, and that I had much reason to be satisfied with the judgement, skill and good taste which he displayed in executing the work. He had many difficulties to contend with, all of which he surmounted with his ability and resources. The working drawings he designed with so great accuracy, that every stone was found to fit the place which it was intended to occupy; nor did a single incident occur during the whole progress of the work, or a labourer or mechanic experience the slightest hurt or injury. I make this statement at the desire of Mr Cottingham and in justice to his merit as an architect. December 7th 1841.'[51]

Armagh has undergone further works of restoration since 1834. In 1888 Cottingham's stone screen was removed and now stands between the regimental chapel and the choir vestry, and in 1903 the chancel walls were raised 8ft and faced with stone. At this date the original oak roofs, dating from the fifteenth century, which had been restored but not renewed by Cottingham, were replaced with an oak groined roof. Over the years Cottingham's pews, carved stalls, ceilings, throne and pulpit have been removed. In 1950 the windows of the nave aisles and the clerestory windows were replaced. Today, only forty years later, they are corroding badly and are still a glaring, light-coloured, unsympathetic stone against the sandstone of the cathedral, perhaps following twentieth-century ethics that recent restoration should be distinct from older work. Cottingham, by contrast, achieved harmony with the old work by painting new stone with 'good lead and oil', a procedure frowned upon by later restorers. Armagh Cathedral still stands today due to Cottingham's advanced technical brilliance which was recognised in his own time. Certainly Armagh was transformed 'as a specimen of nineteenth-century architecture' on the exterior, owing to its total refacing, but Cottingham has never been given credit for trying to preserve, wherever humanly possible, the traces of antiquity, nor for staying close to the spirit and intentions of the mediaeval builders.

BIBLIOGRAPHY
Architectural Magazine, Vol.1, 1835
Carpenter, R. H. and Ingelow, B., *Architects' Report*, 1886, Armagh Cathedral Library, BX XXVI 28 r 28ap
Cottingham, L. N., *Drawings, Plans etc for the restoration of St Patrick's Cathedral, Armagh*, Cathedral Library

Cottingham, L. N., Letters to Dean Jackson, Archbishop Beresford etc from 1834-42, PRONI T2771/1/5/27
Ecclesiologist, New Series Vol.I, 1845; Vol.XIII, 1855
The Gentleman's Magazine, 1834
Paterson, T. G. F. and Davies, O., 'The Churches of Armagh', *Ulster Journal of Archaeology*, Vol.3, 1940
Rogers, E., *Memoir of Armagh Cathedral with an Account of the Ancient City*, Belfast, 1888
Willement, T., *Works in Stained Glass*, London, 1840

Hereford Cathedral: Restoration 1841-9

At Hereford, Cottingham was summoned to undertake the task of saving the mediaeval structure from imminent destruction. The Dean of Hereford, the Reverend John Merewether, published *A Statement on the Condition and Circumstances of the Cathedral Church of Hereford in the Year 1841*, where he described the extent of the dilapidations and the reparations proposed (Figs 49, 50, 51, 52, 53, 54). He expressed his determination to 'instigate sound architectural restoration not mending or patching, nor architectural innovation'. Hereford, like many other cathedrals and churches at this date, had already suffered disasters due to neglect, incompetent repairs, and much-criticised architectural innovation. John Britton, in his *Autobiography*, wrote that Hereford had been an 'object of lament from the circumstances of its decay and fall of the west front with parts of the nave and aisle, on Easter Monday 1786', and its consequent restoration by James Wyatt. The drastic step of rebuilding the triforium and clerestory was taken after the nave vaults collapsed in 1790 due to the failure of Wyatt's earlier works for the security of the fabric. Richard Gough wrote: 'My heart bleeds at the sacrifice already made to the caprices of our modern architects, partly through neglect by Chapters and ill-management of the architects they employ, the lives of 16 men were placed in danger and some killed by the placing of scaffolding in the nave.'[52] Wyatt made designs to form the west front and Britton wrote: 'Instead of harmonising with the old Norman architecture which prevailed throughout the nave his designs showed large pointed arched windows with mullions, tracery, crocketted pinnacles not only out of character but *poor, meagre, tasteless*'.[53] Britton remarked that at that time, as in the preceding age, it was not 'deemed a matter of the slightest consequence in the repair or alteration of Cathedrals to make new correspond with the older and good work'. Wyatt's work on the nave was completed in 1792 and by 1796 exterior works had been undertaken, including the stripping and refacing of the choir, transepts and Lady Chapel, and the roofs of the nave choir and transepts were lowered in pitch to increase the impression of height in the spireless central tower.

Fig.49 East end of the choir before restoration, Hereford Cathedral, 1841
Etching 4×6½ in (10×16.5 cm)

Fig.50 East end of the choir after restoration, Hereford Cathedral, 1841
Etching 4×6½ in (10×16.5 cm)

By 1840 the increasing dilapidation of the fabric was giving rise to alarm. Dean Merewether, a keen antiquary and practising archaeologist who had started excavations on scientific lines at Silbury Hill and was also a member of the Oxford Society for Promoting the Study of Gothic Architecture, was alerted to the serious state of the cathedral by the architect Mr Hardwick, at the time planning alterations to the Bishop's Palace. He said that the east end of the Lady Chapel, which was used as a library, was in immediate danger of collapse. In the spring of 1840 the dean called in Cottingham to examine the extent of the decay, writing:

'The name of Cottingham stands justly high in the estimation of those who have had the opportunity of observing his accurate restorations and splendid designs; his sound taste in ecclesiastical Architecture, and the powerful resources of his skill as a practical engineer –

that very celebrity which he had acquired is itself an unquestionable guarantee of soundness.'

Not content to rely merely on Cottingham's fame, the dean resolved to investigate 'how far these reports of his skill and talent may be depended upon'. He had seen Cottingham's restorations of Magdalen and St Alban's, 'the objects of his minute enquiries', had read an account of Armagh, and conferred with one of the canons on the restoration of Rochester. He then included in his book letters of recommendation confirming Cottingham's ability and integrity in terms of unconditional praise from Archbishop Beresford at Armagh, Verulam, President Routh of Magdalen, William Burge of the Societies of the Inner and Middle Temple, John Field of the Lambeth estate, John Harrison of Snelston Hall, the Reverend Charles Hotham of Roos Church and Sir Robert Inglis of Milton Bryan.[54]

Fig.51 The north arch of the tower, Hereford Cathedral, 1841
Etching $3\frac{1}{2} \times 5\frac{1}{2}$ in (9×14 cm)

Fig.52 The north arch after Cottingham's restoration, Hereford Cathedral, 1841
Etching $4 \times 5\frac{1}{2}$ in (10×14 cm)

Cottingham began his examination in the Lady Chapel with no idea at that time of the full extent of the decay throughout the cathedral. On clearing away whitewash and plaster, cracks 4 inches wide appeared in the soffit of each window arch, showing the exterior and interior ashlar to be unconnected, the rubble masonry having lost all cohesive qualities. The dean noted that this discovery 'refuted all the nonsense about the dilapidation resulting from his clearing away the soil from the base of the walls' which was done to allow air to the crypt. The panelling below the windows and the lath and plaster partitions at the sides of the pillars in the west end of the chapel were removed to follow the extent of the fissures. This resulted in the discovery of the remnants of late fourteenth-century frescoes, the monuments of Joanna de Kilpec and Humphrey de Bohun of the mid fourteenth century, two aumbries both walled up, a double piscina on the south side, the doorway to the forgotten chapel of Bishop Audley dating from the fifteenth century and, especially interesting,

'two of the most beautiful specimens of transitional arches which can be found in any edifice, bearing the Early English form, but ornamented in their soffits with Norman moulding and zig-zag decoration corresponding with the union of Norman intersecting arches on the exterior of the building with its pointed characteristics'.

The stairs to the crypt and adjoining vaults containing interesting relics were also uncovered in lowering the floor to its original level.

Evidence of cracks in the groining above the transept between the Lady Chapel and the altar led to a cautious examination of 'the modern Italian wainscot screen of the Corinthian order' erected by Bishop Bisse in 1717. The architraves of arches with traces of Norman ornament appeared, filled with broken fragments of figures from different monuments, and on the removal of the whole screen the full extent of the damage was revealed. When the screen was erected, ashlar had been removed in four places to receive it, leaving the walls without support and

'the painted boards to represent curtains (what an adornment for a Cathedral Church!) were loosened'.

The dean's disparaging remarks about the Grecian screen echoed Pugin's disgust at such an intrusion, and *The Gentleman's Magazine*, in reporting progress at Hereford, noted 'the removal of the wretched altar screen and equally wretched painted window above, a composition which forms, it will be recollected, the subject of one of Pugin's most forcible contrasts'.[55] The window, by J. Backler, based on Benjamin West's *Last Supper*, on its removal was offered by advertisement to any church willing to preserve it.[56] It would seem that the classically inspired work of Benjamin West was still viewed with disfavour at this date, as twenty years earlier the Dean of Rochester was trying to rid the cathedral of West's oil painting of the *Last Supper*.[57] A further careful examination of the parts walled up behind the screen revealed the original composition of the east end of the choir, and a massive Norman chancel arch, decorated with foliage and zig-zag ornament, its crown cut off and missing but the capitals to the columns supporting the arch perfect, with their foliage and sculpture intact. Above the arch Cottingham discovered three Early English lancets which had been inserted by cutting away the Norman groining, and between the arch and the windows, a blind arcade of Norman columns. At the same time he discovered, just above the blind arcade, Early English openings with cluster columns completing the triforium of the nave.

Cottingham then examined the crossing of the tower and the mass of masonry under the arches. The tower, dating from 1300, rested on four Norman arches and piers which had been increasingly shored up with extra masonry as they showed signs of cracking and bulging. The unsightly infilling and supports had made the situation worse by causing a downward lateral pressure, forcing the piers increasingly out of perpendicular. On removing Wyatt's layers of mortar and whitewash, great fissures were found. At each angle immediately below the Gothic string course were four apertures running diagonally through the walls, wide enough to let in light. The double columns at the angles over these had crushed and fractured the intervening stones, and fissures were found running vertically through the masonry above. The dean wrote in his report of these alarming findings:

'On the removal of a stone from the north-west pier a discharge of dust poured out, emphasising the precarious state. The Architect at this startling discovery was so affected by the apprehension that this beautiful and majestic tower, and with it the whole surrounding fabric might be beyond the power of human skill to save, that without affectation, I firmly believe, he could not refrain from tears.'[58]

Fig.53 First arch of the nave of Hereford cathedral, 1841
Etching $3\frac{1}{2}\times5\frac{1}{2}$ in (9×14 cm)

Fig.54 Arch at the west end of the north aisle before
restoration, Hereford Cathedral, 1841
Etching $3\times5\frac{1}{4}$ in (7.75×13.25 cm)

The crushed mortar, having lost all cohesion, ran out like
sand, indicating that this pier was standing on its outer
casing unaided by any central core. Cottingham further
discovered that the belfry floor and the groining above
the choir were filled with rubble and fragments of
crucifixes, alabaster carvings and the remains of a
fourteenth-century shrine. When two hundred and fifty
cartloads of rubbish were removed, there were to be seen,
not just fissures, but four holes, one big enough for two
men to creep into, with daylight clearly showing through.
Excavations were then made to examine the foundations.
This was absolutely vital and, as the dean pointed out,
answered the charge of 'removing, needlessly as it was
asserted, stalls, organ, and organ screen'.

Cottingham's assessment of the dilapidation was
confirmed by the Reverend Robert Willis, Jacksonian
Professor of Caius College, Cambridge, who at the dean's
request carried out a structural survey. He wrote to the
dean: 'I have not ventured to indicate the exact manner or
extent of the repairs which must be left to the judgement

of your architect whose skill has already been so
successfully exerted in the similar cases of Rochester and
Armagh.'[59]

Willis's knowledge and appreciation of Cottingham's
work at Rochester and Armagh underlines Cottingham's
fame in his own day, and as an internationally known
antiquary Willis's approbation of Cottingham's work was
significant.

B26 (Fig.55)
L. N. Cottingham, proposed alterations to Hereford
Cathedral showing the nave as restored, 1841
Engraving 14×24 in (35.5×61 cm)
Hereford Cathedral Library
Courtesy the Dean and Chapter of Hereford

The means of effecting the task of restoration was left to
Cottingham. The contract for the restoration of the piers
and arches to Cottingham's specifications listed eighteen
drawings and models. He estimated the cost at £17,550

and Carline Brothers, a firm of stonemasons of
Shrewsbury, agreed the contract. Cottingham's full
instructions on every aspect of the restoration procedures
are to be found in the *Chapter Acts Book*.[60]

Cottingham's engineering skills were required to
undertake the dangerous and delicate task of
underpinning the great piers and restoring the
perpendicularity of the whole without removing the
capitals. He clamped the structure with iron ties, and
pinned and wedged the fifty-two columns above the
arches of the tower. Wyatt's plaster groined roof had to
be removed in order to reinstate the piers and was
replaced by a flat ceiling with bosses in Norman styles, as
Dean Merewether said, 'of the utmost accuracy'. The
dean's report was tellingly illustrated with prints of the
dilapidated portions of the cathedral showing crumbling
stonework, blocked-up arches, and the masonry supports
to the arches, contrasted with Cottingham's views of the
same parts, as restored.

Cottingham gave instructions for the restoration of
the piers, clearly stating the necessity, where possible, to
repair rather than renew. The ancient carved capitals at
the top of the main piers of the crossing were to be
restored from plaster models prepared for the carvers and
'such portions of the old stonework as are sound must be
reused and the stone left in natural colour. Casts of the
Norman capitals which have been defaced will be taken to
the Architect's modeller and new enrichments laid on'. In
answer to a discussion between Willis and the dean about
the need fully to replace the piers, Cottingham made it
plain in his specifications that

'such portions of the ancient masonry of the piers etc
may remain if in a sound state, *eg* the lower part of the
semi-column in the nave attached to the north-west pier
of the tower, also a portion of the lower part of the pier at
the north-west angle of the arch at the east end of the
north aisle'.[61]

Clearly stated, too, was the instruction that the
restoration was to be correct with regard to the different
styles of architecture:

'All the arches, capitals, bases, mouldings, and ornaments
throughout the works to be performed in and against the
tower shall be a faithful restoration of the original *now in
existence* [author's italics], and the deficiency made good
in true character. The Clerk of Works to take charge of all
ornamental work taken down and not yet refixed for the
use of masons and carvers to copy from when required.'[62]

In addition to the structural works, the floor of the choir
was renewed with 'encaustic tiles of ancient pattern,
exceedingly rich in effect', and the choir refitted 'with the
original and beautifully carved stalls, but the miserable

square panelled pews will be discarded, and seats of the ancient model with Gothic ends surmounted with appropriate finials'. A new pulpit and litany desk were provided, the organ was removed to the south transept arch, and a screen of 'Norman character', shown in his etching of the nave, was planned to separate the choir from the nave. In fact, the screen, to Cottingham's designs, a simple panelled stone screen, was not erected, but in 1849, a stone carved reredos was erected to the designs of his son, N.J.Cottingham.

The contract of 1843 for the works in the Lady Chapel also showed the same concern for careful and sensitive restoration of the existing fabric, despite the enormity of the structural repairs required. The stone used had to be 'the best description of Capley Wood stone, free from seams of clay blend in accordance with the ancient masonry laid in a proper bed of fine grey limestone mortar'. Other instructions relating to materials used included 'stonework to be soundly stopped with iron cement composed of iron filings and turnings mixed with urine' and where new stone was used to repair tracery, 'the stone to be painted four times, with good lead and oil of dark iron colour otherwise left in natural colour'.

The east end of the Lady Chapel, its disconnected ashlar walls clearly showing in the illustration in the dean's report, had to be taken down and 'reinstated in strict conformity with the original work and the drawings and models furnished, the whole external ashlaring, mouldings, carved capitals to the windows and the return of the buttresses'.

Contemporary comments and debates on the progress of the restoration

Cottingham's restoration of Hereford was widely reported and its progress closely followed in many journals such as *The Gentleman's Magazine*, the *Architect's Journal* and the *Athenaeum*. The *Ecclesiologist* commented on the quality of the works, praising 'the great triumph of modern mechanical skill' and the 'skill and boldness of Mr Cottingham', and trusted that the ecclesiological arrangements would be as satisfactory, 'sincerely hoping that the clergy and choral body would be placed at the eastern extremity of the nave near the altar', and that all seats would be 'good oak benches (movable, of course) or oak chairs': it was further hoped that funds would allow 'the diapering of the roof with proper ecclesiastical patterns'. Articles were published and papers read relating to antiquarian precedents for the most minute details of the structure and its restoration. The *Ecclesiologist*, for example, described the technical details of the restoration of the tower, the discovery of large square bases of the nave piers on the lowering of the

Fig.55 (Cat.b26) Proposed alterations to Hereford Cathedral, 1841
Engraving 14×24 in (35.5×61 cm)

pavement to its original level, and the remains of three apsidal terminations to the choir and choir aisles of the Romanesque church. The journal discussed at length the discovery of the small plinths which served as bases to the double semi-cylindrical face shafts formerly running up the face of the piers. The original face shafts had been removed to make way 'for an incongruous triple vaulting shaft substituted by Wyatt when he erected the meagre triforium with its painfully glaring clerestory'.[63]

Cottingham's restoration of the face shafts from the ancient example remaining had occasioned much argument not only in the committee but amongst others 'loud in their condemnation of them as non-supporting capitals – a supposed grievous architectural anomaly'. The writer supported Cottingham's decision to restore them, pointing out that similar non-supporting shafts appeared in the aisles where the vaulting sprang from corbels detached from the capitals of the face shafts by an interval of several feet, proving 'beyond contradiction that for five centuries they had not provided support for the groining'. The writer went on to give precedents for this feature in the cathedral at Bayeux, S. Ambigio at Milan and the cloisters of S. Trophimus at Arles. At Bayeux,

'the vaulting shafts spring from corbels at the base of the triforium exactly as Mr Cottingham has proposed. Thus he had preserved a rare feature of unusual interest, the occurrence of the double face shaft not being found in any of the pier-ranges of the larger Romanesque buildings of this country, a perfect and complete restoration, separating by a broad line of demarcation, the ancient from the modern, the work of Lozing or Raquelin from the work of Wyatt'.[64]

This testimonial to the archaeological accuracy of Cottingham's work underlines his ability to recognise and preserve 'a very rare feature' of Romanesque architecture, one that appeared in churches on the Continent.

These detailed discussions, the reports in many journals, the exact specifications in the *Chapter Acts Book*, and information in letters written at the time between Cottingham, his son, the dean and others, help now to elucidate areas of doubt and criticism of Cottingham's work. He has been credited with 'rebuilding the piers entirely', 'inserting a triple window in the east end', 'the blank arcading above the eastern arch is Cottingham', and in the nave, 'the vaulting corbels are by Cottingham, before him the shafts rose from the floor without a break' – which as we have seen was not the case.[65] Such comments as these suggest that Cottingham invented certain features or altered existing ones entirely. Meanwhile Wyatt's reputation and his activities at Hereford were defended: 'He has been unjustly maligned

... although he could have saved the Norman gallery his Early English gallery with the simplest Y tracery is not in the least offensive and he repeated the Perpendicular windows in an equally innocuous way. His vault is of timber and the ribbing, self-effacing. The vaulting corbels, of which one cannot quite say that, are by Cottingham.'[66]

Completion of the restoration after Cottingham's death in 1847

After Cottingham's death in 1847, the remaining work to the nave, the aisles, Lady Chapel, stained glass windows, altar reredos and encaustic flooring was continued by his son.[67] The *Chapter Acts Book* noted the dean and chapter's sincere feelings of sorrow and regret at the death of Cottingham and recorded 'their thankful conviction that to his talent and judgement the security of the great central tower of this Church under Divine Providence has been attributable, that in truth that noble structure has been saved from the ruin which threatened it'. They deeply deplored the loss, that they, in common with the country, had sustained at the death of one 'so eminently skilful in all the peculiarities and distinctions of ecclesiastical architecture' and they looked forward to the continuance of the work by his son, who had served a six-year apprenticeship with his father and who had participated in the 'minutiae of the various great and hazardous undertakings'.

The *Chapter Acts Book* records the contract for the completion of the nave and north and south aisles with drawings listed one to twenty, showing the extent of the intended restoration: a plan of one of the nave piers with reinstatement of the double semi-shafts, designs for the tile pavement, working drawings for the restoration of jamb-mouldings to the western doors and doorway and window into the cloisters in the south aisle, plans of nave and aisle ceilings showing intended stencilled diapers, drawings for the restoration of the carved corbels and cappings to the shafts in the triforium supporting the groining of the nave ceilings, and detailed drawings for the underpinning of the nave piers. The specification listed the same requirements as before: care to reuse old stone in all wall-work, 'to accord exactly in colour and appearance with the Mason's work in the choir and Tower already executed', all whitewash to be removed and stone restored to its natural colour, and plaster mouldings to be 'cut and carefully restored in stone in exact accordance with the ancient arches existing'. In the Lady Chapel Nockalls completed the work in accordance with the specifications drawn up by his father in 1845, the work continuing slowly as funds were raised. In addition Nockalls designed the stained-glass windows for the Lady Chapel, the six windows of the north wall depicting

scenes from the Life of Christ and the two windows in the south wall, all in memory of Charles Morgan, canon of Hereford, who died in 1787. The windows are lettered 'Charles A Gibbs pinxit'.[68] Cottingham also designed the glass for the east triplet in 1850. This has been mistakenly attributed to A.W.N. Pugin and Messrs Hardman.[69]

Nockalls, in a letter of 19 October 1849 to R.B. Phillips, a patron of the restoration, wrote: 'I will not fail as speedily as possible to prepare designs for the East windows as a triplet complete. Your wishes as to the pattern window in the Lady Chapel shall also have my best attention.' The dean too wrote to Phillips in January 1850: 'I saw Cottingham here. I believe he is to come again on Saturday. He brought the new plan and designs for the windows and I was charmed with them and entirely approve of the amended designs.' The 'pattern window' was a thirteenth-century window removed from St Peter's Church, Hereford in 1820 and bought by Phillips for £5. He gifted it to the cathedral and N.J. Cottingham inserted it into the chapel. As a memorial to Dean Merewether who died in April 1850, N.J. Cottingham designed the stained glass for the five lancet windows of the Lady Chapel. He wrote to Phillips on 20 February 1851: 'I am truly rejoiced that the windows are approved. I will submit the cartoons to the Memorial Committee. The centre light of the east end of the Choir is nearly completed, the effect will be very gorgeous.'

The triplet in the choir was completed and installed by 14 March 1851. Nockalls also designed the reredos, elaborately carved in Caen stone with figures in crocketed niches, as a memorial to Joseph Bailey MP. The carving of the reredos and the spandrels of the arches behind the altar was executed by Boulton of Lambeth. A large brass eagle lectern that was exhibited at the Great Exhibition of 1851 was also designed by Nockalls. (This lectern is no longer at Hereford Cathedral. The archives relate that it was loaned to Boston Church and was returned, but no trace of it has been found since it was replaced by the present lectern given by Canon Phillot in the 1870s.)

G.G. Scott carried out extensive works of restoration to Hereford Cathedral from 1858. He completely reconstructed the east front and replaced much of the east wall of the Lady Chapel with ornate decoration, turreted angle buttresses and a large east gable, work that was in direct contrast to Cottingham's instructions for the east end 'to be reinstated in strict conformity with the original work'. In the contract between the chapter and Scott of 1858, the massive programme of restoration and the specifications make a telling contrast to Cottingham's insistence that 'such portions of the old stonework as are sound must be reused and the new a faithful restoration of the original work'. The evidence of Scott's approach is there in the *Chapter Acts Book* – 'IT MUST ALL BE NEW'.

BIBLIOGRAPHY

Athenaeum, October 1847

Chapter Acts Book, Contracts and Specifications, L. N. Cottingham, 1843; 1849

Cottingham, N. J., *Letters to R. B. Phillips*, 1849, Belmont Abbey Collection, National Library of Wales, Bundle 29

Frew, J., 'An Aspect of the Gothic Revival in England, 1770-1851', PhD Thesis, Oxford University, 1976

The Gentleman's Magazine, 1842; 1843

Hardman Metalwork Archive, 1850, Birmingham Museum and Art Gallery, *A Brief Description of the Memorials to the Late Very Revd. John Merewether, Dean of Hereford and Joseph Bailey, Esq. MP, recently erected in the Cathedral Church of Hereford*, Hereford, 1852

Merewether, J., *A Statement on the Condition and Circumstances of the Cathedral Church of Hereford in the Year 1841*, London, 1841

Morgan, F. C., *Hereford Cathedral Church Glass*, Leominster, 1979

Pevsner, N. and Metcalf, P., *The Cathedrals of England*, 1989

Willis, R., *Report of a Survey of the Dilapidated Portions of Hereford Cathedral in the Year 1841*, Hereford Cathedral Library

St Mary's Church, Bury St Edmunds: Restoration 1842-9

In 1841, Cottingham was called in to survey, and after its partial collapse, to restore the Norman Tower at Bury St Edmunds. He used his engineering skills to restore the structure without rebuilding. Unfortunately none of the seventeen drawings relating to this work have yet come to light, but contemporary reports provide evidence of the interest the work aroused and of astonishment at the technical feats involved.[70]

When Cottingham was called back to Bury on the collapse of the tower, he was employed at the same time by the Vestry of St James's Parish to give an opinion on cleaning the decorative parts of the roof of St Mary's Church. On going up to the battlements, he discovered extensive evidence of serious dilapidation. He advised a structural survey before any cleaning work was undertaken.[71] His report, printed in full in Samuel Tymms's *Architectural and Historical Account of the Church of St Mary*, gave such an alarming account of the state of the roof and tower that the churchwardens closed the church immediately, arranged for services to be conducted in the chancel and on the following Sunday, the Reverend Phipps Eyre offered up thanksgiving 'for the preservation of minister and people from the imminent and awful peril, which unseen and unthought of had for some time been hanging over their heads'.[72]

Cottingham examined the roof of the nave, a richly carved fifteenth-century timber-framed roof, and found bulging of the embattled stone parapets at the feet of the principal rafters. On removing the gutters and lead covering he found that the ends of the main timbers, the feet of the rafters and the oak plates

'presented a frightful mass of rotten wood, the whole of the timber work, which originally rested on the solid wall, having entirely rotted away, leaving this immense roof covered with heavy lead, no other supports than the small upright helves introduced as ornamental supports for the moulded ribs under the hammer beams'.

These supports were in a very decayed state and crippled by the weight thrown on them. The capitals of the slim shafts on which they rested were also displaced and loosened, 'making it a matter of the greatest surprise how the roof should stand for a single day on such fragile materials'.

The beams and roof timbers had rotted due to accumulated rubbish under the gutter boards, and to rain seeping in through broken gutters and defective leadwork of the roofs where the ends of sheets and seams were soldered together in every direction, causing cracks and fissures. The decay had not extended significantly to the carved work of the roof and Cottingham proposed to encase the ends of the hammer beams in cast-iron sheaths and repair the backs of the principal and common rafters with oak. He concluded that the drastic and expensive recourse of taking the entire roof off could thus be avoided and the repairs could be made without taking any part of the roof down. The stone battlements on the walls of the clerestory had to be restored and the slender buttresses between the windows repaired and underpinned with stones, 'these have been mended with brickbats and tiles which have a very unsightly appearance'.

The roofs of the north and south aisles, also decayed through rain, had to be repaired, the roof of the organ gallery was similarly dilapidated, the mullions, heads and transoms of the west window were loosened, and the walls of the tower were in an insecure state with formidable cracks and fissures, ill-judged repairs, rotting timbers and loose ashlar, requiring iron ties to prevent any further bulging of the walls.

A vestry was called and 'in a liberal spirit' the parishioners voted £1700 for the substantial structural repairs and the minister and churchwardens undertook to raise a subscription for the restoration of 'the ornamental parts'.

Only eighteen months later, in December 1844, *The Gentleman's Magazine* described Cottingham's work at St Mary's as 'one of the finest restorations recently accomplished', mentioning the masterly repair of the roof and the restoration of the carved work, 'every figure of which is a specimen of high art'; the freeing of the pillars and tracery of the windows from whitewash and repairing of defective stonework; the removal of the organ gallery 'which cut in two the fine vista of the nave'; the renewal of the great west window and the insertion of the arms of the neighbouring gentry to the designs of Thomas Willement; the provision of a richly carved font in Caen stone; a pulpit and lectern 'of great boldness and correct styles' in place of a 'Vitruvian tub and bin in mahogany'; an entrance lobby or door screen glazed and elaborately carved; the clearing away of various hoardings and partitions and the replacement of some pews by open seats with foliate finials and bench ends finely carved by Mr Nash: 'the whole of the works under the direction of Mr Cottingham whose research and taste in supplying the deficient parts of the figures is admirable'.[73]

B27 (Fig.56)
Oak throne chair designed by L. N. Cottingham for St Mary's Church, Bury St Edmunds, 1844
Lender: The Parish Church Council
Photograph by Studio Five, Thetford

One of a pair of chairs, of carved oak enriched with pierced Gothic roundels and cusped ornament, which were the gift of Dr W. E. Image of Bury St Edmunds.

B28 (Figs 57, 58, 59)
Interior views of St Mary's Church
Photographs by Studio Five, Thetford

Cottingham designed the oak communion table with traceried panels and bands of pierced quatrefoils, and an aumbrey cupboard. The pulpit of carved oak in the style of the fifteenth century, the period of the church, is of hexagonal form with panels of cinquefoil tracery, separated by angular buttresses and crowned with a cornice decorated with foliage. The staircase has octagonal newels with carved foliage to the capitals and balustrades of pierced quatrefoils and trefoils. The pulpit's hexagonal stem, reinforced by a cast-iron shaft mortised into a stone base, has pointed arch panels with buttressed angles and heavy mouldings, and originally the pulpit was fitted with a 'pair of double branch sconces of polished brass and enamel of rich design'.

B29 (Fig.60)
Caen stone font designed by L. N. Cottingham for St Mary's Church, 1842
National Monuments Record, © RCHME

The old font, illustrated by N. J. Cottingham in Samuel Tymms's *A History of St Mary's Church* of 1845, was

Fig.56 (Cat.B27) Carved oak throne chair, St Mary's Church, Bury St Edmunds, 1844

Fig.57 (Cat.B28) Pulpit of carved oak, St Mary's Church, Bury St Edmunds, 1844

59

Fig.59 (Cat.B28) Carved oak communion table, St Mary's Church, Bury St Edmunds, c.1842

Fig.60 (Cat.B29) Caen stone font, St Mary's Church, Bury St Edmunds, c.1842

60

Fig.58 (Cat.B28) Aumbrey cupboard for St Mary's Church, Bury St Edmunds, 1844

carefully preserved by Cottingham at the time of the restoration. Cottingham's font of deeply carved octagonal form, with armorial shields and stylised foliage, was replaced by the original fifteenth-century font and moved into the Suffolk Chapel. It has since disappeared.

B30 (Fig.61)
Entrance screen of carved oak designed by L. N. Cottingham, c.1842
Photograph by Studio Five, Thetford

The *Bury and Norwich Post* on 4 December 1844 published a long report on the reopening of St Mary's Church, when the bells pealed again after the long silence, giving a full account of the restoration with details of the subscribers, all of whose arms were included in Willements's armorial glass of the restored west window, since replaced. The reviewer noted the high quality of the carvings, the bronzed brass hinges and wrought-iron handles of the entrance lobby of 'exquisite workmanship', the double branch sconces of brass and enamel of rich design, the communion table and high-backed chairs of carved oak, all to Cottingham's designs. The monuments of the Oakes and Sturgeon families had been removed from their 'unsightly situations' against

Fig.61 (Cat.B30) Entrance screen at St Mary's Church, Bury St Edmunds, *c.*1842

the jambs of the chancel arch to the wall of the south aisle, the organ was re-erected in the third bay of the north aisle, while on the removal of the sexton's lumber room at the end of the north aisle remains of early wall paintings were discovered, though too faint to be fully deciphered. The report noted that 'the beautiful North porch, the work of John Notynglas of the fifteenth century, not needing any material repair, has been left untouched with the exception of cleaning the interior' and that the principal at the east end of the nave 'has been repainted and regilded precisely as it was decorated in the fifteenth century from vestiges of the designs remaining'.

The writer concluded by saying that the work 'reflected the highest credit to the professional skill and antiquarian knowledge of the architect. Indeed we know of no other instance in which a similar attempt at restoration has been carried out with more judgement ...' He finished with a statement that characterised Cottingham's restoration work and epitomised his aims:

'Every part of the old work that was defective has been restored with a faithful adherence to the original design and all that is new has been done in the same spirit and made to harmonise with the old.'

There can be no doubt that Cottingham saved national monuments, the Norman Tower, the fifteenth-century St Mary's and other edifices through his immediate and skilful restorations, preserving them for future generations. He brought his expertise to other important churches and to small parish churches. At the fifteenth-century St Mary's Church in Nottingham, his prompt action in 1843 saved the tower from collapse, and at St Mary's Church, in Clifton, Nottinghamshire, he restored the leaning arches and pillars of the nave that were crushed by the weight of the tower, without removing a single stone. Ashbourne Church in Derbyshire, seriously dilapidated and disfigured by an external staircase which gave access to the galleries by way of the mutilated tracery of the west window, was restored in 1841: Great Chesterford in Essex and Horningsheath in Suffolk were extended and restored in 1841: Milton Bryan Church was restored and a new tower erected in 1842; the spire of St James, Louth, struck by lightning in 1844, was skilfully restored: Theberton and Barrow Churches in Suffolk, Roos Church in Yorkshire and Brougham Chapel in Westmorland were all repaired and extended in 1846-7: and in 1847 the ancient Norman Church of Kilpeck and Ledbury Church in Herefordshire were also restored. All these works demonstrate Cottingham's qualities as a sensitive and conservative restorer in advance of his time.[74]

BIBLIOGRAPHY
Bury and Norwich Post, 4 Dec. 1844; 1843, 12 June; 5/745
The Builder, 25 April 1846
Cottingham, L.N., *Report on the Norman Tower at Bury and the Necessary Repairs thereof*, London, 1842
The Gentleman's Magazine, 1843, 1847, Jan. 1849, Dec. 1852
Tymms, S., *An Architectural and Historical Account of the Church of St Mary*, Bury St Edmunds, 1845
Vestry Book, St Mary's, Bury; *Council Proceedings*, 1840-6, Suffolk R.O.

C   Church Furnishings

In addition to carrying out restoration and extension to many churches, Cottingham was commissioned to design ecclesiastical fittings such as pulpits, in wood and stone, bishop's thrones, chairs, communion tables and altars, bench pews, light fittings, lecterns, litany desks, stained glass, monuments, encaustic tiles, screens and fonts. The remaining items of his work have never been reviewed. In the Victoria and Albert Museum's *Exhibition of Victorian Church Art* of 1971, there was no mention of Cottingham as a designer of church art or furnishings except in relation to the Hardman flagon commissioned for Davington Priory where Cottingham possibly carried out restoration for his friend, Thomas Willement, the antiquary and designer of stained glass and armorial paintings.

C1 (Fig.62)
Flagon. Ruby glass body with electrogilt metal mounts
Unmarked, made by John Hardman & Co, and possibly designed by N.J. Cottingham
Height $13\frac{1}{2}$ in (34.5 cm)
St Mary Magdalene's Church, Davington, Kent
Photograph by Portfolio Photographs, Wallington
(See Hardman day-book, 1845-9, p.449 entry 31 March 1849: 'N.J. Cottingham; A large handsome and elaborately worked Cruet, of Ruby glass ... mounted with gilt metal, Engraved etc with design raised on lid, of Pelican and Young in Nest etc etc. £18 10/–'
[See T. Willement, *Historical Sketch of the Parish of Davington*, 1862, p.127])

There is evidence of close links between leading architects such as Cottingham and A.W.N. Pugin and many of the craftsmen in wood and metal who made furniture, fittings, stained glass and carved stone to their designs. Among those craftsmen whom we know worked with Willement, Pugin and Cottingham were Samuel Pratt and his brothers Edward and James, who had workshops and showrooms at 47 New Bond Street and 3 Lower Grosvenor Street in London; Thomas Potter of South Molton Street who provided metal work as well as cast-iron ties for Cottingham's restorations at Bury St Edmunds and Hereford; Messrs Hardman, metalworkers and stained glass designers of Birmingham; W. Boulton of Lambeth, a stone carver; and S.A. Nash, a carver of

Fig.62 (Cat.c1) Silver-gilt flagon, 1849

wood who worked extensively in Suffolk and London.[1] In all specifications and in personal letters to his patrons, Cottingham insisted on the highest quality of materials and craftsmanship in the execution of his meticulously drawn designs. Few working drawings for his ecclesiastical fittings and furniture have come to light apart from those for the carved oak throne and stone screen which he designed for Armagh Cathedral. But some examples of his work in churches have so far escaped the hand of twentieth-century 'improvers'.

Cottingham was in the forefront of promoting and encouraging the revival of encaustic tiled flooring for use in church building and restoration. His interest probably stemmed from his detailed research of mediaeval buildings. At Rochester, for example, in 1842, he preserved the original tile paving comprising fragments of old encaustic tiles.

The *Ecclesiologist* in 1845 noted that 'every day increases our knowledge of ancient pavements and Rochester contains several exquisite specimens'; and the writer expressed disgust at their replacement by 'street-flagging under the direction of Mr Vulliamy'.[2] Cottingham had examples of early tiles in his museum as a source for stylistic accuracy and would have known of the discovery by the Worcester architect, Harvey Eginton, of a mediaeval kiln and deposit of tiles at Malvern in 1833.[3] Eginton had encouraged the Worcester Porcelain Manufacturing Company to produce encaustic tiles, which he used in church restorations such as the church of Stratford-upon-Avon in 1837. Cottingham's discovery in 1841 of the mediaeval tiles in the Chapter House at Westminster was of great importance in stimulating a revival and J. G. Nichols's book on encaustic tiles, with accurate drawings by Cottingham, helped to spread knowledge and interest in mediaeval designs. Most significantly, however, Herbert Minton of Stoke-on-Trent undertook the successful reproduction of tiles from the Chapter House, leading in 1842 to his catalogue entitled *Old English Tile Patterns* which introduced his new range of encaustic tiles. A.W. Pugin, influenced directly by Cottingham and by his father's antiquarian pursuits, was interested in the revival of all aspects of mediaeval art. In Minton's catalogue the first twelve designs in the book were lithographic prints and the remaining fifty designs were connected with Cottingham's Temple Church designs, derived from the Chapter House, and Pugin's tiles for St Giles Church, Cheadle.

Cottingham designed encaustic tiles for many of the churches that he restored and for domestic commissions after the success of the Temple Church designs of 1843. Many of Cottingham's floors have been destroyed in later restorations. For example, at Hereford Cathedral Cottingham's tiles were replaced by G. G. Scott in 1858 when he renewed the flooring with tiles of a more elaborate design. Cottingham's tiles for Hereford were described by the *Ecclesiologist* as 'rather plain'. It is likely that he based his designs on examples of early tiles in his museum and that he used simple two-colour geometric tiles in keeping with the Norman and Early English parts of Hereford. Scott, at Hereford and at Ashbourne Church, replaced Cottingham's geometric and armorial tiles with tiles of intricate design incorporating birds, heraldic beasts, foliage and elaborated armorials of the fifteenth century. Cottingham used tiles with simple Gothic motifs or armorial devices, usually of two or three colours, in his restorations at Market Weston Church, Barrow, Horringer, St Mary's Clifton, Theberton, Roos, and Brougham Chapel, and in his own church of St Helen's, Thorney, where remaining examples may be

seen. For example, at Horringer Cottingham used red and green tiles, the red inlaid with the geometric motifs inlaid in white clay in the manner of thirteenth century tiles such as those discovered at Hailes: the period of these tile designs was in keeping with the Early English arcade and side aisle extension that he designed. He used red tiles inlaid with white again at Barrow Church with a four-tile arrangement of geometric and floral Gothic motifs, again of the late thirteenth- to early fourteenth-century design, in keeping with the church's founding date.

His study of the tiles he discovered at Westminster dating from 1258 gave him precedents for appropriate tile designs. For example, in his work at St Mary's, Clifton, he used the non-figurative designs, described in his article on the Westminster tiles, with circles and foliage and armorials in the centres, composed of a nine-tile design. In his church at St Helen's, Thorney, he used the simple two-colour design based on circles and geometric floral motifs in keeping with the Romanesque ornament of his church.

Cottingham also designed furniture for many of the churches in which he worked. At Rochester, he designed an oak pulpit and bishop's throne, which can be seen in the lithograph of 1842 (see Restoration of Rochester).

C2 (Fig.63)
L. N. Cottingham, carved oak pulpit for Rochester Cathedral, *c.*1825-30
Photograph by Martin & Gray Photography, Rochester. Reproduced by permission of the Dean and Chapter of Rochester

The pulpit of hexagonal form supported on an hexagonal stem is in Early English Gothic of the later period, with the characteristic trefoil in blind tracery panels, crockets to the pointed arches and small bunches of foliage carved at intervals in the hollow mouldings. The staircase curving in two stages to the pulpit has turned balusters with trefoil pointed arches. The bishop's throne has a canopy of similar form to the blind panels of the pulpit with trefoil arched sides, cluster column supports and crocketed pointed arches topped by foliate finials. Both the pulpit and throne echoed the style of the late thirteenth-century choir and transepts, harmonising with the remains of the thirteenth-century woodwork of the pulpitum and the back stalls. Cottingham also designed a stone font in keeping with the Norman nave of the cathedral, of square form with Norman round arch decoration and zig-zag moulding supported on a central column enriched with chevron mouldings and four columns with cushion capitals. The pulpit can still be seen at Rochester (Fig.63). It was removed to the nave (where it looks out of place with the great stone Norman

Fig.63 (Cat.C2) Carved oak pulpit, Rochester Cathedral, c.1825–30

64

pillars) when G. G. Scott replaced it with a very elaborate Gothic pulpit and bishop's throne in 1871.[4] Cottingham's bishop's throne was moved to St Alban's Abbey in 1877 for the enthronement of Dr Claughton as first bishop of that see, and it appears in a lithograph of the nave of St Alban's, but it has now disappeared and cannot be traced.[5] The Norman font was sent to Deptford Parish Church where it looks incongruous in the strictly classical interior of that church.

At Magdalen College Chapel Cottingham's interior remains intact to a large extent. Here he was able to indulge his love of Perpendicular Gothic of the late fifteenth century, in keeping with the chapel's founding date of 1473.

The oak bench pews Cottingham designed for Temple Church in 1841, elaborately carved by S. A. Nash with grotesque masks, crowned heads, fruits and foliage, serpents and birds, ornament in keeping with the thirteenth-century Transitional choir and based on examples in Cottingham's museum, were all destroyed in the bombing of London in 1944. (Illustration remains in the National Monuments Record.)

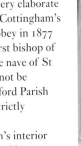

65

Fig.64 (Cat.C3) Tenison Mosse, Interior of Ashbourne Church, 1842
Engraving 33×23¾ in (84×60.5 cm)

Fig.65 (Cat.C4) Wall monument to Lady Boothby, Ashbourne Church, 1840

At Ashbourne Church in Derbyshire, where Cottingham worked from 1839-42, very little remains of his interior furnishing as much was swept away in a later restoration by G. G. Scott. The Reverend Tenison Mosse, however, produced a volume, which gives illustrations of Cottingham's designs.

C3 (Fig.64)
Rev. S. Tenison Mosse, *The Archaeological and Graphic Illustration of Ashbourn Church*, Ashbourne, 1842
Lender: Ashbourne Church, Derbyshire

The author describes the extent of the dilapidations and gives an account of Cottingham's structural repairs, unblocking and restoring of lancet windows, reinstatement of a gallery and removal of a lath and plaster screen which separated the chancel from the nave, repair of damage to the nave piers, 'defaced and cut away to receive monuments', and resiting of the organ in the south transept. Cottingham installed carved oak benches and an oak screen, and, according to Tenison Mosse, also designed a mural monument to Fanny, Lady Boothby, who died on 2 January 1838.

C4 (Fig.65)

L. N. Cottingham, monument to Fanny, Lady Boothby, Ashbourne Church, Derbyshire, 1840
Photograph by Ashbourne Photography, Ashbourne, 1989

The Boothby family were local landowners and patrons of the restoration. Cottingham's Gothic monument to Lady Boothby is divided by slim columns with foliate capitals into three compartments with trefoil heads under pointed arches inset with trefoils and decorated with foliage and armorial shields within roundels. The inscription was written on 'bronzed metal plate in olde English character' with illuminated initials by 'Willement, painter in glass to Her Majesty, the whole executed in London from the designs under the superintendence of Mr Cottingham'.

Fine examples of Cottingham's work still exist in Suffolk, at St Mary's Church, Bury, and in other churches in his home county. Cottingham may well have looked to fifteenth-century Suffolk precedents for his finely carved pulpits, such as the carved oak octagonal pulpit at Theberton Church where he carried out works of restoration in 1846, or Tuddenham Church, the village where he built the school in 1846.

Cottingham, born and bred in Suffolk, knew the locality well and he had been a subscriber in 1827 to a volume by Henry Davy entitled the *Architectural Antiquities of Suffolk, representing the most celebrated remains of Antiquity in the County*. His own museum contained casts of fifteenth-century carved bench ends from Woolpit Church and Westley Church in Suffolk, from Saffron Walden and from Hesset Church in Norfolk. Samuel Tymms, in an article on Woolpit Church, noted in 1859, 'the open seats have been much admired. Pugin copied them, so did Cottingham.' Cottingham's furnishings at St Mary's, as the reviewer at the time said, 'were done in the same spirit and made to harmonise with the old', matching the period of the church itself and the traditions of the area.

At St Mary's Church, Clifton in Nottinghamshire, a twentieth-century restoration has swept away Cottingham's encaustic flooring, decorated with armorial bearings, carved oak screen, decorative ironwork staircase, litany desk and pulpit. The carved oak ceiling of the crossing tower, 'discovered by accident when redecoration started on the ceiling', has now been painted gold, green, red and white in a modern design. All that remains is the font cover of carved oak, studded with brass, the doors to the north porch, and in the chancel, an example of Cottingham's stalls with foliate *poupée*-head finials and pierced quatrefoil decoration. A few of the encaustic tiles remain in the entrance porch.

By contrast, the small parish church of Market Weston, Suffolk, has remained virtually untouched since Cottingham's restoration of 1845. The church, of the early fifteenth century, built in rubble and flint, was in a deplorable state. Cottingham brought the bulging and leaning walls of the nave and tower to upright without rebuilding, rebuilt the chancel which has an open timber-framed roof in common with other small Suffolk churches of this date, and a three-light east window 'glazed by the fair hand of Miss Rickards, the accomplished daughter of the rector of Stowlangtoft', as we are told by the reviewer in the *Bury and Norwich Post* of 1845. The interior, 'neat and pleasing', was accorded new furnishings to Cottingham's designs.

C5 (Fig.66)
Carved oak chair designed by L. N. Cottingham for Market Weston Church, 1845
Lender: Diocese of St Edmundsbury and Ipswich
Photograph by Studio Five, Thetford

C6 (Fig.67)
Carved oak bench designed by L. N. Cottingham for Market Weston Church, 1845
Lender: Diocese of St Edmundsbury and Ipswich
Photograph by Studio Five, Thetford

C7 (Fig.68)
Carved oak lectern designed by L. N. Cottingham for Market Weston Church, 1845
Lender: Diocese of St Edmundsbury and Ipswich
Photograph by Studio Five, Thetford

On each side of the chancel are 'the unostentatious benches and seats for families of the patron and the incumbent', buttressed and panelled with blind cinquefoil tracery, and simple open benches 'for the village schools' with quatrefoil roundels. The nave is filled with solid oak open bench seats with elbows and bookboards, the ends terminating in roundels with combinations of pierced trefoils and quatrefoils in a

66

67

Fig.66 (Cat.c5) Oak throne chair, Market Weston Church, 1845

Fig.67 (Cat.c6) Oak bench, Market Weston Church, 1845

variety of designs. In the nave by the north-east chancel arch is the pulpit 'boldly executed in oak' of octagonal form, simply panelled with blind tracery on a stem with heavy architectural mouldings and a staircase of trefoil arched balusters and hexagonal moulded newel posts. The lectern, also bold and architectural, has pierced roundels, a battlemented top, an octagonal, stepped and buttressed stem and octagonal moulded base with pierced trefoils. Cottingham's stone font, unfinished at the church's reopening in 1844, was replaced in 1889, when a new belfry and vestry were erected and the chancel was raised. Cottingham's interior at Market Weston, where his simple bold designs were in keeping with the period of the church and with the needs of the parish, was described as 'creditable alike to the pious liberality and the improved taste of the age'. (Fig.68)

Fig.68 (Cat.c7) Interior of Market Weston Church after restoration, 1845

Fig.69 (Cat.c8) Interior of Brougham Chapel, Westmorland, 1846

C8 (Fig.69)

Interior of Brougham Chapel, Westmorland, designed by L.N. Cottingham in 1846
Photograph by A.F. Kersting

During his work on Brougham Hall, Westmorland, for the Lord Chancellor, Henry, Lord Brougham, Cottingham also made designs for Brougham Chapel in 1846. Simon Jervis tentatively attributed this work to Cottingham, stating that 'the references to Cottingham's involvement at Brougham are enigmatic, but possibly Cottingham worked there under Lord Brougham. We have no evidence that Cottingham worked on the chapel but it seems likely.'[6]

Jervis noted that the candlesticks and the hinges on the oak aumbrey looked like Cottingham's work while the oak stalls, similar in design to those of Winchester Cathedral but omitting the later pinnacles, 'show a discriminating designer at work'. This supposition can be confirmed

from the letters written by Cottingham and his son to William Brougham. Brougham, a keen mediaevalist, collected English and continental mediaeval fitments for the chapel, reusing ancient fragments of panelling, screens, furniture and other fittings, including a fine Flemish triptych which was incorporated as a reredos at the east end. Cottingham did not superintend the work in the chapel but sent designs for the Norman columns at the windows, the Norman wheel window inserted in the east end, and the pews and carved stalls, and Lord Brougham's builders and carpenters carried out the work of refitting the interior, transforming it from seventeenth-century severely classical interior to a mediaeval chapel. John White, the foreman, wrote in 1843: 'the piece of carving you suggest for the west gable of the chapel will make a good finish ... The sooner you send the plan for the stone table the better ... the flags from the entrance hall are all made ready for the chapel.'[7]

These letters listed the progress of every stage, the fitting of the floor, the painting of the armorials and the painted decoration of the ceiling, the fitting of the pews and the organ cupboard. The seat ends in the chapel and the aumbrey door are illustrated in a booklet, *Antiquarian Gleanings in the North of England* by William B. Scott. In Cottingham's letter of 24 July 1845, there is confirmation that the work was his, for he included a sketch of this aumbrey door showing his designs for the hinges and he also mentioned designs for the font cover. It is possible that Cottingham designed the altar for the chapel, made by Samuel Pratt. In William Brougham's diary of 22 November 1844, he wrote, 'Pratt says he cannot take less than £150 for the altar having refused this from Pugin for Lord Shrewsbury'.[8] The hinges for the aumbrey, and the locks and hinges for the doors of the chapel were made to Cottingham's designs by Thomas Potter of South Molton Street.

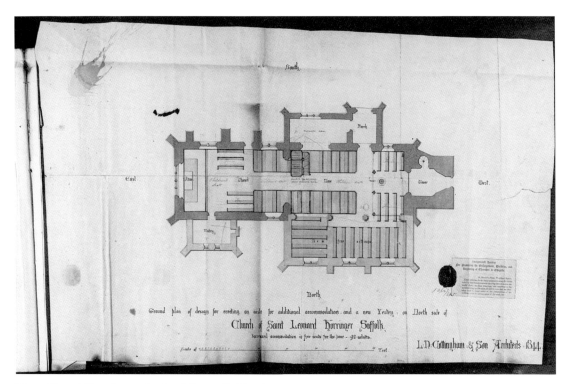

Fig.70 (Cat.C9) Plan of extension for St Leonard's Church, Horringer, 1845
Line and wash $11\frac{1}{2} \times 15\frac{1}{2}$ in (29.25 × 39.5 cm)

Fig.71 (see Cat.C9) Encaustic floor tiles, St Leonard's, Horringer, 1845

Fig.72 (see Cat.C9) Tiles laid in Barrow Church, Suffolk, 1849

C9 (Fig.70)
L. N. Cottingham, plan of extension for St Leonard's Church, Horringer (Horningsheath) Suffolk, restored in 1845
Line and wash $11\frac{1}{2} \times 15\frac{1}{2}$ in (29.25 × 39.5 cm)
ICBS, File no.3577
Courtesy the Archbishop of Canterbury and the Trustees of Lambeth Palace Library

St Leonard's Church, dating from the fourteenth century with Perpendicular additions, was enlarged by Cottingham in 1845. He erected a new vestry, a new north aisle which this plan illustrated, with an Early English arcade in keeping with the date of the nave, allowing ninety-eight more seats for the congregation. The plan shows the three two-light fourteenth-century Gothic windows and buttresses, the whole in keeping with the style and materials used in the original building. He renewed the seating throughout with oak benches with carved finials, altered the position of the pulpit and lectern by 4ft and left the font in its original position opposite the south entrance. Later restorations removed his oak benches but left an example of his encaustic tiling in the chancel, and the door to the vestry, panelled with quatrefoil tracery (Figs 71, 72).

At Barrow Church, close by, the restoration of the dilapidated fabric was completed to the designs of Cottingham's son, Nockalls, 'the walls having been brought upright by Mr Cottingham's process and underpinned'.[9] Another small Suffolk church rescued from dilapidation by Cottingham in 1846 was St Peter's, Theberton, where, without resorting to rebuilding, he saved the round tower which leaned 18in out of perpendicular, and restored the fifteenth-century porch and south aisles with its intricate ornament. In the interior he restored the south aisle and refitted the nave and chancel with 'very handsomely carved seats; those appropriated to Mr Doughty, the patron himself, being of oak and more elaborately wrought, the others of deal'.[10]
Cottingham, as Samuel Tymms pointed out, looked to Woolpit Church for the fifteenth-century precedent and his oak chancel benches have panelled ends with blind tracery and foliate finials, some enriched with carved winged kneeling angels holding shields of arms, very similar to, although not copies of, the bench ends at Woolpit. The deal nave benches, darkened with age to a rich patination, have boldly carved simple foliate finials. Traces of polychromy were discovered on the removal of

whitewash from the south aisle arcade. Cottingham restored the stencilled patterns with great richness of colour in the mediaeval manner, decorative work that was carried out in 1846, the year in which similar work was undertaken by Viollet-le-Duc at La Sainte Chapelle and by A. W. N. Pugin at St Giles, Cheadle, in their efforts to revive the full colour and beauty of the mediaeval interior. Cottingham also restored and redecorated the timbers, spandrels and bosses of the south aisle roof with stencilled patterns in rich colouring. H. M. Doughty, writing in 1910, noted criticism of this in the Davy MS: 'He did not know that Mr Cottingham the eminent church architect had but followed a practice of the period to which the aisle belongs.'[11]

C10 (Figs 73, 74)
Interiors of St Peter's, Theberton
Photographs by Studio Five, Thetford

C11 (Fig.75; Colour Plate 1)
Wall monument to the Hon. Frederica Doughty, designed by L. N. Cottingham, 1845-6
Photograph by Studio Five, Thetford

In the south aisle there is a wall monument to the Hon. Frederica Doughty, designed by Cottingham in the style of fifteenth-century Gothic in keeping with the date of the south aisle itself, with an ogee-pointed crocketed arch surmounted by angels, the whole emblazoned with armorials and intricately carved painted and gilded ornament. Possibly Cottingham looked to the many examples of monuments of the late mediaeval period in his museum, carefully cast from the originals, particularly those at Westminster, or he may have based his Doughty monument, for example, on the monuments to Joanna de Kilpec and Humphrey de Bohn which he had discovered in Hereford Cathedral. It is possible that Thomas Willement executed the monument to Cottingham's designs, for he was responsible for the three stained-glass windows of the restored south aisle at Theberton, depicting the figures of St Peter and St Paul and the Doughty coats-of-arms. Cottingham designed the encaustic tiles for the floor in three patterns but no trace of these remain in the church. They were swept away in later restorations and Cottingham's 'lectern of square form', possibly similar to his lectern for Market Weston, was also replaced. In recent years parts of Cottingham's aisle arcade, the roof of the south aisle and the Doughty monument have been repainted to restore the brilliance of the colours. In Cottingham's restoration of the Norman parish church at Milton Bryan, funds were limited to the structural work. This included a new north porch, a south transept to balance the Inglis Chapel at the north, and a tower to house the seventeenth-century bells. Cottingham reopened the blocked-up west window, a fifteenth-century insertion in the earlier fabric, and the window was later filled with stained glass as a memorial to Sir Joseph Paxton who died in 1871. Cottingham may have designed the brass church plate and corona pierced with Gothic ornament but no documentary evidence has appeared to support the supposition.

BIBLIOGRAPHY
Brougham Papers, Letters from LNC to William Brougham, UCL Library, 1844-6: W. Brougham's diaries, UCL, 1844
Bury and Norwich Post, 3 Jan. 1849, 'Reopening of Barrow Church', *Suffolk Institute of Archaeology*, Vol.7, Theberton Church, 1891
Davy, H., *Architectural Antiquities of Suffolk etc*, Southwold, 1827
Doughty, H. M., *Chronicles of Theberton*, London, 1910
Essex, W. R. H., *Illustrations of the Architectural Ornaments etc of Temple Church*, London, 1845
Exhibition Catalogue, 'The Age of Chivalry'; John Cherry, 'Tiles', Royal Academy, 1989

73

74

75

Fig.73 (Cat.C10) Interior of St Peter's Church, Theberton, Suffolk after restoration, 1846

Fig.74 Carved pews in St Peter's Church, Theberton, 1846

Fig.75 (Cat.C11) Wall monument to the Hon. Frederica Doughty, 1845-6

Exhibition Catalogue, Minton 1798-1910, V&A Museum, 1976
Exhibition Catalogue, Victorian Church Art, V&A Museum, 1971
ICBS, Horringer Church File, No.3577, 1845
Minton, H., *Old English Tile Patterns*, 1842 (V&A Archive)
Myles, J., 'The Church Furnishings of L. N. Cottingham', *Victorian Society Annual*, 1990, pp.23-41
Nichols, J. G., *Example of Inlaid Gothic and Encaustic Tiles*, London, 1845
Rochester Cathedral Archives, Kent R.O. Ref DRC emf 135
Tymms, S., 'Woolpit Church', *Proceedings of the Suffolk Institute of Archaeology*, Vol.II, 1859

D Church Building

St Helen's, Thorney, Nottinghamshire 1845-9

As far as is known, Cottingham only built one church, the small parish church of St Helen, Thorney, on the borders of Nottinghamshire and Lincolnshire. Some difficulties have arisen in the past over the dating and attribution of this church. Nikolaus Pevsner attributed it to L. N. Cottingham, giving the date of building as 1849, two years after Cottingham's death, and for this reason Timothy Mowl, in his thesis on the Norman Revival, attributed it to Cottingham's son.[1] In Cottingham's obituary in *The Art-Union*, the writer suggested that the church was built to Nockalls Cottingham's designs 'from the desire of his father to test his ability'. But Nockalls, writing to William Brougham in June 1846, referred to Thorney in terms which do not confirm that he designed the church: he merely mentioned 'the Norman Church that we are building'.[2] Certainly, due to his father's ill-health, Nockalls was taking on increasing responsibility for all building projects between 1846 and 1847, and the church, clearly under construction by June 1846, was finished by him in 1849, eighteen months after Cottingham's death. St Helen's was erected by the Lord of the Manor, George Nevile of Grove and his son the Reverend Christopher Nevile. The Nevile family succeeded the Hercys as lords of Grove in 1500 and George Nevile bought the Thorney estate in 1567, since when it has been held by the family until the present day.[3] Surviving letters from 1845 indicate that Christopher Nevile and his brothers Henry and Charles and their mother, who donated £1000, raised the bulk of the funds, and the church was built to Cottingham's designs in Romanesque style.[4]

D1 (Fig.76)
St Helen's Church, Thorney, 1845-9, exterior view
Photograph by Roger Mockford Photography, Newark

The *Ecclesiologist* noted in 1845 that 'Mr Cottingham has sent an external view of the Church he is building. It is in Norman style and presents nothing that we can praise, excepting the length of the chancel.'[5] Naturally the *Ecclesiologist* disapproved of Cottingham's choice of neo-Norman, considering Middle-Pointed to be the only true

style for church design. But on its completion in 1849, the journal published a detailed and favourable report suggesting that 'the excellence of the execution and real church-like effect of the interior are entitled to considerable praise'. Cottingham's choice of Romanesque for this church is an interesting one. He had written in various publications on the beauties and merits of Romanesque architecture, giving examples of existing buildings, and shown a detailed knowledge of its history, development and construction, gained not only from the extensive collection of fragments and casts of Romanesque art and architecture that filled his museum, but also from his direct experience of restoring Romanesque buildings, including that of Kilpeck Church in Herefordshire. Cottingham knew this church well. He subscribed, together with Sir Samuel Meyrick, the Reverend Routh, Anthony Salvin, The Cambridge Camden Society, Albert Way, Thomas Willement and others to a volume of 1842 by G. R. Lewis on Kilpeck Church. In his introductory essay, Lewis wrote: 'Kilpeck Church has been but little seen ... it is a work of high imagination. It must be made known the present disgraceful state of this most beautiful church ... it must be taken in hand by the highly educated.'[6] In a letter of 7 June 1845, Nockalls wrote to William Brougham: 'You are probably well acquainted with the beautiful Norman church at Kilpeck – we have lately received the appointment to restore it. Among architecture it is considered a perfect gem, the decoration and arrangement full of symbolic meaning.'[7]

It is significant that Cottingham was chosen as the 'highly educated' restorer of this major example of European Romanesque architecture. Unfortunately no archive material relating to this restoration has come to light and Cottingham's work was overlaid by later works of restoration.

Apart from influence through his own practical experience and study of Romanesque buildings themselves, Cottingham would have studied the early volumes on English and continental Romanesque architecture, as well as those produced by his friends and fellow members of the scholarly societies. No catalogue of Cottingham's library, described as 'extensive', has yet come to light. But it is possible that some of his books, at his death, went to his brother Edwin, whose valuable library was sold in 1859.[8] It contained Cottingham's publications and such volumes as Ducarel's *History of Monastic Orders* (1695), Cressy's *Church History of Brittany from the beginning of Christianity to the Norman Conquest* (1668), Neale and Webb's *Durandus* (1503), Dugdale's *Monasticon* in eight volumes (1817-30), *Vetusta Monumenta*, in five volumes (1747-1835), and Britton and Brayley's *Beauties of England and Wales* (1801-15).

Fig.76 (Cat.DI) St Helen's Church, Thorney, 1846

Fig.77 (Cat.D2) West front of St Helen's Church, Thorney, 1846

Cottingham had made his own study of English Romanesque and the great continental Norman churches, such as St George de Bocherville and St Etienne at Caen, as we know from the casts of architectural features in his museum. And he would have known of other antiquarian publications by his friends, such as A. C. Pugin's *Architectural Antiquities of Normandy* (1828) and Cotman's *Antiquities of Normandy* (1822), Whewell's works on German churches and churches of Normandy and Picardy (1835) and Henry Gally Knight's *Architectural Tours of Normandy, Sicily and Italy*, published between 1835 and 1844. While these writers were known personally to Cottingham, knowledge spread, too, through scholarly interchange at meetings of the antiquarian societies to which Cottingham and these friends all belonged.

Pattern books of the early nineteenth century also showed Romanesque designs as a cheap alternative to classical and Gothic. Several architects such as Blore, Salvin and Ferrey designed in the style, and A. W. N.

Pugin, who had restored the Romanesque church of St Nicholas at Peper Harrow, also built three Neo-Norman churches.

The plan of St Helen's follows the usual Romanesque parish church arrangement of a simple two-celled plan, a nave without aisles, a deep chancel of square end design with a small sacristy to the north, and no tower. It has a gable belfry over the west end with two bells in a round-headed arch enriched with roll-moulding and zig-zag, and columns with volute capitals, billet carving, and below, a corbel course of six grotesque heads. Kilpeck has a similar two-bell belfry in a round-headed arch, and drawings of St Peter's Church at Tickencote in Lincolnshire show a belfry of this form prior to its removal in the restoration of 1792. At St Helen's, between the nave and chancel there is a second bell-turret like a miniature tower, elaborately carved with figures in round arches. The existence of the two belfries was criticised by the *Ecclesiologist* as 'the most glaring defect in the church, being wholly, we believe, without precedent'.[9] Cottingham drew upon his extensive knowledge of the Romanesque to design a church that was archaeologically correct, but instead of slavishly copying original examples, he combined elements to create his own design.

Fig.78 (Cat.D4) Interior view of St Helen's Church, Thorney, 1846

dragons' heads around the church which closely resemble those at Kilpeck.

D3
Dragon heads on north front of St Helen's, Thorney
Photograph by Roger Mockford Photography, Newark

Kilpeck has outstanding examples of the Herefordshire School, a regional variation of the Romanesque style which developed in the 1130s, along with others such as the schemes of decoration at Shobdon and Billesley.[10] The corbel course of grotesque heads under the bell-turret of St Helen's is continued along the north and south sides of the church, again closely resembling those on the apsidal sanctuary of Kilpeck. The side windows of St Helen's are grouped in pairs with side columns, while the sacristy window has a deep zig-zag surround very like the small belfry window at Iffley Church. The south door has further variations of mouldings, beak-head, billet, chevron and wheels; and the square-ended chancel has a triple lancet and a small round window with geometric design.

D4 (Fig.78)
Interior view of St Helen's, Thorney, 1846
Photograph by Roger Mockford Photography, Newark

The interior demonstrated Cottingham's understanding of one of the essential qualities of the Romanesque, that of mass, enlivened by linear geometric decoration. The lofty high-pitched nave roof of hammer-beam construction was praised by the *Ecclesiologist*. The chancel arch is decorated with billet and interlaced cable mouldings and has columns with scalloped capitals, like those of the twelfth-century St Michael and All Angels, Stewkley. It is restrained in elaboration, in comparison to the chancel arch of St Peter's at Tickencote which has six orders each carved with a different design: square-cut foliage with billet moulding, chevron, grotesques, embattled moulding, beak-head ornament and cable moulding. In the chancel of St Helen's, the sedilia is surmounted by an arcade of three round arches with bold roll-moulding and intersecting arches supported on eight columns, showing a variety of decorative chevron and roll-mouldings. Above each seat is a circular carved decoration of simple wheel form with fleur-de-lis, a decoration that appeared in later Norman work.

D5 (Fig.79)
Interior of St Helen's, Thorney, with details of sedilia, chancel arch and chancel, 1846
Photograph by Roger Mockford Photography, Newark

The windows of the church are surrounded by a variety

D2 (Fig.77)
St Helen's, Thorney, exterior view of west front and doorway, 1846
Photograph by Roger Mockford Photography, Newark

The west front doorway at St Helen's has pillars all differently carved with roll-moulding, cable and lattice designs, with cushion, volute and scalloped capitals. The round arch has decorations in bands of roll-moulding, beaded cable and stiff leaf foliage interspersed with human and animal faces, and the hood has a decoration of zig-zags and wheels ending in crowned heads. Above the doorway are three round-arch lancets with pillars and over them a wheel window. The wheel window is more commonly found in Romanesque churches in France but Cottingham's version echoes the one that he discovered in Temple Church, though not an exact copy, and resembles also the wheel window that he inserted in the east end of the chapel at Brougham. The west front of St Helen's has a string course of circles and chip carving that ends in grotesque, projecting dragon or crocodile heads with curled tongues. There are seventeen of these

Fig.79 (Cat.D5) Details of the chancel, St Helen's Church, Thorney, 1846

Fig.80 (Cat.D6) The Ancaster stone font, St Helen's Church, Thorney, 1846

Fig.81 (Cat.D8) Carved oak throne chair, St Helen's Church, Thorney, 1846

of Romanesque geometric mouldings, beak-head to the circular window of the chancel, lozenge, billet and interlaced cable around the narrow lancet window.

D6 (Fig.80)
Carved stone pulpit and lectern designed by L. N. Cottingham for St Helen's, Thorney, 1846
Photograph by Roger Mockford Photography, Newark

The square stone pulpit supported on a carved central shaft and four columns is of Ancaster stone, carved with scenes from the Bible; the details include heads of the twelve Disciples in tiny medallions and the symbols of the four Evangelists. The stone lectern is also of square form with stiff-leaf foliage and the font is of early Norman circular tub form with blind interlaced arches and columns, scroll foliage and a font cover of carved oak.

D7
Interior of St Helen's, Thorney, with details of encaustic tiles in nave and chancel
Photograph by Roger Mockford Photography, Newark

D8 (Fig.81)
Carved oak throne chair designed by L. N. Cottingham
for St Helen's, Thorney, 1846
Lender: The Parochial Church Council of St Helen's,
Thorney

The floor is inlaid with encaustic tiles of two patterns: an
enriched geometric design in the chancel and in the aisle
alternating plain and simple patterned tiles and pierced
cast-iron grilles for heating and ventilation. The pews are
of oak, of simple open-bench form, and the carved oak
throne chair is enlivened with beaded intersecting arches,
nail-head and blind arcading design. Cottingham allowed
the remains of the early church – two pointed arches and
pillars of a mediaeval arcade and a fifteenth-century
window surround, now overgrown with ivy – to stand in
the graveyard as a picturesque ruin. The early
Romanesque stone font, indicative of the church's
earliest building date (and possibly another reason for
Cottingham's choice of the Romanesque) was preserved
and can be seen alongside Cottingham's font, not a copy
of the early one but a bold architectural nineteenth-
century interpretation of Romanesque motifs. The
church today is still in its original state, so far
'unimproved' by later restoration, although now showing
some signs of neglect.

BIBLIOGRAPHY
Anderson, C., *Hints on Church Building or Ancient Models*,
1841
Barr, J., *Anglican Church Architecture*, London, 1842
Ecclesiologist, Vol.XXIX, 1844; Vol.IV, 1847
Fedden, R., 'Neo-Norman', *Architectural Review*,
Vol.116, Dec. 1954
Lewis, G. R., *Illustrations of Kilpeck* etc, 1842
Morris, R. K., 'The Herefordshire School: Recent
Discoveries', in F. H. Thompson ed., *Studies in Mediaeval
Sculpture*, 1983
Mowl, T., 'The Norman Revival in British Architecture,
1790-1870', PhD thesis, Oxford University, 1981,
Appendix
Nevile Family papers, Nottingham Record Office, DDN;
158-83; Ecclesiastical Papers of Rev. C. Nevile, 1839-80;
Building Accounts, 132, 1846
Sale Catalogue, Library of the late Edwin Cottingham
MRCS of Bexley, Kent containing rare and curious books
etc, etc. Messrs S. Leigh Sotheby and J. Wilkinson, 15
June 1859 and three following days

E Domestic Architecture and Design

Cottingham worked for a number of patrons throughout
his career, designing shops, offices, hotels, banks, grand
mansions for eminent patrons, schools and an estate
village. He also carried out extensions to existing houses
as the Gothic Revival gained momentum. His first major
undertaking was a development in Waterloo Bridge Road
where he established his own family home and housed his
museum.

Waterloo Bridge Road Estate, Lambeth 1824-33

Cottingham designed the Waterloo Bridge Road estate for
John Field, on a site at the corner of York Road and
Waterloo Road.[1] It is possible that John Field, one of a
growing breed of speculators, secured the services of
Cottingham through his work as surveyor to the Cooks'
Company, an appointment that placed Cottingham in the
centre of architectural activity in London, giving him
knowledge of likely architectural commissions,
competitions and the latest speculative developments,
and ensuring him a commission for John Field's Lambeth
estate. The Livery Companies of London, mostly dating
from the fourteenth and fifteenth centuries, owned
extensive estates and took part in the great expansion of
building in the Regency period. The Mercers' Company,
for instance, developed ninety acres in Stepney. The
Minutes Book of the Cooks' Company shows that
Cottingham, as surveyor and architect to the company,
designed warehousing, an estate of houses in Wood
Street, Walthamstow, and houses and commercial
premises in Oat, Staining and Lillypot Lanes in the City
of London.[2] The land in Waterloo Bridge Road for the
proposed estate was close to the river and clearly required
the services of a professional surveyor and architect. John
Field himself noted in a letter: 'Cottingham had many
difficulties to contend with in the foundations.'[3] There is
no documentation remaining, but it is likely that
Cottingham employed James Browne of College Street
and Joseph Orlibar Cottingham, a distant cousin of his
father's, to undertake the building works: they both
worked to his specifications for the Cooks' Company at
this date and for the restoration of Rochester Cathedral
in 1826.[4]

Plans and drawings dating from 1826 exist for
numbers 80 to 86 Waterloo Bridge Road, for the houses
on the return front in Boyce Street, formerly Anne
Street, and at the south end of Bazing Place, off Waterloo
Bridge Road.[5] The influence of Cottingham's classical
training is evident in the handling of the proportions and
detail of his restrained façades. Most late eighteenth-
century terraces from Adam's Adelphi scheme of 1771
onwards, and the Regency terrace façades of Nash, were
based on the divisions and proportions of the classical
column. The ground floor (as the base), partly rusticated
as in Cottingham's Duke of York Hotel, the first and
second storeys representing the column, and the
decorative part of the order, the frieze, formed by the
cornice and blocking course of attic storey. The divisions
are clearly defined and the whole is of regular and
symmetrical arrangement.

E1 (Fig.82)
L. N. Cottingham, elevations for numbers 80-86 Waterloo
Bridge Road, and the Duke of York Hotel, 1826
Line and wash $12\frac{1}{2} \times 19$ in (31.75×48.25 cm)
British Museum, Crace Views, XXX5, No.65

Cottingham's drawings for numbers 80-86, originally
numbered 40-43, show neo-classical designs with smooth
walls and windows cut in sharply, reflecting the
fashionable neo-classicism of Nash and also the Laugier-
inspired classicism of Soane. Cottingham knew Soane
and at this date he lived at 66 Great Queen Street, close
to Soane's house museum at Lincoln's Inn Fields. Some
details in Cottingham's classical terraces relate closely to
Soane's decoration such as the long frieze with triglyphs
and the use of indented panels. Numbers 80-86 formed
an impressive terrace in stock brick, composed of four
storeys above pavement level with recessed round arched
windows at the first floor and gauged flat arches and
panelled sills to the windows of the upper floors. Number
80 was the York Hotel and 82-86 had shop fronts. The
divisions between the units were clearly expressed in the
ground-floor detailing and in the indented vertical stress;
the whole composition was strongly united at second-
floor level by a boldly articulated cornice with triglyphs
and again with a parapet surmounted by short pedestals
and acroteria at the ends and over the party walls. The
York Hotel had simple pilaster treatment and surround to
the large shallow-arched windows of the ground floor and
a bold pediment with cornice and parapet at roof level,
which served to stress the end of the block and mark the
return on Boyce Street. Number 86 was Cottingham's
own house, again incorporating a shop front but differing
from numbers 82 and 84 in its treatment of the pilasters
and fascia. Cottingham planned Number 86 with special
provision for his library and museum collection. In his

82

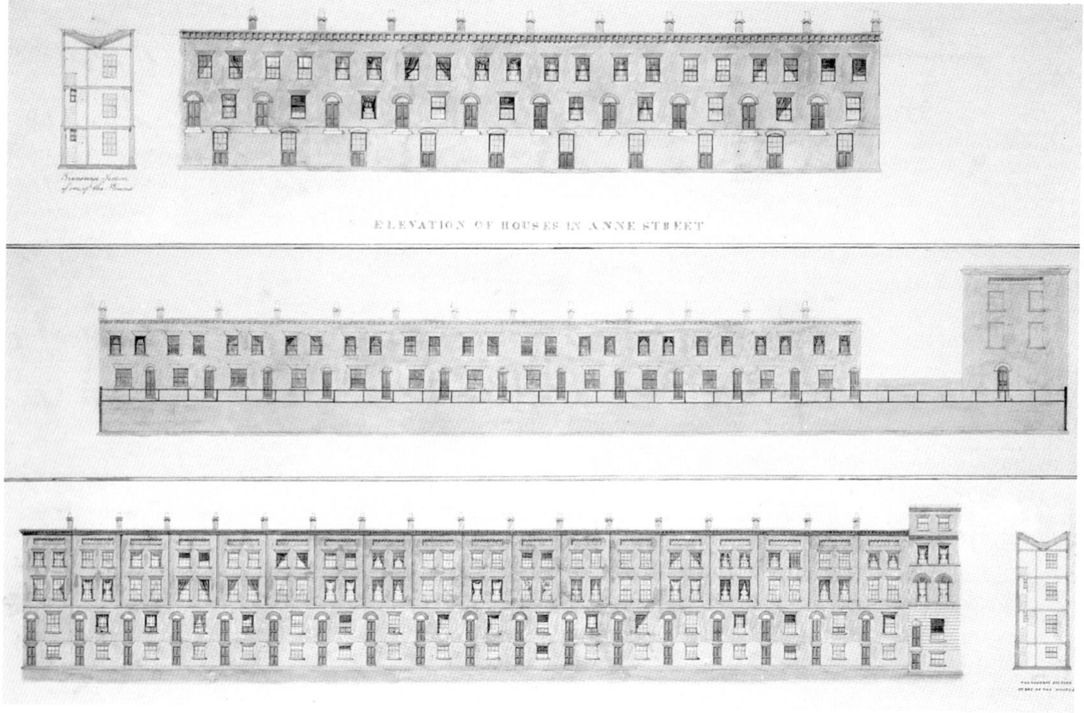

83

Fig.82 (Cat.E1) Elevations for numbers 80-86 Waterloo Bridge Road, and the Duke of York Hotel, 1826
Line and wash 12½×19 in (31.75×48.25 cm)

Fig.83 (Cat.E2) Elevations and plans for Anne Street and Bazing Place, Waterloo Bridge Road, 1826
Line and wash 6×25 in (15.25×63.5 cm)

Plans etc of Henry VII's Chapel of 1822 he intimated that he gave lessons in architecture, using his collection of casts and models, and in 1828 he moved from Great Queen Street to the newly completed Waterloo Bridge Road house with his growing collection of mediaeval antiquities. Cottingham transformed the door of Number 86 on the Boyce Street return by enriching the round arch with Norman zig-zag moulding, possibly assembled from fragments in his collection, and a stone-carved heraldic crest above the arch. This was the only reference on the exterior of the property to the amazing collection of antiquities within, whereas Soane decorated the front of his house museum with classical statues and Gothic brackets from Westminster Hall. Drawings made prior to the demolition of Waterloo Bridge Road in 1951 showed the plaster ceilings to the ground-floor shop at Number 86, with classical decorations of scrolls, fruiting vines and anthemion and the first-floor doors with classical entablatures, ogee mouldings and decorated frieze. Other drawings showed the remaining fittings from Cottingham's museum: Gothic arch doorways, a three-light pointed window with quatrefoils and a richly carved fireplace.[6] Nockalls bought back some lots at the sale of his father's collection which he clearly left *in situ* when he moved in 1852 to his new address at 6 Argyle Place.[7]

E2 (Fig.83)

L. N. Cottingham, elevations and plans for Anne Street and the south end of Bazing Place, Waterloo Bridge Road, 1826
Line and wash 6×25 in (15.25×63.5 cm)
British Museum, Crace Views, xxx5 No.65

Cottingham's drawings, 'View of South End of Bazing Place' showed a terrace of nineteen three-storeyed dwellings reflecting the normal planning for the 1820s, with entrance door and living room at ground level, basement kitchen with entrance, living rooms at first-floor level and bedrooms on the second storey. No ground plans are given but the exterior reflected the changed planning from the eighteenth-century terrace plan of entry direct to the ground-floor living rooms, to the nineteenth-century mode of offset door giving access to a hallway and staircase. Again the end of the terrace was strongly terminated by a four-storey block with attic storey to give emphasis. Architectural details included regular twelve-pane sash windows symmetrically arranged beneath a cornice and an indented panel ornamented with triglyphs. The drawing 'Elevation of Houses in Anne Street' showed a row of simple two-storey dwellings with a large basement window, again with twelve-pane sash windows to the ground and upper storey, bold dentil cornice uniting the design, and chimney stacks with incised Soanean neo-classical ornament.

A testimonial written by John Field in 1832 to the Committee of the Fishmongers' Hall competition stressed the quality of Cottingham's work:

'I beg to state that Mr Cottingham has been employed by me these eight or nine years in laying out an extensive estate and that £80,000 to £90,000 have been expended in buildings thereon under his sole direction and superintendance to my entire satisfaction. He had many difficulties to contend with in the foundations but I can declare with much pleasure that the buildings have not in any instance cracked or given way, but on the contrary are greatly admired both for the design and the substantial manner in which they are constructed. From Mr Cottingham's energy, integrity and ability I have never had cause to regret placing my estate in his hands'.[8]

At the time of his neo-classical plans for the Waterloo Bridge Road estate and his undertakings at Rochester Cathedral, Cottingham was also engaged on drawings and plans for the mansion, Snelston Hall, commissioned by John Harrison, a wealthy Derby lawyer and landowner, and a member of the Society of the Inner Temple, Lincoln's Inn Fields, London.

BIBLIOGRAPHY
Cooks' Company *Minutes Book*, July 1822-5 September 1834, Guildhall Library, Ref MS 3/11/4/5
Cottingham, L.N., *Letters to Fishmongers' Court*, 1832, Guildhall Library, Ref. 516/SAL
Crace Views, XXX5, No.65, Dept of Prints and Drawings, British Museum, London
Dyos, J.H., 'The Speculative Builders and Developers of Victorian London', *Victorian Studies*, Summer 1968
Kaufman, E.N., *The Life and Work of E.B. Lamb 1805-69*, PhD Thesis, Yale University, 1984
Rochester Cathedral Archive, *Dean Stevens's Notebook*, 1825
Survey of London, Vol.23, South Bank, St Mary's Lambeth, LCC, 1951

Snelston Hall and estate village, Snelston, Derbyshire 1822-30

Cottingham began making drawings in 1822 for John Harrison's mansion at Snelston, a small hamlet three miles south-west of Ashbourne, recorded in the *Domesday Book* as Snellestune. The inheritance of the manor passed to John Harrison's son in 1871, then to his grandson Henry Stanton who took up residence in 1906. The Stanton family continues to live at Snelston holding a considerably reduced manor. Snelston Hall was demolished in 1951 despite spot-listing and at that time the stable block was renovated and altered to become the present Snelston Hall.

A fairly comprehensive reconstruction of the Hall and its interiors can be derived from a number of sources of archive material: drawings, watercolours and plans for Snelston in the Derbyshire Record Office, the Stanton family's collection of papers and drawings, drawings and photographs in the National Monuments Record, and eleven sheets of drawings for furniture designs gifted to the V&A by the late Lt Col J.R.G. Stanton.

E3 (Fig.84)
L.N. Cottingham, 'South Elevation of Snelston Hall, the Seat of John Harrison Esq', 18 June 1822
Line and wash $8\frac{1}{4} \times 12\frac{1}{2}$ in (21 × 31.75 cm)
Derbyshire Record Office, Matlock: gift of Lt Col J.R.G. Stanton Ref 157/3021-4095
Photograph by Jeremy Hardman-Jones

John Harrison first commissioned Cottingham to build a large mansion around the upper Hall, rebuilt in classical style after a fire in the eighteenth century. This was to form the west wing of the intended new Hall.

No personal correspondence between Harrison and Cottingham exists to explain Cottingham's commission but it seems likely that Harrison, as a lawyer of the Inner Temple, might have known Cottingham and his collection of mediaeval antiquities close by in Great Queen Street, or would have met him through Cottingham's friends William Twopenny and William Burge, both members of the Inner Temple. Another possible link is through Edward Blore, an antiquary and architect friend of Cottingham. Blore, a descendant of an old Ashbourne family, was born in Derby in 1787. His father, a lawyer, had been articled to Edward Evans of Derby, a relative of Harrison's wife, Elizabeth.[9] Blore may have recommended Cottingham to the Harrisons. On the evidence of the designs Blore prepared for Lambeth Palace in 1829, it is possible to infer that he knew Cottingham's drawings for Snelston of 1826, as these are remarkably similar.[10]

Cottingham's first series of drawings for Snelston of 1822-6 were classical. The earliest, dated 18 June 1822, 'South elevation of Snelston Hall', appeared to be intended as an extension to the existing classical house with a pedimented portico of stark simplicity supported by coupled Greek Ionic columns, twelve-pane sash windows to the three bays and round arch windows, a design reflecting the prevailing Greek Revival of the early 1820s, although the roof with its rectangular indented chimney stacks perhaps related to the remains of the existing building.

E4
L.N. Cottingham, 'Elevation of West Front to Snelston Hall, Derbyshire the Seat of John Harrison Esq', January 1826

Fig.84 (Cat.E3) 'South elevation of Snelston Hall etc', 1822
Line and wash $8\frac{1}{4} \times 12\frac{1}{2}$ in (21 × 31.75 cm)

Line drawing 20 × 28 in (50.5 × 71 cm)
Derbyshire Record Office

By contrast, this elevation for the 'West front of Snelston' dated January 1826, showed a neo-classical façade. It was perhaps intended as a garden front, or possibly designed as an orangery, for the ground floor was entirely glazed with tall sixteen-paned windows. These designs show Cottingham using classical sources, the simplicity of Greek and the variety of Roman, and reinterpreting them in his own way.

In May 1826, Cottingham was proposing Gothic designs. Here was his opportunity to design a Gothic Revival mansion for his patron. He must have persuaded Harrison that Gothic would answer his aspirations as the new inheritor of an ancient manor and a descendant of distant aristocracy by symbolising his position in society as the landed gentry. It was a style that had the power to evoke a period and yet could be adapted to suit modern requirements, as Cottingham had pointed out in his designs for a Gothic mansion in 1822.

The fine watercolour elevation of February 1826 and the line drawings of May 1826 showed designs for a house of modest size in comparison to the twelve buttressed bays and massive cloistered entrance of Cottingham's Gothic mansion designs.

E5 (Fig.85; Colour Plate 4)
L.N. Cottingham, 'Gothic Elevation for Snelston Hall', February 1826
Watercolour $18\frac{3}{4} \times 27\frac{1}{2}$ in (47.5 × 70 cm)
Derbyshire Record Office

Cottingham's Snelston Hall design was battlemented with square-paned windows under hood moulds. It had stair turrets and angled buttresses to the three-storey projecting entrance porch. The building was placed in a Reptonian setting with richly wooded background, with the addition of a Gothic water fountain and lunetted

Fig.85 (Cat.E5) 'Gothic Elevation for Snelston Hall', 1826
Watercolour 18¾×27½in (47.5×70cm)

Fig.86 (Cat.E6) 'Proposed East Elevation of Snelston Hall',
1826
Line drawing 12¾×18in (32.5×45.5cm)

entrance gate to impart a sense of age to the design. The line drawings of May gave further views of the various elevations.

E6 (Fig.86)
L. N. Cottingham, 'Proposed East Elevation of Snelston Hall', May 1826.
Line drawing 12¾×18in (32.5×45.5cm)
Signed
Derbyshire Record Office
Photograph by Jeremy Hardman-Jones

The east elevation for Snelston was of asymmetrical arrangement with asymmetrical twin-turreted entrance porch, an oriel window above a four-centred arch doorway, square-headed square-paned windows with hood moulds, battlements to the octagonal end turrets and roof, and a lower two-storey extension with battlements and pointed lights with mullions and square hood moulds. The battlements and window features were very like those at nearby Haddon Hall and exactly like those of the late fourteenth-century Hever Castle in Kent that Cottingham knew well.

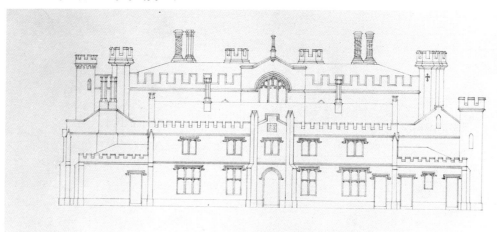

Fig.87 (Cat.E7) 'Proposal for Elevation of the North Front of Snelston Hall etc', 1826
Line drawing 13¼×18in (33.5×45.5cm)

E7 (Fig.87)
L. N. Cottingham,' Proposal for Elevation of the North Front of Snelston Hall as seen from the Shrubberies', May 1826
Line drawing 13¼×18in (33.5×45.5cm)
Signed
Derbyshire Record Office
Photograph by Jeremy Hardman-Jones

The proposed north front shows the lower domestic range of buildings with battlements, an entrance porch with angled buttresses and, beyond, the main block of the house with octagonal turrets, a round tower, a variety of Tudor chimneys and a great hall window of traceried lights.

Fig.88 (Cat.E8) 'Elevation of the West Front of Snelston Hall', 1826
Line drawing 13×18in (33×45.5cm)

E8 (Fig.88)

L. N. Cottingham, 'Elevation of the West Front of
Snelston Hall', May 1826
Line drawing 13×18 in (33×45.5 cm)
Signed
Derbyshire Record Office
Photograph by Jeremy Hardman-Jones

The west front again repeated all these elements but with
battlemented square-pane bay window projections and
five octagonal turrets. The style was reminiscent of the
late fourteenth-century Penshurst Place or Hever in
Kent, but instead of narrow traceried windows,
Cottingham designed large square-paned windows
answering his concerns for 'modern convenience'.

More Gothic designs followed and in January 1827 a
southern view of Snelston was made, inscribed 'without a
Bell Turret'.

E9 (Fig.89)

L. N. Cottingham, 'South-East View of Snelston Hall,
(without the Bell Turret), the Seat of John Harrison,
Esq', January 1827
Line and wash 14×20½ in (35.5×51 cm)
Signed
Derbyshire Record Office
Photograph by Jeremy Hardman-Jones

Fig.89 (Cat.E9) 'South-East View of Snelston Hall (without
the Bell Turret) etc', 1827
Line and wash 14×20½ in (35.5×51 cm)

This elevation showed a bold, confident, fully Gothic
design, a highly irregular mass with strong perpendicular
emphasis in repeating stepped buttresses with tall
crocketed pinnacles, some square-headed and some two-
light pointed windows with mullions, and a two-storey
entrance porch with oriel windows surmounted by
pepperpot turrets, like those at West Stow Hall in
Cottingham's native Suffolk. This design also showed an
octagonal battlemented tower with narrow windows and
beyond, a chapel or great hall with many buttresses, and
great pointed traceried windows.

E10 (Fig.90; Colour Plate 5)

L. N. Cottingham, 'Entrance Front of Snelston Hall, the
Seat of John Harrison Esq', July 1827
Watercolour 19×27½ in (48.25×70 cm)
Signed
Derbyshire Record Office

This watercolour now related closely to the final design as
built with stepped buttresses, crocketed pinnacles, a
flèche, and transomed and mullioned windows of two
lights with pointed heads under square hood moulds but
no crenellations.

E11 (Fig.91)

L. N. Cottingham, 'South-East View of Snelston Hall,
the Seat of John Harrison Esq', dated October (possibly
1827)
Line and wash 14×20½ in (35.5×52 cm)

Fig.90 (Cat.E10) 'Entrance Front of Snelston Hall etc', 1827
Watercolour 19×27½ in (48.25×70 cm)

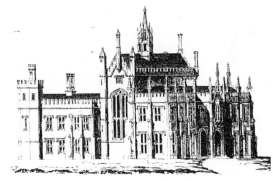

Fig.91 (Cat.E11) 'South-East View of Snelston Hall etc',
c.1827
Line and wash 14×20½ in (35.5×52 cm)

Signed
Derbyshire Record Office

The east view of Snelston (dated October, possibly 1827),
drawn after the foundations were laid, shows the final
version with the main blocks of the house clearly defined,
the east section containing the drawing room, dining
room and the entrance, the lofty central section with the
two-storey great hall and staircase behind a massive
traceried window, and the west wing, formerly the earlier
part of the house, now refaced in keeping with the rest of
the Hall. Two undated ground plans of the ground floor
and the first floor of the Hall show a compact plan, with
the entrance hall leading to a groined vestibule and great
staircase, and ranged around it the main rooms, library,
breakfast room, drawing room. However, a watercolour
(dated May 1828) of the landscape design for Snelston

Hall indicates the final plan of the house as more
irregular, with the main reception rooms on either side of
the great hall and staircase forming a T-shaped inner
space, and more clearly separated from the service wing
which formed an irregular block beyond. Possibly these
changes reflected Harrison's need for grandeur in the
public rooms and the nineteenth-century planning
obsession with having services at a great distance from
the living rooms. The new plan also indicated
development from Cottingham's first 'picturesque'
Gothic drawings of 1826 to a design of an
archaeologically correct rendering of fourteenth-century
Gothic, while answering his attempts to re-create, in his
own words, the 'irregularity, variety and grandeur' of the
mediaeval plans and the appearance of a building having
developed and grown as the need arose.[11]

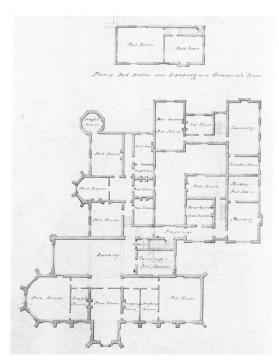

Fig.92 (Cat.E12) 'Chamber Plan of Snelston Hall', 1828
Line drawing 13 × 16½ in (33 × 42 cm)

Fig.93 (Cat.E13) East front of Snelston Hall, *c*.1925, prior to
its demolition in 1952

E12 (Fig.92)
L. N. Cottingham, 'Chamber Plan of Snelston Hall', 1828
(as built)
Line drawing 13 × 16½ in (33 × 42 cm)
National Monuments Record, © RCHME

That conclusion is confirmed by a plan of the first-floor
arrangements, showing three main bedrooms and their
dressing rooms on the east wing, governess's bedroom
and water closets and back staircase off the landing, six
more bedrooms in the west wing and a passage to the
nursery, housekeeper's and servants' rooms in the north
wing. Cottingham, ever mindful of utility and
convenience and interested in advances in technology,
had included water closets and bathrooms in his Gothic
mansion plans even on the ground floor, not an altogether
universal feature of country houses in the early decades
of the nineteenth century.[12] These drawings formed the
ultimate design and plan for the Hall and the foundation
stone was laid by John Harrison junior, then aged eight,
on 11 June 1827.

Snelston Hall was built of red Keuper sandstone on
the site of the ancient upper Hall. Cottingham had
written of the qualities of mediaeval domestic
architecture, its 'rich and splendid assemblage of turrets,
battlements and pinnacles' and wrote, too, of 'the rise and

fall, advance and recess', a movement and variety in the
architecture which 'gave great beauty and grandeur by
powerful contrast without encroaching on utility and
convenience'.[13]

Cottingham, in his work at Snelston and Brougham,
was attempting to revive the true Mediaeval, based on
archaeological study, seeing the assertion of social
position and the revival of feudal values as appropriate to
English architecture. By contrast, Pugin, in his writings,
saw the revival of the Gothic as a moral issue and linked
the architecture, the worth of the architect and the
architect's contribution to society to the idealised
religious and moral values of the mediaeval period.

For his Snelston Hall, Cottingham looked to the
'Third Class' of pointed architecture or the
Perpendicular which he dated from the beginning of the
reign of Richard II in 1377 until the end of Henry VII's
reign in 1509. He extended a comprehensive unity of
design to the whole estate, including the offices, lodges,
farm buildings and estate cottages.

E13 (Fig.93)
Photograph of the East front of Snelston Hall, *c*.1925
prior to its demolition in 1952
Stanton family collection

The eastern front, 100 feet long, was composed of eight
regular bays divided by stepped buttresses terminating in
bold crocketed pinnacles with battlemented parapets.
Cottingham had described the diagonally presented
buttresses which are a feature of Perpendicular Gothic
and these he used for the two-storey battlemented and
gabled, off-centre entrance porch with its large mullioned
and transomed traceried side windows, battlemented
oriel, and four-centred arched entrance with square hood
moulds.

E14 (Fig.94)
Detail of the entrance porch, Snelston Hall, *c*.1925
Stanton family collection

In his discussion of the transition from fortified
mediaeval castles, Cottingham had explained how the
narrow windows and massive walls, 'little suited to
comfort and convenience', gave way to 'windows made
wider and the arches flattened for lightness'. At Snelston
he incorporated many windows based on those of Crosby
Hall, 'an elegant example', with the principal mullion
running 'quite up to the mouldings of the arched heads'
under the square heads used in this period. The east
front of Snelston ended in a large tripartite bay, lighting
the drawing room on the ground floor, and on the south

Fig.94 (Cat.E14) Detail of the entrance porch, Snelston Hall, *c.*1925

porch to form the T-shape, expressive of the interior volume of space. This space formed a staircase area lit by the great window and a central two-storeyed hall rising to a lofty panelled ceiling hung with knopped pendants. At Snelston, Cottingham took Crosby as his source for the archaeologically correct designs for the ceilings with their 'pendant drops'. The antiquarian aspect of Snelston was appreciated by Burke, writing in *Visitations* (1854):

'The interior fully answers to the expectations raised by the first view of this stately edifice ... The principal rooms are fitted up with oaken furniture, carved and massive, according to the ancient fashion, which is so rigidly adhered to, even in the minutest details, as to completely exclude any idea of a modern mansion.'

Snelston was a house of fairly modest size in comparison to Toddington, for example. Snelston had two main reception rooms leading from the great hall where Cottingham used the space to create a sense of grandeur accentuated through the use of slender cluster columns of diamond form and wide obtuse-pointed Gothic arches with foliage in the spandrels formed under the square heads, 'one of the earliest specimens is the entrance porch to Westminster Hall, built at the time of Richard II'.[14] The drawing room, 26 ft by 36 ft, entered from the north, had a carved marble fireplace and overmantel enriched with elaborate ogee-pointed ornament derived from the fifteenth-century Gothic of Henry VII's Chapel (Fig.97), and a plasterwork ceiling based on the council chamber at Crosby Hall. Cottingham used dark oak linenfold panelling in the entrance hall, and throughout the house he used genuine pieces of old timber and panelling for fittings and furniture. The double folding doors, for example, in the hallway were made up of carved oak panels from the time of Henry VII, possibly supplied from Cottingham's own collection.

Continuing his creation of an antiquarian interior derived from 'the best example', Cottingham decorated the hall with six plaster busts of kings and queens of England on brackets, fourteen heraldic shields from the originals in the north and south aisles of Westminster Abbey, and three groups of figures, the coronation of Henry V in England and in France, and Edward the Black Prince crossing the Channel, all cast from the originals in Westminster. From the hall, the grand staircase with carved oak open Gothic tracery and richly carved newels with poppy-head finials, led up to the high south window bordered by stained glass and bearing the monogram and coat-of-arms of John and Elizabeth Harrison (Fig.98). Cottingham's staircase divided into two flights leading into the music gallery, decorated with five plaster figures of saints in niches (Fig.99), the figures cast from the triforium stage of Henry VII's Chapel, richly coloured

front the two-storeyed hall and staircase were lit by a great traceried south window, the focal point of the composition, echoing his Westminster Hall window which he cited as 'the finest of its period'. Beyond was the faceted bay of the library and on the south-east corner a massive four-storeyed battlemented tower surmounted by a small octagonal turret (Figs 95, 96).

Interiors of Snelston Hall

The interior plan of the house, with its emphasis on the ceremonial aspects of circulation, was articulated on the exterior and through the structure of the house. The pitched roof behind the battlemented gable joined another pitched roof running back from the entrance

Fig.95 (see Cat.E14) Snelston Hall from the west, before demolition in 1952

Fig.96 (see Cat.E14) Snelston Hall from the north-east, and landscape gardens, before demolition in 1952

Fig.99 Niches based on Henry VII's Chapel, Snelston Hall, 1952

Fig.97 Gothic overmantel and fireplace, Snelston Hall, 1952   **Fig.98** The staircase, Snelston Hall, 1952

and gilt, and furnished with finely carved oak choir-stalls based on those in Lichfield Cathedral and illustrated in an undated watercolour by Cottingham[15]. Wide flattened arches with slender columns separated the gallery and the corridor leading to the main bedrooms, the Castle Bedroom, Damask, Chippendale and Elizabethan Bedrooms. The dining room, with square panelled plaster ceilings and a finely carved marble fireplace, was furnished with sideboards made to Cottingham's designs from panels believed to have come from Nonsuch Palace[16]. One of the sideboards can just be seen in a photograph of the dining room taken in 1927. The breakfast room and library, part of the original building, formed a double room 'divided by needlework curtains' and were redecorated and furnished to Cottingham's designs with carved oak bookcases and cupboards following the late Gothic designs of the rest of the house and surmounted by busts of famous writers. The octagonal reading room was 'curiously panelled in carton pierre', the designs taken from the Henry VIII panels in the dining room and drawing room, with inset portraits on panel of Tudor kings, reputedly by Holbein, which 'came from an old royal palace in Suffolk'[17]. Much of the furniture and joinery for Snelston Hall was carried out to Cottingham's designs by Adam Bede, the original of George Eliot's *Adam Bede*, who lived and worked nearby in Norbury Parish[18].

Fig.100 (see Cat.E16) Design for a drawing room for
Snelston Hall, 1842–3
Pencil, pen and ink 13 × 19 in (33 × 48 cm)

Furniture designs for Snelston Hall

Cottingham continued to design furniture for John Harrison over the years, for some of his existing drawings for furniture are dated 1842 and 1843.

E15
L. N. Cottingham, line drawing of interior of drawing room, undated
13 × 19 in (33 × 48.25 cm)
Derbyshire Record Office

Cottingham assembled his drawing room furniture designs in one large drawing of the interior which shows the carved fireplace and Crosby Hall ceiling. The principal piece was a massive carved oak display cabinet with tripartite top, richly carved with caryatids and scrolling foliage and grotesque masks, flanked by cross-framed chairs and a pair of carved cabinets on stands pierced with Gothic tracery.

Also included was a large upholstered sofa, the carved frame pierced with quatrefoil decoration and surmounted by a large finial; a Gothic side chair; a 'Divan Couch for Angle of the Room' again pierced with quatrefoil ornament and with barley twist legs; an octagonal table with its octagonal base echoing the form of an early fifteenth-century Gothic chalice; a round stool; a throne-like cross-framed chair; a sofa table; and a 'conversational' sofa composed of pierced Gothic roundels.

Individual drawings for these pieces of furniture are in the V&A Museum and are listed here.

E16 (Figs 100, 101, 102, 103)
L. N. Cottingham, furniture designs for Snelston Hall, 1842-9, Gift of Lt Col J. P. Stanton, 1951, to the Victoria and Albert Museum.
1. The drawing room, Snelston, 1842-3.
Pencil, pen and ink 13 × 19 in (33 × 48 cm).
2. Design and plan for an octagonal table in the Gothic style, c.1842. Signed 'L. N. Cottingham, Architect'. Inscribed with scale and 'Design for Table, Temp. Henry VII, and Plan'.
28 × 20 in (71 × 51 cm).
3. Designs (four on one sheet) for three chairs and a stool for Snelston Hall. Signed 'L. N. Cottingham, Architect, 1842'. Inscribed with scale and 'Designs for Furniture, temp. Henry VII'.
Pen, ink and wash 17 × 19 in (43 × 48 cm).
4. Designs for a couch in the Gothic style for Snelston Hall, inscribed 'Conversational Sofa'. Signed and dated 1842.
Pen, ink and watercolour 15½ × 19½ in (39.5 × 49.5 cm).
5. Design for a Gothic cabinet for Snelston Hall. Signed and dated 1843. Inscribed 'Drawing room Cabinet'.

Pen, ink and watercolour 13¾ × 20 in (35 × 51 cm)
6. Design for a sofa for Snelston Hall. Signed 'L. N. Cottingham, 1843'. Inscribed 'Drawing room sofa'.
Pen, ink and watercolour 13¾ × 20 in (35 × 51 cm).
7. Design for a couch for Snelston Hall, c.1842. Signed 'L. N. Cottingham'. Inscribed with scale and 'Divan Couch for Angle of a Room'.
Pen, ink and watercolour 13½ × 20 in (34 × 51 cm).
8. Design for a Gothic table for Snelston Hall, c.1842. Signed and inscribed 'Sofa Table'.
Pen, ink and watercolour 14 × 20 in (35.5 × 51 cm).
9. Designs (two on one sheet) for hanging shelves with plan and scale in feet, and for a pole screen with plan and section for Snelston Hall.
Pen, ink and watercolour 19¼ × 26¼ in (49 × 66.5 cm)
10. Designs for the sideboard and chairs for the dining room, Snelston Hall, with the wall and ceiling mouldings indicated. Signed 'L. N. Cottingham, Architect'. Inscribed 'Sideboard and Chairs for the Dining room, Snelston Hall, the Seat of John Harrison Esq'.
Pen and ink 12¼ × 18½ in (31 × 47 cm)
11. Designs for wall seats in the form of misericord stalls for the music gallery. Inscribed in pencil 'There are 3 of these stalls 10' each in length, the Outside Ends are with columns and capitals. The seats all turn up on hinges and have different carved objects underneath', and in a later hand, 'Snelston Hall Stalls in the Music Gallery'.
Pen, ink and wash 11 × 19¼ in (28 × 49 cm)

E17 (Fig.104)
L. N. Cottingham, 'Design for a Gothic armoire for the Great Drawing Room of Snelston Hall, the Seat of John Harrison Esq', c.1842, with front and side elevations and plan
Pen, ink and watercolour 14 × 20 in (35.5 × 51 cm)
Signed
Derbyshire Record Office
Photograph by Jeremy Hardman-Jones

This design was clearly intended to display objects from Harrison's collection of mediaeval antiquities: in his drawing Cottingham included Gothic reliquaries, chalices, salvers, goblets, carved caskets, candlesticks and sculpture. Harrison was a discriminating collector of the Mediaeval and of later periods: in Cottingham's museum was a pair of 'very finely modelled dragons after an original pair in bronze by Cellini in the possession of J. Harrison Esq, of Snelston Hall'.

E18 (Fig.105)
Oak hall chair with Harrison family crest, c.1840s, possibly designed by L. N. Cottingham
Lender: Mr John Myles
Photograph by Rupert Drummond-Hoy

101

102

103

Fig.101 (see Cat.E16) Design for 'Drawing Room Sofa' for Snelston Hall, 1843
Pen, ink and watercolour 13¾ × 20 in (35 × 51 cm)
Fig.102 (see Cat.E16) Design for 'Divan Couch for Angle of a Room' for Snelston Hall, 1842
Pen, ink and watercolour 13½ × 20 in (34 × 51 cm)
Fig.103 (see Cat.E16) Design for 'Drawing Room Cabinet' for Snelston Hall, 1843
Pen, ink and watercolour 13¾ × 20 in (35 × 51 cm)

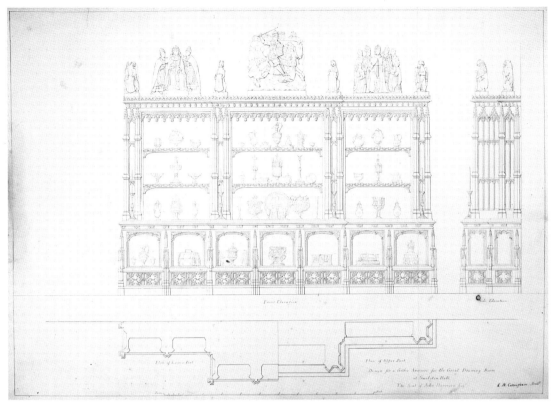

Fig.104 (Cat.E17) 'Design for a Gothic armoire etc' for Snelston Hall, *c.*1842
Pen, ink and watercolour 14×20 in (35.5×51 cm)

Fig.105 (Cat.E18) Oak hall chair with Harrison family crest, *c.*1840s

This is one of the set of nine chairs that came to light in 1984 and started my quest for Cottingham. The crest was the early crest used by the family without authority, of azure three demi-lions or and a canton argent; crest a demi-lion or supporting a chaplet of roses vert. The grant of arms to John Harrison was made by the College of Arms in 1853: the hall chairs were therefore made prior to this date. They are not illustrated in Cottingham's surviving drawings of furniture, but are possibly to his design and may have been made by Adam Bede in a simple solid form of Gothic.

E19

Oak library steps of Gothic design, *c.*1830, possibly designed by L. N. Cottingham
Lender: Mrs J. R. G. Stanton of Snelston Hall

The library steps are in the same category as the hall chairs and were possibly made by Adam Bede to Cottingham's designs.

Cottingham's designs for landscape and farm buildings at Snelston Hall

E20 (Fig.106)

L. N. Cottingham, plan of Snelston Hall and landscape gardens, May 1828
Pen, ink and watercolour $49\frac{3}{4} \times 28\frac{3}{4}$ in (126×73 cm)
Inscribed 'Plan of the Terrace Flower Garden, Snelston Hall'
National Monuments Record (51/114), © RCHME

At Snelston, Cottingham also designed the landscaped setting of the Hall. To the south, a series of stepped terraces led to a massive retaining wall behind which he planned a 'Terrace Flower Garden' shown in his plan, with serpentine paths, choice evergreen trees such as *Yucca gloriosa* and cedars of Lebanon, roses, irregular flower beds leading down to the lake, an aquarium and a Gothic seat. Cottingham was well acquainted with Humphrey Repton's *Observations on the Theory and Practice of Landscape Gardening* (1803), and his *Fragments on the Theory and Practice of Landscape Gardening* (1816). The influence of Repton's theories is evident in these garden designs, and in Cottingham's finished watercolour of Snelston Hall of February 1926. It is clear that Cottingham had looked at Repton's designs for Ashridge, prepared in 1811, and in particular at the fountain or stone conduit in an enclosure of rich masonry which appears in *Fragments*, with a figure and tubs of flowering shrubs. Repton had planned a 'Monk's Garden' but in his plan Cottingham avoided anachronism, demonstrating an awareness of the irrelevance to his patron of a monk's garden, and the planned feature was denominated an aquarium. The figure leaning on the side of the fountain is presumably looking at the fish. Cottingham also included pots of flowers, irregular flower beds shaped like those in Repton's 'rosarium', a drive sweeping up to the entrance porch, and in the foreground cattle grazing close to a low garden wall: elements frequently shown in Repton's designs such as his drawings for Sheringham and Ashton Court.

E21 (Fig.107)

L. N. Cottingham, Gothic garden seat design, signed, and inscribed 'A Gothic Seat Designed for J. Harrison Esq of Snelston Hall, Derbyshire, 1839'
Pen, ink and wash $21\frac{1}{2} \times 13\frac{1}{2}$ in (54.5×34.5 cm)
Derbyshire Record Office
Photograph by Jeremy Hardman-Jones

Cottingham designed garden furniture for Snelston Hall including this hexagonal Gothic garden seat for location under a tree and and an octagonal summerhouse with ogival arched window frames and blind arcaded panels below: the garden seat features in Cottingham's landscape plan.

Fig.106 (Cat.E20) Plan of Snelston Hall and landscape gardens, 1828
Pen, ink and watercolour $49\frac{3}{4} \times 28\frac{3}{4}$ in (126×73 cm)

Cottingham designed the outbuildings, stables and other offices; of these one drawing remains.

E22 (Fig.108)
L. N. Cottingham, 'Design for Pineries and Pine Pits, Gardener's House and sheds for Snelston Hall', 1826
Pen, ink and watercolour $20\frac{1}{2} \times 32$ in (52×81.5 cm)
Signed 'L. N. Cottingham', and giving elevations and plans
Derbyshire Record Office
Photograph by Jeremy Hardman-Jones

The elevation and plans are for 'Gardeners' houses, 'Forcing Houses, Fruit Room, Seed Houses, Kitchen and Parlour', with plans for the supply of water pipes, drainage and heating for growing pineapples and for the vine houses. There are no Gothic embellishments, and the designs are pared down to the essentials of practicality, function and purpose. The existing farm buildings were designed by Cottingham, with Gothic elements in the pointed-arch stable doors and the traceried crew-yard gates (Fig.109. Photograph by Jeremy Hardman-Jones).

When Henry Stanton inherited Snelston Hall in 1906, he commissioned the architect Philip Lockwood to add a

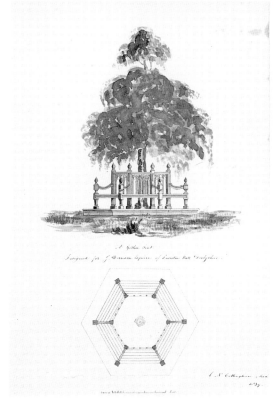

Fig.107 (Cat.E21) Gothic garden seat design, Snelston Hall, 1839
Pen, ink and wash $21\frac{1}{2} \times 13\frac{1}{2}$ in (54.5×34.5 cm)

storey to the old wing of the upper Hall, to redecorate much of the house and to design a stone fireplace for the great hall adorned with the Stanton coat-of-arms and motto.

Cottingham's Snelston Hall was much admired. A view of the house by antiquarian topographer Frederick Nash (1782-1856) was shown at the Watercolour Society in 1829, and in 1854 Burke described Snelston as 'a splendid mansion, modern as to the date of its construction but so closely imitating the character of olden times that it wants nothing but the mantling ivy about its walls and the mellowing tints of age to make it pass for works of other days'.

E23
Frederick Nash, Snelston Hall, c.1830.
Oil on canvas 42×36 in (106.5×91.5 cm)
Lender: Mrs J. R. G. Stanton, Snelston Hall
Photograph by Jeremy Hardman-Jones

E24 (Fig.110)
Frederick Nash, Snelston Hall and its surroundings, c.1829 (exhibited at the Royal Academy)
Watercolour $9\frac{1}{2} \times 12\frac{1}{2}$ in (24×31.75 cm)
Lender: Mrs J. R. G. Stanton, Snelston Hall

John Harrison, too, was pleased with his fine mansion, writing in 1832 in answer to Cottingham's request for testimonials:

'It is with sincere pleasure that I am able to answer your application for my testimonial of your ability as an architect. The house you have erected for me here will I trust, long remain a standing proof of your good taste and ability. It is greatly admired by all, both for the beauty of the external and internal appearance, the convenience of its arrangements, solidity of its construction, and all are astonished at the rapidity with which the work was executed.'[19]

Snelston Hall fell into disrepair during the Second World War and was demolished in 1952 despite spot-listing in 1951. Contemporary comment on its destruction reflected the mid-twentieth century disparagement of Gothic Revival architecture. The *Journal of Derbyshire Archaeological and Natural Historical Society* of 1952 was far from inconsolable: 'Regrets that another mansion has been added to the list of several classic and ancient homes which have disappeared in this country can be tempered by the fact of its comparative modernity and indifferent structure.' And Pevsner, noting in 1953 the destruction of Pugin's Alton Towers and Cottingham's Snelston, which he described as 'a miniature Alton Towers', observed in dismissive terms: 'There is never much hope for the preservation of nineteenth century fantasy in the twentieth century.'[20]

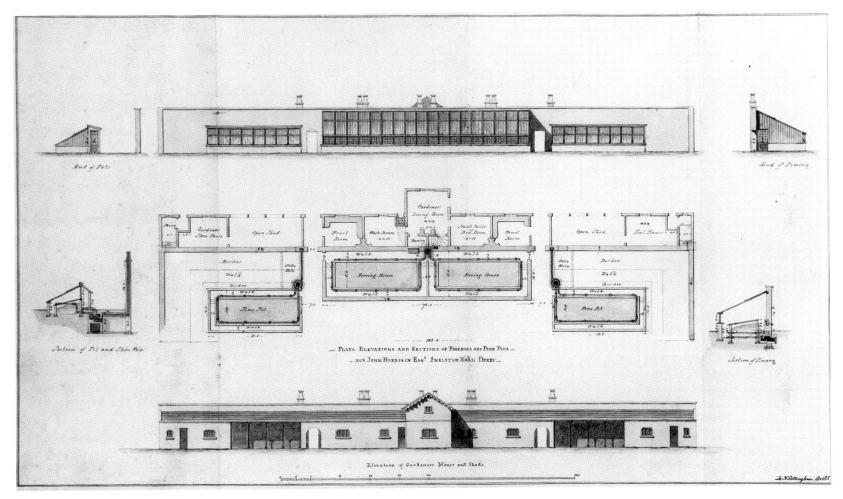

Fig.108 (Cat.E22) 'Design for Pineries and Pine Pits, Gardener's House etc', Snelston Hall, 1826
Pen, ink and watercolour 20½×32 in (52×81.5 cm)

Fig.109 (see Cat.E22) Snelston farm buildings, 1995

To describe Snelston Hall as a 'a nineteenth century fantasy' did little justice to the seriousness of Cottingham's expressed intentions. *A Catalogue of Sale* of the fixtures and fittings of Snelston Hall of June 1952, available prior to its demolition, contained illustrations of the various lots, the great south window, oak-panelled doors, the staircase and Cottingham's carved fireplaces and overmantels and firegrates.[21] Colonel J. P. Stanton renovated the stable block which is now Snelston Hall, incorporating some of Cottingham's fitments removed from the Hall: the traceried staircase, stone carved fireplaces, library bookcase fitments and carved oak doors, cut down in scale and altered to fit, a few remnants of Cottingham's Snelston Hall, described in 1927 as 'one

Fig.110 (Cat.E24) Frederick Nash, Snelston Hall (detail), *c.*1829
Watercolour $9\frac{1}{2} \times 12\frac{1}{2}$ in (24×31.75 cm)

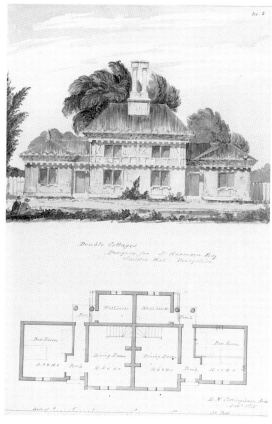

Fig.111 (see Cat.E25) Double Cottages for Snelston Hall, 1825
Watercolour $9\frac{1}{2} \times 13$ in (24×33 cm)

of the best examples of modern Gothic architecture in the country'.[22] Part of the crenellated retaining wall and the turreted archway through which visitors approached John Harrison's splendid new house still stands, a picturesque feature in the landscape and a reminder of Cottingham's Snelston Hall with, in his own words, 'the rich and splendid assemblage of its turrets, battlements and pinnacles'.

Snelston Estate Village

In 1825, in addition to his many proposals for Snelston Hall, Cottingham produced a book of watercolour drawings for the improvement of the Snelston estate village.

E25 (Figs 111, 112, 113; Colour Plate 6)
L. N. Cottingham, 'A Series of Examples for Plain and Ornamental Cottages, Gamekeeper's and Bailiff's Houses, Gate Lodges and other Rural Residences, Designed for the Use and Domain of J. Harrison Esq, Snelston Hall, Derbyshire. December 1825'
Watercolour $9\frac{1}{2} \times 13$ in (24×33 cm)
Lender: Mrs J. R. G. Stanton, Snelston Hall
Photographs by Jeremy Hardman-Jones

The seventeen watercolours reflected the influence of the Picturesque. The series was intended to advertise the accomplishments of the architect, to present possible styles for the patron to consider in creating his estate village of cottages, in contrast to the normal classicism of

the great mansion, and to demonstrate a concern to elevate the landowner's prestige and enhance the estate through the provision of attractive labourers' dwellings. Cottingham did not publish his book of drawings, the originals having remained with the Stanton family. Perhaps his patron wanted to keep the Snelston designs exclusive, or it may have been that Cottingham saw no need to publish his drawings when the market was already saturated with design books. Over a hundred architectural pattern books with designs for cottages and rural residences in Greek, Roman, Chinese, Indian, Gothic and Swiss styles had appeared in Britain between 1790 and 1810, published by such designers as Edmund Aitken, John Plaw, James Malton and Joseph Gandy.[23]

In the Snelston volume, Cottingham produced three severely simple neo-classical designs, numbers 6, 12 and 13. But the other fourteen designs were based on Tudor vernacular with strong Gothic elements, showing a Picturesque variety of materials, thatched and slate roofs, brick roughcast, stone for walls and quoins and rusticated timber for lean-tos as in designs 1, 2 and 9.

Some of the designs incorporated tall Tudor chimneys in a variety of patterns, steeply pitched roofs and gables, diamond lattice-pane casement windows as in the Bailiff's Residence (design number 10), half-timbering as in design number 3, and a variety of bay and oriel windows. Some had pronounced Gothic elements such as the 'Woodman's Cot' (number 1) and a lodge (number 8), with fourteenth-century pointed-arch Gothic windows, pointed-arch and late Gothic four-centred arch doorways and entrances, porches with pierced Gothic traceried

bargeboards, and mullioned two-, three- and five-light pointed windows under square heads with drip moulds.

Cottingham prepared this volume of drawings only five months before his first Gothic designs of May 1826 for Snelston Hall itself. Despite his classical Lambeth estate and other neo-classical designs, Cottingham's mind was seriously turning to a serious consideration of the Gothic as a source of style.

The seventeen drawings, accompanied by meticulous ground plans with measurements, reflected detailed consideration of the possible requirements for Harrison's estate workers. They exhibit a wide variety of accommodation, including one- to four-roomed single-storey dwellings with porches; lean-to woodsheds and attached dairies, dog-kennels and wash-houses; and substantial two-storey houses such as the bailiff's house or the 'Ornamental Cottage for a Game-keeper' with two, three and four rooms on the ground floor and two rooms above. Nine of the designs offered variations on the double cottage plan, similar to many double and

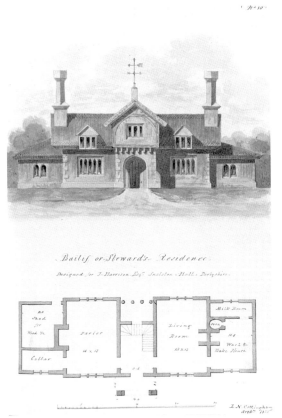

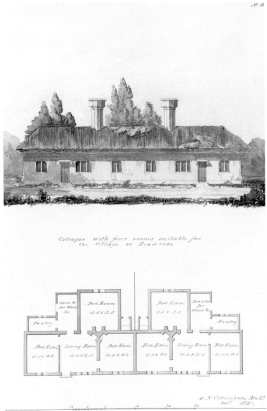

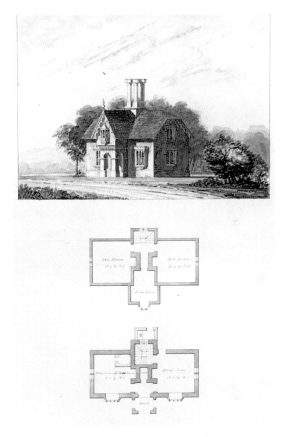

Fig.112 (see Cat.E25) Design for Bailiff's residence, Snelston Hall, 1825
Watercolour 9½×13 in (24×33 cm)

Fig.113 (see Cat.E25) Estate cottages for Snelston Hall, 1825
Watercolour 9½×13 in (24×33 cm)

Fig.114 (Cat.E26) Elevation for the Edlaston Road Lodge, Snelston Hall, 1820
Pen, ink and wash 15×12 in (38×30.5 cm)

quadruple plans in such pattern books as Joseph Gandy's *Designs for Country Houses, Villas and Rural Dwellings* (1800). The planning demonstrated Cottingham's concern for 'convenience and utility': the main rooms in all the designs were of good size, generally 12 ft×15 ft, and centrally placed chimneys for maximum heating efficiency were included. The overall impression one derives from the proposed dwellings is not one of wide Picturesque eclecticism, such as appeared in many pattern books, but rather a strong hint that Cottingham hoped his patron would favour his suggestions for a village that looked to the late mediaeval period for its inspiration.

Snelston Village as built 1827-46

In keeping with the Gothic Snelston Hall, Cottingham's estate village, built between 1827 and 1840, was based largely on four of the Tudor Gothic designs in Cottingham's pattern book: the two-storeyed gabled

double cottage; the half-timbered two-storeyed design number 3 with projecting centre and end bays; the Tudor Gothic entrance lodge; and the bailiff's house. The Picturesque elements such as thatch, which is not a material common to Derbyshire, and the rusticated timber supports, were not used. Instead, Cottingham's village houses were based on utility of plan and undisguised local materials in construction. This was an architecture that looked ahead to the domestic revival works of Pugin, Butterfield, Street and Webb, predating such key buildings as Pugin's St Marie's Grange of 1835 or Butterfield's Baldersby St James of 1855, which were inspired by the English vernacular as a source of style. Drawings were made for the Edlaston Road Lodge which relates to design number 5 in Cottingham's book.

E26 (Fig.114)

L. N. Cottingham, plans and elevation for the Edlaston Road Lodge, Snelston, 1820
Pen, ink and wash 15×12 in (38×30.5 cm)

Derbyshire Record Office
Photograph by Jeremy Hardman-Jones

The lodge is a single-storey house with a gabled porch with pierced bargeboards, flattened pointed-arch doorway with labels of sculpted heads in mediaeval headdress, and five-light pointed-arch mullioned windows. The large living room has a five-light stone mullioned bay window with diamond lattice casements; a large central stack of diamond Tudor form warms the living room and bedrooms; and the bedroom and woodshed (now the bathroom) windows have mullioned three-light windows under hood moulds. The finish is in stucco, possibly of a later date, with local slate roofs. The original entrance gates to the estate remain: stone gate-posts and panelled gates decorated with a wrought-iron design in the form of a capital H for Harrison. The lower lodge, situated close to the church and the village, is of similar plan with steep slate roofs and gabled porch, but is of stucco and timber framing with pierced bargeboards and bay

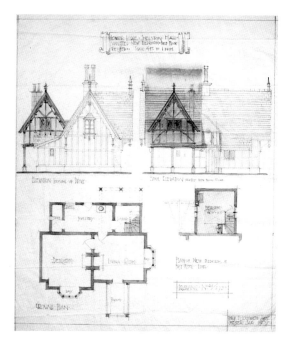

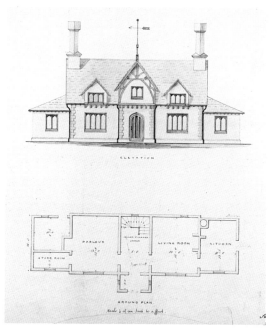

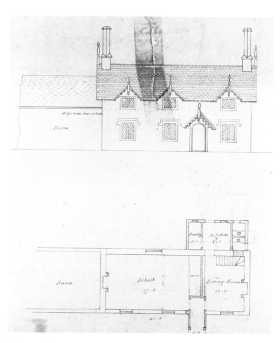

Fig.115 (Cat.E27) Philip Lockwood, designs for alterations to Lower Lodge, Snelston Hall, 1909
Pen, ink and watercolour 20½×21¾ in (52×55.25 cm)

Fig.116 (Cat.E28) Plans and elevations for Bailiff's Cottage, Snelston Hall, c.1826
Pen and ink 13×11¾ in (33×30 cm)

Fig.117 (Cat.E29) Plans and elevation for the Schoolhouse, Snelston Hall, c.1826-9
Pen and ink 13×13 in (33×33 cm)

windows to living room and bedroom. Drawings by Philip Lockwood of 1909 show suggested alterations to Cottingham's lower lodge with the addition of bedroom, scullery, store and larder.

E27 (Fig.115)

P. Lockwood, designs for additions and alterations to the Lower Lodge, Snelston, with elevations and plans, 1909
Pen, ink and watercolour 20½×21¾ in (52×55.25 cm)
Derbyshire Record Office
Photograph by Jeremy Hardman-Jones

Undated line drawings and ground plans exist for the bailiff's house relating closely to design number 10 (apart from the substitution of local slate roof tiles for thatch) and also for the schoolhouse, built in local red sandstone like the Hall.

E28 (Fig.116)

L. N. Cottingham, plans and elevation for the Bailiff's Cottage, Snelston, c.1826
Pen and ink 13×11¾ in (33×30 cm)
National Monuments Record (51/121), © RCHME

The bailiff's house has a projecting centre bay with half-timbered gable, gabled dormer windows, steep slate roofs, double chimney stacks and single-storey lean-to

bays to each side, four-light mullioned windows with decorative leaded light casements under square heads to the ground floor and two- and three-light windows above. (Cottingham had included in his *Smith and Founder's Director* designs for lattice windows as a means of cheaply reproducing the effect of a leaded light window of the late Gothic period.) The plan of the bailiff's house shows a living room and parlour both of 15 ft × 15 ft, a lean-to kitchen and storeroom or woodshed, 10 ft × 15 ft and an 8 ft hallway with staircase and steps down to the larder and cellar. The house is built in local brick and slate with regular stone dressings.

E29 (Fig.117)

L. N. Cottingham, plans and elevation for the Schoolhouse, Snelston, c.1826-29
Pen and ink 13×13 in (33×33 cm)
National Monuments Record, © RCHME

It is clear from the plan that the schoolhouse was built on to an existing barn or cottage in matching ashlar. The schoolroom (27 ft 3 in × 15 ft 2 in) and the schoolteacher's living room, (12 ft × 15 ft) occupied the ground floor with a kitchen and pantry extension beyond the stairs to the first-floor bedrooms. The gables in the drawing and the bargeboard pierced with Gothic trefoils to the shallow

entrance porch, also in the drawing, have been omitted. But the square-mullioned windows with decorative lattice casements remain. Photographs of Snelston village show the inspiration of Cottingham's Gothic watercolour proposals, although no other plans by Cottingham apart from the bailiff's house and schoolhouse have yet come to light. The double cottage by Snelston brook is of two storeys, built of brick in Flemish bond, with fine detailing in the square hood moulds over flattened arch two-light windows, echoing the design of the hall windows, and with single-storey slate roofed projections on either side of the centre gabled bay, steep slate roofs and tall diamond-stack Tudor chimneys. The half-timbered double cottage is of similar plan but with centre gable and dormers, side bays of lower pitch, stone sills and segmental arched windows. The inn, now converted to a private dwelling, followed the same form, built of brick with projecting straight-coped gabled end bays, a steeply roofed entrance porch, large square-headed mullioned and transomed windows at ground level and three one-light mullioned windows above, an attached stable block and courtyard, two tall chimney stacks in clusters of four round brick chimneys, local slate roofs and stone dressings. Another variation of the double cottage appears on the main street of the village, opposite the school. It has two-storey projecting ends, straight-coped gables with mullioned windows fitted with lattice casements of intricate geometric design, and a single-storeyed central bay with the two entrance doorways under four-centred Gothic arched heads, again built in brick with very tall double chimneys to the outside of each gabled bay, fish-scale tiled roof, and regular stone dressings to the mullions and angled buttresses (Figs 118, 119, 120, 121. Photographs by Jeremy Hardman-Jones).

A simpler two-storey double cottage based on one of Cottingham's single-storey three-roomed designs of 1825 has square-headed windows under carved brick hood moulds (the present window frames are replacements), a central chimney stack and entrances in the one-storey kitchen bays.

The details of Cottingham's estate village are discernibly Gothic. The four-centred arch of the late Gothic period is used throughout, with mainly square-headed windows with arched lights or lattice casements. The use of buttresses is minimal, their diagonal placement again relating to Cottingham's '3rd class of Gothic'. Fine brick detailing is seen in drip moulds and ribbed chimneys. Chimney stacks project boldly from the wall from ground level in the mediaeval manner, a feature to be taken up by Pugin. The slate roofs are steep, the chimney stacks very tall, and the interior functions are openly expressed by different roof levels or lean-tos such as porches, one-storey kitchens, woodsheds or kennels. Some of the features are similar to those of the Picturesque cottages of the many pattern books, with gables, mullions, dormers and bay windows, but the

Fig.119 (see Cat.E29) The Schoolhouse, Snelston Hall, 1995

Fig.118 (see Cat.E29) Edlaston Lodge, Snelston Hall, 1995

Fig.120 (see Cat.E29) The Bailiff's Cottage, Snelston Hall, 1995

handling is different. The simple brick walls have an air of austerity and although the outline of the houses may be Picturesque, it is a Picturesque arising from strict utility. The buildings are straightforward and honest in their simple village settings, with no attempt to create the self-conscious irregularity or prettiness of Nash's Blaize Hamlet. Cottingham's village contrasts also with Paxton's Derbyshire village of Edensor of 1840 where he arranged cottages and villas around the church with contrived Picturesque informality, each house being different and showing a wide range of styles including the Italian Villa and the Tudor Cottage. At Snelston simple unpretentious English architecture prevails, based on concern for the climate, utility, simplicity and truthfulness, the whole expressed in practical function and materials and construction based on English mediaeval precedent.

It is possible that Pugin saw Snelston and the estate village when working at nearby Alton Towers from 1838 and drew inspiration from Cottingham's work. At Snelston, Cottingham, in continuing the local traditions of building and the use of local materials, anticipated William Butterfield's Baldersby village houses of 1859 where local rough Yorkshire ashlar was used, with vestiges of Gothic in the four-centred arch and square-headed windows, steep slate roofs, gables, timber framing and massive chimney stacks, houses that are taken as a seminal development in the English domestic revival of the nineteenth century and one that looks ahead to the aims and ideals of the Arts and Crafts architects later in the century.

At Snelston, Cottingham used the stone and brick of Derbyshire. Few places in Derbyshire are far from good building stone, with almost every geological rock type having been worked to provide building materials. The major beds of sandstone in the Millstone Grit, Coal Measures and Keuper such as the fine-grained buff pink of Snelston Hall, have been used for building, walling and paving stone. The shale and clay within these strata, used for brickmaking and roof slating, were worked from the thin-bedded parts of sandstone horizons.[24] Plain tiles, never pantiles, were used widely in the region, with roofs at a very steep pitch, showing them to advantage. Timber-framed houses, too, proliferated in the region although few mediaeval examples remain, apart from Somersal Herbert, the seat of the Fitzherbert family; Mickleover Old Hall, a small manor house; and the small house at South Sitch with close studding under a thatched roof. Cottingham's Mediaeval Revival entrance lodge recalls the once numerous timber-framed houses of Derbyshire. The use of brick was more common, extending from the sixteenth century to present day, and stone dressings were used widely, as at such splendid

Fig.121 (see Cat.e29) Brook Cottages, Snelston Hall, 1995

mansions as Sudbury Hall and in more humble town and village houses.

Throughout Derbyshire, whatever the material used, the most universal and traditional feature is the use of gables, not stepped or shaped as in other regions, but plain and straight and usually coped. Minor houses were often E-shaped with three gables and sometimes a projecting porch, continuing from the late fifteenth century to the early eighteenth century. Ashbourne Mansion in Church Street of 1683, for example, is a twin-gabled house in brick with a wide central bay projecting slightly; and Green Hall, also in Ashbourne, dating from the late seventeenth century, is also a twin-gabled house built of brick with stone dressings. Hazelbadge Hall, dating from 1549, also features the straight-coped gable of Derbyshire, with depressed pointed arches to the windows under square hood moulds, used by Cottingham in his lodges at Snelston. The celebrated houses of Derbyshire would have been well known to Cottingham, as would the lesser yeomen's houses and smaller manor houses in Ashbourne and surroundings.

Cottingham worked widely in the county, beginning with Snelston Church, where he restored the crumbling

piers in 1822 before he began work on Snelston Hall, and later at Elvaston Castle in 1832, and at Ashbourne Church which he surveyed in the 1830s and restored in 1839. In his gabled cottages with their use of brick with stone dressing, steep slate roofs and Gothic detailing, Cottingham clearly looked to the traditional Derbyshire materials and style of architecture of the late fifteenth to eighteenth centuries, although in no sense did he indulge in copying archaic features. The farm and horticultural buildings are pared to a minimum in their concern for function, and in Snelston village, the use of the vernacular Tudor Gothic as a source of style for a domestic Gothic Revival architecture anticipated by many years the intentions of Philip Webb's Red House of 1859.

Snelston village has survived without additions or alterations since Cottingham's time, except that the school, the inn and the bailiff's house are now used as dwellings. Under the Civic Amenities Act of 1967 the village and the surrounding area became a Conservation Area. Until 1975 the entire village was in the Stanton family ownership but low rents, taxation and inflation have led to the sale of properties, a trend likely to continue as others become vacant. Cottingham's village remains unspoilt, a rare remaining example of his work.

BIBLIOGRAPHY
Bowyer, Rev. A. R. C., *The Ancient Parish of Norbury*, Ashbourne, 1843
Catalogue of Sale, Snelston Hall; W. S. Bagshawe & Sons, Ashbourne, 15 July 1946
Catalogue of Sale, Snelston Hall: Sale of Fixtures and Fittings, Allen and Farquhar, 11 June 1952
Cottingham, L. N., *Original Plans and Drawings for Snelston Hall*, Derbyshire Record Office, Ref. 157 3021-4095
Craven, M. and Stanley, M., *Derbyshire Country Houses*, Derbyshire Museum Services, 1982
Jervis, S., 'Furniture Designs for Snelston Hall', V&A Museum Album, 1984
National Monuments Record: *Snelston File*
Pevsner, N., *The Buildings of Derbyshire*, London, 1953
The Queen, 'Mrs Stanton and Her Home', 6 April 1927
Stanton, J. R. G., 'Derbyshire Conservation Areas: Snelston', *Derbyshire Life and Country*, 1984

Brougham Hall, Westmorland *c.*1830-47

Cottingham was commissioned in 1830 to extend and enlarge the modest house in Westmorland belonging to the Lord Chancellor of England, Henry, Lord Brougham. The house was of twelfth-century origin. At Brougham, Cottingham looked to the Romanesque and Early English period to create a 'sternly magnificent' baronial mansion in the tradition of the fortified castles of the north of England. The extent of Cottingham's involvement at Brougham can be established from contemporary accounts in journals such as the *The Gentleman's Magazine*, the Brougham family archive (containing letters from Cottingham), comments and descriptions by contemporary writers such as George Shaw, watercolours, photographs in the National Monuments Record prior to Brougham Hall's demolition, and material collected by the Brougham Hall Trust established in 1988 to conduct an archaeological survey and restore the ruins.

Brougham Hall, Westmorland, situated two miles south-east of Penrith, was the seat of Henry, Lord Brougham and Vaux, an historian, scientist, man of letters and Lord Chancellor in the famous 1830 administration which passed the Reform Bill of 1832. Described variously as 'the bold uncompromising opponent of slavery, the advocate of popular education, courageous counsel at the Bar of the House of Peers, defending the honour of an oppressed Queen, and the daring innovator of legal reforms', Lord Brougham was also widely admired in society, 'despite his gossiping

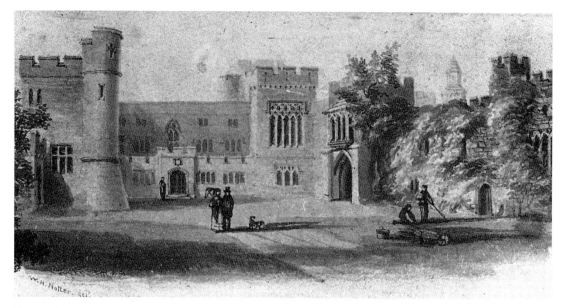

Fig.122 (Cat.E30) W. H. Nutter, Brougham Hall, Westmorland, 1847
Watercolour, dimensions unknown

propensities'. As a journalist noted in the *Illustrated London News* in 1843: 'He has talked more than any human being breathing not excepting that great talker Louis Philippe, the King and Lord Brougham are sworn friends. He visits extensively, men of no parties are exempt of his visitation.'[25] It was important for Lord Brougham to entertain in return at his country seat. In 1829 his younger brother William Brougham, who administered the estate, was put in charge of the rebuilding and refurbishment of the Hall, creating a thirty-bedroomed baronial mansion in keeping with its ancient origins and befitting the seat of the third man in the kingdom.

E30 (Fig.122)
W. H. Nutter, Courtyard of Brougham Hall, *c.*1847
Watercolour
Lender: Brougham Hall Trust

The Hall, in the *PO Directory* of 1858, was described as 'a noble mansion principally modern in the castellated style with embrasured parapets and turrets, the interior decorated and furnished in Old English style with objects of great interest to the admirers of art and lovers of the antiques'. Brougham was also known as 'The Windsor of the North' for it was based on a castle of courtyard type with parts reputedly dating from mediaeval times. Past references to Cottingham's involvement and to the works at Brougham have been ambiguous and inaccurate. *The*

Art-Union obituary of Cottingham merely mentioned in passing ' private works for Lord Brougham at Brougham Castle', and in *Vanishing Houses of England* it was stated that 'Cottingham worked here for Lord Brougham after 1829 by which time the Great Hall had been built and filled with modern stained glass'.[26] This suggests that the castellated extension and rebuilding of the Hall was already completed, possibly to the designs of Robert Smirke who built nearby Lowther Castle for the Earl of Lonsdale in castellated style from 1800-11; and that Cottingham was commissioned to design the interiors after this date. There is no documentary evidence to link Smirke with the work. It was Cottingham who worked from 1830, when the tower was constructed and the major building works began, up to 1846 when he was making drawings for the final details of the interiors.

These undertakings were described in the nineteen surviving letters which Cottingham and his son Nockalls wrote to William Brougham between 1844 and 1846.[27] In a manuscript on Westmorland, the writer gave a chronology of the building works at Brougham, listing the tower (1832); the stone bridge to the chapel (1842); the library and a small turret at the west end (1843); new stables and a vestibule to the south and a 'Norman Room with a groined arch underneath' (1843-4).[28] The writer erroneously continued that 'Richardson the builder was the architect of these alterations and also put up a clock turret and a new staircase.' Joseph Richardson was certainly the building contractor but Cottingham made the designs, a fact confirmed by Richardson in a letter to William Brougham: 'I received your plan of the staircase turret. I think it should not be altered but carried up in the way Mr Cottingham has drawn it ... and we are putting up the clock turret.'[29]

The exact date of the building of the tower can be pinpointed to February and March of 1831, for its construction was described in the diary of George Shaw. Shaw became acquainted with William Brougham, visited the Hall and wrote many letters to Brougham over a period of twenty years commenting on the rebuilding of the Hall. Shaw also described details of the construction and interiors of Brougham in his diaries, and researched antiquarian topics for precedents for the work. In his diary on 1 May 1831, Shaw wrote:

'Since I went on this road before, which was only in January, Brougham has now fronted the Hall in castellated style and added a heavy Norman tower of great height and massive architecture with machicolated embrazure battlements. The effect of the Hall over the top of the aged surrounding woods is sternly magnificent – And if it before merited its appellation 'The Windsor of the North' it now merits it tenfold. The Situation is scarcely to be matched standing as it does on the brow of a commanding eminence, overhanging the river and looking down on the ruins of the Castle.'[30]

Building had been in progress since the previous August to our certain knowledge, for William wrote to Lord Brougham: 'We have had a good deal of rain lately so as to rather hinder the building, and we are accordingly rather in confusion, but I take it for granted you will bring nobody back with you.'[31]

The date of the Norman tower can be firmly established as 1831. Cottingham himself confirmed that he was its architect in a letter to William Brougham in which he spoke of 'the large number of drawings I have made since the commencement of the works at Brougham'. This establishes beyond doubt that Cottingham made plans and advised on all aspects of the work from 1830, and was not, as has been suggested, working from Smirke's drawings or simply completing the interior designs during the 1840s. Certainly, in his letters of 1844-6, Cottingham wrote detailed instructions to the stone carvers working on the finishing of the exterior. These letters give evidence of the wide extent of Cottingham's involvement in the design of the great staircase, the armour hall, carved and gilded ceilings, woodwork, doors, panelling, encaustic flooring, the construction, furnishing and fittings of the Norman bedroom, fireplaces, grates and fire-irons, furniture of every kind, carved oak figures, lions and stags, wall sconces and chandeliers and designs of cornices, pelmets,

curtain fabrics and chair coverings: all part of the furnishings and details of a major architectural project, with Cottingham in overall charge. The project progressed as funds allowed over a period of years from 1830 onward.

The fact that the Hall was known as 'The Windsor of the North' lends some credence to the suggestion that the foundations of the Hall were of mediaeval origin, despite much contemporary scepticism of Lord Brougham's claims to a Saxon ancestry. William Brougham, in a history of the Hall, wrote that it was 'for most part rebuilt but retained some ancient portions', a wall of the twelfth century, another of the fourteenth century, and the entrance gatehouse of Edward I's time with 'some good corbel heads and battlements'.[32] These 'ancient portions' of the late Norman origins, with remains of later centuries, gave Cottingham the archaeological basis for his full mediaeval revival of the Hall. He attempted to create a baronial mansion which reflected the growth and development of a building during the whole mediaeval period.

At this time Lord Brougham – in common with a great many of the minor aristocracy, landed gentry, nouveau-riche industrialists, and families of no clear lineage at all – was much concerned with establishing a pedigree and building or extending a house to reflect social position and British ancestry.[33] His concern with his pedigree was of such importance to him that it led to some exaggeration and distortion of the truth, a fact that did not pass without caustic comment from his contemporaries.[34] Fake mediaeval brasses were displayed in the sanctuary at the Chapel of Ninekirks to substantiate descent from the Nevilles, Earls of Westmorland; and William Brougham, during repairs to Ninekirks Chapel in 1846, discovered what was supposed to be the grave of Odard, Lord of Brougham, who lived between 1140 and 1185.[35] Other graves yielded the supposed skull, sword and prickspur of Gilbert de Burgham and the skull of Edwardus de Burgham, items that Lord Brougham was wont to show his visitors. Mrs Hardcastle, in her *Life of Lord Campbell* described a visit to Brougham Hall in 1848 in lightly ironic language:

'The place is very beautiful and very interesting, having so much to be justly proud of there is nothing he (Henry, Lord Brougham) cares to talk about connected with himself except the antiquity and greatness of his race. In the Church at Brougham there was the grave of an Edwardus de Burgham who accompanied Richard to the Holy Land, my noble and learned friend lately opened his coffin, brought away his skull, framed it and placed it in his baronial hall ... Being called upon to admire the Grinning Crusader I could only say, that I was much struck by the family likeness between him and his

illustrious descendant particularly in the lengthiness of the jaw.'[36]

Present day archaeologists excavating the site of the demolished Hall have discovered, 10 ft below the terrace level, a cobbled area and the foundations of a wall which may be the remains of the seventeenth-century house. But they are unable to determine whether the Broughams demolished this house before building the Hall or whether they incorporated it into their own castellated mansion. However, the description in Shaw's diaries of the exterior, the documented extent of Cottingham's works applied to the interiors, and William's letters describing how some parts were extended and some demolished, all suggest that the existing house, arguably 'Mr Bird's house', was gradually encased and the interior gutted. Shaw wrote in May 1832: 'Brougham has a magnificent looking castle, few people have displayed such taste as he has in the repairs of the place which two or three years ago was a very common looking building.' On a further visit in June, Shaw went on foot to the Hall, making some drawings preserved in his existing sketchbooks, and giving a detailed description helpful in determining the various stages of the building and interior design. The Hall presented on approach 'a grey venerable assemblage of Towers heavy walls and time-worn battlements, with glimpses of towers, windows, stacks of chimneys, and grotesque spouts' appearing through the trees, and an arched gateway, 'apparently partly in ruins' and covered with ivy with two ponderous panelled and studded oak doors giving admittance to a courtyard laid out with lawns and shrubs.

William, in a letter of 1830 to Lord Brougham, had mentioned the planting of creepers and shrubs, and noted that they were doing well. Shaw's description of the Norman tower, 'of great height, massive architecture, with machicolated embrazure battlements', the sketches he made, and the evidence of photographs taken before its demolition in 1935, offer clear evidence of Cottingham's efforts to create an archaeologically correct Norman tower in keeping with the existing twelfth-century perimeter wall and ruins, once again taking advantage of the commanding position of a fortified manor house overlooking a valley (Fig. 123). Cottingham had available to him precedents for his Norman tower in the remains of others close by, such as the ruined Brougham Castle and Pendragon Castle with its twelfth-century pele tower which were among those restored in the seventeenth century by Lady Anne Clifford. At Brougham, Cottingham deliberately created a sense of age and development and a sense that the alterations were in response to changed needs and conditions. In his tower he designed narrow-slit single- and double-light lancet windows to illuminate the upper floors and inserted large

Fig.123 (see Cat.E30) Brougham Hall prior to demolition in 1935

late fourteenth- or early fifteenth-century mullioned windows of three lights with cinquefoil arched heads to light the ground floor. Similarly, the embrazured battlements and round stair turret of the tower, and the large square-headed mullioned and transomed five-light Perpendicular window, very similar to those in the chapel at Naworth, gave the impression of a later insertion to light the armour hall and were all based on ancient precedent.

Shaw went on to describe the 'curious ancient stones' built into the wall near the entrance, a means of preserving the traces of the original archaeological remains. The lofty entrance hall was wainscoted with carved oak, lit by fine stained-glass windows and decorated with portraits, shields of arms and a suit of half-armour, and 'a screen of most beautiful carving' which in Shaw's opinion was of foreign workmanship. The screen concealed a small flight of steps leading to a 'kind of breakfast parlour in an unfinished state' but which contained 'a splendid chimney-piece of carved oak supported on figures with coronets, modern and a very successful imitation of the ancient style'. This room was extended in 1842 to become the drawing room.

Unlike Hopper at Penrhyn, where the 'decorations of the Norman style were not at all in harmony with the requirements of modern times', Cottingham made no attempt to re-create the interior of a twelfth-century Norman keep. But he extended the idea of improvements and developments over the ages by creating interiors that reflected the rich beauty and comfort of the later mediaeval period.[37] From his study of existing examples, Cottingham chose to employ the wainscot, which was normal in great houses of the thirteenth century, but he added the later elaboration of linenfold panelling and high-relief carving. The dining room was also wainscoted with carved panels; its ceiling was of square panelled compartments filled with richly emblazoned armorial bearings; the fireplace was of black marble; and there was an oriel window.

The library immediately above the dining room was a disappointment to Shaw. It contained books in arched recesses behind curtains and the walls were covered with tapestry. A new library was to be formed in the further extensions of 1843-4. Shaw continued his visit by examining Brougham Chapel 'reached by a rustic bridge', one that was later replaced by Cottingham's stone bridge.

The chapel was in a dilapidated state, but the butler, who was obviously giving the visitor a guided tour, informed him of 'his Lordship's intention to repair it and render it fit for worship'. He already had 'some fine old stalls' and intended to 'fit it up entirely with carved oak and windows of stained glass'. The chapel, rebuilt by Lady Anne Clifford in the seventeenth century, was of mediaeval foundation, and Lady Anne made some

attempt to echo the origins in a Gothic Revival building. She used heavy buttresses and simple unarchaeological round arch windows under square drip moulds, but with an interior that reflected the classical simplicity of the seventeenth-century church with plain panelled box pews and no rich Gothic decoration. Cottingham and William Brougham created a full Gothic Revival interior at the Chapel, but retained references to its Norman origins by means of pillars and zig-zag mouldings to the round arch windows in the interior. Shaw concluded his description:

'When I first travelled this road the house was a common, whitewashed sash framed dwelling with nothing to recommend it but its situation and now it arises the baronial mansion of the fifteenth century ... It is certainly the best imitation of an ancient castellated mansion house that I have yet seen, and the imitation is not merely confined to its shape but also to colour which is of a sober grey, the effect of some wash which has been applied with the addition of moss and ivy to render the deception still stronger.'

In these first stages of the project described by Shaw in 1831 and 1832 – with the Norman tower and castellated hall ranged around an inner courtyard giving the appearance of later additions, and with the richly decorated mediaeval interiors incorporating ancient fragments as at Snelston – Cottingham was creating an archaeologically correct revival of the Mediaeval, yet one in keeping with the requirements of his patron. William Brougham, like Hanbury Tracy at Toddington, Meyrick at Goodrich and Tollemache at Peckforton, was passionately interested in the design and antiquarian furnishing of the new castle although 'not wishing to set up as an architect'.[38] William relied upon Cottingham to translate his ideas into a realisable project, for he was anxious that the rebuilding should be carried out with 'true antiquarian feeling' in the best possible way to create a baronial mansion which echoed the true mediaevalism of nearby Naworth. By the late 1830s William was planning further extensions and enlargements. In his letters of 1838 to Lord Brougham, he was suggesting a means of building the new library and an extension to the sitting room. He had examined the conservatory, 'fast decaying from damp and woodwork rotting', and thought that it could be converted into a library; he drew a diagram to show how a sitting room, 'not very wide indeed, but as long as you pleased', could be created by forming an extension from the octagon tower with a bay window. He stressed possible economies: 'the old bricks lying in the garden could be used as a lining of the walls in the library, the bookcases could do again and furnishing might be done gradually'.

Brougham Hall Interiors

Apart from the letters of Cottingham and William, little documentation remains to make possible a full reconstruction of the plan and interiors of Brougham Hall. But George Shaw wrote a description which related to the work completed after his visit and drawings of 1832. In a letter to William Brougham in 1847, Shaw asked him to 'perhaps look at these scribblings and say what alterations should be made before its appearance in the *Manchester Guardian*'.[39] The article was reprinted in an Edinburgh paper and then in *The Gentleman's Magazine* of April 1848.[40] Shaw described the plan of the Hall with the principal suite of rooms occupying three sides of the large court and, in the entrance front, an embattled porch with buttresses; this led through an archway into a 'cloistered Norman passageway' decorated with a painted copy of the Bayeux Tapestry. In this cloistered passageway Cottingham followed the early thirteenth-century practice of painting the walls with richly coloured 'histories'. Among Cottingham's friends listed in his obituary was C. A. Stothard, an antiquary and draughtsman to the Society of Antiquaries, who made copies of the wall paintings discovered in the famous Painted Chamber in the Palace of Westminster in 1819. In that year Stothard made a series of thirty-two hand-coloured engravings of the Bayeux Tapestry, possibly even at Cottingham's suggestion, for few were interested at that date in the art of the mediaeval period and even fewer in the 'crude and barbaric works of the Normans'.[41] Now Cottingham used a copy of the tapestry as an entirely appropriate decoration for a mansion that was once a Norman fortified manor house, in keeping, too, with the Mediaeval Revival cloistered way, and with the aspirations of his patrons to an ancient lineage. George Shaw, in another letter of 1847, commented to Brougham on Cottingham's Norman bedroom, noting the appropriateness of the painted wall decoration: 'the effect of the flattened paintings from the Bayeux tapestry beyond the archway will have a fine effect as it will harmonise in character with the style and date of the room'.[42]

The work of painting the Bayeux copy and the interior of the Norman bedroom was carried out at Brougham by Mr Walton, the painter. In his *Gentleman's Magazine* article, Shaw described how the passage led to the armour hall, with the archaeologically correct screens passage giving access to a newly constructed service wing, the entrance at the end furthest from the high table, a staircase leading to the principal chamber, the Norman bedroom, on the first floor, and a painted and gilded carved oak panelled roof resting on spandrels. The walls were panelled in oak linenfold wainscot to twelve feet,

Fig.124 (see Cat.E30) C. V. Richardson, The Armour Hall, Brougham Hall, *c.*1850
Watercolour $7\frac{1}{2} \times 10$ in (19×25.5 cm)

and above the panels the walls were decorated with demi-suits of armour, weapons, stags' antlers, pennocles, banners and two full suits of armour. The fireplace was based on fifteenth-century designs such as the one at the Bishop's Palace, Wells, with carved stone columns supporting a carved and panelled frieze of five coats-of-arms, and a flattened arch opening with decoration to the spandrels. The floor, 'encaustic tiles with the armorial device of the family was laid during the recent renovation' (Fig.124).

From the armour hall an 'iron clenched door' with a massive box lock, possibly derived from examples in Cottingham's museum, led to the grand staircase with stone arched doorways and openings leading to various landings. Shaw wrote that 'much old oak was brought from Scailes Hall for the recent repairs of this staircase'. Carried away with imparting to his readers this vision of the Broughams' ancient baronial castle, and forgetting that fifteen years earlier he had written that the erstwhile

ordinary, sash-windowed dwelling was the 'best imitation of a castellated mansion he had yet seen', Shaw wrote of Cottingham's Norman bedroom that 'the old armoury had been converted to a bedchamber, the machicolations having been closed and the passageway assumed a Udolphish dreamy character worthy of Mrs Radcliffe'. He described the 'fine old timber roof of the Norman bedroom' and the Norman stone arch which divided the room forming a recess for the bed 'which is to be made from old drawings and illuminations' in an attempt to imitate an oak fourposter bed of the mediaeval period. The chimney piece had Norman zig-zag moulding and an inlaid tiled hearth, the walls were richly decorated in the manner of the thirteenth century, and in the spandrels above the arch were 'two of the Norman Kings on thrones painted from original drawings'.

Shaw concluded his article with a description of the chapel and a history of the Brougham ancestry. Immediately a 'furious critique' of the article was published in *The Gentleman's Magazine*, 'written with the greatest scurrility and insult', according to Shaw, and declaring the whole to be 'one tissue of falsehoods'. The article was entitled 'Brougham Hall, A Modern Antique' and signed 'Old Subscribers'. The writers, with some justification, vigorously refuted the impression given that Brougham was a mediaeval Hall 'lately renovated'. They pointed out that the 'huge square tower' had never been used for missiles of defence as it was new in 1832 'and consequently nothing but chamber missiles would be thrown from that tower since 1832 – yea – the more likely to be so since this strange queer gallery had been turned into a Udolphoish bedroom'. The article went on to point out that out-offices 'of various ages covered with ivy and the weather stain of the centuries' were all erected in the reigns of George III, George IV, William IV and Victoria, though none with the appearance later than Henry VII; the Norman bedroom and staircase were totally new erections in 1843; and all the suits of armour and accoutrements 'of family association' were in reality bought from various curiosity shops in Wardour Street 'since 1830' and 'the like may be said of nearly every article in the house'. The writers grieved at the violence done to archaeological science and felt that it was time that such 'outrageous perversions of historical facts as were foisted on the public's credulity for family gratification should cease'.[43]

Despite his romanticising, Shaw had given a useful impression of the plan of the Hall and description of the interior. Later additions at Brougham, designed by Cottingham up to his death in 1847, included the groined archway with the projecting oriel window of the Norman bedroom, a 'window of later character', as Cottingham described it, and a long battlemented range with pointed two-light windows completed the third side of the courtyard (Fig.125). On the south-facing garden and terrace sides, a series of projecting bays of irregular height and window type gave evidence of the different stages of development: the first bay Lord Brougham's study, the window added 'for more light' as in Perpendicular Gothic developments; the massive two-storey bay with the octagon or drawing room on the ground floor; and in 1849 the billiard room with the old drawing room above completing a structure that echoed the growth of a mediaeval castellated mansion (Figs 126, 127).

Building of the Service Wing 1843-4

The only ground plans that have so far come to light are undated and unsigned, and are plans of the offices at Brougham Hall. The writing, phraseology and style of plan are very similar to those of Cottingham's for Snelston Hall and may be attributed tentatively to him on

125

126

Fig.125 (see Cat.E30) F. W. Hulme, Brougham Hall, 1846
Lithotint, dimensions unknown

Fig.126 (see Cat.E30) South-west front of Brougham Hall, pre-1935

these grounds. The kitchen wing was built in 1843-4 when Richardson was erecting the staircase tower and clock turret 'to Mr Cottingham's drawings'. In a letter to William Brougham of 1 May 1843, Richardson wrote: 'Let me know how you would have the doors and windows of the rooms, oven house, housekeepers room and kitchen finished with mouldings.'

E31
'Plans of the offices at Brougham Hall', possibly by
L. N. Cottingham, undated
Pen and ink 24×36 in (61×91.5 cm)
Lender: Brougham Hall Trust; gift of the late Mr Eric Hill

The plan shows an extensive range of rooms facing north-west, close to the road and the stone bridge to the chapel, with kitchens, housekeeper's room, servants' hall, larders, brewery and baking house and adjoining the new stables, facing on to an inner courtyard, with access from the road through the great oaken doors.

Although professing 'not to set himself up as an Architect', William evidently preferred to superintend the work himself or entrust it to his contractors (John Robinson from 1837 to 1840 and then Joseph Richardson) to carry out the building to Cottingham's designs, perhaps for reasons of expense. In a letter dealing with his patron's complaints about charges Cottingham reminded him 'of the large number of drawings I have made since the commencement of the works at Brougham and the time which must necessarily have been expended on them and the valuable and in some cases unique models, with the trouble I have taken in having your furniture properly executed'.

Cottingham expressed his dissatisfaction at not being on site himself to superintend the work:

'I would far rather make designs for you in the regular way in which I am generally employed, *ie* by personally seeing and superintending the work with my own clerks to take my sketches and dimensions than have to work in the dark, by which so much time is lost from not knowing the effect and situation and circumstances and the labour in consequence is much increased, as verbal directions during the progress of works from the architect frequently supersede the necessity of elaborate drawings.'[44]

It would seem from William's diaries and Cottingham's comments that the cost of labour and materials in Westmorland was far below London prices and that William was constantly trying to make savings and cut costs in the extensive works. 'You get work done at a price that perfectly astonishes me,' Cottingham noted, although he firmly refused to persuade his craftsmen to reduce their charges:

Fig.127 (see Cat.E30) West front of Brougham Hall, pre-1935, showing wrought-iron gates possibly designed by Cottingham

'As regards Mr Potter's charges I really do not see where in justice to take off anything ... and Messrs Robinson & Robinson's bill for the table and washstand is only a fair charge, and though you may have got them done at a cheaper rate at Brougham I consider whatever you get them done for, the real value of such work is very different ... I consider them well worth the money.'[45]

William had to balance the need to control expenditure and his desire to use the very best materials and craftsmen to undertake the work. Joseph Richardson wrote that he had received the plans for the doorcase and continued with a progress report:

'The door into the groined archway passage is put in, the Gateway into the Yard is ready for the arch and the dog-house is arched over ... I have finished the Tower of the Great Staircase, leaving that part clear between the high tower and the other to finish as you think proper ... I received the plans and models for the Hall Ceiling on Friday and directly sent for Robert James, William Scott, and James Scott. R. J. thinks they can be done at a great deal less expense in stucco than in wood ... I think it will be adding a great expense to the work putting in a block of wood at each angle to fix the rossetts to as shown in the plan.'[46]

William consulted Cottingham and two weeks later Robinson wrote: 'I received your note saying the blocks of wood cannot be dispensed with.' Cottingham would not compromise on the quality of the work by using archaeologically incorrect materials such as stucco instead of wood for the armour hall ceiling. William wrote to Lord Brougham in 1843 with a summary of accounts for the work to date, listing all the outstanding bills for labour and materials, interior work still to be finished such as iron casements and firegrates, chimney pieces in stone for the bedrooms and all the furniture, and noting that although 'it had cost so little considering what was done this does not alter the fact that it has cost four times as much as we reckoned on'. Another reason for the high cost was that 'of the old part pulled down everything was so decayed that none of the old material except the stone could be used again and the stone did not pay for the pulling down and the clearing for the foundations so that it is all like new work'. The building accounts were itemised: '3306 yards of walling @ 1/8, fine hewing 1051 feet @ 2/5 per foot, 2187 feet of windows @ 10d, 909½ feet of Doors, 1324 feet of arches, 1514 feet of parapet, 1514 feet of Ashlar work, 1218 feet of coping, 364 feet of stone stairs, 127 feet of corbels.' The total account amounted to £3,348.1s.

The only other drawing for Brougham that has come to light so far is a drawing for a Gothic window.

Fig.128 (Cat.E32) 'Window for Brougham Castle', 1842
Pen and wash 21×26 in (53.5×66 cm)

E32 (Fig.128)
L. N. Cottingham, 'Window for Brougham Castle', with plans and sections
Pen and wash 21×26 in (53.5×66 cm)
Signed, in capitals, and dated 1842. In handwriting, 'the mullions to be prepared for cast iron frames'. Inscribed 'Windows at passage to Long Building'
The reverse is inscribed with addresses, 'To:-Revd. Gilbert Elliot, (or Mr Joseph Richardson), Brougham, Penrith, Pd.20 Dec. 1842. From:- L. N. Cottingham, Bazing Place, Waterloo Road, Lambeth, Surrey'
Lender: The Librarian, University College London, Manuscripts. *Brougham Papers*, WB Property Boxes, Misc, no.2

Completing the Interiors and Furnishings at Brougham, from 1844

In 1844, work was in full progress on the chapel and the Norman bedroom, the armour hall and the grand staircase. William and his builder may have made suggestions but Cottingham, although at a distance, was totally in command and he was consulted on the most minute detail in clarification of his plans and drawings, as his letters and those of Nockalls clearly indicate. Instructions to accompany plans and drawings for the interior design and decoration of the Norman bedroom appear in many of the letters. Designs and diagrams were sent for the intricate laying of a parquetry border to the floor, complicated by the irregular shape of the room, and for the shutters and windows: 'You will see that we have not made the shutters Norman as that would not be right, the window being of a later character. The hinges will of course be gilt, also the handles for pulling the shutters out of their boxings.'[47] The Norman bedroom had a rectangular oriel window described as 'projecting from the building and supported by pillars with a groined arch underneath', a feature dating from the early fourteenth century onward. Cottingham, with his knowledge of the Mediaeval and his concern for correctness, refused to mix the styles in an unarchaeological way.

Casts were sent for the patterns of skirting linings to the windows, a tracing for the hearth of the zig-zag moulded fireplace and designs for the 'grate and appendages'. Cottingham asked if he was to design encaustic tiles for the hearth 'or will you wait for those we shall have for the Norman church we are building?' At this date Cottingham was steeped in studies of Romanesque architecture and design. He was building St Helen's at Thorney in Norman style. He was making detailed surveys of the Norman Tower at Bury St Edmunds. He was engaged in restoring and uncovering early Romanesque parts of Hereford Cathedral. And he had been given the task of restoring the important Norman parish church of Kilpeck in Herefordshire. Cottingham's evident experience led to his patron recommending him in 1844 as the 'best mediaevalist architect' and the only one fit to restore Naworth Castle.

Cottingham made designs for every smallest detail of the Norman bedroom at Brougham and sent instructions to 'tone down the stonework throughout the room with boiled linseed oil having a very small portion of burnt sienna or umber in it, but no paint where stonework is to appear'. A long list of queries concerning the decoration of the Norman bedroom was returned with Cottingham's answers in the margin. The questions help us to imagine the effect of the room and also to appreciate the extent to which William relied on Cottingham's directions. William's litany of queries and Cottingham's responses [in square brackets] are as follows:

'In large arch, the splays against which the two columns rest are coloured red. Is the flat side to be left in its natural state or tinted? [Answer, 'stone'.]

'Are all the parts of the columns which are not shown in the drawing to be red, blue, green or gold, or left in natural stone? [Answer, 'Yes'.]

'Is the margin that surrounds the wattle work to be stone or vellum colour like the plain squares of the wattle work? [Answer, 'Yes, vellum colour, The principle adopted in this room has been to heighten the effect of stone walls with colour and gold'.]

'I presume I am right in supposing you intend the Doorcase, chimney piece and window arch with all their ornaments to be left in stone? [Answer, 'Yes'.]

'The door and other oak being made of old wood are black as ebony. Ought not the oak ground of the ceiling and especially the oak shown in the beams to be rather dark, and if so how many shades lighter than the door? In your drawing it is much like pale gingerbread. [Answer, 'The drawing would have looked heavy coloured very dark. The oak of the ceiling and indeed throughout the room should have the effect of being of one age'.]

'Is the Norman panel for the window to be continued as if cut in one plane, without any jointing or framing? The panel is 2 ft and includes three of the circles. If the above method is the correct one it will I think look better than a framework. [Answer, 'No framework'.][48]

George Shaw, in one of his letters to William, also made suggestions and passed comment on the Norman room, which he described as 'a bold and daring attempt and has so far succeeded wonderfully'. He investigated precedents for tiles, mentioning some in the collection of Cottingham's friend Francis Douce, and commented on the decorations: 'I can believe the old Kings look glorious, but cannot readily understand the good effect produced by the grotesque heads if at all like the specimens placed between the beams when I saw the room.'[49]

The kings were painted in the spandrels above the Norman arch. Shaw also approved of the use of the Bayeux Tapestry as 'harmonious decoration', but clearly found Cottingham's archaeologically correct use of grotesque Romanesque masks as bosses for the beams not at all pleasing.

The great staircase was also discussed in detail in Cottingham's letters and its progress noted in William Brougham's diary. The entry for 12 June 1844 read: 'Called Mr Cottingham, settled all drawings for the great staircase'. On 22 August William and his family returned from holiday in France and William noted in his diary: 'Infinitely disgusted at finding house in such confusion. Postern only up to the door tops and staircase full of scaffolding. H. (Lord Brougham) arrived at 12 much pleased with the new work but annoyed to find house so backward. Nobody to come to sleep till 1st Sept. which will give time to get bedrooms ready.'

By May 1845, the staircase was installed with queries about final details being answered in Cottingham's letters. Drawings for screen and brackets under the staircase were forwarded to Samuel Pratt. Favourable reports of progress were noted. Lions and stags of carved oak, like those for Sir Edward Blackett's staircase at Matfen Hall, where Cottingham was also engaged in works, were to be carved as newel posts. Cottingham wrote to Sir Edward: 'I think you will like the lions and stags much. There is however a great deal of labour in them and as I have

insisted on the master man himself doing them I must crave your patience a little longer. They are so near the eye they must be very well and carefully carved.'

The repetition of the half-baluster newels for the staircase was discussed in detail. Cottingham explained that these were not always adopted in ancient staircases but that there were numerous examples of their use: 'It is a mere matter of expense and as you have really got your staircase at half its value it would be better to have the half parts as a considerable improvement to the general effect.'

Cottingham's advice was taken, for the Sale Catalogue of the Hall, prior to its demolition, included the 'fine oak staircase' with ten octagonal newel posts each surmounted by lions bearing heraldic shields.[50] It was also decided to dispense with ramps. Nockalls wrote: 'My father says all newels must be of the same height on the landings. You are however mistaken in supposing ramps a modern invention, one among many instances of them is to be found in Henry VII's Chapel at Westminster.' The question of using foreign oak for the work, as a less expensive alternative to English oak, had been raised previously by the builder John Robinson. Nockalls continued his letter: 'My father says that such oak as the staircase is made of is worth all the foreign wood in existence and PRAY USE NO VARNISH!'

The wood for the staircase had come from Scailes Hall, a former home of the Broughams before Henry, Lord Brougham, fell heir to the Hall, and no doubt had the rich, dark patination of ancient oak. Cottingham, as an expert on mediaeval timber and early oak and walnut furniture, knew that there was no need for varnish, which would ruin the natural patination. No illustrations remain of Cottingham's grand staircase at Brougham, but it was probably very similar to the staircase he designed for Sir Edward Blackett at Matfen, a monumental staircase rising in a two-storeyed hall and mounting in flights at right angles to each other, a design dating from the end of the fifteenth century.

Cottingham designed furniture which was made up by Samuel Pratt and his sons Edward and James of New Bond Street in London. William, ever conscious of costs, noted in his diary of 14 June 1844: 'Settled drawings of Hall table with Mr Cottingham, then to Pratt who undertakes it, Top (solid oak) for £8, frame and legs, £27, £35 in all, which is not dear – the oak is old English. Pratt undertakes it will be at Brougham before 2nd August with 20 chairs'. On Tuesday 6 August, William wrote 'hall table and some of the chairs arrived from Mr Pratt's – very handsome'. No drawings of the furniture have yet come to light but in the Sale Catalogue of the remaining contents of Brougham Hall of 21 June 1932, lots 929 and 930 were sets of chairs, one of which was photographed.[51] This chair had a deep carved frieze to the base with Gothic roundels, almost identical to the bishop's chair Cottingham designed for St Mary's, Bury St Edmunds in the same year, 1844, and it may be attributed to him. The Brougham chair, as a dining chair, had upholstered seat and back, with carved roundels echoing the base. Cottingham had instructed: 'I advise you to lower the seats of the chairs if they require it – on no account cut the legs.' The watercolour of the armour hall by C.V. Richardson depicts a chair of similar base but with a low back composed of pierced roundels.

E33 (Fig.129)
Carved oak dining chair for Brougham Hall designed by L. N. Cottingham, made by Samuel Pratt, New Bond St, London, 1844
Lender: Dr Clive Wainwright (ex Sotheby's Sale, 14 July 1989)

Other furniture is mentioned in the letters and diaries, such as sitting room and hall tables, solid oak dressing tables with 'looking glass frames', wash-stands and chairs. Pratt made valances for the beds, dining-hall curtains and 'a Gothic cornice and window curtains'. Writing in September 1845, Pratt reported that 'The Gothic firescreen with bellows, two velvet cushions and four tappets were sent off together. The sofa, armour and other things go tomorrow'.

Pratt also made furniture for the Norman bedroom. George Shaw wrote later: 'How well this room has come out Mr Pratt's old bed I see standing in its tapestried niche.' Pratt may have supplied an antique bed but more likely he composed a four-poster bed, using ancient fragments of carved oak from a variety of sources.

Armour was supplied to decorate the armour hall, some by a Mr Falcke, but mostly by Pratt. William wrote in his diary of 4 July 1844: 'Settled about armour with Mr Pratt. Cap à pie suit, H.VII for £45 with sword complete' and on the 5 July he went to the Tower and 'learnt a good deal'. He was 'much struck with the H.VIII suit sent to him by Emperor Maximilian: fine suit Rd.III (worn by Lord Waterford at Eglinton) and some curious helmets'.

The metalwork was carried out to Cottingham's designs by Thomas Potter of South Molton Street, who made locks, door handles, hinges and a massive door knocker from a cast of the Durham knocker, stair rods and wall sconces. Cottingham had a cast of the Durham knocker in his collection and doubtless considered it a perfect example of early mediaeval design and entirely appropriate for the mediaevalising of Brougham. The concern for archaeological correctness extended to every detail. For example, Nockalls wrote in reply to William's queries about light fittings: 'Pray do not have the "neither

one thing nor the other" sconces or branches – there was never anything like what you name', and with the authority of a mediaeval expert continued: 'If you have sconces they must be with spikets, thus ...' He made a sketch of a sconce similar to one dating from the time of Henry V in his father's museum: 'The candle might be Mr Palmer's imitation Japan tube but *nothing* will ever look in place but the chandelier: both my father and self sincerely hope you will decide on it.'[52]

William noted in his diary on 1 July 1844 that 'Potter can't finish the chandelier in time – settled to have 7 silver sconces which will be beautiful for Hall or Library'. A chandelier was made, however, described in the *Sale Catalogue* as a 'massive six light gas chandelier hung in the staircase hall'. George Shaw wrote to William to ask for a 'tracing of the drawing for the flamboyant chandelier of very good design in the grand staircase at Brougham'. Other sconces and light fittings were made and Cottingham noted: 'Mr Potter will have 10 sconces finished very shortly – we have managed some capital

Fig.129 (Cat.E33) Carved oak dining chair for Brougham Hall, 1844

enamel on copper as cheap as china for the sconces.' For metalwork that was to be made at Brougham, Cottingham sent instructions and drawings: 'I enclose a working drawing for the work to the Postern doors – all the work to be in wrought metal: when finished to be heated red hot and dipped in grease. This prevents rust and gives a fine permanent iron black colour far superior to paint, bronze etc'.

Cottingham, armed with his knowledge of the design and use of metals, reflected in his *Director* and in his work on church restoration, was able to advise on the technicalities of preserving ironwork. He urged William 'to see the shields of Arms for the Hall and lions in Caen stone which we are having executed in town for Sir Edward Blackett'. For the armour hall floor, Cottingham advocated red and grey stone paving: 'We naturally look for something richer over our heads than under our feet, and this mode of paving has a picturesque repose about it from its colour.'

Carpeting was also part of the final design of the Hall and was supplied by Alfred Lapworth of 22 Old Bond Street. In 1844, he despatched green carpet with a border for the grand staircase, 'French carpet' with plain borders, and hearth rugs.[53] Interior pictures of Brougham Hall before its demolition in 1935 survive. Although cluttered with a wealth of Edwardian 'bric à brac' Cottingham's mediaeval armour hall can be seen, with its fifteenth-century roof, Gothic arch spandrels and boldly panelled compartments. The *Sale Catalogue of Fixtures and Fittings* described the armour hall, 'where you dine in baronial splendour', as with fitted cupboards and sideboards made out of linenfold and carved oak panels representing pastoral and scriptural scenes, surmounted by ten coats-of-arms and shields. The catalogue described the dining room filled with linenfold panelling and a ceiling richly carved; the library, the drawing room, the chancellor's study, all panelled with oak or Spanish leather; finely carved fireplaces in stone and marble, massive doors with high relief carving and great brass locks and hinges; and the fine oak staircase with ten octagonal newel posts each surmounted by lions bearing heraldic shields that Cottingham took such care to have carved by the finest craftsman[54] (Fig.130).

Surviving photographs show the process of demolition: the clock turret with weather vane and grotesque mediaeval stone bracket that Richardson found 'the most difficult work of any' with its eight-day tower clock by Vulliamy of 1846: the Norman bedroom fireplace revealed amidst the rubble with its zig-zag mouldings and supporting columns: and the finely carved oak shields of arms, the simplicity of the arms denoting their mediaeval origin in the ceiling of the staircase hall (Fig.131).

130

Fig.130 (see Cat.E33) The Armour Hall at Brougham Hall prior to demolition, 1935

Fig.131 Brougham Hall in the process of demolition, 1935

Fig.132 (Cat.E34) Anon., The Clock Court at Brougham Hall, 1844
Watercolour $5\frac{1}{2} \times 8\frac{3}{4}$ in (14×22.25 cm)

E34 (Fig.132)
Anonymous watercolour of the ice house and clock tower with the Vulliamy clock of 1846, designed by L. N. Cottingham dated 12 November 1844
Lender: Mr Tom Marshall

Photographs pick out a few remaining details after the demolition: a traceried window frame and an arch with corbel heads intact, a reminder of Cottingham's instructions: 'the ornament is all birds, tell your carver not to study to make them all exactly alike or too true to nature'.

The Brougham Hall Trust plan to restore what remains of Brougham Hall – part of the castellated extension of 1832, the entrance tower with its twelfth-century foundations – the intention being to establish

131

132

craft workshops, and a museum in the rebuilt stable block. A model and plan of Brougham Hall based on excavations and photographic evidence was made and indicates the extent of the ambitious programme to rebuild Brougham Hall.

BIBLIOGRAPHY
The Art-Union, 1847, Obituary of L. N. Cottingham
Brougham Papers: WB's diaries 1844-5; letters from LNC and NJC to WB; George Shaw: letters from tradesmen and accounts; letters from WB to Henry, Lord Brougham, etc. University College Library, London Castle Howard Archive, letter from WB to Earl of Carlisle, 25 Nov. 1844
The Gentleman's Magazine, April 1848, pp.369-76; pp.618-20
Hardcastle, Mrs M. S., *A Life of Lord Campbell*, 1881
Hill MS Collection, Brougham Hall, History of Westmorland, Vol.5, 1850, Cumbria Record Office
Illustrated London News 1844, p.340; 1843, p.323
Saddleworth Museum, Letters from Thomas King to George Shaw, 1841-2; Sir S. Meyrick, Goodrich, 1843 and 1845: Ref H/How/GS
Sale Catalogue, Brougham Hall Interior & Exterior Fixtures & Fittings, Wed. 18 July 1934, Messrs Perry & Phillips Ltd, 59 High St, Bridgnorth
Sale Catalogue, Contents of Brougham Hall of 21 June 1932, Garland Smith & Co, Mount St, London
Scot, D., Brougham Hall, Penrith, 1897
Shaw, G., *Diaries*, 1831-3; 34-35; *Sketchbooks 1830-50*; Manchester Central Library, MS 927.2.515.
Tyler, D., 'A History of Brougham Hall', Pamphlet, 1988

Designs for Elvaston Castle, Matfen Hall, Adare Manor and Coombe Abbey

In the 1830s Cottingham was fully employed by aristocratic patrons in addition to Lord Brougham to carry out Mediaeval Revival additions and interiors to their stately mansions. This reflected the growing tide of Gothic Revivalism and was indicative too of Cottingham's fame as a leading antiquarian architect designer.

Elvaston Castle, Derbyshire 1830s

E35 (Fig.133)
Elvaston Castle, east front, designed by L. N. Cottingham, *c.*1830
Print 7½ × 5½ in (19 × 14 cm)
Derbyshire Local Studies Library

Cottingham was commissioned by the Earl of Harrington to design a Gothic east front at his country seat Elvaston Castle in Derbyshire, and to redecorate parts of the interior.[55] Elvaston had been remodelled and Gothicised

Fig.133 (Cat.E35) East front of Elvaston Castle, Derbyshire, *c.*1830
Print 7½ × 5½ in (19 × 14 cm)

by Robert Walker in 1818 to the designs of James Wyatt. The extension owed little to the original parts of the house, which dated from 1633. Wyatt had created a symmetrical entrance front of seven bays, ashlar-faced with an embattled and turreted entrance porch and a projecting end bay echoing the form of the original brick house with its early gabled form clearly discernible.[56] This bay, with its square-headed mullioned and transomed windows, was embattled and angle-turreted to match Wyatt's new work.

By the mid-1830s Cottingham had completed nearby Snelston Hall which the earl may well have seen. He was making designs for Brougham Hall and at Coombe Abbey for the Earl of Craven and was possibly recommended to Earl Harrington by one of these patrons.

Cottingham, in the three-storeyed nine-bay east front, retained the symmetry of Wyatt's entrance front, echoing his crenellated parapet turrets and square-headed windows under hood moulds. The central projecting bay had battlemented bay windows to two storeys flanked by turrets and three panels above carved with Harrington

coats-of-arms, surmounted by a crest. Cottingham omitted Wyatt's two-light cinquefoil-headed windows with transoms and mullions under square hood moulds and designed large sash windows under square heads with a minimum of Gothic detailing to the architraves. In order to retain some sense of harmony with Wyatt's Gothic, Cottingham echoed the overall rectangular form of the fenestration with the late Gothic hood moulds and slim turrets. But in omitting the cinquefoil heads and inserting sash windows, and adopting a symmetrical two-storey façade with attic storey, Cottingham was perhaps trying to relate the house more closely to its seventeenth-century English Renaissance date. Possibly, too, he designed this east front in accordance with his theories of the development of architecture based on fitness for purpose and 'utility and convenience' and inserted the many large sash windows to reflect the classical regularity of the interior and to light the high-ceilinged rooms; the overall impression is one of classical symmetry, a very different approach to the mediaevalism of Brougham Hall or the Perpendicular Gothic of Snelston.

Cottingham redecorated Wyatt's Gothic Hall and it was renamed the 'Hall of the Fair Star'. Lord Harrington, known as Charles Stanhope, Viscount Petersham, before inheriting the title at his father's death, was a well-known eccentric figure in London society. In 1831 he married Maria Foote, an actress of some notoriety. Mark Girouard, in *The Return to Camelot* (1981), gives an account of this romantic episode and relates how the earl and his bride, shunned by society, retired to Elvaston where the 'Hall of the Fair Star' was a shrine and a reminder of the earl's knight-errantry. Wyatt's Gothic fan-vaulted ceiling with pendants was richly gilded and the cinquefoil-pointed niches with ogee-cusped arches were filled with knights in armour and the walls hung with swords and lances, the doors, stained-glass windows and alcoves decorated with appropriate chivalric mottoes – 'Fayre Beyond the Fayrest', 'Beauty is a Witch', 'Faithful and to Beauty and Honour' – and symbols of flaming hearts, lover knots, quivers of arrows, lyres and rare birds of paradise. The theme was extended to the gardens, landscaped from 1830-50 by William Barron, and described in E. Adveno Brooke's *The Gardens of England* (1857). The garden included rare new specimens of American conifers, a Moorish temple, and a topiary garden laid out with box-edged flower beds in the form of a star surrounded by topiary sentry boxes and four kneeling knights set within a thick serpentine clipped edge.

Unfortunately, all plans, drawings and even personal family papers relating to Elvaston have disappeared. The present Lord Harrington, who lives in Ireland, left Elvaston when he was seven years old and has no knowledge of Elvaston Castle and its history.[57] Derby Corporation bought the castle in 1964, when all the archive material was burnt (in order to destroy evidence of mismanagement of the estate, according to unsubtantiated rumours); the gardens were greatly altered and some garden buildings were destroyed.[58] It is, however, a surviving example of Cottingham's domestic work, showing his ability to devise a harmonious extension to an existing building and bring his antiquarian and literary knowledge of mediaeval art to the creation of the 'Hall of the Fair Star'. Pevsner, in writing of Elvaston, did not acknowledge Cottingham by name but wrote in unequivocal praise: 'It is the best nineteenth century interior.'[59]

Matfen Hall, Northumberland

At Matfen in Northumberland Thomas Rickman was employed to build a mansion for Sir Edward Blackett, owner of extensive estates as well as coal and lead mines in Northumberland. Rickman, a keen antiquary and architect, had written an influential book, *An Attempt to Discriminate the Styles of English Architecture* (1817), a chronological account of the progress of Gothic which went into many editions with enlargements and improvements. He was a builder of churches, mainly in Midlands industrial towns. Like Cottingham he was forward-looking in his use of cast iron although his use of it for tracery in churches, such as his Church of St George, Birmingham of 1819-22, was criticised later as unsuitable by the Ecclesiologists and A. W. N. Pugin alike.

Rickman had begun drawings for Matfen Hall in 1828, but difficulties arose over Sir Edward's preference for Elizabethan style rather than Rickman's earlier Gothic, with Sir Edward constantly altering Rickman's drawings.[60] Rickman prevailed and Matfen is a Gothic mansion with severe ashlar façades, mullioned and transomed square-headed windows, stepped gables, many projecting bays and a front entrance of a great oak door within a flattened arch with square hood moulds, the spandrels carved, and above, an oriel window. Rickman designed a mediaeval great hall, the centre of the house, with Early English arcade and aisle leading to a sequence of three reception rooms to the south with curved bays, a lofty hammer-beam roof and, on the west wall, a great stained-glass window of fourteen lights depicting saints, kings and prelates. Relations with his patron became strained as the building progressed and in February 1835 Rickman was dismissed. Sir Edward, who claimed that he had 'chiefly planned and superintended' the building himself, took charge of finishing the work.[61] However, the great staircase was a major difficulty that required expert assistance and Sir Edward commissioned Cottingham to undertake the work. By October 1836 Cottingham had made designs and in a letter accompanying three drawings for the staircase he wrote:

'I am very sorry to have trespassed so long on your patience and am truly grieved to think you should attempt to go on with such an important finishing in your house as the grand staircase without assistance ... I propose in this design to get the whole of the open panelling cast in iron, also tracery to be laid on the strings of the stairs.'[62]

As Sir Edward was impatient to complete his house, Cottingham went on to suggest an alternative method of making the newels:

'I likewise recommend you to have the newels glued up out of 1½ inch dry wainscot or oak with a deal case in the centre of each – I have had some executed on this plan which stand remarkably well and take much less time than carving them out of the solid, indeed, unless the oak has been seasoned for years, it is almost impossible to prevent cracking and warping.'

Cottingham had been asked to make drawings not only for the staircase but also for the 'Hall door and chimney piece'. He in turn asked, 'Do you require a design for the door case as well as the Elizabethan door?' None of Cottingham's drawings survive in the archive, but in a sketchbook of the 1830s in the Avery Library in New York, Cottingham noted 'jamb for Sir E. Blackett's chimney piece'.[63] Cottingham concluded his letter of 1 October: 'You will perceive in my design for the staircase there are no nosings to the steps. I never saw an ancient Gothic staircase with moulded nosings beyond the first step ...'

Cottingham, as antiquary, looked to Crosby Hall as a fine example of late Gothic domestic architecture. His staircases at Snelston, Brougham and now at Matfen, borrowed much from the Crosby Hall staircase, with its flights of stairs at right angles, rising in a two-storeyed hall, with heavily moulded banister rail, Gothic pierced balusters and boldly architectural newel posts. Rickman had designed a great mediaeval two-storeyed hall at Matfen with early Gothic elements such as the Early English pointed arcade. Cottingham's staircase was a suitably monumental design in keeping with Rickman's Gothic interiors.

Cottingham may have made alternative designs for oak panelling, or Sir Edward may have altered the proposed cast iron to wood, for the staircase is solid oak throughout, forming a striking and impressive feature of the great hall. It starts in the west wall, the octagonal moulded newels surmounted by a carved oak lion and lioness bearing the Blackett coat-of-arms, passes the great stained-glass window, and rises along the north to meet the east corridor screened from the hall by an arcade of columns which continues round the south wall. The staircase is of massive boldness and simplicity, with cinquefoil-arched balusters inset with cinquefoil roundels and coats-of-arms, and architectural banister rail.

Cottingham continued to make designs for Sir Edward for some years. In 1845 he told William Brougham that he wanted to show him some shields of arms that were being executed in London for Sir Edward Blackett to hang in his hall at Matfen, and, in 1847, he rendered an account 'for preparing designs and working drawings for the rustic summerhouse and finishing same accordingly'.[64] Matfen Hall is now used as a Cheshire Home and extensive changes have been made to the interior of the building. It is impossible to determine which chimney piece or doorcase was designed by Cottingham. The lions and the summerhouse too have disappeared but Cottingham's fine staircase remains unaltered and intact.

Adare Manor, County Limerick, Ireland

Lord Dunraven was another eminent patron and self-styled architect who employed Cottingham. His task was to assist in making designs during a major rebuilding programme at Adare in County Limerick. A modest Georgian house of 1730 was demolished and between 1832 and 1860 Lord Dunraven constructed a massive Gothic mansion. Dunraven and his wife Caroline had begun work at Adare in 1825-9 when James Pain, a pupil of John Nash, submitted designs for a new house. During the 1830s, the kitchen wing, offices, a long gallery 132 ft in length, and private apartments for the Dunravens on the ground floor were built in Tudor Revival style.[65] Lord Dunraven, being a traveller and antiquary, was a member, like Cottingham, of the Society for Promoting the Study of Gothic Architecture and a frequent visitor to London to attend Parliament. He employed Thomas Willement to design heraldic stained-glass windows for the great gallery and wrote to his wife in 1839: 'One could run up and down stairs all day to look at it. It is so very beautiful.' He was delighted with the effect: 'I never saw the place look so strikingly handsome, but the Gallery almost looks like a Cathedral, I do not know how we shall ever fill it.'[66] During their travels of 1834 and 1836 the Dunravens bought Flemish carved oak which was incorporated into the stalls in the gallery. Fifteenth-century carvings were used to make up the gallery doors. And during 1840 Lord Dunraven bought extensively, writing to tell his wife of such purchases as a full-length portrait of Sir Reginald and Lady Mohun: 'Nothing looks so well in old places,' he wrote, 'as old portraits and old glass. We have plenty of each.'[67]

He also made an extensive tour of English historic houses, visiting Warwick Castle, Hardwicke Hall, the ruins of Fonthill, Chatsworth, where he noted the 'vast gallery covered with portraits and acres of tapestry and needlework', Wyatville's Windsor Castle, which he greatly admired, and Haddon Hall and its 'graceful irregularities'.[68] It is quite likely that he also saw Cottingham's Snelston Hall for Ashbourne, and its historic church, which Cottingham was restoring in 1840, was frequently visited and written about by antiquaries. Lord Dunraven visited nearby Alton Towers, which he did not like, calling it the 'worst style of Modern Gothic', although he admired the chapel. At this time he summarily dismissed Pain, who had been designing the extensions and building works at Adare, with the explanation:

'I did not cease to employ you professionally for the purpose of placing myself in any other professional hands. Building is my amusement and I am a dabbler in architecture and I have for some years now been carrying on the new work entirely from my own designs and without any assistance whatsoever.'[69]

This was some exaggeration, for in March 1840 he employed Cottingham 'to put his plans for Adare in tangible form'. He wrote to his wife that he 'had spent most of the morning with Willement and Cottingham' and in April 1840, he wrote to her:

'I was most of the day yesterday with Mr Cottingham, I like him much. He entered clearly into my ideas and is to draw up the elevation and all the details. But I was obliged to write to Adare for the exact thickness of the walls, size of rooms, and many such things, without which he could not begin to draw ...'

Lord Dunraven had decided to lengthen the drawing room, adding two oriel windows to the south. 'I decided upon that when I saw the oriel in St Mary's Hall at Coventry, and it happens to be just what Cottingham likes.' The dining room was to be altered, moving the door, taking down the exterior wall and creating 'a great projection, a second fireplace, with windows to the south for sun and the east and west for views ... I found it impossible to make the front regular and it will be much handsomer as it is now planned.' Lord Dunraven also wanted to consult Cottingham about the conservatory, to have him make further plans for the new wall, of full height to accommodate bedrooms, and to have a music gallery in the dining room, over the door from the saloon. He continued in a letter to his wife: 'The end of the drawing will be an octagon, projecting from the present room where the bay window does now, with an arch springing from corbels, which will enable the roof to be different from the rest of the room and that part may be arranged for musical instruments.' Cottingham made sketches and plans for all these works and in May Lord Dunraven required him to make working drawings of 'the open work of the parapet and cornice of the house as that cannot be improved, but the rest of the elevations would have to be considered on the spot at Adare before making a final decision'.[70]

At this time Lord Dunraven was having portraits of himself and his wife painted, and he wrote that he was thinking 'of getting the pictures put up in fixed frames inserted in great carved work up to the ceiling'. Cottingham made designs for frames which did not meet with the earl's approval, as he told his wife: 'He had prepared a drawing of the frames for the pictures today quite different from what I directed and not well suited at all, and now he must draw a fresh one.' Ultimately the portraits were mounted together, as the earl intended, in one massive gilt frame which hung over the fireplace in the long gallery. None of Cottingham's designs have

Fig.134 (Cat.E36) Library bookcase from Adare Manor, c.1840

survived and it is difficult to attribute to him with any certainty even those parts of the building for which he made working drawings, partly due to the fact that the earl claimed to have done them all himself. Some furniture, however, was executed to Cottingham's designs and in Christie's *Sale Catalogue* of Adare Manor on 9 June 1982, three oak library bookcases were attributed to Cottingham: the cornices pierced with quatrefoils, the open shelves framed by stepped columns joined by ogival arches and the doors with arcaded panels. The bookcases are very similar in design to Cottingham's Snelston bookcases and to Pugin's fitments for the Palace of Westminster, and take inspiration from Perpendicular Gothic of the late fifteenth century.

E36 (Fig.134)

Library bookcase from Adare Manor, possibly by L. N. Cottingham, c.1840
Illustration from Christie's *Sale Catalogue*, 9 June 1982

Six carved oak throne chairs were attributed to Cottingham in the catalogue; they have blind tracery to the Gothic arched backs, pierced quatrefoil roundels in the sides (a motif seen in his Brougham chairs and those for St Mary's, Bury) and the arms carved with recumbent heraldic beasts surmounting coats-of-arms, and some with leopard mask and winged seraph head capitals to the legs.

Fig.135 (Cat.E37) Oak throne chair from Adare Manor, *c.*1840

E37 (Fig.135)
L. N. Cottingham, carved oak throne chair, designed for Adare Manor, *c.*1840
Lender: V&A Museum: ex Christie's Sale of 9 June 1982

A. W. N. Pugin also worked for Lord Dunraven from 1846, making designs for the hall ceiling, staircase, dining room, library and terrace. Pugin's work was never fully executed due to increasing ill-health, and P. C. Hardwick was to complete the house for the third earl from 1850–62, making use of Pugin's drawings and possibly those of Cottingham appropriated by Lord Dunraven, for details on doorcases, chimney pieces and panelling.

Coombe Abbey, Warwickshire 1833-4

E38 (Fig.136; Colour Plate 7)
L. N. Cottingham, 'View of the South Front of Coombe Abbey for the 2nd Earl Craven'
Pencil and watercolour 19¼×37 in (49×94 cm)
Signed
Exhibited Royal Academy, 1834
Lender: The Christopher Wood Gallery

136

137

Fig.136 (Cat.E38) 'View of the South Front of Coombe Abbey etc', 1834
Pencil and watercolour 19¼×37 in (49×94 cm)

Fig.137 (Cat.E39) 'A Louis XIV Drawing room etc' for Coombe Abbey, 1834
Pencil and watercolour 19¼×37 in (49×94 cm)

E39 (Fig.137; Colour Plate 8)
L. N. Cottingham, 'A Louis XIV Drawing room, Design for the 2nd Earl Craven'
Pencil and watercolour $19\frac{1}{4} \times 37$ in (49×94 cm)
Signed
Exhibited Royal Academy, 1834
British Architectural Library, RIBA, London

In the 1830s Cottingham was also involved in making designs for the Earl Craven at Coombe Abbey in Warwickshire, designs which he exhibited at the Royal Academy in 1834. The designs included an Elizabethan entrance hall and gallery and a Louis XIV drawing room, although none appears to have been carried out.

Coombe was largely demolished and, according to Howard Colvin, archive material relating to this period is very sparse.[71] Several of Cottingham's working sketchbooks have survived but these throw little light on his commissions, consisting mainly of sketches of architectural features, details and working drawings: very few have any notation. (Cottingham evidently took a sketchbook everywhere with him and as a keen antiquary he would make drawings, mainly details from Gothic monuments and churches and early domestic architecture.) However, two sketchbooks in the Avery Library, New York, contain details of Coombe Abbey. Sketchbook number 4, inscribed 'L. N. Cottingham at Coombe Abbey, March 1833', contains pencil drawings, some very faint, with notations that give an idea of his proposed works. These included such details as 'elevations of Elizabethan fireplace' (possibly a preliminary sketch for his exhibited drawing for an Elizabethan entrance hall and gallery at Coombe); 'chimney piece and panelling above in bedroom over North Cloister at Coombe'; 'foliage on Elizabethan chimney piece'; 'west side of his Lordship's parlour; 'plan of recess, Beauty room'; ' the west side of Mrs Clarke's room, southern elevation of Coombe'; 'ceiling to Northern cloisters, Coombe'; 'western elevation of East cloisters with rooms over'; 'west elevation of Coombe'; 'south-east angle of walled garden'. Cottingham drew innumerable details of foliage on pilasters, 'ancient doorways', details of the coach house, stables, engine house, the brewhouse, the gardener's house and the walled garden. Again, his sketchbook number 5 has many details of Coombe: 'details of chimney piece, Lady Louisa's room'; 'flue to Elizabethan room'; and many drawings of heraldic ornament, architectural details and measurements, as well as drawings made at other houses such as Wikens, near Coombe, and Benham Park, Berkshire.

Cottingham would have found Coombe Abbey of great interest for it was built in 1150 by Richard de Camvill. The Norman work of the Cistercian monks remained in an undercroft in the east wing, and the mansion was

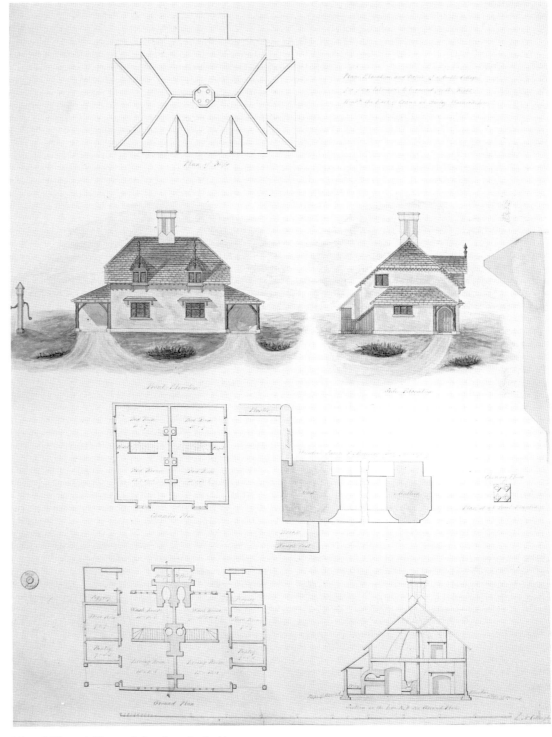

Fig.138 (Cat.E40) 'Plans and elevations of a double cottage for farm labourers etc', Binley, Warwickshire, c.1833
Pen, ink and watercolour $24\frac{1}{2} \times 19\frac{3}{4}$ in (62.25×50 cm)

enlarged in successive ages with Gothic windows preserved in the cloisters, Jacobean forecourt and south-west building, with a Palladian west and north elevation. None of Cottingham's sketches for Coombe are finished drawings for the sketchbooks are small, only 8 in × 11 in, and are clearly an architect's working notebook. It is impossible to tell from them which are Cottingham's proposals for alterations and which are jottings of existing features. They were used to develop his proposals for extensions, however, for in an inventory of Coombe made in 1916, five watercolours by Cottingham were listed, described as 'South west view of Coombe Abbey and four interiors of the same – proposed alterations and extension'. One other finished drawing for Coombe Abbey by Cottingham has come to light, and that was among the Snelston Hall drawings in the Derbyshire Record Office archive. The drawing is inscribed 'Plans Elevations and Sections of Double Cottages for Farm Labourers erected for the Rt Hon Earl of Craven at Binley Warwickshire'. It is undated but we can perhaps assume the date 1833 when Cottingham was working at Coombe.

E40 (Fig.138)

L. N. Cottingham, 'Plans and elevations of a double cottage for farm labourers to be erected for the Rt Hon Earl of Craven at Binley, Warwickshire', c.1833
Pen, ink and watercolour 24½ × 19¾ in (62.25 × 50 cm)
Derbyshire Record Office (Snelston Hall archive), Matlock
Photograph by Jeremy Hardman-Jones

The double cottage is of one storey with a hipped tiled roof and dormer windows, with square-headed mullioned windows and diamond lattice panes to the ground floor. The entry is through a single-storey lean-to at the side and a central chimney stack served each room of the two units. Gothic detailing is kept to a minimum with Gothic pierced trefoils to the dormer window bargeboards and a four-centred arch to the entrance door, drawing inspiration from the late mediaeval or early Tudor period when Gothic elements continued into the sixteenth century. As in the Snelston estate village watercolours, a Picturesque element appears in the rustic timber supports to the lean-to sections. But, as at Snelston, Cottingham gives evidence in his Coombe cottages that he has taken account of the vernacular architecture of the area. Thus he uses a hipped thatched roof, dormer windows , and plastered whitewashed finish to the walls. The interior plan shows two rooms of 15 ft × 12 ft on the ground floor, with built-in oven and a 'privy', and in the single-storey section a stove, pantry and piggery, with two bedrooms to the first floor, an arrangement close to the two-unit baffle entry plan common to the vernacular architecture of Warwickshire, here adapted to two

separate units. We have no way of knowing now whether Cottingham's extensions and interior designs for the main building were carried out, but the *Catalogue of Sale* of the Coombe Abbey Estate of 1923 listed four pairs of estate cottages at Binley, no doubt built to the designs of Cottingham's simple, harmonious double cottage plans of 1833.

BIBLIOGRAPHY

Elvaston Castle
Girouard, M., *The Return to Camelot*, London 1981
Matlock Record Office, information on lack of Elvaston material; confirmed by M. Craven of Derby Museum Service

Matfen Hall
Avery Architectural Library, New York, Ref. AA2620
Cottingham, L. N., Sketchbooks, Vol.5, p.47
Macaulay, J., *The Gothic Revival 1745-1845*, 1971
Northumberland Record Office, *The Blackett Papers*, Ref. ZBL list 34; 260

Adare Manor
Cornforth, J., 'Adare Manor, County Limerick', *Country Life*, 15 May 1969
Dunraven Papers, Public Record Office of Northern Ireland, Ref. D3196/J/1-30
Oxford Historical Society, *Draft Reports*, 1841, Bodleian Library; Letters and Pamphlets by H. Markland OHS
Sale Catalogue, Adare Manor, 9 June 1982, Christie Manson & Woods, Introduction by Knight of Glin – Caroline, Countess of Dunraven, *Memorials of Adare Manor*, Oxford, 1865

Coombe Abbey
Catalogue of Sale, Coombe Abbey Estate, 21 August 1923, Messrs Winterton & Sons, Lichfield
Colvin, H., 'The Rebuilding of Coombe Abbey', *The Walpole Society*, Vol.50, pp.248-53
Cottingham, L. N., Sketchbooks, 5 Vols, Avery Architectural Library, Ref. AA 2620
Craven Archives, Ref. 372, Bodleian Library
Robinson, S. M., 'Farming on a Princely Scale', *Architectural Review*, Vol.160, 1976

F Commercial and School Building

The Savings Bank, Bury St Edmunds 1844-6

At the time of his restoration of the Norman Tower and St Mary's, Bury St Edmunds, Cottingham was commissioned by the Savings Bank Committee to design a new bank on the site of the demolished houses which had endangered the stability of the Norman Tower. The bank, incorporating a caretaker's house, was to form the end of a terrace with frontage on to Crown Street and overlooking St James's Churchyard at the rear, situated 20 ft to the south side of the Norman Tower. In May 1844, the Vestry Book of the Parish of St James noted the removal 'of Mr Lenny's house and the clearing away of twenty feet of Mr Deck's house', and voted the 'site being applied to a Savings Bank'.[1] A Savings Bank Committee was formed and in the minutes of their meeting on 18 June 1844, it was resolved 'to examine minutely Mr Cottingham's plans'. Further meetings in 1845 considered alterations to the plans and the tenders for the work, and expressed satisfaction with 'Mr Cottingham's explanation of the Designs' which would not increase the expenses and unanimously adopted them, offering Mr Cottingham their 'thanks for the care he had taken to perfect the Design of the Savings Bank'.[2]

Cottingham's bank is built of local red brick inset with soft black diapering in a variety of patterns and stone dressings, forming a subtle link with the mid-eighteenth-century brick town houses further along Crown Street and the ancient stone of its neighbour, the Norman Tower. The difficulties of the site, which required a building that took into account an adjoining existing Georgian terrace, a deep drainage channel between the Norman Tower and the site, and the close proximity of its overpowering neighbour, enabled Cottingham to base the form of his Mediaeval Revival building genuinely on 'utility and convenience' and on irregularity arising from necessity. The design is asymmetric and freely functional Tudor Gothic in form, but on the street frontage Cottingham echoed the roof slope and symmetry of fenestration of its Georgian neighbours. The corner section has a striking oriel window of three mullioned and transomed Gothic pointed-arch lights, and above, a steep-pointed gable with finely detailed cut and rubbed brick copings and finials.

F1 (Figs 139, 140)
The Savings Bank, Crown Street, Bury St Edmunds,
designed by L. N. Cottingham, 1846
Exterior views
Photographs by I. R. G. Spencer

The main entrance is to the side facing the tower, with
four-centred arch stone canopy supported on moulded
columns, its pointed gable echoing that of the entrance
porch to the tower, and a Gothic panelled oak door with
wrought-iron hinges and studding. The fenestration to
the side is asymmetrically arranged with a variety of
single, double and triple stone-mullioned, transomed
pointed lights with lattice panes, under square heads with
random ashlar architrave surrounds, and one massive
rectangular window of seven arched lights. The side
elevation has two steep gables with brick coping and
boldly articulated chimney stack with diapering and the
date AD 1846, steeply pitched roofs, fish-scale tiling and
groups of tall Tudor brick-patterned chimneys. The rear
of the building has the entrance to the caretaker's house,
two steep gables, an oriel window of rectangular plan
with three lights and a frieze carved with blind
quatrefoils, and continuous hood moulds above a
rectangular five-light mullioned, transomed square-
leaded window, random stone quoins, and a tall staircase
turret, the whole inset with diapers. Further committee
meetings of April 1847 noted requests for estimates for
completing the bank, for supplying and fitting iron doors,
making all parts exposed to the next property fireproof
and obtaining a perpendicular boundary between the
property of the bank and that of a Mr Law, in a straight
line from the passage of the bank to the churchyard,
creating a kitchen under the waiting room and a footway
to the entrance into the bank. By January 1848 Nockalls
Cottingham was rendering his final accounts for the work
to the interior, the fireproofing, iron strongroom doors,
and all furniture such as oak benches for the waiting
room, committee chairs and a president's chair, a large
table with drawers for the bank and stools for clerks as
well as chimney pieces, hearths, encaustic tiles, grates,
fire irons and fenders, kitchen range and dresser, door
handles, coathooks, stoves, shoe scrapers, wallpaper,
umbrella stands and coal scoops. All these items were
listed with individual prices, the total amounting to
£304 12s 8d.[3]

The interior of the bank has been altered to
accommodate modern office arrangements, the fireplaces
and the original staircase having been removed. But in the
caretaker's cottage the original features remain, such as
its groined entrance lobby of carved and painted oak, the
two-light inner-pointed arch door with linenfold panels
and a cast-iron fireplace with Tudor rose ornament,
traceried columns and a leafy branch support to the shelf.

Figs 139 and 140 (Cat.F1) Two views of the Savings Bank,
Bury St Edmunds, 1846

Contemporary interest in Tudor and Elizabethan precedent had been stimulated by the choice of Elizabethan or Gothic for the Houses of Parliament Competition, and by the publication of various works during the 1830s and 1840s such as Thomas Hunt's *Tudor Architecture* (1830), C. J. Richardson's *Architectural Remains of the Reigns of Elizabeth and James I* (1840), and particularly Joseph Nash's *The Mansions of England in Olden Time*s (1839-49), with lithographs of Elizabethan country houses. Cottingham, however, had been one of the first to suggest as early as 1822 a study of ancient architecture as a source of style, and he had long been interested in sixteenth-century domestic architecture. His museum contained many examples of fifteenth- and sixteenth-century architecture and design, and he brought his knowledge of ancient precedent in structure and design to his Tudor Revival Savings Bank.

Other architects had designed Gothic Revival buildings with Tudor elements, such as Philip Hardwick the elder, whose grammar school at Stockport in Cheshire of 1831 was in sixteenth-century style, built of brick with stone dressings, the schoolroom with open timber roof and double-height mullioned bay window. With his son P. C. Hardwick, he designed buildings for Lincoln's Inn in 1839 in red brick with diapering, stone dressings, square towers and ogival pinnacled turrets. However, as Hermione Hobhouse pointed out in *Seven Victorian Architects*, Hardwick's Gothic was never more than skin-deep, for his buildings have no concession to Gothic planning such as Cottingham introduced into his Savings Bank, with their strictly symmetrical plans and exterior Tudor elements.[4] It is interesting to note that Hardwick and Cottingham were exact contemporaries, Hardwick taking up his post as surveyor to the Goldsmith's Company in 1829 at a time when Cottingham was surveyor to the Cooks' Company. Hardwick, too, shared antiquarian interests and it is possible that the two knew each other well, resulting in mutual influence.

It may be that Cottingham looked at sixteenth-century domestic architecture of Suffolk as a suitable style, harmonising in materials and style with its surroundings. Suffolk has some remaining examples of brick architecture that Cottingham knew well, such as the family home of his antiquary friend John Gage, Hengrave Hall of 1538; Helmingham Hall of 1500 with diapering and tall brick chimneys; the Cliftons at Clare, again with a rich variety of intricately patterned brick chimneys; and West Stow and Melford Halls. Another quite unmistakable source for Cottingham's Savings Bank is Layer Marney in Essex, built about 1520-30. The great 70 ft, eight-storey gatehouse which still stands was completed but building stopped in 1530 before the

proposed main courtyard could be finished. In Cottingham's day, although partly demolished, some of the buildings of the courtyard still remained. Cottingham had panelling from Layer Marney in his collection, and he had made casts of various architectural details. J. H. Parker's illustration of Layer Marney in his *Some Account of Domestic Architecture in England* (1851) shows how closely Cottingham's Savings Bank echoes early sixteenth-century East Anglian domestic architecture: all-over diapering is used in the asymmetric structure; the detail on the Layer Marney chimneys protruding from the wall is repeated in the Savings Bank design, as are continuous hood moulds, and a variety of square-headed windows. Bury St Edmunds had few surviving examples of its sixteenth-century brick dwellings. In his Savings Bank, Cottingham chose to revive the style for an imposing town property, drawing for his source upon East Anglia's mediaeval past. Pevsner dismissed the bank as a 'rather unfortunate effort in the Victorian Tudor Gothic, irregular, diapered, red, turreted', and again omitted the name of the architect.[5] A juster appraisal would cite Cottingham's Savings Bank as an example of English Gothic Revival architecture, based upon principles of truth to materials and fitness for purpose, a forerunner, like the Snelston village estate, of the English domestic revival architecture later in the century that looked, not to English or European ecclesiastical Gothic for its inspiration, but to the English mediaeval tradition as a source of style.

Tuddenham School, Suffolk 1846

In a letter to William Brougham of June 1846, Cottingham described a preparation for the treatment of wood which he had used very successfully at a number of works including 'the endowed school at Tuddenham'.[6] Research revealed that in 1725 in the will of J. Cockerton Esq, a Charitable Trust was set up to buy land to build a Free School for children of the poor, with a salary for the schoolmaster and money for its upkeep.[7] The resulting school at Tuddenham had fallen into a sad state of disrepair by 1795. In 1855 *White's Suffolk Directory* stated that 'the house and school' were rebuilt in 1846 but made no mention of the architect. However, the receipts and payments account book of the trustees of Cockerton's Charity records the following payment in 1846: 'Mr Cottingham, Architect, for Plans, Drawings and Superintendence upon the erection of Tuddenham School £30'. The trustees' records contain no plans, drawings or correspondence relating to the work, but Cottingham's village school, now used as a private house, has remained largely unspoilt and unaltered.

F2 (Figs 141, 142)
Tuddenham School, Suffolk, 1846, designed by L. N. Cottingham
Photographs by Studio Five, Thetford

J. Cockerton, at the early date of 1725, was an enlightened benefactor, for generally it was not until after 1775 that a new sympathy for the poor became widespread. The Society of Friends had foreshadowed this new attitude with their concern for education, the oldest Quaker foundation being a warehouse school in Clerkenwell in 1702. But in general, before the establishment of education for all children by the Elementary Education Act of 1870, there was no national system of schooling, with secondary education available only to the more fortunate and higher education to the privileged few. Charitable benefactors like J. Cockerton of Suffolk, voluntary societies such as the National Society for Education representing Anglican interests and the British and Foreign School Society, helped in the expansion of primary education. Some writers such as Joseph Lancaster in the early nineteenth century were conscious of the importance of the school building and its internal plan. In his *Improvements in Education* (1805) he advocated a new arrangement of desks facing the master, allowing seven feet per child, aisles five feet wide, low ceilings for lessening of noise, white limewashed walls, novel heating arrangements of flues at floor level instead of open fires, and adequate sanitary accommodation. These ideas were adopted by the National Society for the new elementary schools like the Daventry school of 1826, of rather gaunt and barn-like appearance.[8] In parish schools, however, the school would be small, of simple plan with one large schoolroom, cloakroom and porch, and usually relied on one teacher who would live in part of the building.

In the 1820s and 1830s most of the schools were classical in style. But Gothic, often a secular Tudor Gothic, gradually made an appearance, a reflection of its use for scholastic building during the great educational expansion of Tudor and Stuart times, and was generally used for schools with any claim to architectural pretensions. Examples of such schools were John Shaw's Christ's Hospital, Newgate Street of 1820-32; Edward Blore's Harpur Street School in Bedford of 1829; and King Edward's School in Birmingham by Charles Barry and A. W. N. Pugin of 1838. The secular Tudor style for schools grew in popularity during the 1830s, but by the 1840s ecclesiastical Gothic became widespread due to the influence of the Oxford Movement and the Ecclesiologists: and school building had come to be viewed as second only in importance to church building. In 1847 the *Ecclesiologist* advocated certain architectural

Figs 141 and 142 (Cat.F2) Two views of Tuddenham School, Suffolk, 1846

of the day, and would seem to place education on a Christian footing.'[9]

Before 1840, only the major public school foundations had the services of an architect. But now a plea for professionally designed village schools was made in Henry Kendall's *Designs for Schools and School Houses* (1847). In the Preface he wrote that 'styles of the Middle Ages ... are best suited for school houses for the buildings themselves, like pious institutions of olden times, partake of a semi-ecclesiastical character'. He did not consider purity of style an essential and his designs combined all styles of Gothic and mixed Tudor with 'the fantastic medley manner of building in the time of James I'. Kendall's School for Poor Boys of 1842, one of three designed by Kendall and built at Bury St Edmunds, is of red brick, diapered with knapped flint, copings with corbelled pinnacles, buttresses and battlements in white Suffolk brick, and mullioned and transomed traceried windows of fir, grained and varnished.

By complete contrast, Cottingham's school at Tuddenham, like Pugin's Roman Catholic Spetchley School in Worcestershire of 1841, relied on the use of local materials for 'reality', with minimal Gothic detail, drawing upon evidence of vernacular architecture where late Gothic elements had lingered through the sixteenth and into the early seventeenth centuries. A fine Suffolk example was Sir John Leman's School at Beccles of 1631 with mullioned lights, a Tudor arch doorway under square hood moulds and dormer windows in the pantiled roof.

The plan of Cottingham's school is very similar to Pugin's Spetchley, a single-storey centre section with entrance porch and steep pantiled roofs, a high hammer-beam schoolroom at one end, and at the other end, set at right angles, the schoolmaster's two-storeyed dwelling attached to the school. Cottingham used local materials to create a simple unprententious English architecture based on mediaeval precedent: Suffolk knapped flint ranging in colour from dark to pale grey for the walls, contrasting with functionally necessary smooth-cut ashlar architraves of the square-headed mullioned windows and doorways, and moulded gable copings and finials; and local red brick for the quoins, bases and chimney stacks with a decorative stepped edging between the stone copings and the flint walls. Gothic detailing in the Tuddenham school is kept to a minimum, as at Snelston estate village, with no buttresses or traceried windows: and the four-centred arch is used simply for doors, entrance porch arches and the centre light of the large schoolroom windows. The separate functions of the building are clearly expressed on the outside, each section with its own roof, and the massive chimney stacks with their diamond chimney pots project boldly from the walls. The gabled schoolroom with hammer-beam roof

requirements such as a separate roof for the schoolroom and the master's house, with the classrooms set at right angles and a lean-to cloakroom. Boys and girls were to be separated wherever possible and the school should be 'real' in every way, the internal fittings, the desks and paper for the walls should be good and 'real' without archaism: 'A school with its gable crosses, its crested ridge, its Middlepointed windows, simple and beautiful, its well carved fittings, its holy pictures, its roses or Virginia creepers, need not cost more than the erections

has three windows to its front elevation, mullioned and transomed two-light rectangular windows on either side of a large three-light centre window, with flattened arch architrave, and above, a small square-headed garret window. The school is of substantial size, larger than the average nineteenth-century parish school, with two schoolrooms, each with its own heating stove and chimney stack, separate entrances, and lean-to cloakroom with entry from the playground and the single-storey schoolroom. The *Ecclesiologist*'s school plan instructions of 1847 could have been modelled on Tuddenham School, although they advocated the ecclesiastical style of the Middle Pointed period.

The schoolmaster's house is gabled, two storeys high and one room deep on the vernacular baffle entry plan, with two reception rooms, one with a large side bay window, a gabled entrance porch with Gothic arch oak door with cast-iron hinges, two-light windows, stone copings and finials, and a lean-to kitchen and woodshed with the third bedroom and gabled dormer above. Access to the schoolrooms was through an inner lobby and doorway leading from the rear entrance of the schoolmaster's house to the single-storey central classroom. The irregular fenestration of the house reveals the two-bay plan. The bedroom above the sitting room has a two-light window to the front and a three-light window to the side elevation, with a small garret window above. The staircase is lit by a small single light, the living room with two double-light windows, and above a three-light window, all with stone mullions and transoms. The general scheme of Cottingham's school echoed the mediaeval H-shaped hall house with the single-storey centre hall with a massive chimney stack to the rear, and two cross wings, a layout ideally suited to the needs of a school with master's house attached. An example Cottingham knew well was the fourteenth-century Little Chesterford Farm close by in Essex and near Great Chesterford, where he was involved in church restoration and school building at this date. A surviving sketchbook gives evidence of his study of buildings at Little Chesterford, with drawings of the church and architectural details taken from other structures.[10]

The principles of the Ecclesiologists and such publications as Kendall's ecclesiastical designs of 1847 widely influenced parish school designs. Butterfield's plan for a model village school of 1852 reflected these ideas, and G. E. Street used local materials and Gothic detailing in his small school at Inkpen in Berkshire of 1850. The work of Butterfield and Street in their simple village schools of the 1850s clearly reflected an influence, hitherto attributed solely to Pugin, but stemming also from Cottingham's earlier examples of an architecture based on the vernacular.

The interior of Cottingham's Tuddenham School suffered minor alterations in its transition from school to private house in 1969. A mezzanine floor with bedroom and bathroom was inserted in the large schoolroom and the open-timbered roof boarded over. Some of the stone mullions have been replaced with modern wooden frames, and cast-iron stoves and encaustic flooring have given way to central heating and wall-to-wall carpeting. However, apart from an injudicious use of brilliant white paint over the stone arched entrance porches, the exterior of the building is in original condition. The former school is a fine, hitherto unknown example of Cottingham's work, perfectly suited to its English village setting.

Great Chesterford School, Essex 1846

Also in 1846 Cottingham gained the commission to build another school close by in Essex at the village of Great Chesterford.[11] He had restored the parish church of Great Chesterford in 1841 under the patronage of the Reverend Lord Charles Aurelius Hervey, Vicar of Great Chesterford from 1839, and fifth son of the First Marquis, the Earl of Bristol.[12] Lord Charles's brother, the fourth son, the Lord Arthur Hervey, later Bishop of Bath and Wells, was the patron of much of Cottingham's church restoration work in Suffolk. Both brothers, in their interest in architecture, took after their grandfather, the eccentric Earl of Bristol and Bishop of Derry who instigated grandiose building schemes at Ickworth and in Northern Ireland. Cottingham also had close family connections in the area. His maternal grandmother lived in Great Chesterford until her death in 1813 aged eighty-eight, and his brother Robert Martin Johnson Cottingham, a farmer and church warden, lived there for sixty years.[13]

Lord Charles Hervey initiated a number of building schemes but, as the second youngest of six sons, he could not rely on patrimony and had very limited personal resources. Parochial finance limited his ambitions but to him goes the credit for the building of the National School. He worked at fund raising, taking a detailed interest in Cottingham's plans, and due to his efforts the school remained in the management of the Church of England.[14] Unlike the Tuddenham school, funded by a Charitable Trust, the Great Chesterford school received a government grant towards its building through the Committee of Council on Education. In answer to the pressing need for elementary schools, the government had instigated grants for education in 1833 and the committee ruled that all grant-aided schools should be inspected and building plans approved. The school promoters, who had to raise at least half the cost of the

school by subscription, had to apply directly to the committee, leaving the National and British School Societies to make their own building grants.

F3 (Figs 143, 144)
Great Chesterford School, Essex, designed by L. N. Cottingham, 1846
Photographs by I. R. G. Spencer

None of Cottingham's plans or drawings has come to light but reference is made to payments from the school building fund for plans dated January to February 1845 and for specifications from Cottingham of 1847. The site of the school, in the middle of the village, was the gift of the Marquess of Bristol in 1845, and the draft application to the Committee of Council on Education, dated October 1846, included a full description of the proposed building materials, referring to a complete set of plans.[15] Cottingham chose a more noticeably ecclesiastical Gothic style than Tuddenham for the Great Chesterford project, no doubt because it was a church school and the plans and designs had to be approved by the committee. Once again, he used the traditional materials of the Suffolk/Essex border, with flint walling, stone-mullioned windows, architraves and quoins, white Suffolk brick for the base plinth of the building and for the clustered chimney stacks, and tiled roof with alternating bands of straight and semi-circular fish-scale tiles. The single-storey schoolroom, before its alterations and extension of 1857, had a steep gabled roof, four stone-mullioned three-light windows with trefoil heads in ogee-pointed arches, entrance doors to the south elevation, buttressed and gabled west and east elevations with straight stone coping and Gothic finials, two double chimney stacks with diagonal pots to heat each large schoolroom, and a lean-to cloakroom with square-headed windows, entered from the schoolyard and from the schoolroom.

The master's two-storeyed home set at right angles to the school is of substantial size, two rooms deep and three bays wide with two three-light ogee-pointed stone-mullioned windows to match the school and one single-light ogee trefoil-pointed window inset with a trefoil to the west elevation, with three gabled dormers above having two-light cinquefoil wooden-framed windows, trefoil arched bargeboards and Gothic finials. A lean-to projection to the north end forms a kitchen with arched entrance doorway and two-light mullioned window. To the rear, the east-facing elevation again has three mullioned windows and dormers above with three lean-to projections of reducing roof heights as woodshed, wash-house and stores. A lean-to entrance lobby in the angle of the schoolroom and house mirrors the one to the front of the building giving access to the school and the

Figs 143 and 144 (Cat.F3) Two views of Great Chesterford School, Essex, 1846

master's house. Two massive chimney stacks of flint walling with stone quoins and four diamond pots in cut and moulded brick indicate fireplaces in the living rooms and bedrooms.

F4
Plans and elevations for alterations to Great Chesterford School, and proposed additions, 1875
Essex Record Office

In 1875 the school was enlarged by the addition of a classroom 16 ft × 14 ft projecting from Cottingham's south elevation, in exact imitation of his building, with matching two-light mullioned windows in the west and east faces and a large three-light fourteenth-century Gothic window with trefoil and quatrefoil tracery. The plans showing the proposed alterations indicate that the two traceried windows on either side of Cottingham's buttresses to the west elevation were later additions as they are not evident on the plan showing 'present schoolroom'. Cottingham's two central schoolroom windows were altered to connect with the extension, forming eccentric corner windows to the inner angles of the new classroom. The interiors have been altered over the years. In Cottingham's large schoolroom the lofty timber-framed ceiling remains but the fireplaces have been removed. The schoolmaster's house, now used as school administration offices, has suffered such alterations as the removal of fireplaces, one staircase and partition walls.

For his Great Chesterford school Cottingham looked to local precedent and materials, in particular, the old village school dating from the seventeenth century, which still stands in School Street opposite Cottingham's building. The small single-storey classroom is built of knapped flint with brick dressing, the large window having a flattened Gothic arch and the attached schoolmaster's house is of plaster and thatch.

The decorative roof tiling of Cottingham's school, of alternating square and rounded tiles, appears in the late sixteenth-century vernacular architecture of the Home Counties and southern parts of East Anglia. Nearby Little Chesterford Manor Farm, where Cottingham made sketches and could examine local domestic architecture of the fifteenth and sixteenth centuries, incorporates the clunch and flint of the Essex Cambridgeshire borders, still visible in parts, although painted over in recent years, the muted red tiles reflecting the variations in the composition of clays of the district: a fine surviving example of mediaeval vernacular exploitation of local materials, echoed in Cottingham's school. Little Chesterford Manor Farm had developed from a thirteenth-century two-storeyed house built of flint rubble strengthened with clunch and limestone, an aisled hall added at right angles just before the end of the thirteenth century and another wing added in the late fourteenth century, completing an H-shaped dwelling. Both Tuddenham and Great Chesterford Schools showed Cottingham's use of the Mediaeval as a source, and his concern for local materials and building methods. At Great Chesterford the use of Gothic was taken as a style appropriate to a school which depended on the patronage of the church.

Cottingham's schools of 1846 were early examples of Gothic Revival architect-designed schools that were to become widespread by 1860, although later schools, influenced by the Ecclesiologists and Ruskin's promotion of European Gothic, were built in an increasingly elaborate and ornate ecclesiastical style. *The Builder*, in 1850, gave many designs for Gothic schools, noting that even the Quakers, 'of all men the most indifferent to the claims of art', were losing their distrust of mediaeval styles. In 1860, Harry Chester, the Assistant Secretary to the Committee of Council for Education, said that where, before 1840, schools were 'low, thin, dingy, and ill-drained', now the land was 'adorned with schools, the most celebrated architects undertaking to design these buildings'. Thus school building was established as a recognised branch of architecture and an important part of the Gothic Revival.[16]

BIBLIOGRAPHY

Savings Bank, Bury St Edmunds
Cook, O., *The English House through Seven Centuries*, Weybridge (1968), 1983
Fawcett, J., (ed.) *Seven Victorian Architects*, Chapter 2 by Hermione Hobhouse, 1976
Lloyd's Bank Archives, File No.7048 c1b/51: Letters of Minutes of Public Committee of the Savings Bank re new office; letters, tenders, invoices etc from N.J. Cottingham
Parker, J.H., Source *Account of Domestic Architecture etc*, Oxford, 1851
Pevsner, N., and Radcliffe, E., *The Buildings of England: Suffolk*, 1961 Revised 1974
Wood, M., *The English Mediaeval House*, (1963), 1985

Tuddenham School
Cottingham, L.N., letter to W. Brougham, 19 June 1846, Brougham Papers UCL
Ecclesiologist, New Series XIX, January 1847
Kendall, H., *Designs for Schools and School Houses*, London, 1847
Seaborne, M., *The English School; its Architecture & Organisation, 1370-1870*, Routledge & Kegan Paul, 1971
Suffolk Record Office, Bury St Edmunds, Charitable Trust of J. Cockerton Esq. FL/644/M/13.1

Great Chesterford School
Cottingham, L.N., Sketchbook: (1) Drawings of Canterbury Cathedral, (2) Drawings of Little Chesterford etc 1846-7, British Museum: Dept of Manuscripts
Deacon, M., 'Great Chesterford: All Saints in the 19th Century,' *Unpub Ms*, Ref EROC4. Essex R.O.
Essex Record Office: Churchwarden's Meeting 1840, Churchwardens, R.M.J. Cottingham and Robert Cottingham
Essex Record Office: Draft Application to Committee of Council on Education, 29 Oct. 1846, Refer to LNC's drawings, D/P/10/28/4
Essex Record Office: Great Chesterford School, Ref. Acc 7444 D/P/10/28/1-6
ICBS, No.2985, Application 3 Dec 1841, LNC, Lambeth Palace Archive
Suffolk Record Office, Parish Register, FC80/L2/14-19, (Death of LNC's grandmother) S.O. Johnson, widow of M. Johnson (surgeon)

G Designs for Unexecuted Works 1821-36

Salters' Hall Competition, 1821

As far as we know, Cottingham entered three competitions for public works, and these are revealing of aspects of his development as an architect, of architectural practice and of contemporary patronage and of the changing taste of the early nineteenth century.

Cottingham's plans of 1821 and 1832 reflect the prevailing classicism of the day, and the choice of Gothic by the authorities for the Houses of Parliament Competition of 1836 is a highly significant pointer to the change in styles from the classical to the mediaeval, a development in which Cottingham himself had played a major role. Other aspects of Cottingham's attitude and approach to his work are revealed: his integrity and honesty in all his dealings, the thorough and meticulous preparation of plans and drawings, his concern for the practicality and function of the buildings designed, and his concern to provide the highest possible quality of craftsmanship, materials and service to his patrons. It may be that one reason for Cottingham's neglect, despite his undoubted eminence in his own day, is that he never won a commission for a major public building. His disgust at the corruption, 'jobbery and jealousy' that surrounded the instigation and conduct of competitions in the first half of the century precluded his attempting any more after his entry for the Houses of Parliament Competition.

Fig.145 (Cat.G1) 'Sketch for Principal Front for the Salters' Hall', 1821
Pen, ink and wash $16\frac{1}{2} \times 11\frac{1}{2}$ in (42×29 cm)

G1 (Fig.145)

L. N. Cottingham, 'Sketch for Principal Front for the Salters' Hall', 20 June 1821, and 'Plan of Butler's pantry adjoining Livery dining hall', 27 July 1833 (two on one sheet)

Pen, ink and wash $16\frac{1}{2}$ in $\times$ $11\frac{1}{2}$ in (42 x 29 cm)

Guildhall Library; ref. 516/SAL (1)

Cottingham entered designs for the Salters' Hall Competition in 1821. Two of the drawings remain, a front elevation of extremely simple, stripped neo-classicism and a ground plan showing the staircase plan and entrance hall. Virtually nothing is known of the competition and no prizes were awarded. The little remaining archive material relates that the company's surveyor, H. Carr, designed a building based on several of the entries to the competition. However, Cottingham's drawings and letters relating to the Fishmongers' Hall survive, permitting a more complete examination of his competition entries of 1832.

Fishmongers' Hall Competition, 1832

The old Fishmongers' Hall had been demolished in 1830 ready for the building of the new London Bridge, and a Building Committee composed of Wardens of the Fishmongers' Company was set up to determine the requirements of the new Hall. The company's surveyor, Richard Suter, and the New London Bridge Committee envisaged a new Hall that would accord with the detail, scale and mass of the bridge and Suter himself prepared plans and proposals. The committee decided, however, to instigate an open competition, offering premiums for the three best designs. The requirements were for a building with two important frontages, one to the river and one to the viaduct leading to the bridge. The difference in level between the wharf side and the road level was to be used as a basement area for warehousing, cellars, offices and Hall kitchens; the upper storeys were to be faced with Bath or Portland stone and the lower parts faced with granite. The details were sent to 223 architects and there were eighty-three entries including Cottingham's.[1]

Cottingham had hopes of winning this competition, expressed in a letter to Dr Routh at Magdalen College, Oxford:

'I am one of the successful candidates and as I expect all three architects whose designs are approved will have to undergo a strict examination as to their capability of carrying their plans into effect, I have some hope of being employed as architect to it, having taken very great pains with the estimate'.[2]

He went on to ask Dr Routh for a written testimonial of his professional ability, required by the Fishmongers'

Fig.146 (Cat.G2) 'Design for the Fishmongers' new Hall etc', 1832
Pen, ink and watercolour 25 $\times$ 38 in (63.5 $\times$ 96.5 cm)

Court, 'if my proceedings at Magdalen College Chapel should have given you satisfaction'. The decision, however, went against Cottingham. Henry Roberts was awarded the first premium, John Davies the second, and Cottingham received the third prize for his designs.

The remaining sixteen plans and drawings of Cottingham's competition folio confirms the quality of his work, his skill as an artist and draughtsman, and his meticulous attention to detail.

G2 (Fig.146)

L. N. Cottingham, 'A Perspective View of a Design for the Fishmongers' new Hall as it would appear from the North approach to the new London Bridge', 1832

Pen, ink and watercolour 25 $\times$ 38 in (63.5 $\times$ 96.5 cm)

Inscribed 'Tobit No.2'

Guildhall Library, Folio III, ref s831

The view of the Hall from the approach to London Bridge shows an imposing building of classical symmetry on a podium with two identical storeys and a third Palladian storey of lower height; the entrance at ground-floor level approached by a flight of steps had tetrastyle-attached Ionic columns of a giant order; a massive attic storey and entablature with dentil cornice and pediment enriched with arms of the Fishmongers' Company, and the whole surmounted by a dome expressing the great central two-storey Hall within. The detail of the building was restrained and elegant, with the battered effect of the architraves creating a subtle sense of movement. Cottingham had hoped to design a portico but severe shortage of space for the building on the available site rendered this impossible. His concern for the cramped quality of his entrance led him to write to the Fishmongers' Court suggesting the inclusion of a clause in the Bill before the House of Commons for improving the approaches to the New London Bridge which would 'allow you to bring the columns out to where the steps commence being in a line with the West side of the foot pavement, a portico thus formed would add greatly to the comfort as well as the importance of the building with very little addition to any present estimate.'[3] This improvement would have answered the criticism levelled at Cottingham's design in the Barbican Art Gallery Catalogue, *Getting London in Perspective* (1984) that 'the Ionic portico on the East side is disconcertingly close to the top of the bridge stairs which would have resulted in ferry passengers tangling with dinner guests and the dome above the East front would have looked off-centre from the Bridge'.[4]

G3 (Fig. 147)
L. N. Cottingham, 'Eastern or Bridge front from the South approach to London Bridge', 1832, Fishmongers' Hall
Line and wash 20 × 26 in (51 × 68 cm)
Guildhall Library, ref. 232/FIS

Cottingham's perspective view of the Fishmongers' Hall as it would appear from the east approach to London Bridge, the front facing the river, showed a boldly rusticated basement of open plan to allow for unloading from the wharf. Here Cottingham echoed the heavily rusticated arches and square pillars – for example of Queen's College Library, Oxford of 1693 or William Chambers's Somerset House of 1780 – but he changed the strict regularity by alternating large wide arches with narrow smaller ones, producing a rhythm to contrast with the measured symmetry of the fenestration of the three upper storeys. Above the projecting basement arcade, he placed a covered walkway or verandah with coupled columns, again of subtle rhythm, in turn supporting the balcony of the second storey at riverside level, which was the entrance floor at road level. The columns were articulated in the balustrading of the balcony and capped by pairs of classical urns. The attic storey was surmounted by a large plinth and a boldly modelled reclining figure with a spouting dolphin, possibly to represent a merman and dolphin from the Fishmongers' coat-of-arms. Cottingham's handling of this river front showed originality of composition with the arrangement of his arcaded basement, its varied arches creating an almost Piranesi-like effect as they receded beneath the building, totally in keeping with the massive vaulting of the new bridge. Cottingham's river front made an interesting contrast to Roberts's winning design.

Roberts unified his block facing the river with a massive engaged hexastyle range of Ionic columns of a giant order raised on a basement podium of regular rusticated arches. Here Roberts created the impression of a Greek temple which happened to be placed at a riverside. But Cottingham, whilst creating an imposing front, conveyed a sense of the building's use, reflecting perhaps the form of the eighteenth-century warehousing along the river front and, in his fine watercolour elevation, he stressed his intention by depicting men at work unloading from the wharf to the basement cellars.

G4 (Fig. 148)
L. N. Cottingham, 'A geometrical elevation of the Eastern or Bridge Front of the Hall, showing its connection with the Bridge approaches and Thames St', 1831,

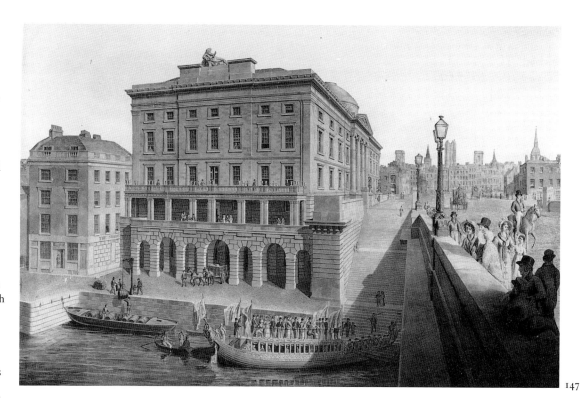

147

148

Fig. 147 (Cat.G3) Fishmongers' Hall Competition design, 1832
Line and wash 20 × 26 in (51 × 68 cm)

Fig. 148 (Cat.G4) Fishmongers' Hall Competition design, 1831
Line and wash 25 × 38 in (63.5 × 96.5 cm)

Fishmongers' Hall
Line and wash 25×38 in (63.5×96.5 cm)
Inscribed 'Tobit No.1'
Guildhall Library, Folio III

Other drawings included an elevation of the east front designed to show the fireproof warehouses and cellarage stores below the finished line of the bridge pavement and an elevation of the south front showing warehousing and wharves. The planning of these areas was of importance for the basement was to 'produce the greatest possible Value or Rental'.

G5

L. N. Cottingham, 'Geometrical Elevation of the South or River Front of the Hall showing its connection with the 'Shades' Bridge', 1831, Fishmongers' Hall
Line and watercolour 25×38 in (63.5×96.5 cm)
Inscribed 'Tobit No.1'
Guildhall Library, Folio III

G6

L. N. Cottingham, 'An Elevation of the North or Thames Street Front of the Hall showing its connection with the archway under the Bridge Road', 1831, Fishmongers' Hall
Line and watercolour 25×38 in (63.5×96.5 cm)
Inscribed 'Tobit No.1'
Guildhall Library, Folio III

G7 (Fig.149)

L. N. Cottingham, 'Perspective View of the Interior of the Great Hall looking North towards the Music Gallery end', 1832, Fishmongers' Hall
Line and watercolour 25×38 in (63.5×96.5 cm)
Inscribed 'Tobit No.3'
Guildhall Library, Folio III

Cottingham wrote on the drawing: 'This Hall is 70' long and 36' wide, the height from the floor to the centre of the Dome is 44 feet and from the floor to the centre flowers in the segmental part of the Ceiling 33 feet. Recess for the great side board under the Music gallery'. Here Cottingham used two storeys to create a magnificent space made more imposing by a central coffered dome. The central dome was flanked by a boldly coffered elliptical ceiling and the two tiers of windows of twelve panes and six panes had finely reeded and strongly defined architraves with full-height Corinthian pilasters on either side. The view looking north also depicted the music gallery, intricately wrought with classical motifs and supported on Corinthian columns. As is clear from his *Smith and Founder's Director*, Cottingham was well acquainted with the drawings of Percier and Fontaine, Charles Tatham and Thomas Hope, and it is possible to see these influences in his interior design for his Fishmongers' Great Hall.

Fig.149 (Cat.G7) Fishmongers' Hall Competition design, 1832
Line and wash 25×38 in (63.5×96.5 cm)

G8

L. N. Cottingham, 'A transverse section through the Great Hall, Entrance Hall and Grand Staircase showing the Base Hall to Offices, Entrances to Warehouses and Stone Staircases leading to the Cellars below Thames St', 1832, Fishmongers' Hall
Line and watercolour 25×38 in (63.5×96.5 cm)
Inscribed 'Tobit No.13'
Guildhall Library, Folio III

This plan showed the arrangement of his main reception rooms, with the large entrance hall divided by Corinthian columns leading to the west end of the grand staircase and the entrance to the dining room and above, a two-storey domed court.

G9

L. N. Cottingham, 'Plan of the Ground Floor of the Hall which is designed to be eight feet above the level of the Foot pavement at the principal entrance', 1832, Fishmongers' Hall
Line and watercolour 25×38 in (63.5×96.5 cm)
Inscribed 'Tobit No.5'
Guildhall Library, Folio III

Cottingham was gratified to be awarded one of the premiums in the competition but must have been very disappointed to lose in the final selection to Henry Roberts. In a letter of 15 February 1832 thanking the court for awarding him a prize, Cottingham hinted at the irregularities that frequently attended the running of architectural competitions at this time: 'I cannot but express the high satisfaction that I feel at my plan having so far met with your approbation as it was completed without the advantage of a conference with anyone from which I might doubtlessly have been better enabled to meet your wishes and conveniences which you may deem requisite.'[5] He continued that he had made a complete set of drawings of the old Hall before its demolition which in some measure assisted him, but he hoped that he could have an interview for the purpose of 'entering further into explanation upon the plan' in order to make any minor alterations that may be necessary. These could be arranged without materially affecting the principle of the design 'which is a practical one with due consideration of the mode of carrying all its details into effect'. He stressed that he had made careful specification of the works, correct estimates of expenses and was prepared to produce respectable builders who would give ample security to perform and complete the work at the amounts stated in the particulars. J. S. Curl, in his *Life and Work of Henry Roberts*, points out that Roberts had been a pupil of Smirke, had worked with him during the erection of the New Post Office, the British Museum and the restoration of the Custom House, and that at the time of the Fishmongers' Hall Competition, Smirke was supervising the planning of the approaches to the New Bridge.[6] Inevitably, some competitors assumed that Smirke had persuaded the committee in favour of his young assistant. But Cottingham in his letter made it plain that he was aware that other competitors may have had unfair advantages in the form of deeper discussion on the requirements, which in the original instructions had been fairly brief and unspecific; and he also distanced himself from architects of lesser quality who would enter drawings of fine picturesque effect and no practical value, and totally unrealistic estimates of cost. These were aspects of the competition system that were to bring Cottingham bitter experience four years later in the competition for the building of the New Houses of Parliament.

Houses of Parliament, Competition Designs, 1836

The destruction by fire of the main part of the Palace of Westminster, including the House of Commons and the House of Lords on 16 October 1834, provided the opportunity for the major architectural competition of the nineteenth century. Accommodation at the Palace of Westminster had been increasingly strained in the 1830s. Since the sixteenth century 500 members had been housed in St Stephen's Chapel, which was altered by Wren in 1692 and again in 1707 when the number was increased by the forty-five Scottish members. The chamber of the House of Lords in Parliament House was equally overcrowded and with the additions of the Irish Peers after the Union with Ireland, they moved into the old Court of Requests. St Stephen's Chapel was partially destroyed to make room for the Irish Members of the

Commons and additions were made piecemeal by Wyatt and Soane.[7] A Select Committee of 1833, under the chairmanship of Joseph Hume, the radical MP, heard lengthy evidence including a long interview with James Savage on the proposed rebuilding, and plans were drawn up by several architects and amateurs. Among them were J. Soane, B. Wyatt, J. Savage, J. Deering, E. Blore, F. Goodwin, Decimus Burton, G. Basevi, J. Wyattville, George Allen and Hanbury Tracy.[8] Savage's own design was classical with a Grecian portico and rotunda. After the fire Sir Robert Smirke carried out temporary works, including reroofing the House of Lords for use by the Commons, and the Lords moved into the Painted Chamber. Smirke's Gothic designs for a new Palace of Westminster were abandoned in favour of an open competition. This idea, in tune with a Reformed Parliament, was promoted by Hume and by the Tory Sir Edward Cust. Having the support of all parties, a Select Committee for Rebuilding the Houses of Parliament was appointed in March 1835. Members included the Chancellor Lord Russell, the Marquess of Chandos, Lord Stanley, Sir Robert Peel, Sir J. Hobhouse, Sir J. Graham, Lord Egerton, Sir R. Vyvyan, Mr O'Connell, Mr Hume, Sir R. Inglis, Mr Hanbury Tracy and Mr Bernal.[9] On 5 June, the committee published the terms of the open competition. The style was to be Gothic or Elizabethan, reflecting the developing Gothic Revival and notions of nationalism, the entries were to be on a scale of twenty feet to one inch and in monochrome, Westminster Hall was to be preserved, three perspectives only from set viewpoints were allowed, and no models or estimates were required.[10]

A great deal of research and writing has been devoted to the competition. And there has been extensive analysis of the controversies surrounding the choice of Gothic or Elizabethan as opposed to classical; the composition of the committee of judges, soon to be dubbed the 'gentlemen amateurs'; the complex requirements of the specifications and the exigencies of the site; contemporary reporting of the progress of the competition; the accusations of corruption and 'jobbery'; the unrealistic time allowed for preparation of designs and the time allowed for properly judging ninety-seven entries and some 1400 plans; the controversy over exhibiting the competitors' designs and those of the four winners; considerations of the value or demerit of competitions for public buildings; criticism of the committee's decision-making; the inability of English architects to plan on a massive scale; the over-ecclesiastical nature of most of the designs; and, finally, the choice of Charles Barry, protégé of Sir Edward Cust, winner of the competition, whose designs (the ground plan and general designs) were declared by Hanbury

Tracy to be 'far superior to any other plan that has been submitted'. It will be sufficient here to consider Cottingham's drawings and Cottingham's complaints arising from the competition, previously overlooked in published accounts.

Cottingham in his entries created from mediaeval precedent his own vision for the seat of government and took the opportunity in his designs to make plain his position as a preserver of the Gothic by including a full restoration of St Stephen's Chapel and Westminster Hall to their former mediaeval splendour. Cottingham's three plans for the competition following the prescribed viewpoints survive and include a perspective view of the new House, the Speaker's residence and the restoration of St Stephen's.

G10 (Fig.150)
L. N. Cottingham, 'A Perspective View of the New House, Speaker's residence and restoration of St Stephen's Chapel, given from the pavement in front of Westminster Bridge on the Surrey side of the river at the Bridge foot', 1836, Houses of Parliament Competition
Line and watercolour $19\frac{3}{4} \times 53\frac{1}{2}$ in (50×136 cm)
The British Architectural Library, RIBA, London (Ref. 051/14)

G11 (Fig.151)
L. N. Cottingham, 'A Perspective View of the South West front, given from a point on the West of Abingdon Street', 1836, Houses of Parliament Competition
Line and watercolour $34\frac{1}{2} \times 54$ in (87.5×137 cm)
The British Architectural Library, RIBA, London (Ref. 051/14)

G12
L. N. Cottingham, 'A Perspective View of the Entrance Gates to the Speaker's New Residence, the Servant's office attached to Westminster Hall and the North West fronts of the Law Courts as seen from the north east angle of St Margaret's Churchyard', 1836, Houses of Parliament Competition
Line and watercolour $26\frac{1}{2} \times 53\frac{1}{2}$ in (67.5×136 cm)
The British Architectural Library, RIBA, London (Ref. 051/14)

Few of the architects attempted to handle a monumental façade using the thousand feet of available river front and Cottingham was no exception.

Instead he used the long narrow north-eastern rectangle between the Hall and the river for his massive Speaker's House, forming a distinct unit. He enlarged the Old Palace Yard by removing the ruins of the old Court of Common Pleas and revealing two full bays of St Stephen's Chapel. Westminster Hall, with its surviving

150

151

Fig.150 (Cat.G10) Houses of Parliament Competition
design, 1836
Line and watercolour $19\frac{3}{4} \times 53\frac{1}{2}$ in (50×136 cm)

Fig.151 (Cat.G11) Houses of Parliament Competition
design, 1836
Line and watercolour $34\frac{1}{2} \times 54$ in (87.5×137 cm)

flêche, he restored without addition or embellishment. Pulling down the ruin of the Palladian Royal Courts of Justice, he rebuilt them in mediaeval fortified Gothic but retained the scale and mass of the original. Cottingham drew upon his detailed study of the Gothic of Edward III's and Richard II's time, describing Perpendicular Gothic as 'the invention of a noble minded race of men who dared to look at hill and dale – at rise and fall, advance and recess, and by imitating nature, introduced into their designs beauty and grandeur, by powerful contrast without encroaching on utility and convenience'.[11]

Cottingham achieved this looked-for movement and grandeur in his New House by designing eight great projecting five-storey square castellated and pinnacled towers with six recessed bays divided by stepped buttresses on either side of a hexagonal centre section. A three-stage Perpendicular octagonal flêche, reminiscent of Ely Cathedral, surmounted the whole and had flying buttresses, pierced quatrefoils and crocketed pinnacles similar to the late fourteenth-century Oxford Colleges such as New Hall or the quadrangle of Magdalen. For his Speaker's residence he again used symmetrical bays, here divided by projecting tall octagonal battlemented turrets with narrow slit windows and blind tracery. The central buttressed bay was dominated by a two-storey turreted gatehouse tower or *porte cochère* with Perpendicular windows, niches for statues and blind quatrefoil tracery. The Law Courts attached to Westminster Hall, by contrast, were simpler rugged battlemented Gothic or mediaeval domestic architecture such as the northern fortified castles and manor houses like Aydon and Naworth and Warkworth, all known to Cottingham, while his tall octagonal turrets revealed his knowledge of the great houses such as Nonsuch Palace and Layer Marney in Essex.

Cottingham attempted to achieve a unity of design and effect, without tame repetition, an aim shared by several architects such as H. E. Kendall and Thomas Hopper, who claimed to have treated 'the entire mass of building ... as a single edifice'. Some preferred to compose in a variety of styles to avoid what Cottingham described as 'the all-round-alike monotony of ditto repeated'. *The Architectural Magazine* of 1836 published a critical survey of many designs, dismissing Mr Hakewill's as 'extremely poor', Mr Cockerell's as 'having some beauties' and Mr Salvin's, 'though possessing originality would look infinitely better as a state prison or a hospital than as a Senate House'. Cottingham's designs were awarded a full paragraph but were considered to be

'scattered about in such a way that you can get no pleasing view of them, but by the help of a little manoeuvre he makes one good group in his design. A spire is placed on Westminster Abbey and it just comes in

the centre of the Speaker's House at that particular point which the view is taken from, but move it a little or left and the charm is gone.'[12]

The Gentleman's Magazine reported that the exhibition afforded 'a convincing proof that the architecture of their own country has formed no part of the study of our present race of architects'. Instead some architects had looked to continental models for inspiration. Morgan, for instance, borrowed features from old German domestic architecture, Donaldson incorporated a 260 ft tower and spire apparently based on Brussels and Bruges, and Salvin's massive designs reflected his knowledge of German Renaissance architecture. Architects largely drew upon ecclesiastical sources for their designs, or as *The Gentleman's Magazine* pointed out, 'ransacked Britton's *Antiquities of Great Britain* (1821) for precedents.[13]

The problems of style and precedents for the architects were only part of their difficulties. Charles Fowler wrote:

'No unity of design can be preserved, and the Hall and St Stephen's Chapel being mixed up with the new building will not only fetter the arrangement but will frustrate all the skill and endeavours of the architect ... the magnificent monuments will lose their own proper identity and the whole will be rendered confused and ineffective.'[14]

The Gentleman's Magazine noted that 'restoration as a prominent and valuable feature of the general design has been almost entirely overlooked'. But Cottingham, as a fervent preservationist, welcomed the instruction to retain Westminster Hall and he included a complete restoration of St Stephen's Chapel in his designs. He also made a model to demonstrate the feasibility of this restoration.[15]

A storm of protest arose after the first prize in the competition was awarded to Barry. Cottingham was one of several architects including Thomas Hopper, William Wilkin, James Savage and C. R. Cockerell who met at the Thatched House Tavern in St James's Street to formulate their protest at the manner in which the competition had been planned and judged. A sub-committee of the architects organised a petition signed by thirty-four of them. It was presented to the Commons by Hume, a member of the Committee of Taste who had been critical of proceedings.[16] The petition requested a Commission of Inquiry before the decision of Barry's favour was finalised. The petitioners protested that the decision was made by a consideration of elevation alone, instead of by plan; they included a print of Barry's ground plan to demonstrate its deficiencies, and put their

case to the Chancellor of the Exchequer and to Sir Robert Peel.[17]

Cottingham, in particular, protested that Barry had appropriated his ground plan for the Houses of Parliament after it was exhibited. Unfortunately Cottingham's ground plan has not come to light for us to compare and analyse the two plans and the changes that Barry allegedly made. Cottingham felt so strongly that he went to the length of petitioning the House of Commons to order an inquiry into the matter and redress the injustice, stating that 'the unacknowledged appropriation of the essential and peculiar arrangements of his plan' was a wrong that should be remedied, for the use of it now rendered Mr Barry's plan practicable where before it 'was manifestly defective'.[18] Cottingham's serious allegations of plagiarism have been dismissed as 'a disgruntled competitor's attempts to upset the award'.[19] Sir Edward Cust, writing in defence of the committee said: 'Few architects would be found willing to compete if a professional brother was to be made the depository of any little novelty or ingenuity their talents had devised and of which they would be most unwilling that another in their profession should take advantage.' He then cited Cottingham, who thought that the public exhibition of his design 'had furnished a hint to Mr Barry on the revisal of his original plan'. He dismissed this as jealousy and the 'unjustifiable exertion of those who were straining every nerve to deprive Mr Barry of the prize'.[20] Thomas Hopper, in forceful reply to Sir Edward, supported Cottingham's accusations:

'The Commission stated that Mr Barry's plan, although richer in appearance was infinitely less costly than many others and would not exceed £500,000. Parliament ... required an estimate, the Commission met again when, instead of the prize plan another plan was laid before them estimated at £724,984, which plan appears more Cottingham's than Mr Barry's. If Mr Cottingham's drawings have been copied into Mr Barry's plans, ought he not to be paid for them?'[21]

Sir Edward Cust had said that Cottingham thought his 'plans had furnished a hint to Mr Barry'. Hopper declared bluntly: 'Mr Cottingham said no such thing, he alleged that the plan was in essential parts his, and the exhibition of the drawing afterwards enabled him to detect the piracy and prove the fact'. The reluctance of the commission to exhibit the prize drawings was due mainly to their consciousness that 'a great portion of his plans had been transferred to Mr Barry's'.

Cottingham's friend James Savage also contributed to the controversy by writing an important and hard-hitting analysis of the faults of the competition, with observations on issues of copyism and the role of the architect, but to no avail.[22] The petitions were not successful and according to H. M. Port, Hanbury Tracy had 'little difficulty in showing the specific allegation to be largely unfounded'.[23]

Another aspect of Barry's plan was brought into question at a later date. When works were in progress, fears as to the fate of St Stephen's were voiced. Cottingham had planned a full restoration of St Stephen's as a fine example of thirteenth-century Gothic, but in 1842 a controversy arose over Barry's intentions. In the *Ecclesiologist*, letters were written quoting Barry's description of his designs for the competition in which he stated that the 'crypt and cloister are proposed to be restored'.[24] The *Athenaeum*, too, 'misunderstood' Barry, describing ' the fine effect that will be produced by the eye ranging upwards through the old Chapel of St Stephen's with its light attached pillars and richly groined roof'.[25] Barry replied that it was an error to suppose that the restoration was a part of his designs. The only portions he intended to retain of the ancient palace were the crypt and cloisters. A perfect restoration of St Stephen's was 'impracticable in every way; it could be restored and used for ecclesiastical purposes, but according to my plans adopted, it was impossible'.[26]

The *Ecclesiologist* retorted that 'such a want of true feeling for ancient art was to be lamented in an architect of such high standing and eminent talent'.[27] In commenting on Barry's lack of provision for St Stephen's restoration and seeming confusion between his plans and apparent intentions, the journal was in effect echoing Cottingham's and others' protests at the manner in which Barry's plans were adopted by the committee without proper consideration in every particular, and without concern to ensure that all the requirements of the specifications were fulfilled. Cottingham had protested in 1836 at Barry's lack of adequate provision of space and planning and the subsequent adoption of his own superior arrangements in their place. Now the *Ecclesiologist* highlighted the preservationist issue. By 1842, it was increasingly influential in the concerns for the restoration of churches and the preservation of mediaeval remains, and the journal was blunt in its condemnation of Barry's 'want of true feeling for ancient art'. According to Barry, a restoration was 'impracticable', but expediency and the excuse that his plans 'as those adopted' must stand overcame the *Ecclesiologist*'s objection and those of the preservationist lobby. The *Ecclesiologist* implied that Barry might be an architect 'of eminent talent', able with the advice of the Gothicist Pugin to supply the required Gothic Houses of Parliament, but no true mediaevalist imbued with a passion for the mediaeval English heritage could have dispensed with St Stephen's Chapel on so slight an excuse.

Cottingham maintained a dignified silence following the failure of his petition and the highly contentious matter of Barry's success. But it would not be unreasonable to assume that the patronage offered him later by Sir Robert Inglis, a member of the Select Committee, was to some degree a consciously proffered act of compensation for this patent lack of justice. It is hardly surprising that Cottingham did not enter any further open competitions for public buildings. Instead he relied upon the recognition of the quality of his work and his name as a mediaevalist to gain commissions through a network of patronage.

BIBLIOGRAPHY

Salters' Hall
Cottingham, L. N., *Salters' Hall Plans*, Guildhall Library, Folio III Ref. S 831, 1821

Fishmongers' Hall
Cottingham, L. N., *Fishmongers' Hall Competition*, Guildhall Library, Folio III Ref. S 831, 1831
Cottingham, L. N., *Letters to Fishmongers' Court*, 1832, Guildhall Library, File 2, MS 5843
Cottingham, L. N., Letters to Dr Routh, 1832, 13 Feb., Magdalen College Archives, MS 735
Curl, J. S., *The Life and Work of Henry Roberts, 1803-76*, Chichester, 1983
Metcalf, P., *The New Hall of the Fishmongers' Court*, London, 1977

Houses of Parliament
Architectural Magazine, 16 April, Editorial comment on House of Parliament Plans, Vol.III, 1836
Commons Journal, XCII, Appendix to the Report of the Select Committee of the House of Commons on Public Petitions, 10 May 1837, App. 652
Cottingham, L. N., *Plans for the Houses of Parliament Competition*, 1836. RIBA Drawings, Ref. 051/14
Cust, The Hon. Sir Edward, 'Thoughts on the Expedience of Control and Supervision over Buildings erected at the Public Expense and on the subject of Rebuilding the Houses of Parliament', 1837
Ecclesiologist, Vol. VIII, May 1842; No.XVI, Oct. 1842
Fowler, C., 'On the Proposed Site of the New Houses of Parliament', 1836, p.7, RIBA Pamphlets
The Gentleman's Magazine, 1836, I p.523
Hopper, T., 'Hopper versus Cust, on the subject of rebuilding the Houses of Parliament,' London, 1837, pp.7-9
Mirror of Parliament, III, 2487
Port, M., (ed.) *The Houses of Parliament*, Yale UP, 1976
Savage, J., *Observations on Style in Architecture with suggestions on the best mode of procuring Designs for Public buildings and Promoting Improvement of Architecture especially with recommendation in the report of the Commissioners on the Design of the New Houses of Parliament*, London, 1836
Minutes of Evidence, before the Select Committee, 1833, RIBA Library

Notes to Part Two

A: Cottingham's Publications

1 King's School Archive. It was possible for parents to obtain a 'Nomination' from those who gave donations towards the founding of the school. LNC obtained a 'Nomination' from the Reverend Ireland in 1832. (Information received from Frank Miles, King's School archivist)
2 *Douce Mss*, Bodleian Library, MSD26, letters to FD from William Capon, 4 June 1827, 13 June, 1827; Thos Walmsley (grandson of Capon), Sept. 1827; Lucy Capon, 13 June 1828, 26 June 1828
3 Pugin, A. W. N., *Contrasts*, 1836, reprint, New York, 1969, Introduction by H. R. Hitchcock, p.17
4 RCHM (England), London, *Westminster Abbey*, Vol.1, 1924, p.14
5 McCarthy, M., *The Origins of the Gothic Revival*, New Haven and London, Yale UP, 1987, p.59, plates 73, 74
6 *The Gentleman's Magazine*, 1832, pp.103-6
7 ibid., 1826, Vol.1, p.163
8 ibid., 1837, Vol.1, p.68
9 ibid., 1832, Vol.1, p.38, Report of Meeting, 5 Jan.; Mr Weston, a banker, proposed demolition
10 Restoration of the Lady Chapel, Southwark, *Report of a Meeting* held at Freemason's Tavern, 28 Jan., 1832, BL
11 ibid., Resolution 4
12 *The Gentleman's Magazine*, 25 Feb. 1832, pp.103-6: letter from E. I. Carlos
13 Stevens, R., DD, *Repairs to Rochester Cathedral 1825-26*, 'Mr Cottingham, Architect'. Transcript of notebook kept by Robert Stevens, Dean of Rochester (1820-70), 1825, p.1, Kent R.O.
14 ibid., pp.6-8
15 Lister, R., *Decorative Cast-Ironwork in Great Britain*, London, 1960, pp.5-7, pp.86-7
16 Robertson, F. G. and J., *Cast Iron Decoration: A World Survey*, London, 1977, p.16
17 Harris, J., *A Catalogue of British Drawings in American Collections*, New York, 1971. The volume by Isaac Ware was inscribed, 'L.N. Cottingham'
18 Percier, C. and Fontaine, P. F. L., *Recueil de Décoration Intérieure*, Paris, 1801-11, Introduction
19 Robertson, op. cit., p.16
20 Pugin, A. W. N., *True Principles etc*, 1841
21 Ruskin, J., *Seven Lamps of Architecture*, 1849, Chapter 2
22 op. cit., Pugin
23 Viollet-le-Duc, E. M., *Entretiens Sur L'Architecture*, translated, Bucknall, 1877-81: Watkin, D., *Morality and Architecture*, Oxford, 1977, p.24
24 A Report from The Select Committee on Arts and their connection with Manufacturers, with minutes of evidence, House of Commons, 9 Sept. 1835

B: Church Restoration

1 *The Gentleman's Magazine*, Jan. 1825, p.76
2 Hope, W. H. St John, *The Architectural History of St Andrew at Rochester*, 1900, p.114
3 *Chapter Acts Book*, Rochester Cathedral, p.1873, Kent R.O.
4 Spence, C., *A Walk Through Rochester Cathedral*, London, 1840, p.11
5 Palmer, G. H., *Rochester, the Cathedral and See*, 1899, p.107
6 *Douce Mss*, Bodleian Library, D26; Letters of 5 April 1828; 11 May 1828; 21 May 1831
7 *Annales Archéologiques*, 'Promenade en Angleterre', Didron, Vol.5, 1846, p.284
8 Fawcett, J., (ed.), *The Future of the Past: Attitudes to Conservation 1174-1976*, London, 1976, p.103
9 Spence, op. cit., p.8
10 *A Perspective Account of the Cathedral Church of Rochester*, Anon, Rochester, 1839, p.112
11 Magdalen College Archive, *New Building Account Book*, 20 March 1829, Ref. CP2152; LNC, letter to Fishmongers' Court, 15 Feb. 1832
12 *Book of the Chapel*, Magdalen College Archive, MS732
13 Ingram, J., *Memorials of Oxford*, 3 Vols, 1837, Vol.11, p.21
14 Buckler, J., *Observations on the Original Architecture of St Mary Magdalen College*, (pub. anon), 1823, p.109
15 ibid., p.173
16 LNC to Dr Routh, 11 Jan. 1830, Magdalen College Archive, MS735
17 ibid.
18 ibid., letter from J. H. Browne to Dr Routh, 27 March 1830
19 Harper, J., 'The Organ of Magdalen College, Oxford', *The Musical Times*, May 1986, pp.293-6
20 Ingram, op. cit., p.23
21 Ferrey, B., *Recollections of A.W.N. Pugin*, 1861, pp.86-7
22 *The Gentleman's Magazine*, 1832, p.100
23 Cottingham, L. N., *Preservation of St Alban's Abbey*, Hertford R.O., D/228, 224: leaflet and etching of interior
24 Pevsner, N. and Metcalf, P., *The Cathedrals of England: Southern England*, 1985, p.245
25 Hertford R.O., St Alban's Abbey Archive, D/288
26 *The British Magazine*, Vol.11, 1832, pp.207-8
27 Hertford R.O., 1832, D/EX50021
28 *The British Magazine*, Vol.11, 1832, pp.485-6
29 Scott, G. G., *Personal and Professional Recollections by the late Sir G. G. Scott*, 1879, p.61
30 *The Gentleman's Magazine*, 1832, Report from Society of Antiquaries, p.546
31 *The British Magazine*, 1832, p.485
32 Hertford R.O., D/EX50021
33 *The British Magazine*, 1832, pp.485-6
34 Paterson, T. G. F. and Davies, O., 'The Churches of Armagh', *Ulster Journal of Archaeology*, Vol.3, 1940, pp.82-103. The 'Book of Armagh' was compiled by a scribe of the School of Armagh in 1807
35 *Ecclesiologist*, Vol.XIII, 1855, pp.8-15
36 Cottingham, L. N., letters to Dean Jackson, etc from 1834-42, PRONI, T2771/1/5/27
37 Carpenter, R. H., and Ingelow, B., *Architect's Report*, 1886, St Patrick's Library, BXXXVI28 V28ap2
38 *The Gentleman's Magazine*, 1834, p.296
39 PRONI, T2771/1/5/27, letters, Dean Jackson to Archbishop Beresford, 2 June 1837
40 *The Architectural Magazine*, Vol.1, 1835, p.278
41 Carpenter and Ingelow, op. cit., p.6
42 *Ecclesiologist*, Vol.XIII, 1855, p.8
43 ibid.
44 Rogers, E., *Memoir of Armagh Cathedral etc*, Belfast, 1888, p.129
45 PRONI, T2771/1/5/27, letter, Mr Paton to Archbishop Beresford, 31 May 1837
46 ibid., 7 June 1838
47 ibid., 29 July 1837
48 ibid., 27 May 1837
49 ibid., 29 July 1837
50 ibid., 20 July 1837
51 Merewether, J. A., *A Statement on the Condition and Circumstances of the Cathedral Church of Hereford in the Year 1841*, Hereford, 1841, p.7
52 *The Gentleman's Magazine*, 30 Jan. 1790, p.172
53 Britton, J., *Autobiography of John Britton*, Vol.1, 1850, p.176
54 Merewether, op. cit., pp.35-42
55 *The Gentleman's Magazine*, 1843, p.286
56 Morgan, F.C., *Hereford Cathedral Church Glass*, Leominster, 1979, p.23
57 Stevens, R., *Repairs to Rochester Cathedral 1825-6*, 'Mr Cottingham, architect', Transcript of notebook kept by Dean R. Stevens, 1825
58 Merewether, op. cit., p.23
59 Willis, Rev. R., *Report of a Survey of the Dilapidated Portion of Hereford Cathedral in the Year 1841*, Hereford, 1841
60 *Chapter Acts Book*, Hereford Cathedral, Contract and Specifications, LNC, 1843, pp.96-103
61 ibid.
62 ibid.
63 *Ecclesiologist*, Vol.VI, 1848, pp.32-7; paper by F.R. Haggitt
64 ibid., pp.345-7
65 Pevsner and Metcalf, op. cit., pp.165, 171
66 ibid., p.171
67 *Chapter Acts Book*, op. cit., Sept. 1849, pp.389-99
68 Morgan, op. cit., pp.12-13
69 Pevsner and Metcalf, op. cit., p.174, (source of information was Morgan, 1967) and Morgan, op. cit., p.23.
See Cottingham, N. J., letter to R. B. Phillips, 19 Oct. 1849, Belmont Abbey, Bundle 29; this confirms NJC as the designer, supported by evidence in Hardman's archive, JH to NJC, p.107, 1850, Birmingham Museum and Art Gallery
70 See Myles, J., PhD Thesis, 1989, Vol.II, pp.189-97
71 *Vestry Book of the Parish of St James: Council Proceedings*, 1840-6, Suffolk R.O., Ref 2571/1/2
72 Tymms, S., *An Architectural and Historical Account of the Church of St Mary, Bury St Edmunds*, 1854, p.94
73 *The Gentleman's Magazine*, Dec. 1844, p.632
74 Myles, op. cit., Vol.2, Appendix IV

C: Church Furnishings

1 *Brougham Papers*, University College Library; Magdalen Chapel Accounts, Magdalen College Library Archive
2 *Ecclesiologist*, 1845, p.121
3 Cottingham's pupil George Truefitt went to work for Eginton. (See obit., RIBA Journal, Vol.9, 1901-2, p.461.) LNC and Eginton had mutual friends such as Willement and a patron, The Earl of Craven
4 Palmer, G.H., *Rochester Cathedral and See*, London, 1899, p.92
5 Benham, W., *Rochester Cathedral* (*English Cathedrals*), London, 1900, p.39
6 Jervis, S., letter to Miss Dawson, 1979, Brougham File, V&A Archives
7 *Brougham Papers*, letters from LNC and NJC to W. Brougham, 31 July,1844 to 2 Oct. 1846; and letters from John White, Joseph Robinson, 1843-6
8 *William Brougham's Diaries*; Brougham Papers, UCL
9 *Bury and Norwich Post*, 3 Jan. 1849
10 *Suffolk Institute of Archaeology*, Vol.7, 'Theberton Church', 1891, p.253
11 Doughty, H.M., *Chronicles of Theberton*, 1910, pp.335-44

D: Church Building

1 Mowl, T., 'The Norman Revival in British Architecture, 1790-1870', PhD Thesis, Oxford, 1981, Appendix
2 *Brougham Papers*, letter 19 June 1846, NJC to WB
3 Nevile Family Papers, Nottingham R.O., Ref. DDN
4 ibid., Ecclesiastical Papers, 1839-85; letters of 1845; Building Accounts
5 *Ecclesiologist*, Vol.1, 1845, p.169
6 Lewis, G.R., *Illustrations of Kilpeck Church etc etc*, 1842; Introduction, p.xvii
7 *Brougham Papers*, 7 June 1845
8 *Sale Catalogue*, 'The Valuable Library of the late Edwin Cottingham, MRCS, of Bexley, Kent, etc etc', Sold by Messrs Leigh Sotheby and John Wilkinson, 15 June 1859, and three following days
9 *Ecclesiologist*, Vol.NVI, 1849, p.203
10 Morris, R.K., 'The Herefordshire School: recent discoveries' ; *Studies in Mediaeval Sculpture*, ed. F.H. Thompson, 1983, pp.198-201

E: Domestic Architecture and Design

1 *Survey of London*, Vol.23, South Bank, St Mary's Lambeth, LCC, 1951, p.28
2 *Cooks' Company Minute Books*, July 1822; 15 Sept. 1834; Guildhall Library, Ref. MS 3111/4/5
3 Merewether, J.A., *A Statement on the Condition and Circumstances of the Cathedral Church of Hereford in the Year 1841*, Hereford, 1841, p.7
4 Cooks' Company, *Minutes of Proceedings July 1822 - Sept. 1834*. MSS 31114-5, Guildhall Library Archive; Stevens, R., *Repairs to Rochester Cathedral 1825-6*, Transcript of notebook kept by Dean R. Stevens, 1825
5 *Crace Views*, XXX5, No.65, BM, Dept of Prints
6 Survey of London, op. cit., p.29, and information from Chesham House. Most of the original buildings of Waterloo Bridge Road, nos 79-119 have been demolished – Waterloo Station, Union Jack Club, and Cottingham's estate were removed to make a site for the Festival of Britain
7 *Catalogue of Sale*, 'Museum of Mediaeval Art collected by the late L.N. Cottingham, FSA', 3 Nov. 1851, Foster & Son; handwritten notes in the V&A Library copy give evidence of the buyers
8 Merewether, op. cit., p.7
9 *Derby Evening Telegraph*, 19 June 1949, article on Blore
10 *Survey of London*, Vol.XXIII, South Bank and Vauxhall, Lambeth Palace, see p.180
11 Cottingham, L.N., Plans for the Houses of Parliament Competition, *Catalogue of Designs*, 1836
12 Girouard, M., *Life in the English Country House*, Yale UP, 1978, p.265
13 Cottingham, L.N., *Plans etc of King Henry VII's Chapel*, 1829, Preface
14 Britton, J., *Graphic Illustrations with Historical and Descriptive Accounts of Toddington, Gloucs. The Seat of Lord Sudeley*, 1840
15 *Sale Catalogue*, 'Snelston Hall', Bagshawe & Sons, Ashbourne, 15 July 1946, lots 182-184
16 *The Queen*, 'Mrs Stanton and her Home', 6 April 1927, pp.5-7: See Aslin, E., *Early Victorian Furniture*, 1978, p.30. Aslin refers to 'bills remaining for ancient material bought for this purpose' but gives no reference. Mrs Stanton may have been in possession of them at the time of her interview in 1927. See also Cottingham's *Sale Catalogue*; 'panelling from the destroyed palace of Nonsuch'
17 *The Queen*, op. cit., p.6
18 Mottram, W., (a grand-nephew of Adam Bede), *The True Story of George Eliot in Relation to Adam Bede*, London, 1905
19 Derby Local Studies Library, Ashbourne RDC, *Listed Buildings*, p.40
20 Pevsner, N., *The Buildings of Derbyshire*, London, 1953
21 *Catalogue of Sale*, 'Snelston Hall, Derbyshire. Sale of Valuable Fixtures and Fittings', Allen & Farquhar, Ashbourne
22 *The Queen*, op. cit., p.6
23 Blutman, S., 'Books of Designs for Country Houses, 1780-1850', *Architectural History*, XI, 1968, p.25
24 Craven, M., and Stanley, M., *The Derbyshire Country House*, Derbyshire Museum Service, 1982, p.11
25 *Illustrated London News*, 1843, p.133
26 Strong, R., Harris, J., Binney, M., *Vanishing Houses of England*, 1974, p.100
27 *Brougham Papers*, WB's personal diaries, May 1844 to June 1845: letters from LNC and NJC to WB; letters from G. Shaw; letters from tradespeople; building accounts; letters from WB to Henry, Lord Brougham etc
28 Hill Mss Collection, Brougham Hall: *History of Westmorland*, Vol.5, 1850; Cumbria R.O.
29 *Brougham Papers*, letter, J. Richardson to WB, 25 Jan. 1844
30 Shaw, G., *Diaries*, 1831-3; 1834-5: *Sketchbooks*, 1830-50, Manchester City Library, MS927.2.515: Entry for 10 June 1832
31 *Brougham Papers*, letter, WB to HB, Aug. 1830
32 Parker, J.H., *Some Account of the Domestic Architecture in England, the Conquest to the end of the Thirteenth Century*, 1851, pp.222-5: an account of Brougham Hall written by WB and included verbatim
33 Tyler, D., *A History of Brougham Hall*, 1988. Tyler, in this booklet, traces the background of the de Burgham family and the division of the manor from 1315 to 1654
34 *Illustrated London News*, 1843, p.323
35 Tyler, op. cit., p.27
36 Campbell, Lady, M.S., (afterwards Mrs Hardcastle), *A Life of Lord Campbell*, 1881, p.244; visit to Brougham Hall, 11 Sept. 1848
37 *Shaw Correspondence*, letter from Stanhope to Shaw, 10 Oct. 1863
38 Brougham, W., letter to the 7th Earl of Carlisle, 25 Nov. 1844, Castle Howard Archive, J19/1/38/87
39 *Brougham Papers*, letter, G. Shaw to WB, 27 Oct. 1847
40 *The Gentleman's Magazine*, April 1848, pp.369-76
41 *Exhibition Catalogue*, 'English Romanesque Art 1066-1200', London, 1984, p.391
42 *Brougham Papers*, letter, G. Shaw to WB, 6 Oct. 1847; 15 Oct. 1847
43 *The Gentleman's Magazine*, June 1846, pp.618-20. Shaw wrote a reply (published 'grievously shorn and mutilated' as he told WB) in the July issue of the *GM*. Shaw suggested that an attorney in Appleby was the anon. writer and further, it had been repeated to him that Wordsworth had read the article with 'disapprobation – this looks like Lowther Castle interference as Wordsworth is notorious for his partisanship to the Lonsdale family'. This critique and Shaw's response perhaps serve to refute the suggestion in Tyler, (op. cit.), that the whole case of Bird v. Brougham was a publicity stunt to allow the Broughams publicly to reinforce their claims to ancestry
44 *Brougham Papers*, letter, LNC to WB, 7 Sept. 1844
45 ibid., letter, LNC to WB, 24 July 1845
46 ibid., letter, J. Richardson to WB, 20 May 1843
47 ibid., letter, NJC to WB, 24 April 1844
48 ibid., letter NJC to WB, 27 May 1846
49 ibid., letters, G. Shaw to WB, 6 Oct. 1847; 15 Oct. 1847
50 *Sale Catalogue*, Contents of Brougham Hall, 21 June 1932, Garland Smith & Co, Mount Street, London
51 ibid., lots 929, 930
52 *Brougham Papers*, letter, NJC to WB, 25 June 1845
53 *Brougham Papers*, letters, accounts, Lapworth to WB, 1844-57
54 *Catalogue of Sale*,' Brougham Hall Interior & Exterior Fixtures and Fittings,' Wed. 18 July 1934, Messrs Perry & Phillips Ltd, 59 High Street, Bridgnorth
55 *The Art-Union*, Obituary of LNC, 1847, p.377
56 Craven, M., and Stanley, M., op. cit., p.33
57 Personal communication from Lord Harrington, 15 Jan. 1986
58 Information from Matlock R.O.; Craven M., and Stanley, M., op. cit.
59 Pevsner, op. cit., *Derbyshire*, 'Elvaston Hall'
60 Macaulay, J., *The Gothic Revival*, 1745-1845, 1971, p.307
61 ibid., p.309
62 Northumberland R.O., *The Blackett Papers*, Ref. 2BL, List 34; letter, LNC to Sir Edward Blackett, 1 Oct 1836, Ref. ZBL 260
63 Cottingham, L.N., *Sketchbooks*, Vol.5, p.47, 'Jamb for Sir E. Blackett's chimney piece'

64 *The Blackett Papers*, Northumberland R.O., Ref. 2BL, letter NJC to Sir Edward Blackett, 16 Nov. 1847

65 *Sale Catalogue*, Adare Manor, 9 June 1982, Christie, Manson & Woods. See Introduction by The Knight of Glin, p.9. Source used, *Memorials of Adare Manor*, 1865, by Caroline, Countess of Dunraven

66 *Dunraven Papers*, PRONI, Ref. D3196/J/1-30; letter from Lord D. to Lady Caroline, Oct. 1839

67 ibid., Ref. D3196/E/7/19

68 ibid., letter, 31 March 1840; 4 April 1840

69 ibid., letter, Lord D. to Pain, Feb.1842

70 ibid., letter, Lord D. to Lady C., April 1846

71 Colvin, H., 'The Rebuilding of Coombe Abbey', *The Walpole Society*, Vol.50, pp.248-53

F: Commercial and School Building

1 Suffolk R.O., Bury St Edmunds, *Vestry Book of St James*, 1834, Meetings of 30 May 1844, Ref. 541/1/4

2 Lloyds Bank Archive, File no.7048, c1b/51; letters of Minutes of Committee of Savings Bank re new office at Bury St Edmund's: letters, tenders, invoices from NJC and T. Farrow of Diss

3 ibid., account from NJC dated 5 Jan. 1848

4 Fawcett, J., (ed.), *Seven Victorian Architects*, Chapter 2, 'P. & P.C. Hardwick', by Hermione Hobhouse, 1976, p.37

5 Pevsner, N. and Radcliffe, E., *The Buildings of England: Suffolk*, (1st edition, 1961), revised, 1974, p.150

6 *Brougham Papers*, letter, LNC to WB, 19 June 1846

7 Suffolk R.O., Charitable Trust of J. Cockerton Esq, Ref. FL/644/m/13.1

8 Seaborne, M., *The English School; its Architecture and Organisation, 1370-1870*, London, 1971, pp.112,137,150

9 *Ecclesiologist*, New Series, Vol. XIX, Jan. 1847, pp.1-6

10 Cottingham, L.N., *Sketchbooks*: No.1, 'Drawings of Canterbury Cathedral': No.2, 'Drawing of Little Chesterford', 1846-7, Dept of Manuscripts, British Museum

11 Essex R.O., Great Chesterford School, Ref. Acc 7444D/P/10/28/1-6

12 ICBS No.2985, 3 Dec. 1841, 'L.N. Cottingham, architect', Lambeth Palace Library

13 Suffolk R.O., FC80/L2/14-19, No.5, Death, S.O. Johnson, widow of Martin Johnson (Surgeon), Great Chesterford Parish, aged 88, 1813; Ref. D/P/10/5, 8 Nov. 1840, and 13 Nov – Meetings of Churchwardens, R.M.J. Cottingham and Robert Cottingham, (LNC's nephews)

14 Deacon, M., *Great Chesterford: All Saints in the 19th Century*, Unpub. MSS Ref. EROC4 pp.16-17, Essex R.O.

15 Essex R.O., Draft Application to Committee of Council on Education, 29 Oct. 1846. Refers to a complete set of drawings, D/P/10'28/4

16 *The Builder*, IX, 1850, p.91: Seaborne, op. cit., p.216

G: Designs for Unexecuted Works

1 An account of the rebuilding of the Fishmongers' Hall is to be found in: Metcalf, P., *The New Hall of the Fishmongers' Court*, 1977, and in Curl, J.S., *The Life and Work of Henry Roberts, 1803-1876*, Chichester, 1983

2 Cottingham, L.N., letter to Fishmongers' Court, 23 Feb. 1832, Guildhall Library, File 2, MS 5843

3 ibid.

4 *Exhibition Catalogue*, 'Getting London in Perspective', Barbican Art Gallery, London, 1984, p.30; also quoted in Metcalf, op. cit.

5 Guildhall Library, File 2, MS 5843

6 Curl, op. cit., p.66

7 Port, M., (ed.), *The Houses of Parliament*, Yale UP, 1976, See Chapter 2

8 *Minutes of Evidence*, before the Select Committee on the Rebuilding of the New House of Commons, 1833, RIBA

9 'The Select Committee, appointed 9 Feb. 1836, for the Rebuilding of the Houses of Parliament', RIBA Pamphlets

10 Port, op. cit., p.28-32

11 *Catalogue of Designs for the Houses of Parliament*, 1836

12 Editorial comment on the Exhibition of HOP Plans, 16 April, *The Architectural Magazine*, Vol.III, 1836, p.206

13 *The Gentleman's Magazine*,1836, p.206

14 Fowler, C., 'On the Proposed site of the New Houses of Parliament', 1836, p.7, RIBA Pamphlets

15 *The Gentleman's Magazine*, 1836, p.523: See LNC's *Sale Catalogue*, lot 829, Model of St Stephen's Chapel

16 Port, op. cit., p.79

17 *Mirror of Parliament*, III, 2487

18 *Commons Journal*, XLII, Appendix to the Report of the Select Committee of the House of Commons on Public Petitions, 10 May 1837, App. 652

19 Port, op. cit., pp.50,79: Cottingham's petition was not transcribed in detail

20 Cust, Hon Sir Edward, 'Thoughts on the Expedience of Control and Supervision of Public Buildings etc, 1837, RIBA Pamphlets

21 Hopper, T., 'Hopper versus Cust: on the subject of the rebuilding of the Houses of Parliament', 1837, pp.7-9

22 Savage, J., 'Observations on Style in Architecture with Suggestions etc etc on the Design for the New House of Parliament', 1836

23 Port, op. cit., p.80

24 *Ecclesiologist*, Vol. VIII, May 1842, p.117: No.XVI, Oct. 1842, p.18

25 ibid., 1842, p.18

26 ibid., 1842, May, p.18

27 ibid., Nos.XI, XIII, p.183

Biographical Appendix

The unsigned obituary of Cottingham which appeared in the monthly journal *The Art-Union* for October 1847 is reproduced in full in this appendix. Comparison with the other main obituaries confers on it primary necrological status. Thus the anonymous obituary published in *The Gentleman's Magazine* July – December 1847 is almost identical textually and it is noteworthy that all the qualitative judgements in *The Art-Union* are reproduced verbatim. The unsigned obituary in *The Builder* of 23 October – which had reported in its 16 October issue the passing of this 'long well-known ... ecclesiastical architect' – is altogether shorter than the accounts of Cottingham in *The Art-Union* and the *The Gentleman's Magazine* and the judgements of his professional achievement echo those of the other two journals. In the *Athenaeum* of 16 October 1847 the anonymous columnist suggested that Cottingham 'understood and appreciated the several distinctions of style in Gothic architecture; and had accomplished a good deal towards the revival of a true taste among us'; and concluded that the 'restorations at Hereford are just as carefully executed as the restorations at Ely – and that is high praise'.

A brief notice of Cottingham's death in the *Ipswich Journal* of 23 October 1847 drew attention to the restorations at Magdalen College, Oxford, and Rochester Cathedral; and, with a forthrightness not found in this context in the national obituaries, pointed out that his 'design for the new Houses of Parliament was rejected in favour of Mr Barry, and his design for Fishmongers' Hall, *somewhat unfairly, in favour of an inferior architect.*' [my italics]. It is perhaps worth adding that I was unable to trace in *The Times* any obituary of Cottingham. On the other hand, it was evident from an examination of this newspaper that there was no established tradition of a regular obituary column, necrologies being few and far between in the issues examined.

Cottingham appears in *The Dictionary of National Biography* (DNB) in the volume published in 1887. The entry is signed by L.C., that is Sir Lionel Cust (1859-1929: see *Who Was Who*, 1929-1940), art historian and, as such, an astonishingly prolific contributor to the DNB (760 articles according to Gillian Fenwick's *The Contributor's Index to The Dictionary of National*

Biography 1885-1901, Winchester and Detroit, 1989). *The Times* (14 October 1929) obituary of Cust described him as an historian of art specialising in early English portraiture: not, in retrospect, an obvious qualification for assessing the work of an ecclesiastical architect. L. Binyon's entry on Cust in the DNB 1922-1930 pointed out the accuracy and painstaking research characteristic of his biographies of artists. However, Cust inadequately evaluates Cottingham's main publications (1822-9) as containing drawings 'rather coarsely executed if also interesting as the first of their kind': while Cottingham made no claim for them as fine engravings, they were far from coarse and their significance, missed by Cust, lay in their promotion of a 'correct' revival. Cust rightly states that Cottingham 'did a great deal to promote the revival of mediaeval Gothic architecture', but his claim that Cottingham was 'now [1887] esteemed more for his draughtsmanship than the works that he carried out' reflects the contemporary decline of the Gothic Revival. Cust's most unjustly damaging and enduring judgement is that Cottingham's 'enthusiasm for the Gothic revival frequently overcame his discretion in handling the buildings entrusted to his care'. Here Cust merely echoed the prevailing view that all earlier restorers subscribed to a drastic unity of style approach to restoration. The main thrust of this book is to demonstrate that Cottingham was not in that category.

Binyon's essay on Cust notes that 'the extraordinary accuracy of his memory enabled him to dispense with note-books'. Cust was, however, occasionally mistaken, for he wrongly cites *The Builder* of 2 December 1856 as a source. Cottingham is referred to in the 1 June 1850 and 8 and 22 November 1851 issues of that journal.

Three entries on Cottingham in earlier works of reference are worth noting. The article on him in the first volume (APS: 1848) of *The Dictionary of Architecture* edited by Wyatt A. Papworth reflected the general view at that time, that 'the chief grounds for his reputation ... were the numerous important repairs and restorations which he directed'. Even in 1878, Samuel Redgrave, in his *A Dictionary of Artists of the English School* (George Bell, revised edition) could record that 'the successful execution of these works (Rochester, Magdalen, St

Alban's) gave him a reputation as a Gothic architect', and that Armagh 'gave room for his constructive and mechanical skill'. And in 1885, Cottingham still rubs shoulders with the great and the good in T.H. Ward's *Men of the Reign : A Biographical Dictionary of Eminent Persons etc* (Routledge).

Two years later, as we have seen, Cottingham's reputation, courtesy of Cust (DNB), is in decline. Nearly seventy years later, Cust's evaluation still finds reflection in *A Biographical Dictionary of English Architects 1660-1840* (Murray, 1954) where H.M. Colvin suggests that 'although somewhat drastic by modern standards his restorations were inspired by a genuine love of Gothic architecture, and he showed considerable technical ability in dealing with the structural problems with which he was faced at Hereford and elsewhere'.

The Art-Union, October 1847, pp.377-8

OBITUARY: LEWIS NOCKALLS COTTINGHAM FSA
This distinguished architect died at his residence in the Waterloo Bridge-road on the 13th ult, after a long and painful illness.

He was born in 1787, at Laxfield, in Suffolk, of an ancient and highly respectable family. One of his ancestors was Abbot of St Marie's Abbey at York in the year 1438; and many early documents and contracts for works in the palmy days of Gothic Architecture, which are in the possession of his family, contain the name of Cottingham honourably mentioned, as artists of high merit, engaged in rearing the matchless ecclesiastical edifices of England in the Middle Ages; so that his peculiar bent might be said to be in some degree inherited.

He, very early in life, evinced unequivocal marks of a genius for Science and the Arts, and was consequently, according to the frequent practice of those days, apprenticed to an extensive builder at Ipswich, in Suffolk. He there acquired the fundamental principles of that particular skill and knowledge which have been so fully shown in his works. After several years spent, as his early drawings and studies prove, in most industriously making himself acquainted with all the branches of his art, he proceeded to London, and there placed himself for further improvement with a skilful architect and surveyor.

He commenced his professional career in 1814, and for many years, at his residence in the vicinity of Lincoln's Inn Fields, steadily and perseveringly worked himself up to that eminence which subsequently obtained for him the numerous important public works we now proceed to enumerate.

His first public appointment was that of architect and surveyor to the Cooks' Company in the year 1822, which he held for a number of years; and soon after this, John Harrison Esq., of Snelston Hall, Derbyshire, became one of his principal patrons. He erected for this gentleman the above-mentioned mansion in the perpendicular style of Gothic architecture.

In the year 1825 he was nominated by the Dean and Chapter of Rochester, architect to their Cathedral, where he effected very extensive works, including a new central tower, with the restoration of many portions of the fabric; and on their completion received a most flattering testimonial, accompanied by a handsome pecuniary compliment in addition to his professional charges, as an expression of the high opinion entertained of his ability and taste. In 1829 he was the successful competitor for the restoration etc., of the interior of the Chapel of Magdalen College, Oxford; and this work may justly be considered one of the first steps towards the revival of the correct taste and feeling for the English ecclesiastical architecture, which, since then, has happily been so widely extended. In 1833 he was intrusted with the restoration and repairs of St Alban's Abbey Church, and there carried out, in a most satisfactory manner, very considerable works.

The next large work on which he was engaged was the Cathedral at Armagh, in Ireland, which, with the exception of a very small portion, was entirely rebuilt from his designs. This elaborate undertaking occupied him several years, and gave full opportunity for a display of the great mechanical skill which he possessed, as well as his sound taste and feeling as an English ecclesiastical architect, of both of which it will ever furnish the strongest evidence.

He was exceedingly strenuous in his exertions to aid in the restoration of the Ladye Chapel, St Saviour's, Southwark.

In 1840 he was called in by the Societies of the Inner and Middle Temple, to report upon the proposed restoration of the Temple Church; and he afterwards, in various ways, materially aided in the beautiful restoration there accomplished.

The reparation of the tower and spire of St James's, Louth, Lincolnshire which had been rent from the top to its foundations by lightning, was confided to his care, and has been restored with the utmost skill and accuracy.

The extensive and able restorations at St Marie's Church, Bury St Edmunds; the Norman Tower in the same town, which has been completely restored in a truly admirable manner; the new Bank adjoining, which he erected; with other works in churches, etc., in the neighbourhood, will long cause his name to be honourably remembered in his native county; and especially by the many noblemen, and gentlemen of taste on the several committees, who have so zealously aided his endeavours to preserve and restore the fine examples of our ancient English architecture in which Bury St Edmunds abounds.

He was subsequently occupied most extensively in the ecclesiastical and civil branches of his profession; and from among many others, may be mentioned the following:– The restoration of the churches at Ashbourne, Derbyshire; Chesterford, Essex; Milton Bryan, Beds. – where, in addition to other works, he erected a new tower at the north-west angle of the nave; Clifton, Notts; Roos, Yorkshire; Theberton, Suffolk; Market Weston, Suffolk; and private works for Lord Brougham at Brougham Castle, Westmorland; the Earl of Harrington, at Elvaston Castle, Derby; the Earl of Dunraven, at Adare Abbey, Ireland; and the Earl of Craven, at Coombe Abbey.

Among his numerous patrons may be also mentioned the late Earl of Verulam, the Hon. and Rev. Lord C. Hervey, Sir Robert H. Inglis, Sir Edward Blackett etc. etc.

In the years 1824 and 1825, he published several most valuable practical works connected with the study of Gothic architecture; among which may be specially mentioned a large folio work on Henry VII's Chapel, as restored; a folio work of 'The Details of Gothic Architecture'; and a quartowork on Ornamental Metal Work. His last great work, remaining to be completed by his son, was the restoration of Hereford Cathedral. Here it is that all his efforts have been directed, for some years past, to bring into full action the fruits of his long experience in the restoration of this splendid fabric. So much had been done in former times to deface and destroy the beautiful proportions and detail of the early parts of the building, that it was, till his practised eye undertook the task, considered almost beyond the possibility of authentic renovation.

All difficulties have, however, been overcome by the unceasing thought and care bestowed; and the works there executed will ever be a noble monument to his genius and ability.

The great central tower had been disfigured internally by unsightly modern groining, and the introduction of barbarous supports under the great north and south arches, together with the mutilations of the four grand piers sustaining the tower, by the insertion of large blocks of masonry of the rudest description: all this, together with most serious fractures, presented so formidable appearance that it was considered by eminent men next to impracticable to effect a work of such difficulty and danger.

The four main piers of the tower have been, with the aid of exceedingly skilful shoring, perfectly reinstated with new ones of the original Norman design; sufficient remains of which were discovered to decide, with the most minute accuracy, every moulding. The modern groining has been removed, and the four great Norman arches, with the interesting stone lantern above, restored; and a new timber ceiling, richly decorated in gold and colour, placed under the bell-chamber floor.

The adjoining portions abutting on the tower have likewise been restored in corresponding style.

He next proceeded with the work of restoration in the Ladye Chapel, with its exceedingly rich and beautifully designed east end of early English date. This latter had become so dilapidated, from the hand of time exercising its effects on stone of inferior quality, that what the carved stone had been was, with the utmost difficulty, ascertained. All has, however, been renewed with the most perfect fidelity; and an examination of the exquisitely varied nature of the very elaborate and numerous ornamental details will fully convince every observer, of the talent and thought bestowed on all parts, however minute. The roof has been raised nearly twenty feet to its original pitch, covered with lead, and surmounted with a rich metal cresting, with pierced inscriptions and glory, and at the west end terminated by a metal cross of early character. The eastern gable which was of very low pitch to correspond with the former roof, and with embrasures in its coping, has been also raised, and an exceedingly elaborate wheel window, with vesica panel above, and arched panels on each side, introduced; the whole surmounted with a splendid stone cross, embodying in its design appropriate emblems.

In the interior, the entire Ladye Chapel has been completely and faithfully restored; and the whole of this most gorgeous work, which has been visited by most of those who, from their well-known taste in the Arts, are best calculated to judge, is now pronounced equal to any specimen of its date in England, and a triumph of skill and taste worthy of any age.

The third contract, which is now in progress, comprises the complete restoration of the choir, with its fine end, shown in the engraving published for the subscribers at the comencement of the works; and will, if possible, surpass, when completed, all that we have before described.

We have been thus particular in describing the minute points of this, his last work, as only the day before his decease, a county meeting was held to raise the funds required to render the building fit for Divine service, for which the sum of £25,000 is required. This, however, it appears from the published accounts, there is every probability will be raised; and it remains for his son to finish a work in which we feel sure his whole heart and feelings must be centred, and which will truly be a labour of love; connected as it must be, with the many associations of his deeply-lamented father.

About the year 1825, Mr Cottingham undertook the management and arrangement of the very extensive estate belonging to the late John Field, Esq. of Tooting, and thereon erected the principal portion of the houses forming the large parish of St John's, Lambeth, immediately surrounding his own residence. This also he built, and provided with large suites of rooms attached, for the purpose of depositing the valuable works of Art and the library; which he had with the true and earnest zeal of an artist devoted to his profession, spared neither trouble nor expense to acquire. During the subsequent two and twenty years, this collection has constantly been added to, and may justly be considered as unique, comprising as it does specimens and relics of all the rarest examples in the different styles of architecture, arranged in chronological order, in numerous apartments appropriately furnished.

Of necessity arising from his long affliction, his elder son, whom he has with unceasing care and solicitude educated to the profession, has long been actively engaged in almost solely carrying on his most extensive practice; which, added to other advantages, places him in a position to pursue his professional career with equal advantage to his country, and, we trust, fame and profit to himself.

A new church, of costly description, now erecting near Lincoln, is exclusively from young Mr Cottingham's designs, though not hitherto publicly known to be so, from the desire of his father to test his ability, and which fact it was the intention of the latter not to promulgate till its completion. The numerous elaborate and difficult works in progress at Hereford Cathedral, besides very many other buildings now in course of erection or under restoration by him, may be mentioned as proofs of the good use he has made of the opportunities afforded him, and serve to gain for him that confidence which his father enjoyed.

The late Mr Cottingham was a member of many of the scientific societies, and had, from a very early period, been on intimate terms with most of the celebrated artists, architects, and scientific men of his time, among whom we may mention his friendship with Flaxman,

Stothard, the well-known John Carter, Mr Gayfere (who restored Henry VII's Chapel, Westminster), Mr Capon the antiquary; and others now no more; and a numerous list might be added of those whom he has left to mourn his loss.

His temper and feeling with regard to his profession might by the stranger be considered enthusiastic; but his heart and his affections were equally ardent, and those who once knew him ever entertained the greatest esteem and friendship for his amiable domestic habits, and generous, benevolent disposition. Many who have enjoyed his friendship, and those who have received the advantage of his sound and able instruction, and since attained eminence in their profession, will feel this to be but a just eulogy to the memory of so highly-gifted and true-hearted a man.

He married, in the year 1822, Sophia, second daughter of Robert Turner Cotton, Esq., of Finsbury, and has left two sons and one daughter; the elder son, Nockalls Johnson Cottingham, succeeded him in his profession; and the younger, Edwin Cotton Cottingham, practising in the medical profession in Suffolk.

His remains were interred on Friday, Oct. 22, in the family vault at the east end of the north aisle of Croydon Church, Surrey.

Bibliography

Primary Sources
Unpublished Reports, Letters, Manuscripts etc.

Atkinson and Browne, *Bill of Sundry and Artificers Works employed in the Restoration of the Inner and Outer Chapels of Magdalen Chapel, Oxford during the years 1830, 1831, 1832, and 1833*, Goswell Street, London. Magdalen College Archive

Atkinson and Browne, *Letter to Dr Routh re Fittings for Magdalen College Chapel as described by L. N. Cottingham*, 27 March 1830, Magdalen College Archive

Atkinson and Browne, *Sundry Works in Labour and Materials employed in the Restoration of Magdalen College Chapel agreeable to the plans and specifications furnished by L.N. Cottingham and under his direction, 1830-1833*, Magdalen College Archive

Beresford Papers, PRONI, Letters re Armagh Cathedral, 1834-1837, Vol.V, T2772/1

Blackett, Sir E., *Blackett Family Papers*, Northumberland R.O., List 34, compiled by H. A. Taylor

Bloxham, Rev. J. R., *The Architectural Changes at Magdalen College, Oxford*, MS 732, Magdalen College Chapel Archive

Brougham, William, *Personal Diaries, May 1844-1845; Letters to Henry, Lord Brougham*, Brougham Papers, University College Library Archive, London

Brougham, William, *Letters to the 7th Earl of Carlisle*, Castle Howard Archive, 5 19/1/38/87, 1846-56

Bury St Edmunds, *Vestry Book of St James*, 1834-1844, MS2571, Suffolk R.O.

Bury St Edmunds, Council Proceedings from 1 Jan 1841-1844, MS 2571, Suffolk R.O.

Capon, W., *Letters to Francis Douce*, 1827-1828, *Douce Mss*, Bodleian Library

Carline, J., *Letter from J.C. Carline to R.C. Carline re Hereford Cathedral Restoration*, Dec. 1847, Hereford Cathedral Library Archive

Cooks' Company, *Minutes of Proceedings July 1822-Sept 1834*, MSS 31114-5, Guildhall Library Archive

Cottingham, L.N., *A Series of Plain and Ornamental Cottages, Gamekeeper's and Bailiff's Houses, Gatelodges and Other Rural Residences, Designed for J. Harrison of Snelston Hall. December, 1825*, Stanton Family

Cottingham, L.N., *5 Sketchbooks*, 1830s, Avery Library Collection, University of Columbia, New York

Cottingham, L.N., *Letters to Dr Routh from LNC, Magdalen College, Oxford*, 11 Jan,1830; 13 Feb, 1832; MS 735, Magdalen College Archive

Cottingham, L.N., *32 Drawings for Restoration of Armagh Cathedral*, Armagh Cathedral Archive

Cottingham, L.N., *8 Letters to the Fishmongers' Court from LNC*, 20 Sept. 1831-17 March 1832, Guildhall Library

Cottingham, L.N., *Fishmongers' Hall Competition Plans*, 1832, Folio III, Ref. S831, Guildhall Library Archive

Cottingham, L.N., *Sketchbook of Canterbury Cathedral*, 1835, British Museum

Cottingham, L.N., *Letter to Sir E. Blackett*, 1 Oct. 1836, Northumberland R.O.

Cottingham, L.N., *Letters to Lord Beresford re Armagh Cathedral*, 1830-59, PRONI, Beresford Papers

Cottingham, L.N., *Louth Church Spire Drawings*, 1840, Lincs R.O.

Cottingham, L.N., *Letter to Savings Bank Committee*, 18 Nov. 1844, Lloyds Bank Archive

Cottingham, L.N., *Plans for Extensions to Horringer Church*, ICBS, 1844

Cottingham, L.N., and N.J., *19 Letters to W. Brougham*, 31 July-2 Oct. 1846, University College Library Archive, London

Cottingham, L.N., *Plans of Great Chesterford School*, 1846, Essex R.O.

Cottingham, L.N., *5 Letters to Francis Douce, Douce Mss*, Bodleian Library

Cottingham, L.N., *Last Will and Testament*. P.R.O. PROB11/2072

Cottingham, N.J., *Schedule of Work and Estimate for Extra Works and Fittings requiring to be executed at Savings Bank, Bury St Edmunds, 10 January, 1845*, Lloyds Bank Archive

Cottingham, N.J, *Letter to Sir E. Blackett*, 16 Nov. 1847, Northumberland R.O.

Cottingham, N.J., *Sketchbook of Little Chesterford, Essex*, 1847, British Museum, 25,356

Cottingham, N.J., *Letters to the Savings Bank Committee, 18 Jan 1847 - 24 Aug 1848*, Lloyds Bank Archive

Cottingham, N.J., *Letter to R.B. Phillips, 1849*, Belmont Abbey Collection, National Library of Wales

Douce, Francis, *Correspondence, Douce Mss*, Bodleian Library

Dunraven Papers, *Letters of Caroline, Lady Dunraven, and Lord Dunraven*, 1834-6, PRONI

Ellis, Sir H., *Letters to F. Douce*, 1828, *Douce Mss*, Bodleian Library

Great Chesterford, *Churchwarden's Accounts*, 8 Nov. 1840, Essex R.O., D/P/10/5

Hereford Cathedral, *Register Book,1844-51: Chapter Acts Book, 1844*: Hereford Cathedral Library

Howard, G.W.F., Earl of Carlisle, *Letters to W. Brougham*, 1846, Brougham Papers, UCL Archive

Incorporated Church Building Society Reports, ICBS Archive, Lambeth Palace Library

Inglis, Sir Robert, *Diaries, Correspondence, Parliamentary Reports*, 1841-52, Kent R.O.

Jervis, S., *Letter to Miss Dawson and Miss Bouch*, Brougham Hall File, V&A Archive, London

King's School, Wimbledon, Archive, *School Records, Prize Lists, etc*

Lapworth, Alfred, *Letters to W. Brougham*, 1844, UCL Archive

Lockwood, P., *Plans for Proposed Alterations to Snelston Hall, 1907*, Derbyshire R.O., Ref D 157

Louth, *Churchwardens' Accounts*, June 1843-April 1844, Lincs. R.O., 6/7/12

Love, H.W., *The Beresford Restoration of Armagh*, MSS, undated

Magdalen College, *Book of the Chapel*, Hom. 1477, MS 824, Magdalen College Archive

Meyrick, Sir S., *Letter to F. Douce*, Aug. 1830-Nov. 1830, *Douce Mss*, Bodleian Library D27

Millar, S.M., *2 Letters to Dr Routh re Estimates for Restoration of Magdalen College Chapel, 13 July, 1833*, Magdalen College Archive

Nevile, Rev. C., *Nevile Papers, Thorney Church*, Notts R.O.

Newman, J., *Letter to R.B. Phillips*, 11 Nov. 1852, Belmont Abbey Collection, National Library of Wales

Oxford Architectural Society, *Correspondence, 1839-49, 1844-58; Calendar of Letters; OAHS Accounts 1839-1902; Memorandum Book 1845-50; Minute Book 1844-7 etc*, Bodleian Library

Oxford University Genealogical and Heraldic Society, 1835-9; Oxford Society for Promoting the Study of Gothic Architecture, 1840; *Report of Proceedings*, V&A Library

Parker, J.H., *Correspondence with Albert Way, etc*. Society of Antiquaries, Burlington House

Phillips, R.B., *Draft of Letter; Appeal for Restoration of Hereford Cathedral*, 1847, Belmont Abbey Collection, National Library of Wales

Potter, T., *Letters to W. Brougham*, Sept. 1844, Brougham Papers, UCL Archive

Pratt, Edward, *Letters to W. Brougham*, Sept. 1844-5, Brougham Papers, UCL Archive

Pugin, A.W.N., *Letters re Restoration of St Mary's Church, Beverley*, Humberside R.O.

Rawlins, Rev. R., *Survey of Parish Churches of Derbyshire*, MSS in 3 Parts, 1843, Derbyshire R.O.

Richardson, C.J., *Drawings and Sketches*, Prints and Drawings, V&A, 93H18

Richardson, J., *Letters to W. Brougham*,1834-48, Brougham Papers, UCL Archive

Robinson, J., *Letters to W. Brougham*, Feb. 1839-Aug. 1840, UCL Archive

Rochester Cathedral. *Lithographs by Harris of Rochester: Reports by LNC and G.G. Scott etc*, Emf 65-7; Emf 76-7, Kent R.O.

Savage, H., *A Memoir of James Savage*, 1852, RIBA Library

Savage, J., Observations on Style etc etc, 1856, RIBA Pamphlets

Savings Bank, Bury St Edmunds, *Minutes Book of the Building Committee*, File 7045, Lloyds Bank Archive

Scott, Sir W., *Letters to F. Douce*, inserted in *Sir Tristram*, *Douce Mss*, Bodleian Library, E264

Shaw, George, *Letters to W. Brougham 1844-52*, Brougham Papers, UCL; *Diaries 1831-5; Sketchbooks, 1830-50*, Manchester City Library

Shaw, Henry, *Letters to F. Douce*, 18 June 1830, *Douce Mss*, Bodleian Library

Society of Antiquaries, *Minute Books*, 1823-33, Burlington House, London

Stevens, Rev. R., *Notebook of Repairs to Rochester Cathedral 1825-6*, Kent R.O.

Twopenny, W., *Letters to Douce*, 1830-1, *Douce Mss*, 145, Bodleian Library

Verulam, Earl of, *Diaries of the 1st Earl, 1819-43 and 1846-95*, Herts R.O.

Way, Albert, *Letter to R.B. Phillips*, 1843, Belmont Abbey Collection, National Library of Wales

Willement, T., *Letters to Douce*, *Douce Mss*, D27, Bodleian Library

Willis, Rev. R., *Report of a Survey of the Dilapidated Portions of Hereford Cathedral in the year 1841*, Hereford Cathedral Library

Secondary Sources

Allibone, J., *Anthony Salvin, Pioneer of Gothic Revival Architecture*, Cambridge, Lutterworth, 1988

Apted, Beer, and Saunders, (eds), *Ancient Monuments and Their Interpretations; Essays Presented to A.J. Taylor*, London, Phillimore, 1977

Barker, F. and Hyde, R., *London As It Might Have Been*, London, 1982

Baylis, T.H., *Temple Church*, London, G. Philip & Son, 3rd ed., 1900

Billings, R.W., *Architectural Illustrations and Account of Temple Church*, London, Isbister & Co, and R.W. Billings, 1838

Blackeburne, E.L., *An Architectural and Historical Account of Crosby Place*, London, John Williams, 1834

Boe, Alf, *From Gothic Revival to Functional Form*, Oslo University Press & Basil Blackwell, Oxford, 1978

Britton, J. (ed.) and Pugin, A.C., *Specimens of Gothic Architecture*, The Authors, 1821

Brown, R. (ed.), *The Architectural Outsiders*, London, Waterstone, 1985

Brunskill, R.W., *Illustrated Handbook of Vernacular Architecture*, London, Faber, 1970

Burge, W., *The Temple Church, An Account of its Restoration and Repairs*, London, W. Pickering, 1843

Carpenter, R.H. and Ingelow, B., *Architect's Report, Armagh Cathedral*, Armagh, 1886

Carter, J., *The Ancient Architecture of England*, 2 Vols., London, John Carter, 2nd ed., 1845

Christie and Manson, *Descriptive Memoir of the Museum of Mediaeval Architecture and Sculpture formed by the late L.N. Cottingham*, FSA, London, 1850

Clark, K., *The Gothic Revival*, London, Constable, 1928

Clarke, B.F.L., *Church Builders of the Nineteenth Century*, London, SPCK, 1938

Cocke, T.H., *The Ingenious Mr Essex, Architect*, Cambridge, Fitzwilliam Museum, 1984

Cole, D., *The Work of Sir George Gilbert Scott*, London, Architectural Press, 1980

Cottingham, L.N., *Westminster Hall*, London, Priestley and Weale, 1822

Plans, Sections, Elevations of the Magnificent Chapel of King Henry VII at Westminster and a Faithful Account of its Restoration, London, Priestly and Weale, 1822

The Smith and Founder's Director Containing a Series of Designs and Patterns of Ornamental Iron and Brass Work, London, L.N. Cottingham, 1823, 1824, 1840

Working Drawings of Gothic Ornament and a Design for a Gothic Mansion, London, Priestley and Weale, 1823

Some Account of an Ancient Tomb Discovered at Rochester Cathedral, 1825

Description of the Sepulchral Effigy of John de Sheppie, discovered in Rochester Cathedral, 1825, London, 1832

and Savage, J., *Reasons Against Pulling Down the Lady Chapel at the East End of St Saviour's Church, Southwark*, 1832

Report on the Present State and Necessary Repair Thereof: Norman Tower at Bury St Edmunds, S. Gross, Bury St Edmunds, 1842

Crook, J. Mordaunt and Port, M.H., *The History of the King's Works*, (Vol.VI), 1782-1851, London, HMSO 1973

Crook, J. Mordaunt, 'John Britton and the Genesis of the Gothic Revival', in *Concerning Architecture*, ed. Summerson, J., London, Allen Lane, 1968

Darley, G., *Villages of Vision*, London, Architectural Press, 1975

Delheim, C., *The Face of the Past*, Cambridge UP, 1982

Dixon, R. and Muthesius, S., *Victorian Architecture*, London, Thames and Hudson, 1978

Eastlake, C.L., *A History of the Gothic Revival*, London, Longmans Green, 1872; 2nd ed., Crook, Leicester, Leicester University Press, 1971

Essex, W.R.H. and Smirke, R., *The Architecture of the Temple Church*, London, John Weale, 1845

Evans, J., *A History of the Society of Antiquaries*, London, Society of Antiquaries, 1956

Fawcett, J. (ed.), *The Future of the Past: Attitudes to Conservation, 1174-1976*, London, 1976

Ferrey, B., *Recollections of A.W.N. Pugin*, London, E. Stanford, 1861

Ferriday, P. (ed.), *Victorian Architecture*, London, Cape, 1963

Frankl, P., *Gothic Architecture*, Harmondsworth, Penguin, 1962

The Gothic, Literary Sources and Interpretation, Through Eight Centuries, Princeton, NJ, London, Princeton UP, Oxford UP, 1960

Franklin, J., *The Gentleman's Country House and its Plan, 1835-1914*, London, Routledge and Kegan Paul, 1981

Frew, J.M., 'An Aspect of the Gothic Revival in England c.1770-1815; The Antiquarian Influence with reference to the career of James Wyatt', PhD Thesis, Oxford, 1976

Germann, G., *Gothic Revival in Europe and Britain*, London, Lund Humphries for the Architectural Association, 1972

Girouard, M, *The Return to Camelot*, London, New Haven, Yale, 1981

Life in the English Country House, New Haven, London, Yale UP, 1978

Gloag, J. and Bridgwater, D., *History of Cast Iron in Architecture*, London, Allen & Unwin, 1948

Gwynn, D., *Lord Shrewsbury, Pugin and the Gothic Revival*, London, Hollis & Carter, 1946

Harris, J., *English Decorative Ironwork, 1610-1836*, London, Tiranti, 1960

Catalogue of British Drawings 1550-1836 in American Collections, Upper Saddle River, NJ, 1971

Harrison, M., *Victorian Stained Glass*, London, Barrie & Jenkins, 1980

Harvey, J., *The Mediaeval Architect*, London, Wayland, 1972

Hermann, W., *Laugier and 18th Century French Theory*, London, Zwemmer, 1962

Hobhouse, H., *Lost London*, London, Macmillan, 1971

Hope, A. J. Beresford, *The English Cathedral of the Nineteenth Century*, London, 1861

Humphrey, S. C., *Primary Sources for Nineteenth Century Churches*, London, 1981

Hunt, W. Holman, *Pre-Raphaelitism and the Pre-Raphaelite Brotherhood*, 2 Vols, London, Macmillan, 1905

Jenkins, F., *Architect and Patron*, London, Oxford UP, 1961

Jervis, S., *High Victorian Design*, Woodbridge, 1983

Kaye, B., *The Development of the Architectural Profession in England*, London, Allen & Unwin, 1960

Law, H. W. and I., *The Book of the Beresford Hopes*, London, Heath Cranton, 1925

Lenoir, A., *Musée Imperiale des Monuments Français*, Paris, 1815

Lewis, G. R., *Illustrations of Kilpeck Church*, London, G. R. Lewis, 1842

London County Council, *Survey of London*, Vol.23, 1951

Macaulay, J., *The Gothic Revival, 1745-1845*, London, 1970

Madsen, S. Tschudi, *Restoration and Anti-Restoration. A Study in English Restoration Philosophy*, Oslo, Universitetsforlaget, 1975

Marshall, D., *The English Poor in the Eighteenth Century*, London, Routledge, 1926

McCarthy, M., *The Origins of the Gothic Revival*, New Haven and London, Yale UP, 1987

McLeod, R., *Style and Society, 1835-1914*, London, RIBA, 1970

Merewether, J. A., *A Statement on the Condition and Circumstances of the Cathedral Church of Hereford in the Year 1841*, Hereford, 1841

Metcalf, P., *Halls of the Fishmongers' Company*, London, 1980

Minton & Co., *Examples of Old English Tiles Manufactured by Minton & Co.*, 1842, Reprint 1979

Mowl, T., 'The Norman Revival in British Architecture 1790-1870', PhD Thesis, Oxford, 1981

Myles, J., 'L. N. Cottingham 1787-1847, Architect: His Place in the Gothic Revival', PhD Thesis, Leicester Polytechnic, 1989

Nichols, J. G., *Examples of Decorative Inlaid Tiles, Sometimes called Encaustic*, London, 1845

Palmer, G. H., *Rochester Cathedral and See*, London, George Bell & Sons, 1899

Perkin, H., *Origins of Modern English Society, 1780-1880*, London, Routledge & Kegan Paul, 1969

Pevsner, N., *Nottinghamshire*, Harmondsworth, Penguin, 1951

Suffolk, Harmondsworth, Penguin, 1951

Derbyshire, Harmondsworth, Penguin, 1953

Herefordshire, Harmondsworth, Penguin, 1963

Ruskin and Viollet-le-Duc: Englishness and Frenchness in the Appreciation of Gothic Architecture, London, Thames & Hudson, 1969

Some Architectural Writers of the Nineteenth Century, Oxford, Clarendon Press, 1972

and Sherwood, J., *Oxfordshire*, Harmondsworth, Penguin, 1974

and Metcalf, P., *The Cathedrals of England*, London, Viking, 1985

Port, M. H., *600 New Churches: A Study of the Church Building Commission*, London, SPCK, 1961

(ed.), *The Houses of Parliament*, Yale UP, New Haven, London, 1976

Pugin, A. C., *Architectural Antiquities of Normandy*, Lomdon, The Author, 1828

Gothic Ornament Selected from Various Buildings in England and France, 1831

and A. W. N., *Examples of Gothic Architecture from Measured Drawings of 1832*, 2 Vols, London, The Authors, 1832

and Willson, E. J., *Specimens of Gothic Architecture Selected From Various Edifices*, 2 Vols, London, J. Taylor, 1821-3

Pugin, A. W. N., *Contrasts: A Parallel Between the Noble Edifices of the MA, and Corresponding Buildings of the Present Day: Shewing the Present Decay of Taste*, London, Charles Dolman, 1836

The True Principles of Pointed or Christian Architecture, etc, London, Henry Bohn, 1841

Robertson, E. G. and J., *Cast Iron Decoration: A World Survey*, London, Thames & Hudson, 1977

Rogers, E., *Memoir of Armagh Cathedral, With an Account of the Ancient City*, Belfast, 1888

Royal Commission for Historic Monuments, England, London, *Westminster Abbey*, London, HMSO, Vol.1, 1924; Vol.2, 1925

Saint, A., *The Image of the Architect*, New Haven, London, Yale UP, 1983

Scott, G. G., *Personal and Professional Recollections*, London, 1879

Seaborne, M., *The English School etc.*, 2 Vols, London, Routledge & Kegan Paul, 1971-7

Shaw, H., *Specimens of Ancient Furniture – Drawn from Existing Authorities*, London, William Pickering, 1836

Steegman, J., *Victorian Taste: A Study of Art and Architecture from 1830-1870*, London, Nelson, 1970

Strong, R., Harris, J. and Binney, M., *The Destruction of the Country House*, London, Thames & Hudson, 1974

Stroud, D., *Sir John Soane*, London, Faber, 1984

Suckling, Rev. A., *The Suckling History & Antiquities of Suffolk*, 2 Vols., London, John Weale, 1846-8

Summerson, J. (ed.), *The Architectural Association, 1847-1947*, London, AA, 1947

(ed.), *Concerning Architecture*, London, Allen Lane, 1968

Victorian Architecture, New York, London, Cambridge UP, 1970

Survey of London, *St Saviour's, Southwark; South Bank and Vauxhall*, Vol.XXIII, London, LCC, 1950

Taylor, F. H., *The Taste of Angels*, Boston, Mass., Little, Browne & Co, 1948

Thompson, F. M. L., *English Landed Society in the 19th Century*, London, Routledge & Kegan Paul, Toronto UP, 1965

Tymms, S., *An Architectural and Historical Account of the Church of St Mary, Bury St Edmunds*, Bury St Edmunds, 1845-54

Vaux, C., *Villas and Cottages*, New York, 1857

Viollet-le-Duc, *Entretiens Sur L'Architecture*, translation, Bucknall, 1877-81, 2 Vols, reprint, 1959

Wainwright, C., 'The Antiquarian Interior in Britain, 1780-1885', PhD Thesis, University of London, 1986

Watkin, D., *Morality in Architecture*, Oxford, Clarendon Press, 1977

Wedgwood, A., *A. W. N. Pugin and the Pugin Family*, London, V&A, 1985

Willement, T., *A Concise Account of the Principal Works in Stained Glass by Thomas Willement*, FSA, London, 1840

Historical Sketch of Davington, London, (one of thirty copies), 1862

Willis, Rev. R., *The Architectural History of Some English Cathedrals*, (1843), 2nd ed., Chicheley, 1972

Wood, M., *The Mediaeval House*, London, Bracken Books, 1965

Exhibition and Sale Catalogues

Adare Manor, Co. Limerick, *Sale Catalogue*, 10 June 1982, Christie, Manson & Woods

Arts Council of Great Britain, 'English Romanesque Art 1066-1200', *Exhibition Catalogue*, 1984

Barbican Gallery, 'Getting London in Perspective', *Exhibition Catalogue*, London, 1984

Baron Taylor, *Catalogue of Sale*, Paintings, 24 Feb. 1880, Drouot, Paris

Brougham Hall, Westmorland, *Sale Catalogue*, 21 June 1932, Garland Smith & Co, 100 Mount St, London

Carter, J., *Sale Catalogue*, Library and Collection of John Carter, Sotheby's, London, 1818

Coombe Abbey Estate, *Catalogue of Sale*, 21 Aug., Messrs Winterton & Sons, Lichfield, and Mr E. Whittendale, Hereford, 1923

Cottingham, E., *Sale Catalogue*, 'The Valuable Library of Edwin Cottingham, MRCS, containing rare and curious books by early English printers (incl. a copy of Caxton), extensive collection of Historical, Theological, Antiquarian, Classical Works, etc etc', Messrs S. Leigh Sotheby & John Wilkinson, 15 June and 3 days, London, 1859

Foster & Son, *Sale Catalogue*, Museum of Mediaeval Art Collected by the Late L.N. Cottingham FSA, 3 No. 1851

Gallery Lingard, 'Buildings in Perspective: 1830-1939', *Exhibition Catalogue*, 1984

Gallery Lingard, 'On the Face of it; an Exhibition of British and European Elevations, 1830-1950', *Exhibition Catalogue*, 1985

Gallery Lingard, 'Softs and Hards; Drawings by Victorian and Edwardian Architects', *Exhibition Catalogue*, 1986

Gallery Lingard, 'Greeks and Goths: 1830-1939', *Exhibition Catalogue*, 1987

Gough, R., *Catalogue of Sale*, The Library of Richard Gough, Leigh S. Sotheby, 1810

Magdalen College Chapel, *Sale Catalogue*, Fixtures and Fittings, T. Hallam, Oxford, 14 Dec. 1837

Pugin, A. C., *Sale Catalogue*, The Library etc etc of A. C. Pugin, Messrs Wheatley & Son, 4 June 1833

Royal Academy of Arts, 'Age of Chivalry', *Exhibition Catalogue*, London, 1987-8

Smirke, S., *Catalogue of Sale*, Libraries of S. Smirke and W. Railton, and the Remainder of W. E. Frost, 21 March 1878, Leigh S. Sotheby and J. Wilkinson

Smirke, Sir R., *Catalogue of a Portion of the Library of the late Sir R. Smirke*, Bodleian MS Bib. 1118579(7)

Snelston Hall, *Sale Catalogue*, Bagshaw & Sons, Uttoxeter, 15 July 1946

Snelston Hall, *Catalogue of Sale*, Fixtures and Fittings of Snelston Hall, Allen & Farquhar, Derby, 11 June 1952

Soane, Sir J., *Catalogue of the Library of Sir John Soane*, Sir John Soane Museum

Victoria and Albert Museum, 'Victorian Church Art', *Exhibition Catalogue*, 1971

Victoria and Albert Museum, 'Marble Halls', *Exhibition Catalogue*, 1972-3

Periodical Articles: Signed

Adams-Acton, M., 'Vandals in English Churches: the Defacement of Ecclesiastical Art', *Connoisseur*, 1949, pp.72-8

Blutman, S., 'Books of Designs for Country Houses, 1780-1815', *Architectural History*, XI, 1968, p.25

Boase, T. S. R, 'An Oxford College and the Gothic Revival', *Journal of the Warburg and Courtauld Institutes*, Vol XVIII, 1955, pp.145-188

Bordeschi, M. D., 'From Johnson to J. Soane: an analysis and history of two Museum Houses', *Domus*, No.631, Sept. 1982, pp.44-8

Branner R., 'Villard de Honecourt, Reims, and the Origin of Gothic Architectural Drawing', *Gazette des Beaux-Arts*, March 1963, pp.129-140

Caumont, Arcisse de, *Bulletin Monumental*, Paris, 1834-7; 1838-9; 1840-1

Clarke, B. F. L., 'An Ecclesiological Crusade; Church Restoration in the 19th Century', *Country Life*, 1972, 2 Nov. pp.1148-52; 9 Nov. pp.1236-40

Codrington, K. de B., 'The Making of the 19th Century Museum', *Country Life*, XIX, 1936

Colvin, H., 'The Rebuilding of Coombe Abbey', Vol.50, *The Walpole Society*, pp.248-53

Cornforth, J., 'Adare Manor, County Limerick', 15 May, 1969, *Country Life*, pp.1230-1

Cottingham L. N., Petition to the House of Commons, *Commons Journal*, XLII 367, 10-19 May 1837

Letter of 17 December, re Temple Church, *The Gentleman's Magazine*, 1841, p.18

Letter to the Editor, re Temple Church, *Archaeologia*, XXIX, 1841, p.399

Letter to Sir H. Ellis, 'Communicating the result of an examination of the floor of the Chapter House at Westminster', *Archaeologia*, XXIX, 1841, p.390

Report on the Norman Tower at Bury, *Architect, Engineer and Surveyor*, 1842, pp.22, 23, 57

Report on St Mary's Church, Nottingham, *Architect, Engineer and Surveyor*, 1843, p.43

Letter to the Editor, *The Gentleman's Magazine*, 1847, p.157

Crook, J. M., 'Sir Robert Peel: Patron of the Arts', *History Today*, Jan. 1966, pp.3-11

'The Pre-Victorian architect: professionalism and patronage', *Architectural History*, 1969, p.62

'The Restoration of the Temple Church: Ecclesiology and Recrimination', *Architectural History*, Vol.II, 1964, pp.39-45

'Sir Robert Smirke: A Pioneer of Concrete Construction', *Transactions of the Newcomen Society*, Vol.XXXVIII, 1965-6, pp.5-22

Didron (aîné), 'Promenade en Angleterre', *Annales Archéologiques*, Vol.V, 1846, p.284

Duncan, G., 'A Basket of Destiny', *Nautical Magazine*, Vol.174, 1955, p.210

Dyos, H. J., 'The Speculative Builders and Developers of Victorian London', *Victorian Studies*, Summer, Vol.XI, 1968, pp.641-90

Fedden, R., 'Neo-Norman', *Architectural Review*, Vol.116, no.696, Dec. 1954, pp.381-5

Ferriday, P., 'The Church Restorers', *Architectural Review*, 1964, p.87

Frew, M., 'Gothic Is English', *Art Bulletin*, Vol.64, June 1982, pp.315-19

Goodhart-Rendell, H.S., 'Rogue Architects of the Victorian Era', *RIBA Journal*, Vol.56, April 1949

Haggit, F. R., 'Hereford Cathedral', *Ecclesiologist*, Vol.NVI, 1848 pp.32-7

Jervis, S., 'Furniture Designs for Snelston Hall', *V&A Museum Album*, 1985

Johnson, J. R., 'The Stained Glass Theories of Viollet-le-Duc', *Art Bulletin*, Vol.45, 1963, pp.121-34

Jordan, W. J., 'Sir George Gilbert Scott RA, Surveyor to Westminster Abbey, 1849-1878', *Architectural History*, 1980, 23, pp.60-77

Kempe, A. J., 'Description of the Sepulchral Effigy of John de Sheppey, etc', *Archaeologia*, Vol.XXV, pp.122-6

Kindler, R., 'Periodical Criticism 1815-1840', *Architectural History*, 1973-4, p.25

Lamb, E. B., Letter to the British Museum calling for a Gallery of British Antiquities, *Civil Engineer and Architect's Journal*, Aug. 1844

Mark, R., 'Viollet-le-Duc and Willis; the Structural Approach to Gothic', *Architectura*, 1977, p.52

McMordie, M., 'Picturesque Pattern Books: Pre Victorian Designers', *Architectural History*, XVIII, 1975, p.43

Meeks, C. V. L., 'Romanesque Before Richardson in the US', *Art Bulletin*, March 1953, p.19

Meller, H., 'Edward Blore: From Engraver to Architect', *Country Life*, 19 Oct. 1978, pp.1205-6

Merewether, J., 'The Condition of Hereford Cathedral in 1841', *The Gentleman's Magazine*, 1843, p.286

Middleton, R. D., 'The Abbe de Cordemoy and the Graeco-Roman Ideal', *Journal of the Warburg and Courtauld Institutes*, XXV, 1962, p.278

Miele, C., 'The West Front of Rochester Cathedral in 1825: Antiquarianism, Historicism and the Restoration of Mediaeval Buildings', *Archaeological Journal*, 151, 1994, pp.400-19

Morris, R. K., 'The Herefordshire School: Recent Discoveries', *Studies in Mediaeval Sculpture*, Occasional Papers, III, Society of Antiquaries, 1983, p.195

Myles, J., 'The Church Furnishings of L. N. Cottingham', *Victorian Society Annual*, 1990, pp.23-42
'L. N. Cottingham and Magdalen College Chapel', *The Magdalen College Record*, 1991, pp.81-91
'L. N. Cottingham, Gothic Revivalist', *The Journal of the York Georgian Society*, 1993, pp.18-24

Old Subscribers, 'Brougham Hall, A Modern Antique', *The Gentleman's Magazine*, 1843, p.286

Paterson, T. G. F. and Davies, O., 'The Churches of Armagh'. *Ulster Journal of Archaeology*, Vol.3, 1940, pp.82-103

Port, H. M., 'The Office of Works and Building Contractors in the Early 19th Century', *Economic History*, XX, 1967, pp.94-110

Reichensperger, A., 'Cologne Cathedral', *Kölner Domblatt*, 30 Nov. 1845

Robinson, J. M., 'Farming on a Princely Scale', *Architectural Review*, Vol.160, July-Dec. 1976, pp.276-81

Rosenau, H., 'English Church Plans', *RIBA Journal*, June 1944, p.206

Shaw, G., 'Brougham Hall', *The Gentleman's Magazine*, Vol.1, 1848, pp. 369-76; Vol.11, p.31

Stanton, Col. J., 'Snelston Hall', *Derbyshire Life and Country*, Oct. 1883, pp.38-9

Wainwright, C., 'Davington Priory', *Country Life*, 9 Dec. 1971, pp.1650-3 and 16 Dec. 1971, pp.1716-19
'The Romantic Interior in England', *NACF Review*, 1985, pp.81-90

Wells, C., '15th Century Woodcarvings in St Mary's, Bury', *Mediaeval History*, No.9, 31965, NMRO

West, Rev G. H., 'The late E. E. Viollet-le-Duc: Some Personal Reminiscences', *RIBA Journal*, 3rd Series, Vol.XXVIII, 1930

Wethered, C., 'The late Viollet-le-Duc', *RIBA Transactions*, 1883-4, pp.210-17

White, W., 'Restoration versus Conservation', *The Builder*, 1878, p.115

Whitehead, D., 'The Mid-Nineteenth-Century Restoration of Hereford Cathedral by Lewis Nockalls Cottingham, 1842-1850', *The British Archaeological Association Conference Transactions*, XV, 1995, pp.177-87

Wicks, J., 'Robert Turner Cotton, H. Cotton and L. N. Cottingham', *Blackmansbury*, Dec. 1968, Vol.V, pp.110-20

Wilton-Ely, J., 'The Architectural Models of Sir John Soane', *Architectural History*, 12, 1969, p.6

Worsley, G., 'Naworth Castle: The Seat of The Earl of Carlisle', *Country Life*, 12 Feb. 1987, pp.74-9: Part 11, 26 Feb. pp.88-91

Periodical Articles: Unsigned

Archaeological Journal, Review of Meetings on The Conservation of Historic Monuments, Caen, Vol.1, 1844, p.81

Architect, Engineer and Surveyor, Review of book by J. Addison on the Temple Church, 1843, pp.18-19

Architect's Journal, Hereford Cathedral, 1841, pp.242, 248

Architectural Magazine, (ed. J. Loudon), Armagh Cathedral, 1835, Vol.III, p.45: Criticism of the Houses of Parliament Designs, 1836, Vol.III, p.202: Catalogue of Designs for HOP, 1836, pp.201-302

Athenaeum, Obituary of L. N. Cottingham, 16 Oct. 1847, pp.1082-3; Account of Crosby Hall Meeting, 1832, p.338

British Magazine, St Alban's Abbey Church, Vol.II, 1832, pp.207-8, 485-6: 1833, Vol.III, p.112

The Builder, St Mary's, Bury, 1844, p.473
Market Weston Church, Suffolk, 1844, p.378
St Mary's Church, Nottingham, 1845, p.299
Rochester Cathedral, 1845, p.466
St Mary's Church, Clifton, Notts., 1846, p.250
Norman Tower, Bury St Edmunds, 1846, pp.200, 245, 473

Sale of LNC's Museum of Mediaeval Art, 1851, p.742

Civil Engineer and Architect's Journal, Temple Church, 1842, p.392
Market Weston Church, 1844, p.332
Norman Tower at Bury St Edmunds, 1846, pp.238-9

Derby Mercury, The Re-opening of Ashbourne Church, 10 June 1840

Ecclesiologist, Cottingham and Moffat at St Mary's, Nottingham, 1845, Vol.II, p.162
Restoration of St Mary's, Bury St Edmunds, Vol.VI, 1848, p.415
St Helen's Church, Thorney, Vol.VI, 1848, pp.202-3
Hereford Cathedral, Vol.VI, pp.205, 345-7
Armagh Cathedral, Vol.XIII, 1855, pp.8-15
N. J. Cottingham's Stained Glass at Ely Cathedral, Vol.XI, 1853, p.7
Church Restoration (including comments on LNC's work at Armagh), Vol.XXII, 1856, p.144

The Gentleman's Magazine, Rochester Cathedral Restoration, 1825, p.36
Bishop Sheppie's Tomb, 1825, p.76
Armagh Cathedral, 1834, p.203
Houses of Parliament Plans, 1836, p.523
Samuel Pratt's Exhibition of Armour, 1836, p.532
Temple Church, 1841, p.18
Willement's lancet window, 1842, p.654
Temple Church, 1842, p.521
Designs for St Alban's Abbey, 1842, pp.649, 1123
Hereford Cathedral, 1842, p.193
The Norman Tower at Bury St Edmunds, 1843, pp.42, 74
LNC's print of St Mary's, Bury St Edmunds, 1843, p.74
Temple Church Restoration, 1843, p.30
St Mary's Church, Nottingham, 1843, p.300
Market Weston Church, 1844, p.304
Church Restoration, 1844, p.632
The Norman Tower, Bury St Edmunds, 1846, p.519
Letter from E. I. C., (possibly E. I. Carlos), re The Norman Tower, 1847, pp.43, 157
LNC's Museum, 1850, p.629
The Norman Tower at Bury St Edmunds, 1852, p.669
LNC's Museum, 1852, p.60

Hereford Times, Reports on the Hereford Cathedral Restoration, 2 Oct. 1847: 20 Jan. 1849: 27 Jan. 1849

Illustrated London News, Crosby Hall, 1842, p.249: Temple Church, p.411: Bury St Edmunds, 1860, p.236

Landscape Design, 'British Influences on F. L. Olmstead', Aug. 1981, pp.13-15

Nautical Magazine, Vol.174, 1955, p.210

RIBA Journal, Architectural Training, XXI, 1924, p.631

West Bridgford and Clifton Standard, St Mary's, Church, Clifton, Notts, 28 Dec. 1968: 4 Jan. 1969

Index